J. Theodore Bent

Ruined Cities of Mashonaland

A record of Excavation and Exploration in 1891

J. Theodore Bent

Ruined Cities of Mashonaland
A record of Excavation and Exploration in 1891

ISBN/EAN: 9783337384937

Printed in Europe, USA, Canada, Australia, Japan

Cover: Foto ©ninafisch / pixelio.de

More available books at **www.hansebooks.com**

THE RUINED CITIES

OF

MASHONALAND

BEING A RECORD OF

EXCAVATION AND EXPLORATION IN 1891

BY

J. THEODORE BENT, F.S.A. F.R.G.S.

AUTHOR OF 'THE CYCLADES, OR LIFE AMONGST THE INSULAR GREEKS' ETC.

WITH A CHAPTER ON THE
ORIENTATION AND MENSURATION OF THE TEMPLES
BY R. M. W. SWAN

NEW EDITION

LONGMANS, GREEN, AND CO.
LONDON, NEW YORK, AND BOMBAY
1896

All rights reserved

PREFACE

TO

THE THIRD EDITION

Since the appearance of the second edition of this book I have received many communications about the Mashonaland ruins, considerable additional work in excavation has been done, and many more ruins have come to light as the country has been opened out. Of this material I have set down the chief points of interest.

Professor D. H. Müller.—Professor D. H. Müller, of Vienna, the great Austrian authority on Southern Arabian archæology, wrote to me on the subject, and kindly drew my attention to passages in his work on the towers and castles of South Arabia which bore on the question, and from which I now quote. Marib, the Mariaba of Greek and Roman geographers, was the capital of the old Sabæan kingdom of Southern Arabia, and celebrated more especially for its gigantic dam and irrigation system, the ruin of which was practically the ruin of the country. East-north-east of Marib, half an hour's ride brings one to the great ruin called by the Arabs the Haram of Bilkis or the Queen of Sheba. It is an elliptical building with a circuit of 300 feet, and the plan given by the French traveller, M. Arnaud, shows a remarkable likeness to the great circular temple at Zimbabwe.

Again, the long inscription on this building is in two rows, and runs round a fourth of its circumference; this corresponds to the position of the two rows of chevron pattern which run round a fourth part of the temple at Zimbabwe. Furthermore, one half of the elliptical wall on the side of the inscription is well built and well preserved, whereas that on the opposite side is badly built and partly ruined. This is also the case in the Zimbabwe ruin, where all the care possible has been lavished on the side where the pattern and the round tower are, and the other portion has been either more roughly finished or constructed later by inferior workmen.

From the inscriptions on the building at Marib we learn that it was a temple dedicated to the goddess Almaqah. Professor Müller writes as follows:—

There is absolutely no doubt that the Haram of Bilkis is an old temple in which sacred inscriptions to the deities were set up on stylæ. The elliptically formed wall appears to have been always used in temple buildings; also at Sirwah, the Almaqah temple, which is decidedly very much older than the Haram of Bilkis, was also built in an oval form. Also these temples, as the inscriptions show, were dedicated to Almaqah. Arabian archæologists also identify Bilkis with Almaqah, and, therefore, make the temple of Almaqah into a female apartment (haram).

From Hamdani, the Arabian geographer, we learn that Ialmaqah was the star Venus; for the star Venus is called in the Himyaritic tongue Ialmaqah or Almaq, 'illuminating,' and hence we see the curious connection arising between the original female goddess of the earlier star-worshipping Sabæans and the later myth of the wonderful Queen Bilkis, who was supposed to have constructed these buildings.

It seems to me highly probable that in the temple of Zimbabwe we have a Sabæan Almaqah temple; the points of comparison are so very strong, and there is furthermore a strong connection between the star-worshipping Sabæans and the temple with its points orientated to the sun, and built on such definite mathematical principles.

Professor Sayce called my attention to the fact that the elliptical form of temple and the construction on a system of curves is further paralleled by the curious temples at Malta, which all seemed to have been constructed on the same principle.

Mr. W. St. Chad Boscawen's interesting communication to the preface of the second edition receives confirmation from details concerning the worship of Sopt at Saft-el-Henneh, published by Herr Brugsch in the Proceedings of Biblical Archæology. Sopt, he tells us, was the feudal god of the Arabian nome, the nome of Sopt. At Saft-el-Henneh this god is described upon the monuments as 'Sopt the Spirit of the East, the Hawk, the Horus of the East' (Naville's 'Goshen,' p. 10), and as also connected with Tum, the rising and setting sun (p. 13). M. Naville believes that this bird represents not the rising sun, but one of the planets, Venus, the morning star; that is to say, that Sopt was the herald of the sun, not the sun itself. Herr Brugsch, however, believes that it was really the god of the zodiacal light, the previous and the after glow. If M. Naville's theory is correct, we have at once a strong connection between Almaqah, the Venus star of the Sabæans, and the goddess worshipped at Marib and probably at Zimbabwe, and the hawk of Sopt, the feudal god of the Arabian nome, which was closely connected with the worship of Hathor, 'the queen of heaven and earth.'

Sir John Willoughby conducted further excavations at Zimbabwe, which lasted over a period of five weeks. He brought to light a great number of miscellaneous articles, but unfortunately none of the finds are different from those which we discovered. He obtained a number of crucibles, phalli, and bits of excellent pottery, fragments of soapstone bowls. One object only may be of interest, which he thus describes:—

> This was a piece of copper about six inches in length, a quarter of an inch wide, and an eighth of an inch thick, covered with a green substance (whether enamel, paint, or lacquer, I am unable to determine), and inlaid with one of the triangular Zimbabwe designs. It was buried some five feet below the surface, almost in contact with the east side of the wall itself.

Sir John also found some very fine pieces of

pottery which would not disgrace a classical period in Greece or Egypt. Furthermore, he made it abundantly clear that the buildings are of many different periods, for they show more recent walls superposed on older ones.

Mr. R. W. M. Swan, who was with us on our expedition as cartographer and surveyor, has this year returned to Mashonaland, and has visited and taken the plans of no less than thirteen sets of ruins of minor importance, but of the same period as Zimbabwe, on his way up from the Limpopo river to Fort Victoria. The results of these investigations have been eminently satisfactory, and in every case confirming the theory of the construction of the great Zimbabwe temple.

At the junction of the Lotsani river with the Limpopo he found two sets of ruins and several shapeless masses of stones, not far from a well-known spot where the Limpopo is fordable. Both of these are of the same workmanship as the Zimbabwe buildings, though not quite so carefully constructed as the big temple; the courses are regular, and the battering back of each successive course and the rounding of the ends of the walls are very cleverly done. The walls are built of the same kind of granite and with holes at the doorways for stakes as at Zimbabwe. But what is most important, Mr. Swan ascertained that the length of the radius of the curves of which they are built is equal to the diameter of the Lundi temple or the circumference of the great round tower at Zimbabwe. He then proceeded to orientate the temple, and as the sun was nearly setting he sat on the centre of the arc, and was delighted to find that the sun descended nearly in a line with the main doorway; and as it was only seventeen days past the winter solstice, on allowing for the difference in the sun's declination for that time, he found that a line from the centre of the arc through the middle of the doorway pointed exactly to the sun's centre when it set at the winter solstice. The orientation of the other ruin he found was also to the setting sun. 'This,' writes Mr. Swan, 'places our theories regarding orientation and geometrical construction beyond a doubt.'

Continuing his journey northwards, Mr. Swan found two sets of ruins in the Lipokole hills, four near Semalali, and one actually 300 yards from the mess-room of the Bechuanaland Border Police at Macloutsie camp. Owing to stress of time Mr. Swan was not able to visit all the ruins that he heard of in this locality, but he was able to fix the radii of two curves at the Macloutsie ruin, and four curves at those near Semalali, and he found them all constructed on the system used at Zimbabwe. The two ruins on the Lipokole hills he found to be fortresses only, and not built on the plan of the temples. The temples consist generally of two curves only, and are of half-moon shape, and seem never to have been complete enclosures; they are all built of rough stone, for no good stone is obtainable, yet the curves are extremely well executed, and are generally true in their whole length to within one or two inches.

Further up country, on the 'Msingwani river, Mr. Swan found seven sets of ruins, three of which were built during the best period of Zimbabwe work. He measured three of the curves here, and found them to agree precisely with the curve system used in the construction of the round temple at Zimbabwe, and all of them were laid off with wonderful accuracy.

Another important piece of work done by Mr. Swan on his way up to Fort Victoria was to take accurate measurements of the small circular temple about 200 yards from the Lundi river. This we had visited on our way up; but as we had not then formed any theory with regard to the construction of these buildings, we did not measure the building with sufficient accuracy to be quite sure of our data.

With regard to this ruin, Mr. Swan writes:—

> One door is to the north and the other 128° and a fraction from it; so that the line from the centre to the sun rising at mid-winter bisects the arc between the doorways. If one could measure the circumference of this arc with sufficient accuracy, we could deduce the obliquity of the ecliptic when the temple was built. I made an attempt, and arrived at about 2000 B.C.; but really it is impossible to measure with sufficient accuracy to arrive at anything definite by this method, although from it we may get useful corroborative evidence.

From this mass of fresh evidence as to the curves and orientation of the Mashonaland ruins we may safely consider that the builders of these mysterious structures were well versed in geometry, and studied carefully the heavens. Beyond this nothing, of course, can really be proved until an enormous amount of careful study has been devoted to the subject. It is, however, very valuable confirmatory evidence when taken with the other points, that the builders were of a Semitic race and of Arabian origin, and quite excludes the possibility of any negroid race having had more to do with their construction than as the slaves of a race of higher cultivation; for it is a well-accepted fact that the negroid brain never could be capable of taking the initiative in work of such intricate nature.

Mr. Cecil Rhodes also had another excavation done outside the walls of the great circular ruin, and the soil carefully sifted. In it were discovered a large number of gold beads, gold in thin sheets, and $2\frac{1}{2}$ ounces of small and beautifully made gold tacks; also a fragment of wood about the tenth of an inch square, covered with a brown colouring matter and a gilt herring-bone pattern.

Mr. Swan thus describes these finds:—

> Very many gold beads have been found; also leaf gold and wedge-shaped tacks of gold for fixing it on wood. Finely twisted gold wire and bits of gilt pottery, also some silver. The pottery is the most interesting; it is very thin, only about one-fifteenth of an inch thick, and had been coated with some pigment, on which the gilt is laid. On the last fragment found the gilding is in waving lines, but on a former piece there is a herring-bone pattern. The work is

so fine that to see it easily one has to use a magnifying glass. The most remarkable point about the gold ornaments is the quantity in which they are found. Almost every panful of stuff taken from anywhere about the ruins will show some gold. Just at the fountain the ground is particularly rich. I have tested some of the things from Zimbabwe, and, in addition to gold, find alloy of silver and copper, and gold and silver.

One of the most interesting of the later finds in Mashonaland is a wooden platter found in a cave about 10 miles distant from Zimbabwe, a reproduction of which forms the frontispiece to this edition. Mr. Noble, clerk of the Cape Houses of Parliament, to whom I am indebted for the photograph of this object, thus describes it:—

In the centre of the dish, which is about 38 inches in circumference, there is carved the figure of a crocodile (which was probably regarded as a sacred animal) or an Egyptian turtle, and on the rim of the plate is a very primitive representation of the zodiacal characters, such as Aquarius, Pisces, Cancer, Sagittarius, Gemini, as well as Taurus and Scorpio. Besides these there occur the figures of the sun and moon, a group of three stars, a triangle, and four slabs with triangular punctures (two of them being in reversed positions), all carved in relief, and displaying the same rude style of art which marked the decorated bowl found by Mr. Bent in the temple at Zimbabwe. A portion of the rim of the plate has been eroded by insects, probably from resting on damp ground. Altogether, the relic presents to the eye an unquestionable specimen of rare archaism, which has been remarkably preserved through many centuries, probably dating back even before the Christian era. Previous observation and measurements of Zimbabwe, by Mr. R. Swan, established the presumption that the builders of it used astronomical methods and observed the zodiacal and other stars; and this plate shows that the ancient people, whether Phœnician, Sabæan, or Minæans—all of Arabian origin—were familiar with the stellar grouping and signs said to have been first developed by the Chaldeans and dwellers in Mesopotamia.

Another interesting find in connection with this early civilisation is a Roman coin of the Emperor Antoninus Pius (A.D. 138); it was found in an ancient shaft near Umtali at a depth of 70 feet, and forms a valuable link in the chain of evidence as to the antiquity of the gold mines in Mashonaland.

Concerning the more recent ruins discovered in Matabeleland, north of Buluwayo, we have not much definite detail to hand at present. Mr. Swan writes that he has seen photographs of them, and that 'many of the ruins are of great size. One can clearly see that in most cases the mason work is at least as good as that at Zimbabwe, and the decorations on the wall are at least as well constructed and are more lavishly used. In one ruin you have the chevron, the herring-bone, and the chessboard patterns.'

J. THEODORE BENT.

13 GREAT CUMBERLAND PLACE;
October 31, 1894.

PREFACE
TO
THE SECOND EDITION

In looking over this work for a second edition, I find little to add to the material as it appeared in the first, and next to nothing to alter. Sir John Willoughby has kindly supplied me with details concerning five weeks' excavation which he carried on the summer following the one which we spent there, the results of which, however, appear only to have produced additional specimens of the objects we found—namely, crucibles with traces of gold, fragments of decorated bowls, phalli, &c.—but no further object to assist us in unravelling the mystery of the primitive race which built the ruins.

No one of the many reviewers of my work has criticised adversely my archæological standpoint with regard to these South African remains: on the contrary, I continue to have letters on the subject from all sides which make me more than ever convinced that the authors of these ruins were a northern race coming from Arabia—a race which spread more extensively over the world than we have at present any conception of, a race closely akin to the Phœnician and the Egyptian, strongly commercial, and eventually developing into the more civilised races of the ancient world.

Professor D. H. Müller, of Vienna, endorses our statements concerning the form and nature of the buildings themselves in his work 'Burgen und Schlösser' (ii. 20), to which he kindly called my attention; and Mr. W. St. Chad Boscawen has also favoured me with the following remarks on certain analogous points that have struck him during an archæological tour in Egypt this last winter:—

The Hawks Gods over the Mines in Mashonaland.

A curious parallel and possible explanation to the birds found in Mashonaland over the works at Zimbabwe seems to me to be afforded by the study of the mines and quarries of the ancient Egyptians. During my explorations in Egypt this winter I visited a large number of quarries, and was much struck by noticing that in those of an early period the hawk nearly always occurs as a guardian emblem.

Of this we have several examples.

In the Wady Magharah, the mines of which were worked for copper and turquoise by the ancient Egyptians of the period of the Third and Fourth Dynasties, especially by Senefru, Knfu, and Kephren, the figure of the hawk is found sculptured upon the rocks as the special emblem of the god of the mines. Another striking example of this connection of the hawk with the mines is afforded by a quarry worked

PREFACE TO THE SECOND EDITION

for alabaster, which I visited in February of this year. The quarry is situated in the Gebel-Kiawleh, to the east of the Siut road. It is a large natural cave, which has been worked into a quarry yielding a rich yellow alabaster, such as was used for making vases and toilet vessels. Over the door were sculptured the cartouches of Teta, the first king of the Sixth Dynasty, but, as may be seen from the accompanying sketch, in the centre of the lintel was a panel on which is sculptured the figure of a *hawk*. This quarry was only worked during Sixth and Twelfth Dynasties, as in the interior were found inscriptions of Amen-em-hat II. and Usortesen III. A third example of this association of the hawk and the mines is afforded by a quarry of the period of the Eighteenth Dynasty. In the mountains at the back of the plain of Tel-el-Amarna is a large limestone quarry. On one pillar of this great excavation extending far into the hill is sculptured the cartouche of Queen Tii. On another column we have the

hawk and emblems of the goddess Hathor, , to whom all mines were sacred. This seems to show that the hawk was the emblem of the goddess Hathor, to whom all mines were sacred, as we know from the inscription at Denderah, where the king says, 'I bestow upon thee the mountains, to produce for thee the stones to be a delight to see.' And it must be remembered that the region of Sinai was especially sacred to the goddess Hathor. This association of mines with Hathor especially explains the birds, as, according to Sinaitic inscriptions, she was in this region particularly worshipped. Here were temples to her where she was worshipped as 'the sublime Hathor, queen of heaven and earth and the dark depths below'; and here she was also associated with the sparrow-hawk of Supt, 'the lord of the East.' This association with Sinai, and also with Arabia and Punt, which is attached to the goddess Hathor, and her connection with the mines in Egypt, seems to me to be most important in connection with the emblem of the hawk in the mines at Zimbabwe.

According to the oldest traditions of the Egyptians there was a close association between Hathor, the goddess of Ta-Netu, 'the Holy Land,' and Punt. She was called the 'Queen and Ruler of Punt.' Now, Punt was the Somali coast, the Ophir of the Egyptians; but, at the same time, there was undoubtedly a close association between it and Arabia, and indeed, as Brugsch remarks, there is no need to limit it to Somali land, but to embrace in it the coasts of Yemen and Hydramaut. 'Here in these regions,' he says ('Hist. Eg.' p. 117), 'we ought to seek, as it appears to us, for those mysterious places which in the fore ages of all history the wonder-loving Cushite races, like swarms of locusts, left in passing from Arabia and across the sea to set foot on the rich and blessed Punt and the "Holy Land," and to continue their wanderings into the interior in a northerly and western direction. We may also bring this connection between Punt, Sinai, and Egypt more close in the time of the Eighteenth Dynasty, when we see on a rock-cut tablet at Sinai, in the Wady Magharah, the dual inscription of Hatsepsu and Thothmes III., who present their offerings to the "lord of the East, the sparrow-hawk Supt, and the heavenly Hathor."'

With all these facts before us there seems little doubt that the association between the hawks and the mines and miners is a very ancient one, and may be attributed to either ancient Egyptian, or rather, I think, to very ancient Arabian times; for, as we know from the inscriptions of Senefru, the builder of the Pyramid of Medum, the mines in Sinai were worked by 'foreigners,' who may have been Chaldeans or ancient Arabians.

Another point which seems to me to throw some additional light upon this subject, and again imply a possible

Arabian connection, is the remarkable ingot mould discovered at Zimbabwe. The shape is exactly that of the curious objects, possibly ingots of some kind, which are represented as being brought by the Amu in the tomb of Khemmhotep at Beni Hasan, an event which took place in the ninth year of the reign of King Usortesen II., of the Twelfth Dynasty. The shape is very interesting, as it has evidently been chosen for the purposes of being tied on to donkeys or carried by slaves. The curious phalli found at Zimbabwe may also resemble the same emblems found in large numbers near the Speos Artemidos, the shrine of Pasht, near to Beni Hasan, and may have been associated with the goddess Hathor. There are many other features which seem to me to bear out a distinctly Arabo-Egyptian theory as to the working of this ancient gold-field, and future study will no doubt bring these in greater prominence.

W. ST. C. BOSCAWEN.

Certain critics from South Africa have attacked my derivations of words. I admit that the subject is open to criticism; almost anyone could state a derivation for such words as Zimbabwe, Makalanga, Mashona, and they would all have about the same degree of plausibility. Some people write and tell me that they are quite sure I am right; others, again, write and tell me that they are quite sure I am wrong. Such being the case, I prefer to let the derivations stand as I originally put them until positive proof be brought before me, and for that I feel sure I shall have to wait a long time.

J. THEODORE BENT.

13 GREAT CUMBERLAND PLACE:
 May 26, 1893.

CONTENTS

PART I

ON THE ROAD TO THE RUINS

CHAP.		PAGE
I.	THE JOURNEY UP BY THE KALAHARI DESERT ROUTE	3
II.	FIRST IMPRESSIONS OF MASHONALAND	31
III.	CAMP LIFE AND WORK AT ZIMBABWE	60

PART II

DEVOTED TO THE ARCHÆOLOGY OF THE RUINED CITIES

IV.	DESCRIPTION OF THE VARIOUS RUINS	95
V.	ON THE ORIENTATION AND MEASUREMENTS OF ZIMBABWE RUINS, BY R. M. W. SWAN	141
VI.	THE FINDS AT THE GREAT ZIMBABWE RUINS	179
VII.	THE GEOGRAPHY AND ETHNOLOGY OF THE MASHONALAND RUINS	223

PART III

EXPLORATION JOURNEYS IN MASHONALAND

CHAP.		PAGE
VIII.	DOWN TO THE SABI RIVER AND MATINDELA RUINS	247
IX.	FORT SALISBURY AND THE OLD WORKINGS AND RUINS OF THE MAZOE VALLEY	270
X.	OUR EMBASSY TO THE CHIEF 'MTOKO	301
XI.	THE RUINED CITIES IN MANOWENDI'S, CHIPUNZA'S, AND MAKONI'S COUNTRIES	336
XII.	THE JOURNEY TO THE COAST	361

APPENDICES

A. NOTES ON THE GEOGRAPHY AND METEOROLOGY OF MASHONALAND, BY R. M. W. SWAN 389

B. LIST OF STATIONS IN MASHONALAND ASTRONOMICALLY OBSERVED, WITH ALTITUDES, BY R. M. W. SWAN . . . 398

C. ADDENDA TO CHAPTER V., BY R. M. W. SWAN . . 401

D. PROGRESS IN MASHONALAND SUMMARISED FROM NOVEMBER 1891 TO MAY 1893 405

INDEX 413

ILLUSTRATIONS

	PAGE
WOODEN PLATTER FOUND IN A CAVE ABOUT TEN MILES FROM ZIMBABWE . . . . *Frontispiece*	
MR. THEODORE BENT	3
MAKING THONGS OF OX-HIDE	19
WOODEN PILLOW	36
ANCIENT EGYPTIAN PILLOW IN THE BRITISH MUSEUM . . .	37
WOODEN DOLLASSES OR DIVINING TABLETS	38
BONE DOLLASSES	39
GOURDS FOR BALING WATER	40
WOODEN MORTAR, BOWL, AND PORRIDGE BOWL . . .	41
WOMAN'S GIRDLE, WITH CARTRIDGE CASES, SKIN-SCRAPERS, AND MEDICINE PHIALS ATTACHED	44
WOODEN HAIR COMB, CHIBI'S COUNTRY	45
GRANARY DECORATED WITH BREAST AND FURROW PATTERN .	46
WOODEN PILLOW REPRESENTING HUMAN FORM	47
IRON SKIN-SCRAPER, AND NEEDLES IN CASES	48
MRS. THEODORE BENT	61
UMGABE AND HIS INDUNAS	67
HATCHET	70
CARVED KNIVES	71
BONE ORNAMENTS	72
WOODEN SNUFF-BOXES	74
BOY BEATING DRUM	77

	PAGE
DRUM DECORATED WITH 'BREAST AND FURROW' PATTERN, AND PLAIN DRUM	78
PLAYING THE PIANO	80
MAKALANGA PIANO	81
HUT AT UMGABE'S KRAAL WITH EUPHORBIA BEHIND	89
AT CHERUMBILA'S KRAAL	91
RUIN ON THE LUNDI RIVER	97
GENERAL VIEW OF ZIMBABWE	101
MAIN ENTRANCE OF CIRCULAR RUIN AT ZIMBABWE	100
LARGE CIRCULAR RUIN, ZIMBABWE	107
PATTERN ON LARGE CIRCULAR RUIN AT ZIMBABWE	109
LARGE ROUND TOWER IN CIRCULAR RUIN, ZIMBABWE	113
ROUND TOWER AND MONOLITH DECORATION ON THE FORTRESS AT ZIMBABWE	123
APPROACH TO THE ACROPOLIS	125
THE PLATFORM WITH MONOLITHS, ETC., ON THE FORTRESS AT ZIMBABWE	127
APPROACH TO THE FORTRESS BY THE CLEFT, ZIMBABWE	133
BAOBAB TREE IN MATINDELA RUINS	136
WALLED-UP ENTRANCE AND PATTERN ON MATINDELA RUINS	137
MAP OF ZIMBABWE DISTRICT	143
THE TWO TOWERS	149
COIN OF BYBLOS SHOWING THE ROUND TOWER	150
THE TRIPLE WALLS AT ZIMBABWE	153
WITHIN THE DOUBLE WALLS, ZIMBABWE	171
SOAPSTONE BIRD ON PEDESTAL	180
SOAPSTONE BIRDS ON PEDESTALS	181
FRONT AND BACK OF A BROKEN SOAPSTONE BIRD ON PEDESTAL	183
BIRD ON PEDESTAL	184
BIRD ON PEDESTAL FROM THE ZODIAC OF DENDERAH	185
MINIATURE BIRDS ON PEDESTALS	187
ORNATE PHALLUS, ZIMBABWE; AND PHŒNICIAN COLUMN IN THE LOUVRE	189

ILLUSTRATIONS

	PAGE
Long Decorated Soapstone Beam in two Pieces	190
Decorated Soapstone Beams	191, 192
Collection of Strange Stones	193
Fragment of Bowl with Procession of Bulls	194
Fragment of Bowl with Hunting Scene	195
Bowl with Zebras	196
Fragment of Soapstone Bowl with Procession	197
Fragments of Soapstone Bowls with Ear of Corn and Lettering	198
Letters from Proto-Arabian Alphabet	199
Letters on a Rock in Bechuanaland, copied by Mr. A. A. Anderson	199
Soapstone Bowls	200, 201
Fragment of Bowl with Knobs	202
Soapstone Cylinder from Zimbabwe	202
Object from Temple of Paphos, Cyprus	203
Glass Beads, Celadon Pottery, Persian Pottery, and Arabian Glass	205
Fragment of Bowl of Glazed Pottery	206
Fragments of Pottery	207
Top of Pottery Bowl, Pottery Sow, and Whorls	208, 209
Weapons	210
Iron Bells and Bronze Spear-head	211, 212
Battle-axes and Arrows	213, 214
Gilt Spear-head	216
Tools	217
Ancient Spade	218
Soapstone Ingot Mould, Zimbabwe	218
Ingot of Tin found in Falmouth Harbour	219
Soapstone Object	219
Bevelled Edge of Gold-smelting Furnace	220

	PAGE
Crucibles for Smelting Gold found at Zimbabwe.	221
Fragments of Pottery Blow-pipes from Furnace	222
Metzwandira	240
Chief's Iron Sceptre, and Iron Razor.	253
Rock near Makori Post Station	254
Knitted Bag	255
Larder Tree	256
Reed Snuff-boxes and Grease-holder.	257
Decorated Hut Door.	259
Straw Hat	260
Decorated Heads	262
Chief's Tomb	271
Interior of a Hut	274
Household Store for Grain, with Native Drawings	275
Native Drawings.	276
Native Bowl from the Mazoe Valley	286
Ruin in Mazoe Valley	298
Three Venetian Beads; one Copper Bead; three old White Venetian Beads; Bone Whorl, Medicine Phials, and Bone Ornaments	297
Tattooed Women from Cridi's, Gambidji's, and Kunzi's Countries	304
Wooden Bowl from Musunoaikwa's Kraal.	305
Makalanga Iron Smelting Furnace	308
Goatskin Bellows and Blow-pipe for Iron Smelting	309
Woman's Dress of Woven Bark Fibre	310
Bracelets.	313
Wooden Platter from Lutzi	316
Earring, Stud for the Lip, and Battle-axe	320
Powder-horn	321
A Collection of Combs.	322
Wooden Spoon. Lutzi	323

ILLUSTRATIONS

	PAGE
Bushman Drawings near 'Mtoko's Kraal	832, 833
Manowendi's Kraal	838
Bushman Drawings from Nyanger Rock	845
Chipunza's Kraal	849
Decorated Post	858

PART I

ON THE ROAD TO THE RUINS

CHAPTER I

THE JOURNEY UP BY THE KALAHARI DESERT ROUTE

MR. THEODORE BENT

In a volume devoted to the ruined cities of Mashonaland I am loth to introduce remarks in narrative form relating how we got to them and how we got away. Still, however, the incidents of our journeyings to and fro offer certain features which may be interesting from an anthropological point of view. The study of the natives and their customs occupied our leisure moments when not digging at Zimbabwe or travelling too fast, and a record of what we saw amongst them, comes legitimately, I think, within the scope of our expedition.

For the absence of narrative of sport in these pages I feel it hardly necessary to apologise. So much has been done in this line by the colossal Nimrods who have visited South Africa that any trifling experiences we may have had in this direction are not worth the telling. My narrative is, therefore, entirely confined to the ruins and the people; on other South African subjects I do not pretend to speak with any authority whatsoever.

Three societies subscribed liberally to our expedition—namely, the Royal Geographical Society, the British Chartered Company of South Africa, and the British Association for the Advancement of Science—without which aid I could never have undertaken a journey of such proportions; and to the officers of the Chartered Company, with whom we naturally came much in contact, I cannot tender thanks commensurate with their kindness; to their assistance, especially in the latter part of our journey, when we had parted company with our waggons and our comforts, we owe the fact that we were able to penetrate into unexplored parts of the country without let or hindrance, and without more discomforts than naturally arise from incidents of travel.

Serious doubts as to the advisability of a lady undertaking such a journey were frequently brought before us at the outset; fortified, however, by previous experience in Persia, Asia Minor, and the Greek Islands, we hardly gave these doubts more than a passing thought, and the event proved that they were wholly unnecessary. My wife was the only one of our party who escaped fever, never having a day's illness during the whole year that we were away from home. She was able to take a good many photographs under circumstances of exceptional difficulty, and instead of being, as was prophesied, a burden to the expedition, she furthered its interests and contributed to its ultimate success in more ways than one.

Mr. Robert McNair Wilson Swan accompanied us in the capacity of cartographer; to him I owe not only the plans which illustrate this volume, but also much kindly assistance in all times of difficulty.

We three left England at the end of January 1891, and returned to it again at the end of January 1892, having accomplished a record rare in African travel, and of which we are justly proud—namely, that no root of bitterness sprang up amongst us.

We bought two waggons, thirty-six oxen, and heaps of tinned provisions at Kimberley. These we conveyed by train to Vryberg, in Bechuanaland, which place we left on March 6. An uninteresting and uneventful 'trek' of a week brought us to Mafeking, where we had to wait some time, owing to a deluge of rain, and from this point I propose to commence the narrative of my observations.

Bechuanaland is about as big as France, and a country which has been gradually coming under the sphere of British influence since Sir Charles Warren's campaign, and which in a very few years must of necessity be absorbed into the embryo empire which Mr. Cecil Rhodes hopes to build up from the Lakes to Cape Town. At present there are three degrees of intensity of British influence in Bechuanaland in proportion to the proximity to headquarters—firstly, the Crown colony to the south, with its railway, its well-to-do settlements at Taungs, Vryberg, and Mafeking, and with its native chiefs confined within certain limits; secondly, the British protectorate to the north of this over such chiefs as Batuen, Pilan, Linchwe, and Sechele, extending vaguely to the west into the Kalahari Desert, and bounded by the Limpopo River and the Dutchmen on the east; thirdly, the independent dominions of the native chief Khama, who rules over a vast territory to the north, and whose interests are entirely British, for with their assistance only can he hope to resist the attacks of his inveterate foe King Lobengula of Matabeleland.

Two roads through Bechuanaland to Mashonaland were open to us from Mafeking: the shorter one is by the river, which, after the rains, is muddy and fever-stricken; the other is longer and less frequented; it passes through a corner of the Kalahari Desert, and had the additional attraction of taking us through the capitals of all the principal chiefs: consequently, we unhesitatingly chose it, and it is this which I now propose to describe.

We may dismiss the Crown colony of Bechuanaland with a few words. It differs little from any other such colony in South Africa, and the natives and their chiefs have little or no identity left to them. Even the once famous Montsoia, chief of the Ba-rolongs of Mafeking, has sunk into the lowest depths of servile submission; he receives a monthly pension of 25*l*., which said sum he always puts under his pillow and sleeps upon; he is avaricious in his old age, and dropsical, and surrounded by women who delight to wrap their swarthy frames in gaudy garments from Europe. He is nominally a Christian, and has been made an F.O.S., or Friend of Ally Sloper, and, as the latter title is more in accordance with his tastes, he points with pride to the diploma which hangs on the walls of his hut.

From Mafeking to Kanya, the capital of Batuen, chief of the Ba-Ngwatetse tribe, is about eighty miles. At first the road is treeless, until the area is reached where terminates the cutting down of timber for the support of the diamond mines at Kimberley, a process which has denuded all southern Bechuanaland of trees, and is gradually creeping north. The rains were not over when we started, and we found the road saturated with moisture; and in two days, near the Ramatlabama River, our progress was just one mile, in which distance our waggons had to be unloaded and dug out six times. But Bechuanaland dries quickly, and in a fortnight after this we had nothing to drink but concentrated mud, which made our tea and coffee so similar that it was impossible to tell the difference.

On one occasion during our midday halt we had all our oxen inoculated with the virus of the lung sickness, for this fatal malady was then raging in Khama's country. Our waggons were placed side by side, and with an ingenious contrivance of thongs our conductor and driver managed to fasten the plunging animals by the horns, whilst a string steeped in the virus was passed with a needle through their tails. Sometimes after this process the tails swell and fall off; and up country a tailless ox has a value peculiarly his own. It is always rather a sickly time for the poor beasts, but as we only lost two out of thirty-six from this disease we voted inoculation successful.

I think Kanya is the first place where one realises that one is in savage Africa. Though it is under British protection it is only nominally so, to prevent the Boers from appropriating it. Batuen, the chief, is still supreme, and, like his father, Gasetsive, he is greatly under missionary influence. He has stuck up a notice on the roadside at the entrance to the town in Sechuana, the language of the country, Dutch, and English, which runs as follows: 'I, Batuen, chief of Ba-Ngwatetse, hereby give notice to my people, and all other people, that no waggons shall enter or leave Kanya on Sunday. Signed, September 28th, 1889.' If any one transgresses this law Batuen takes an ox from each span, a transaction in which piety and profit go conveniently hand in hand.

Kanya is pleasantly situated amongst low hills

well clad with trees. It is a collection of huts divided into circular kraals hedged in with palisades, four to ten huts being contained in each enclosure. These are again contained in larger enclosures, forming separate communities, each governed by its hereditary sub-chief, with its *kotla* or parliament circle in its midst. On the summit of the hill many acres are covered with these huts, and there are also many in the valley below. Certain roughly-constructed walls run round the hill, erected when the Boers threatened an invasion; but now these little difficulties are past, and Batuen limits his warlike tendencies to quarrelling with his neighbours on the question of a border line, a subject which never entered their heads before the British influence came upon them.

All ordinary matters of government and justice are discussed in the large *kotla* before the chief's own hut; but big questions, such as the border question, are discussed at large tribal gatherings in the open *veldt*. There was to be one of these gatherings of Batuen's tribe near Kanya on the following Monday, and we regretted not being able to stop and witness so interesting a ceremony.

The town is quite one of the largest in Bechuanaland, and presents a curious appearance on the summit of the hill. The *kotla* is about 200 feet in diameter, with shady trees in it, beneath which the monarch sits to dispense justice. We passed an idle afternoon therein, watching with interest the women of Batuen's household, naked save for a skin loosely thrown around them, lying on rugs before the palace, and teaching the children to dance to the sound of their weird music, and making the air ring with their merry laughter. In one corner Batuen's slaves were busy filling his granaries with maize just harvested. His soldiers paraded in front of his house, and kept their suspicious eyes upon us as we sat; many of them were quaintly dressed in red coats, which once had been worn by British troops, and soft hats with ostrich feathers in them, whilst their black legs were bare.

Ma-Batuen, the chief's mother, received us somewhat coldly when we penetrated into her hut; she is the chief widow of old Gasetsive, Batuen's father, a noted warrior in his day. The Sechuaua tribes have very funny ideas about death, and never, if possible, let a man die inside his hut; if he does accidentally behave so indiscreetly they pull down the wall at the back to take the corpse out, as it must never go out by the ordinary door, and the hut is usually abandoned. Gasetsive died in his own house, so the wall had to be pulled down, and it has never been repaired, and is abandoned. Batuen built himself a new palace, with a hut for his chief wife on his right, and a hut for his mother on the left. His father's funeral was a grand affair; all the tribe assembled to lament the loss of their warrior chief, and he was laid to rest in a lead coffin in the midst of his *kotla*. The superstitious of the tribe did not approve of the coffin, and imagine that the soul may still be there making frantic efforts to escape.

All the Ba-Ngwatetse are soldiers, and belong to certain regiments or years. When a lot of the youths are initiated together into the tribal mysteries generally the son of a chief is amongst them, and he takes the command of the regiment. In the old ostrich-feather days Kanya was an important trading station, but now there is none of this, and inasmuch as it is off the main road north, it is not a place of much importance from a white man's point of view, and boasts only of one storekeeper and one missionary, both men of great importance in the place.

After Kanya the character of the scenery alters, and you enter an undulating country thickly wooded, and studded here and there with red granite *kopjes*, or gigantic boulders set in rich green vegetation, looking for all the world like pre-Raphaelite Italian pictures. Beneath a long *kopje*, sixteen miles from Kanya, nestles Masoupa, the capital of a young chief, the son of Pilan, who was an important man in his day, and broke off from his own chief Linchwe, bringing his followers with him to settle in the Ba-Ngwatetse country as a sort of sub-chief with nominal independence; it is a conglomeration of bee-hive huts, many of them overgrown with gourds, difficult to distinguish from the mass of boulders around them. When we arrived at Masoupa a dance was going on —a native Sechuana dance—in consequence of the full moon and the rejoicings incident on an abundant harvest. In the *kotla* some forty or more men had formed a circle, and were jumping round and round to the sound of music. Evidently it was an old war dance degenerated; the sugar-cane took the place of the assegai, many black legs were clothed in trousers, and many black shoulders now wore coats; but there are still left as relics of the past the ostrich feather in the hat, the fly whisk of horse, jackal, or other tail, the iron skin-scraper round the neck, which represents the pocket-handkerchief amongst the Kaffirs with which to remove perspiration; the flute with one or two holes, out of which each man seems to produce a different sound; and around the group of dancing men old women still circulate, as of yore, clapping their withered hands and encouraging festivity. It was a sight of considerable picturesqueness amid the bee-hive huts and tall overhanging rocks.

Masoupa was once the residence of a missionary, but the church is now abandoned and falling into ruins, because when asked to repair the edifice at their own expense the men of Masoupa waxed wroth, and replied irreverently that God might repair His own house; and one old man who received a blanket for his reward for attending divine service is reported to have remarked, when the dole was stopped, 'No more blanket, no more hallelujah.' I fear me the men of Masoupa are wedded to heathendom.

The accession of Pilan to the chiefdom of Masoupa is a curious instance of the Sechuana marriage laws.

A former chief's heir was affianced young; he died at the age of eight, before succeeding his father, and, according to custom, the next brother, Moshulilla, married the woman; their son was Pilan, who, on coming of age, turned out his own father, being, as he said, the rightful heir of the boy of eight, for whom he, Moshulilla, the younger brother, had been instrumental in raising up seed. There is a distinct touch of Hebraic, probably Semitic, law in this, as there is in many another Sechuana custom.

The so-called purchase of a wife is curious enough in Bechuanaland. The intending husband brings with him the number of bullocks he thinks the girl is worth; wisely, he does not offer all his stock at once, leaving two or more, as the case may be, at a little distance, for he knows the father will haggle and ask for an equivalent for the girl's keep during childhood, whereupon he will send for another bullock; then the mother will come forward and demand something for lactation and other maternal offices, and another bullock will have to be produced before the contract can be ratified. In reality this apparent purchase of the wife is not so barefaced a thing as it seems, for she is not a negotiable article and cannot again be sold; in case of divorce her value has to be paid back, and her children, if the purchase is not made, belong to her own family. Hence a woman who is not properly bought is in the condition of a slave, whereas her purchased sister has rights which assure her a social standing.

From Pilan's the northward road becomes hideous again; and may henceforward be said to be in the desert region of the Kalahari. This desert is not the waste of sand and rock we are accustomed to imagine a desert should be, but a vast undulating expanse of country covered with timber—the *mimosa*, or camel thorn, the *mapani* bush, and others which reach the water with their roots, though there are no ostensible water sources above ground.

The Kalahari is inhabited sparsely by a wild tribe known as the Ba-kalahari, of kindred origin to the bushmen, whom the Dutch term *Vaal-pens,* or 'Fallow-paunches,' to distinguish them from the darker races. Their great skill is in finding water, and in dry seasons they obtain it by suction through a reed inserted into the ground, the results being spat into a gourd and handed to the thirsty traveller to drink. Khama, Sechele, and Batuen divide this vast desert between them; how far west it goes is unknown; wild animals rapidly becoming extinct elsewhere abound therein. It is a vast limbo of uncertainty, which will necessarily become British property when Bechuanaland is definitely annexed; possibly with a system of artesian wells the water supply may be found adequate, and it may yet have a future before it when the rest of the world is filled to overflowing.

We saw a few of these children of the desert in our progress northwards; they are timid and diffident in the extreme, always avoiding the haunts of the white man, and always wandering hither and thither where rain and water may be found. On their shoulders they carry a bark quiver filled with poisoned arrows to kill their game. They produce fire by dexterously rubbing two sticks together to make a spark. At nightfall they cut grass and branches to make a shelter from the wind; they eat snakes, tortoises, and roots which they dig up with sharp bits of wood, and the contents of their food bags is revolting to behold. They pay tribute in kind to the above-mentioned chiefs—skins, feathers, tusks, or the *mahatla* berries used for making beer—and if these things are not forthcoming they take a fine-grown boy and present him to the chief as his slave.

Sechele is the chief of the Ba-quaina, or children of the *quaina*, or crocodile. Their *siboko*, or tribal object of veneration, is the crocodile, which animal they will not kill or touch under any provocation whatsoever. The Ba-quaina are one of the most powerful of the Bechuanaland feud tribes, and it often occurred to me, Can the name Bechuanaland, for which nobody can give a satisfactory derivation, and of which the natives themselves are entirely ignorant, be a corruption of this name? There have been worse corruptions perpetrated by Dutch and English pioneers in savage lands, and Ba-quainaland would have a derivation, whereas Bechuanaland has none.

Sechele's capital is on the hills above the river Molopolole, quite a flourishing place, or rather group of places, on a high hill, with a curious valley or *kloof* beneath it, where the missionary settlement is by the river banks. Many villages of daub huts are scattered over the hills amongst the red boulders and green vegetation. In the largest, in quite a European-looking house, Sechele lives. Once this house was fitted up for him in European style; it contained a glass chandelier, a sideboard, a gazogene, and a table. In those days Sechele was a good man, and was led by his wife to church; but, alas! this good lady died, and her place was supplied by a rank heathen, who would have none of her predecessor's innovations. Now Sechele is very old and very crippled, and he lies amid the wreck of all his European grandeur; chandelier, sideboard, gazogene, are all in ruins like himself, and he is as big a heathen and as big a sinner as ever wore a crown. So much for the influence of women over their husbands, even when they are black.

Sebele, the heir apparent, does all the executive work of the country now, and the old man is left at home to chew his sugar-cane and smoke his pipe. Around the villages and in the hollow below the native gardens or fields are very fertile; maize, kaffir corn, sugar-cane, grow here in abundance, and out of the tall reeds black women came running to look at us as we passed by, whose daily duty it is at this season of the year to act as scarecrows, and save their crops from the birds. Beneath the corn and mealies they grow gourds and beans, and thereby thoroughly exhaust the soil, which, after a season or two, is left fallow for a while; and if the ground becomes too bad around a town they think nothing of moving their abodes elsewhere, a town being rarely established in one place for more than fifty years.

From Sechele's town to Khama's old capital, Shoshong, is a weary journey of over a hundred and thirty miles through the Kalahari Desert, and through that everlasting bush of mimosa thorn, which rose like impenetrable walls on either side of us. Along this road there is hardly any rising ground; hence it is impossible to see anything for more than a few yards around one, unless one is willing to brave the dangers of penetrating the bush, returning to the camp with tattered garments and ruffled temper, if return you can, for when only a few yards from camp it is quite possible to become hopelessly lost, and many are the stories of deaths and disappearances in this way, and of days of misery spent by travellers in this bush without food or shelter, unable to retrace their steps. The impenetrableness of this jungle in some places is almost unbelievable: the bushes of 'wait-a-bit' thorn are absolutely impossible to get through; every tree of every description about here seems armed by nature with its own defence, and lurking in the grass is the 'grapple plant,' the *Harpagophytum procumbens*, whose crablike claws tear the skin in a most painfully subtle way. The mimosas of many different species which form the bulk of the trees in this bush are also terribly thorny; the Dutch call them camel thorns, because the giraffes, or, as they call them, the camel leopards, feed thereon. Why the Dutch should be so perverse in the naming of animals I never can discover; to them the hyæna is the wolf, the leopard is the tiger, the kori-bustard is the peacock, and many similar anomalies occur.

The botanist or the naturalist might here enjoy every hour of his day. The flowers are lovely, and animal life is here seen in many unaccustomed forms; there are the quaint, spire-like ant-hills tapering to pinnacles of fifteen feet in height; the clustered nests of the 'family bird,' where hundreds live together in a sort of exaggerated honeycomb; the huge yellow and black spiders, which weave their webs from tree to tree of material like the fresh silk of the silkworm, which, with the dew and the morning sun upon it, looks like a gauze curtain suspended in the air. There are, too, the deadly puff adders, the night adders, and things creeping innumerable, the green tree snake stealthily moving like a coil of fresh-cut grass; and wherever there is a rocky *kopje* you are sure to hear at nightfall the hideous screams of the baboons, coupled with the laugh of the jackal. But if you are not a naturalist these things pall upon you after the sensation has been oft repeated, and this was the case with us.

The monotony of the journey would now and again be relieved by a cattle station, where the servants of Sechele or Khama rear cattle for their chiefs; and these always occur in the proximity of water, which we hailed with delight, even if it was only a muddy *vley*, or pond, trampled by the hoofs of many oxen. These cattle stations are generally large circular enclosures surrounded by a palisade, with a tree in the middle, beneath which the inha-

MAKING THONGS OF OX-HIDE

bitants sit stitching at their carosses, or skin rugs, in splendid nudity. All manner of skins hang around; hunks of meat in process of drying; hide thongs are fastened from branch to branch like spiders' webs, which they stretch on the branches to make 'reims' for waggon harness; consequently the air is not too fragrant, and the flies an insupportable nuisance.

One evening we reached one of these kraals after dark, and a weird and picturesque sight it was. Having penetrated through the outer hedge, where the cattle were housed for the night, we reached inner enclosures occupied by the families and their huts. They sat crouching over their fires, eating their evening meal of porridge, thrusting long sticks into the pot, and transferring the stiff paste to their mouths. In spite of the chilliness of the evening, they were naked, save for a loin-cloth and their charms and amulets. A man stood near, playing on an instrument like a bow with one string, with a gourd attached to bring out the sound. He played it with a bit of wood, and the strains were plaintive, if not sweet.

Another night we reached a pond called Selynia, famed all the country round, and a great point of rendezvous for hunters who are about to penetrate the desert. In this pond we intended to do great things in the washing line, and tarry a whole day for this purpose; but it was another disappointment to add to the many we had experienced on this road, for it was nothing but a muddy puddle trampled by oxen, from which we had difficulty in extracting enough liquid to fill our barrels. Needless to say, we did not stay for our proposed washing day, but hurried on.

It was a great relief to reach the hills of Shoshong, the larger trees, the cactus-like euphorbia, and the richer vegetation, after the long flat stretch of waterless bush-covered desert, and we were just now within the tropic of Capricorn. The group of hills is considerable, reaching an elevation of about 800 feet, and with interesting views from the summits. In a deep ravine amongst these hills lie the ruins of the town of Shoshong, the quondam capital of the chief Khama and the Ba-mangwato tribe. It is an interesting illustration of the migratory spirit of the race. The question of moving had long been discussed by Khama and his head men, but the European traders and missionaries at Shoshong thought it would never take place. They built themselves houses and stores, and lived contentedly.

Suddenly, one day, now three years ago, without any prefatory warning, Khama gave orders for the move, and the exodus commenced on the following morning. The rich were exhorted to lend their waggons and their beasts of burden to the poor. Each man helped his neighbour, and, in two months, 15,000 individuals were located in their new home at Palapwe, about sixty miles away, where water is plentiful and the soil exceedingly rich. Thus was Shoshong abandoned. Scarcity of water was the immediate cause of the migration, for there was only one slender stream to water the whole community, and whole rows of women with their jars would stand for hours awaiting their turn to fill them from the source up the valley, which in the dry season barely trickled.

Everything was arranged by Khama in the most beautiful manner. He and his head men had been over at Palapwe for some time, and had arranged the allotments, so that every one on his arrival went straight to the spot appointed, built his hut, and surrounded it with a palisade. Not a murmur or a dispute arose amongst them. In reality it was the knowledge of British support which enabled Khama to carry out this plan. Shoshong, in its rocky ravine, is admirably situated for protection from the Matabele raids. When a rumour of the enemy's approach was received, the women and children were hurried off with provisions to the caves above the town, whilst Khama and his soldiers protected the entrance to the ravine. Palapwe, on the contrary, is open and indefensible, and would be at once exposed to the raids of Lobengula were it not for the camp of the Bechuanaland Border Police at Macloutsie, and the openly avowed support of Great Britain.

The desolate aspect of the ruined town, as seen to-day, is exceedingly odd. The compounds or enclosures are all thickly overgrown with the castor-oil plant. The huts have, in most cases, tumbled in; some show only walls, with the chequered and diaper patterns still on them so beloved by the inhabitants of Bechuanaland; others are mere skeleton huts, with only the framework left. The poles which shut in the cattle kraals have, in many instances, sprouted, and present the appearance of curious circular groves dedicated to some deity. The brick houses of European origin are the most lasting, the old stores and abodes of traders, but even these can now hardly be approached by reason of the thick thorn bushes which, in so short a space of time, have grown up around them. Far up the ravine is the missionary's house, itself a ruin overlooking the ruined town. Baboons, and owls, and vicious wasps now inhabit the rooms where Moffat lived and Livingstone stayed. There is not a vestige of human life now to be seen within miles of Shoshong, which was, three years ago, the capital of one of the most enlightened chiefs of South Africa.

I must say I looked forward with great interest to seeing a man with so wide a reputation for integrity and enlightenment as Khama has in South Africa. Somehow, one's spirit of scepticism is on the alert on such occasions, especially when a negro is the case in point; and I candidly admit that I advanced towards Palapwe fully prepared to find the chief of the Ba-mangwato a rascal and a hypocrite, and that I left his capital, after a week's stay there, one of his most fervent admirers.

Not only has Khama himself established his reputation for honesty, but he is supposed to have inoculated all his people with the same virtue. No one is supposed to steal in Khama's country. He regulates the price of the goat you buy; and the milk vendor dare not ask more than the regulation price, nor can you get it for less. One evening, on our journey from Shoshong to Palapwe, we passed a loaded waggon by the roadside with no one to guard it save a dog; and surely, we thought, such confidence as this implies a security for property rare enough in South Africa.

The aspect of Palapwe is very pleasant. Fine timber covers the hill slopes. A large grassy square, shaded by trees, and with a stream running through it, has been devoted to the outspanning of the many waggons which pass through here. There are as yet but few of those detestable corrugated-iron houses, for the Europeans have wisely elected to dwell in daub huts, like the natives. Scattered far and wide are the clusters of huts in their own enclosures, governed by their respective *indunas*.

High up on the hillside Khama has allotted the choicest spot of all to his spiritual and political adviser, Mr. Hepburn, the missionary. From here a lovely view extends over mountain and plain, over granite *kopje* and the meandering river-bed, far away into the blue distance and the Kalahari. Behind the mission house is a deep ravine, thick set with tropical vegetation, through which a stream runs, called Foto-foto, which at the head of the gorge leaps over steep rocks, and forms a lovely cascade of well-nigh a hundred feet; behind the ravine, on the rocky heights, baboons and other wild animals still linger, perturbed in mind, no doubt, at this recent occupation of their paradise.

Everything in Khama's town is conducted with the rigour—one might almost say bigotry—of religious enthusiasm. The chief conducts in person native services, twice every Sunday, in his large round *kotla*, at which he expects a large attendance. He stands beneath the traditional tree of justice, and the canopy of heaven, quite in a patriarchal style. He has a system of espionage by which he learns the names of those who do not keep Sunday properly, and he punishes them accordingly. He has already collected 3,000*l.* for a church which is to be built at Palapwe.

The two acts, however, which more than anything else display the power of the man, and perhaps his intolerance, are these. Firstly, he forbids all his subjects to make or drink beer. Any one who knows the love of a Kaffir for his porridge-like beer, and his occasional orgies, will realise what a power one man must have to stop this in a whole tribe. Even the missionaries have remonstrated with him on this point, representing the measure as too strong; but he replies, 'Beer is the source of all quarrels and disputes. I will stop it.' Secondly, he has put a stop altogether to the existence of witch doctors and their craft throughout all the Ba-mangwato—another instance of his force of will, when one considers that the national religion of the Sechuana is merely a belief in the existence of good and bad spirits which haunt them and act on their lives. All members of other neighbouring tribes are uncomfortable if they are not charmed by their witch doctor every two or three days.

Like the other Bechuana tribes, the Ba-mangwato have a *totem* which they once revered. Theirs is the *duyker*, a sort of rocbuck; and Khama's father, old Sikkome, would not so much as step on a *duyker*-skin. Khama will now publicly eat a steak of that animal to encourage his men to shake off their belief. In manner the chief is essentially a gentleman, courteous and dignified. He rides a good deal, and prides himself on his stud. On one occasion he did what I doubt if every English gentleman would do. He sold a horse for a high price, which died a few days afterwards, whereupon Khama returned the purchase money, considering that the illness had been acquired previous to the purchase taking place. On his waggons he has painted in English, 'Khama, Chief of the Bamangwato.' They say he understands a great deal of our tongue, but he never trusts himself to speak it, always using an interpreter.

An instance of Khama's system of discipline came under our notice during our stay at Palapwe. Attracted by the sound of bugles, I repaired very early one morning to the *kotla*, and there saw men in all sorts of quaint dresses, with arms, and spades, and picks, mustering to the number of about 200. On enquiry, I was told that it was a regiment which had misbehaved and displeased the chief in some way. The punishment he inflicted on them was this: that for a given period they were to assemble every day and go and work in the fields, opening out new land for the people. There is something Teutonic in Khama's imperial discipline, but the Bechuana are made of different stuff to the Germans. They are by nature peaceful and mild, a race with strong pastoral habits, who have lived for years in dread of Matabele raids; consequently their respect for a chief like Khama—who has actually on one occasion repulsed the foe, and who has established peace, prosperity, and justice in all his borders—is unbounded, and his word is law.

Khama pervades everything in his town. He is always on horseback, visiting the fields, the stores, and the outlying kraals. He has a word for every one; he calls every woman 'my daughter,' and every man 'my son;' he pats the little children on the head. He is a veritable father of his people, a curious and unaccountable outcrop of mental power and integrity amongst a degraded and powerless race. His early history and struggles with his father and brothers are thrilling in the extreme, and his later development extraordinary. Perhaps he may be said to be the only negro living whose biography would repay the writing.

The blending of two sets of ideas, the advance of the new and the remains of the old, are curiously conspicuous at Palapwe, and perhaps the women illustrate this better than the men. On your evening walk you may meet the leading black ladies of the place, parasol in hand, with hideous dresses of gaudy cottons, hats with flowers and feathers, and displaying as they walk the airs and graces of self-consciousness. A little further on you meet the women of the lower orders returning from the fields, with baskets on their heads filled with green pumpkins, bright yellow mealy pods, and rods of sugar cane. A skin caross is thrown over their shoulders, and the rest of their mahogany-coloured bodies is nude, save for a leopard-skin loin-cloth, and armlets and necklaces of bright blue beads. Why is it that civilisation is permitted to destroy all that is picturesque? Surely we, of the nineteenth century, have much to answer for in this respect, and the missionaries who teach races, accustomed to nudity by heredity, that it is a good and proper thing to wear clothes are responsible for three evils—firstly, the appearance of lung diseases amongst them; secondly, the spread of vermin amongst them; and thirdly, the disappearance from amongst them of inherent and natural modesty.

It had been arranged that on our departure from Palapwe we should take twenty-five of Khama's men to act as excavators at the ruins of Zimbabwe. One morning, at sunrise, when we were just rising from our waggons, and indulging in our matutinal yawns, Khama's arrival was announced. The chief walked in front, dignified and smart, dressed in well-made boots, trousers with a correct seam down each side, an irreproachable coat, a billycock hat, and gloves. If Khama has a vice it is that of dress, and, curiously enough, this vice has developed more markedly in his son and heir, who is to all intents and purposes a black masher and nothing else. Khama is a neatly-made, active man of sixty, who might easily pass for twenty years younger; his face sparkles with intelligence; he is, moreover, shrewd, and looks carefully after the interests of his people, who in days scarcely yet gone by have been wretchedly cheated by unscrupulous traders. Behind him, in a long line, walked the twenty-five men that he proposed to place at our disposal, strangely enough dressed in what might be termed the 'transition style.' Ostrich feathers adorned all their hats. One wore a short cutaway coat, which came down to the small of his back, and nothing else. Another considered himself sufficiently garbed with a waistcoat and a fly whisk. They formed a curious collection of humanity, and all twenty-five sat down in a row at a respectful distance, whilst we parleyed with the chief. Luckily for us our negotiations fell through owing to the difficulties of transport; and, on inspection, I must say I felt doubtful as to their capabilities. Away from the influence of their chief, and in a strange country, I feel sure they would have given us endless trouble.

We left Khama and his town with regret on our journey northwards. A few miles below Palapwe we crossed the Lotsani River, a series of semi-stagnant pools, even after the rainy season, many of which pools were gay just then with the lotus or blue water lily (*Nymphœa stellata*). The water percolates through the sand, which has almost silted it up, and a little further on we came across what they call a 'sand river.' Not a trace of water is to be seen in the sandy bed, but, on digging down a few feet, you come across it.

The future colonisation and development of this part of Bechuanaland is dependent on the question of water, pure and simple. If artesian wells can be sunk, if water can be stored in reservoirs, something may be done; but, at present, even the few inhabitants of Khama's country are continually plunged in misery from drought.

North of Palapwe we met but few inhabitants, and, after passing the camp of the Bechuanaland Border Police at Macloutsie, we entered what is known as the 'debatable country,' between the territories of Khama and Lobengula, and claimed by both. It is, at present, uninhabited and unproductive, flat and uninteresting, and continues as far as Fort Tuli, on the Shashi River, after crossing which we entered the country which comes under the direct influence of Lobengula, the vaguely defined territory which under the name of Mashonaland is now governed by the Chartered Company.

CHAPTER II

FIRST IMPRESSIONS OF MASHONALAND

We left Fort Tuli on May 9, 1891, and for the ensuing six months we sojourned in what is now called Mashonaland; of our doings therein and of our wanderings this volume purports to be the narrative. Besides our excavations and examinations into the ruins of a past civilisation, the treatment of which is necessarily dry and special, and, for the benefit of those who care not about such things, has been, as far as possible, confined within the limits of Part II., we had ample time for studying the race which now inhabits the country, inasmuch as we employed over fifty of them during our excavations at Zimbabwe, and during our subsequent wanderings we had them as bearers, and we were brought into intimate relationship with most of their chiefs. The Chartered Company throughout the whole of this period kept us supplied with interpreters of more or less intelligence, who greatly facilitated our intercourse with the natives, and as time went by a certain portion of the language found its way into our own brains, which was an assistance to us in guiding conversations and checking romance.

All the people and tribes around Zimbabwe, down to the Sabi River and north to Fort Charter—and this is the most populous part of the whole country—call themselves by one name, though they are divided into many tribes, and that name is Makalanga. In answer to questions as to nationality they invariably call themselves Makalangas, in contradistinction to the Shangans, who inhabit the east side of the Sabi River. 'You will find many Makalangas there,' 'A Makalanga is buried there,' and so on. The race is exceedingly numerous, and certain British and Dutch pioneers have given them various names, such as Banyai and Makàlaka, which latter they imagine to be a Zulu term of reproach for a limited number of people who act as slaves and herdsmen for the Matabele down by the Shashi and Lundi Rivers. I contend that all these people call themselves Makalángas, and that their land should by right be called Makalangaland.

In this theory, formed on the spot from intercourse with the natives, I was glad to find afterwards that I am ably supported by the Portuguese writer Father dos Santos, to whom frequent allusion will be made in these pages. He says, 'The Monomatapa and all his vassals are Mocarangas, a name which they have because they live in the land of Mocaranga, and talk the language called Mocaranga, which is the best and most polished of all Kaffir languages which I have seen in this Ethiopia.' Couto, another Portuguese writer, bears testimony to the same point, and every one knows the tendency of the Portuguese to substitute *r* for *l*. Umtali is called by the Portuguese Umtare;[1] 'blanco' is 'branco' in Portuguese, and numerous similar instances could be adduced; hence with this small Portuguese variant the names are identical. Father Torrend, in his late work on this part of the country, states, 'The Karanga certainly have been for centuries the paramount tribe of the vast empire of Monomatapa,' and the best derivation that suggests itself is the initial Ma or Ba, 'children,' ka, 'of,' langa, 'the sun.' They are an Abantu race, akin to the Zulus, only a weaker branch whose day is over. Several tribes of Bakalanga came into Natal in 1720, forced down by the powerful Zulu hordes, with traditions of having once formed a part of a powerful tribe further north. Three centuries and a half ago, when the Portuguese first visited the country, they were then all-powerful in this country, and were ruled over by a chief with the dynastic name of Monomatapa, which community split up, like all Kaffir combinations do after a generation or so, into a hopeless state of disintegration.'[2]

[1] M', which looks so mysterious in all African books, is supposed to express that the first syllable may be pronounced either *um* or *mu*; there are four correct ways of pronouncing the name in question, Umtali or Mutare, Umtare or Mutali. The English have adopted the first and the Portuguese the second.

[2] *Vide* Chap. VII.

Each petty chief still has his high-sounding dynastic name, like the Monomatapa or the Pharaoh of his day. Chibi, M'tegeza, M'toko, and countless lesser names are as hereditary as the chiefdoms themselves, and each chief, as he succeeds, drops his own identity and takes the tribal appellative. Such, briefly, is the political aspect of the country we are about to enter.

This is a strange, weird country to look upon, and after the flat monotony of Bechuanaland a perfect paradise. The granite hills are so oddly fantastic in their forms; the deep river-beds so richly luxuriant in their wealth of tropical vegetation; the great baobab trees, the elephants of the vegetable world, so antediluvian in their aspect. Here one would never be surprised to come across the roc's egg of Sindbad or the golden valley of Rasselas; the dreams of the old Arabian story-tellers here seem to have a reality.

Our first real intercourse with the natives was at a lovely spot called Inyamanda, where we 'outspanned' on a small plain surrounded by domed granite *kopjes*, near the summit of one of which is a cluster of villages.

Here we unpacked our beads and our cloth, and commenced African trading in real earnest; what money we had we put away in our boxes, and never wanted it again during our stay in the country. The naked natives swarmed around us like flies, with grain, flour, sour milk, and honey, which commodities can be acquired for a few beads; but for a sheep they wanted a blanket, for meat is scarce enough and valuable amongst this much-raided people. We lost an ox here by one of the many sicknesses fatal to cattle in this region, and the natives hovered round him like vultures till the breath was out of his body; they then fell on him and tore him limb from limb, and commenced their detestable orgy. As one watched them eat, one could imagine that it is not so many generations since they emerged from a state of cannibalism.

We found it a tough climb to the villages through the luxuriant verdure of cactus-like euphorbia, india-rubber tree, the castor-oil, and acacia with lovely red flowers. At an elevation of five hundred feet above our waggons were the mud huts of the people, and up here every night they drive their cattle into extraordinary rock stables for safety. Perched on the rocks are countless circular granaries, constructed of bright red mud and thatched with grass. One would think that a good storm of wind would blow them all away, so frail do they seem.

Rounding a corner of the hill we came across a second village, nestling amongst stupendous boulders, and ascending again a little higher we reached a third by means of a natural tunnel in the rock, fortified, despite its inaccessible position, with palisades.

The natives were somewhat shy of us, and fled to rocky eyries from whence to contemplate us, seated in rows in all sorts of uncomfortable angles, for all the world like monkeys. They are utterly unaccustomed to postures of comfort, reclining at nighttime on a grass mat on the hard ground, with their necks resting on a wooden pillow, curiously carved; they are accustomed to decorate their hair so fantastically with tufts ornamentally arranged and tied up

WOODEN PILLOW

with beads that they are afraid of destroying the effect, and hence these pillows.

These pillows are many of them pretty objects, and decorated with curious patterns, the favourite one being the female breast, and resting on legs which had evidently been evolved out of the human form.

They bear a close and curious resemblance to the wooden head-rests used by the Egyptians in their tombs to support the head of the deceased, specimens of which are seen in the British Museum. They are common all over Africa, and elsewhere amongst savage

ANCIENT EGYPTIAN PILLOW IN THE BRITISH MUSEUM

tribes where special attention is paid to the decoration of the hair.

A Makalanga is by nature vain, and particular about the appearance of his nudity; the ladies have fashions in beads and cloths, like our ladies at home, and before visiting a fresh kraal our men used to love to polish themselves like mahogany, by chewing the monkey-nut and rubbing their skins with it, good-naturedly doing each other's backs and inaccessible corners. Somehow they know what becomes them too, twisting tin ornaments, made from our meat tins, into their black hair. Just now they will

WOODEN DOLLASSES OR DIVINING TABLETS

have nothing but red beads with white eyes, which they thread into necklaces and various ornaments, and which look uncommonly well on their dark skins; and though it seems somewhat paradoxical to say so of naked savages, yet I consider no one has better taste in dress than they have until a hybrid civilisation is introduced amongst them.

From many of the huts at Inyamanda were hanging their *dollasses*—wooden charms, on which are drawn strange figures. Each family possesses a set of four tied together by a string. Of these four one always has a curious conventional form of a lizard carved on it; others have battle axes, diamond patterns, and so forth, invariably repeating themselves, and the purport of which I was never able to ascertain. They are common amongst all the Abantu races, and closely bound up with their occult belief in witchcraft; they are chiefly made of wood, but sometimes neat

BONE DOLLASSES

little ones of bone are found, a set of which I afterwards obtained.

On the evening of the new moon they will seat themselves in a circle, and the village witch doctor will go round, tossing each man's set of dollasses in the air, and by the way they turn up he will divine the fortune of the individual for the month that is to come.

There are many odds and ends of interest scattered about a Makalanga village; there is the drum, from two to four feet in height, covered with zebra or other skin, platted baskets for straining beer, and long-handled gourds, with queer diagonal patterns in black done upon them, which serve as ladles. Most of their domestic implements are made of wood—wooden pestles and wooden mortars for crushing

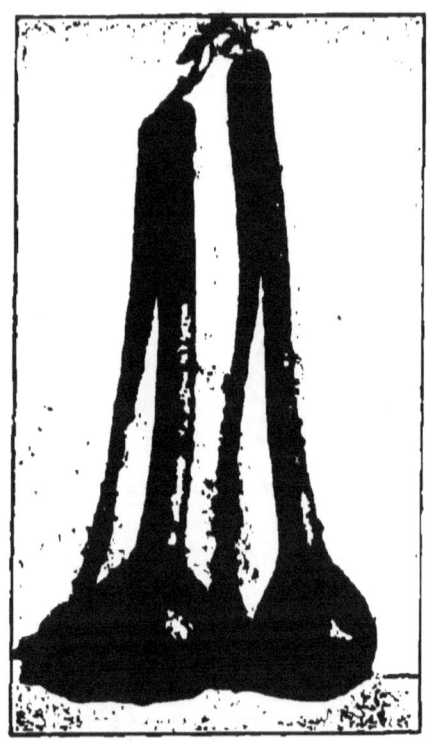

GOURDS FOR BALING WATER

grain, wooden spoons and wooden platters often decorated with pretty zigzag patterns. Natural objects, too, are largely used for personal ornaments. Anklets and necklaces are made out of mimosa pods; necklaces, really quite pretty to look upon, are constructed out of chicken bones; birds' claws and beaks, and the seeds of various plants, are constantly employed for the same purpose. Grass is neatly woven into chaplets, and a Makalanga is never satisfied unless he has a strange bird's feather stuck jauntily in his woolly locks.

Never shall I forget the view from the summit of Inyamanda Rock over the country ruled over by the

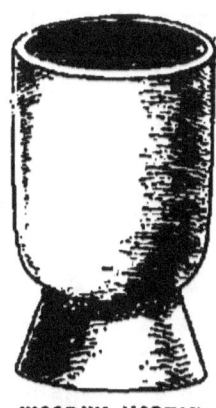
WOODEN MORTAR

WOODEN BOWL

WOODEN PORRIDGE BOWL

chief Matipi; the horizon is cut by countless odd-peaked *kopjes*, some like spires, some like domes, grey and weird, rising out of rich vegetation, getting bluer and bluer in the far distance, and there is always something indescribably rich about the blueness of an African distance. As we descended we passed a wide-spreading tree hung with rich yellow maize pods drying in the sun. Here, too, the bright coral red flowers of the *Erythrina kaffra* were just coming out. Richness of colour seemed to pervade everything.

It was immediately on crossing the Lundi River, the threshold of the country as it were, that we were introduced to the first of the long series of ancient ruins which formed the object of our quest. By diligent search amongst the gigantic remains at Zimbabwe we were able to repeople this country with a race highly civilised in far distant ages, a race far advanced in the art of building and decorating, a gold-seeking race who occupied it like a garrison in the midst of an enemy's country. Surely Africa is a mysterious and awe-inspiring continent, and now in the very heart of it has been found work for the archæologist, almost the very last person who a short time ago would have thought of penetrating its vast interior. *Quid novi ex Africa?* will not be an obsolete phrase for many generations yet to come.

The Lundi River was the only one of the great rivers which flow through this portion of the country which gave us any real trouble. Our waggons had to be unloaded and our effects carried across in a boat, and the waggons dragged through the rushing stream by both teams of oxen; it was an exciting scene, and the place was crowded with people in the same condition as ourselves. On reaching the left bank we halted in a shady spot, and encamped for two days, in order to give our oxen rest and to study the ruin. It was a very charming spot, with fine rocky *kopjes* here and there, rich vegetation, and the dull roar of the fine stream about fifty feet below us. From one of the *kopjes* we got a lovely view up the river, over the thickly wooded flats on either side and the Bufwa range of mountains beyond.

The country beyond the Lundi is thickly populated, with native villages perched on rocky heights, many of which we saw as we wended our slow way through the Naka pass. One hill is inhabited by a tribe of human beings, the next by a tribe of baboons, and I must say these aborigines of the country on the face of it seem more closely allied to one another than they are to the race of white men, who are now appropriating the territory of both. The natives, living as they do in their hill-set villages on the top of the granite *kopjes*, are nimble as goats, cowardly yet friendly to the white stranger. They are constantly engaged in intertribal wars, stealing each other's women and cattle when opportunity occurs, and never dreaming of uniting against the common enemy, the Zulu, during whose periodical raids they perch themselves on the top of their inaccessible rocks, and look down complacently on the burning of their huts, the pillaging of their granaries, and the appropriation of their cattle. Under the thick jungle of trees by the roadside as we passed along we saw many acres under cultivation for the produce of sweet potatoes, beans, and the ground or monkey nut (*Arachis*). They make long neat furrows with their hoes beneath the trees, the shade of which is necessary for their crops. They are an essentially industrious race, far more so than the Kaffirs of our South African colonies. Here the men work in the fields, leaving the women to make pots, build granaries, and carry water. In the Colony women are the chief agriculturists.

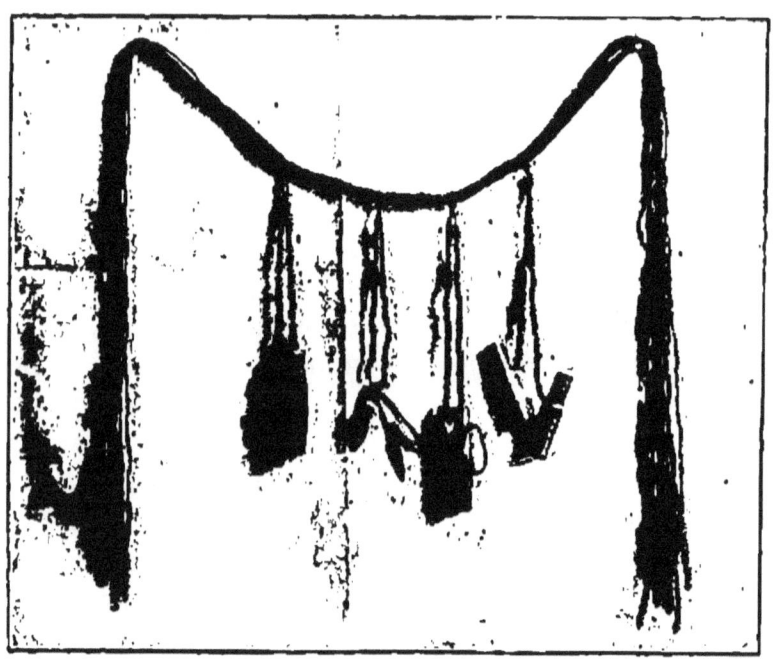

WOMAN'S GIRDLE, WITH CARTRIDGE CASES, SKIN-SCRAPERS, AND MEDICINE PHIALS ATTACHED

We spent a long and pleasant day within a few yards of another village called M'lala in Chibi's country, also perched on a rocky eminence, where many objects of interest came before our notice.

Here for the first time we saw the iron furnaces in

which the natives smelt the iron ore they obtain from the neighbouring mountains. This is a time-honoured industry in Mashonaland. Dos Santos alludes to it in his description, and so do Arab writers of the ninth and tenth centuries, as practised by the savages of their day.[1] In Chibi's country iron-smelting is a great industry. Here whole villages devote all their time and energies to it, tilling no land and keeping no cattle, but exchanging their iron-headed assegais, barbed arrow-heads, and field tools for grain and such domestic commodities as they may require. I am told also of villages which, after the same fashion, have a monopoly of pot-making. This industry is mostly carried on by the women, who deftly build up with clay, on round stands made for the purpose, large pots for domestic use, which they scrape smooth with large shells kept for this object, and then they give them a sort of black glaze with plumbago. In

WOODEN HAIR COMB, CHIBI'S COUNTRY

[1] Chap. VII.

exchange for one of these pots they get as much grain as it will hold.

The native iron furnace is a curious object to look upon. It is made of clay, and is another instance of the design being taken from the human form, for it is made to represent a seated woman; the head is the chimney, decorated in some cases with eyes, nose, and mouth, resting on shoulders; the legs are stretched out and form the sides of the furnace, and to complete the picture they decorate the front with breasts and the tattoo decorations usually found on female stomachs.[1] They heat the charcoal in the furnace by means of air pumped out of goat-skin bellows through clay blow-pipes fixed into the embers. It is a quaint sight to see them at work with all their commodities—pillows, knives, and assegais, fixed on to the reed walls which shut off the forge from the outer world.

GRANARY DECORATED WITH BREAST AND FURROW PATTERN

At M'lala too we were first introduced to the women who have their stomachs decorated with many long lines, or cicatrices. Between thirty and forty of these lines ran across their stomachs, executed with

[1] *Vide* illustration, ch. x.

FIRST IMPRESSIONS

surprising regularity, and resembling the furrows on a ploughed field. In vain we tried to photograph and count them. On one occasion I succeeded in counting sixteen furrows, when the bashful female ran away, and

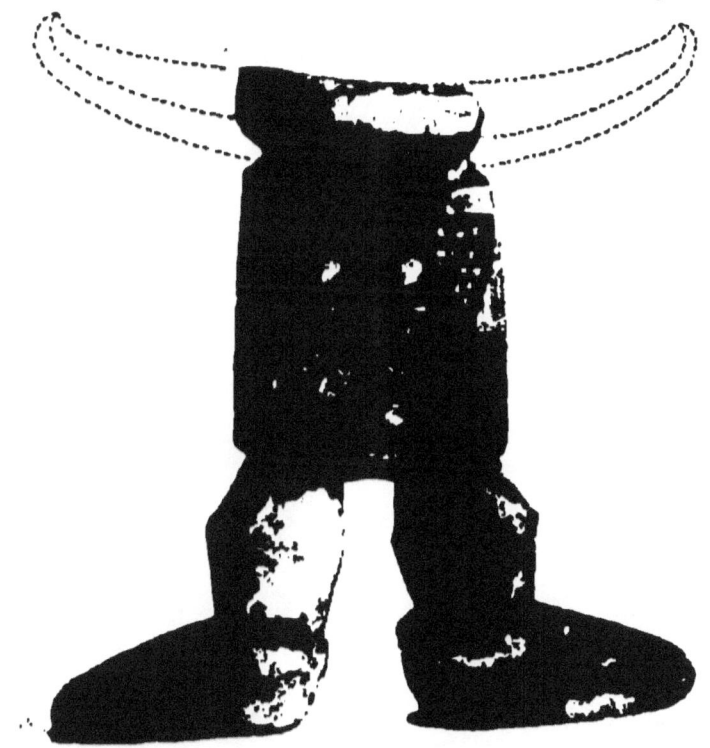

WOODEN PILLOW REPRESENTING HUMAN FORM

I think I had done about half. This is the favourite pattern in Chibi's country and with the neighbouring dependent tribes for female decoration, and they admire it so much that they put it also on their drums, on their granaries, and on their pillows, and, as I have said, on their forges. 'The breast and furrow' pattern, one might technically term it, and I fancy it has to do with an occult idea of fertility.

One of these oddly marked ladies was busily engaged in building a granary on a rock. She first lays a circular foundation of mud, into which she puts

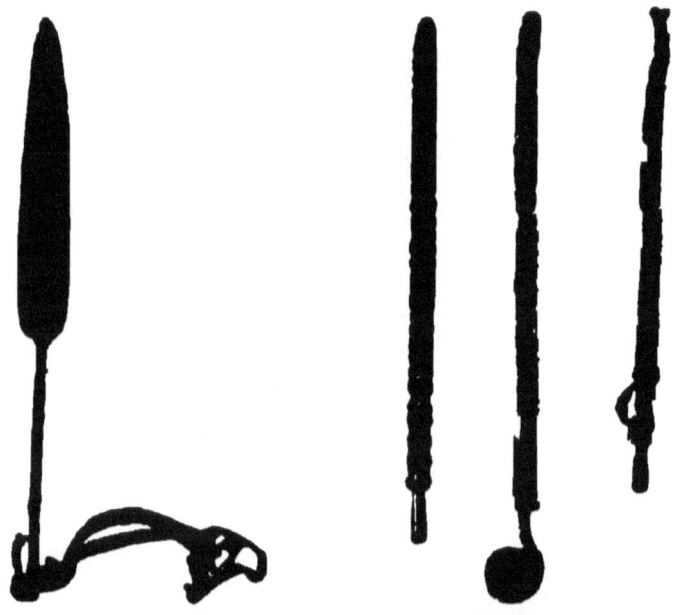

IRON SKIN-SCRAPER.   NEEDLES IN CASES

sticks. On to these she plasters mud until the funnel-shaped thing is about three feet high. A hole is left near the top for inserting and extracting the grain, and it is then thatched with grass; and it effectually keeps out the many rats and mice which swarm in these parts. The costume of these natives is extremely limited. A man is content with two cat-skins, one in front and one behind, though the latter is not always *de rigueur*. The women wear leathern aprons and girdles, tied so tightly as almost to cut them in two, and made of several long strips of leather, like boot-laces fastened together. On to these they hang all the necessaries of their primitive life. At present old cartridge cases are the fashion for holding snuff, or decorated reeds, or wooden cases. Then they have a few decorated bone ornaments, evidently of a mystic character; a skin-scraper or two with which to perform their toilette, which articles are of the form and shape of the strigil known to us from classical times, and the ends of the boot-laces are elegantly finished off with brass or copper beads. The needle, too, is a feature seldom absent from the man's neck and girdle, being a sharp-pointed bit of iron or brass with which they pierce the skins and fasten them together with threads of bark; these needles are fitted into a wooden case, which the more fanciful decorate with bands of brass wire.

At M'lala too we saw the blind witch-doctor of the village, dressed in all his savage toggery. Small gourds with seeds inside to rattle were tied to his calves. These are the fruit of the *Oncoba spinosa*. A buck's horn with a chain was hung round his neck, with which he made a hideous noise. Odd chains of beads decorated his neck, made out of the pods of the *Acacia litakunensis*, and his arms and legs were a mass of brass bracelets and anklets; and his hair resplendent with feathers completed the fantastic appearance of this poor blind man, who danced before us unceasingly, and made such hideous noises that we were obliged to give him some beads and ask him to stop.

The pass through which the road leads up from the river country to Fort Victoria is now called 'Providential,' by reason of the fact that the pioneer force of the Chartered Company did not know how to get over the range of hills rising to the north of the Tokwe River, until Mr. Selous chanced to hit on this gully between the mountains leading up to the higher plateau. Its scenery, to my mind, is distinctly overrated. It is green and luxuriant in tropical vegetation, with the bubbling stream Godobgwe running down it. The hills on either side are fairly fine, but it could be surpassed easily in Wales and Scotland, or even Yorkshire. In point of fact, the scenery of Mashonaland is nothing if not quaint. Providential Pass is distinctly commonplace, whereas the granite *kopje* scenery is the quaintest form of landscape I have ever seen.

Fort Victoria has no redeeming point of beauty about it whatsoever, being placed on a bare flat plateau, surrounded in the rainy season by swamps. Nearly everybody was down with fever when we got there; provisions were at famine prices—for example, seven shillings for a pound of bacon and the same price for a tin of jam—and the melancholy aspect of affairs was enhanced by the hundred and fifty saddles placed in rows within the fort, which had once belonged to the hundred and fifty horses brought up by the pioneers, all of which had died of horse sickness.

The diseases to which quadrupeds are subject in this country are appalling. One man of our acquaintance brought up eighty-seven horses, of which eighty-six died before he got to Fort Victoria. The still mysterious disease called horse sickness is supposed to come from grazing in the early dew, but of this nobody is as yet sure; the poor animals die in a few hours of suffocation, and none but 'salted horses,' *i.e.* horses which have had the disease and recovered, are of any use up here. Our three horses were warranted salted, but this did not prevent one of them from having a recurrence of the disease, which gave us a horrible fright and caused us to expend a whole bottle of whisky on it, to which we fondly imagine it owes its life. Another horse also gave us a similar alarm. One morning its nose was terribly swollen, and the experienced professed to see signs of the sickness in its eye. Nevertheless nothing came of it, and in due course the swelling went down. On close enquiry we discovered that it had been foolishly tied for the night to a euphorbia tree, and had pricked its nose with the poisonous thorns.

As for oxen, the diseases they are subject to make one wonder that any of them ever get up country alive; besides the fatal lung sickness they suffer from what is called the 'drunk sickness,' a species of staggers. When we reached Zimbabwe nearly all our oxen developed the mange and swollen legs, but recovered owing to the long rest. Besides these casualties they often die from eating poisonous grasses; also in some parts the unwholesome herbage, or 'sour *veldt*,' as it is known amongst the drivers, produces kidney diseases and other horrors amongst them.

All around Fort Victoria, they told us, the grass was sour, so we only remained there long enough to make our preparations for our excavations at Zimbabwe. Tools of all descriptions we had luckily brought with us from Fort Tuli, as there were none here when we arrived. In fact the dearth of everything struck us forcibly, but by this time doubtless all this will be remedied, for we were amongst the first waggons to come up after the rains, and now Fort Victoria, with the recent discovery of good gold reefs in its immediate vicinity, is bound to become an important place.

From Fort Victoria our real troubles of progression began. It is only fourteen miles from there to the great Zimbabwe ruins by the narrow Kaffir path, and active individuals have been known to go there and back in a day. It took us exactly seven days to traverse this distance with our waggons. The cutting down of trees, the skirting of swamps, the making of corduroy bridges, were amongst the hindrances which impeded our progress. For our men it was a perpetual time of toil; for us it was a week of excessive weariness.

For two nights we were 'outspanned' by the edge of a deep ravine, at the bottom of which was a swampy stream. This had to be bridged with trees and a road made up and down the banks before our waggons could cross over it. A few hundred yards from this spot the river M'shagashi flowed, a considerable stream, which is within easy reach of Zimbabwe and eventually makes its way down to the Tokwe. On its banks we saw several crocodiles basking, and consequently resisted the temptation to bathe.

By diving into the forests and climbing hills we came across groups of natives who interested us. It was the season just then in which they frequent the forests—the 'barking season,' when they go forth to collect large quantities of the bark of certain trees, out of which they produce so much that is useful for their primitive lives. They weave textiles out of bark; they make bags and string out of bark; they make quivers for their arrows, beehives for their bees, and sometimes granaries, out of bark. The bark industry is second only to the iron-smelting amongst the Makalangas.

At the correct season of the year they go off in groups into the forests to collect bark, taking with them their wives and their children, carrying with them their assegais, and fine barbed arrows with which they shoot mice, a delicacy greatly beloved by them; they take with them also bags of mealies for food, and collect bags of caterpillars—brown hairy caterpillars three inches long, which at this season of the year swarm on the trees. These they disembowel and eat in enormous quantities, and what they cannot eat on the expedition they dry in the sun and take home for future consumption. Their only method of making a fire is by rubbing two sticks dexterously together until a spark appears, with which they ignite some tinder carried in a little wooden box attached to their girdles. At night time they cut down branches from the trees, and make a shelter for themselves from the wind. It is curious to see a set of natives asleep, like sardines in a box, one black naked lump of humanity; if one turns or disturbs the harmony of the pie they all get up and swear at him and settle down again. One man is always told off to watch the fire to keep off wild beasts, and then when morning comes they pack their belongings, their treasures of bark, mice, and caterpillars, and start off along the narrow path in single file at a tremendous pace, silent for a while, and then bursting forth into song, looking for all the world like a procession of black caterpillars themselves.

These forests around Zimbabwe are lovely to wander in, with feathery festoons of lichen, like a fairy scene at a pantomime; outside the forests are long stretches of coarse grass, towering above our heads in many cases, and horrible to have to push through, especially after a fall of rain. They were then in seed, and looked just like our harvest fields at home, giving a golden tinge to the whole country.

Fine trees perched on the summit of colossal ant-hills cast a pleasant shade around, and if by chance we were near a stream we had to be careful not to fall into game pits, deep narrow holes hidden by the long grass, which the natives dig in the ground and towards which they drive deer and antelope, so that they get their forelegs fixed in them and cannot get out.

All around Zimbabwe is far too well watered to be pleasant; long stretches of unhealthy swamps fill up the valleys; rivers and streams are plentiful, and the vegetation consequently rich. Owing to the surrounding swamps we had much fever in our camp during our two months' stay; as we had our waggons with us we could not camp on very high ground, and suffered accordingly. This fever of the high *veldt* with plenty of food and plenty of quinine is by no means dangerous, only oft-recurring and very weakening. Of the fourteen cases we had under treatment none were really dangerously ill, and none seemed to suffer from bad effects afterwards when the fever had worn itself out. The real cause of so much mortality and misery amongst the pioneer force during their first wet season in the country was the want of nourishing food to give the fever patients and the want of proper medicine.

As for the natives themselves, I cannot help saying a few words in their favour, as it has been customary to abuse them and set their capabilities down as nought. During the time we were at Zimbabwe we were constantly surrounded by them, and employed from fifty to sixty of them for our work, and the only thing we lost was half a bottle of whisky, which we did not set down to the natives, who as yet are happily ignorant of the potency of fire-water. Doubtless on the traversed roads and large centres, where they are brought into contact with traders and would-be civilisers of the race, these people become thieves and vagabonds; but in their primitive state the Makalangas are naturally honest, exceedingly courteous in manner, and cowardice appears to be their only vice, arising doubtless from the fact that for generations they have had to flee to their fastnesses before the raids of more powerful races. The Makalanga is above the ordinary Kaffir in intelligence. Contrary to the prognostications of our advisers, we found that some of them rapidly learnt their work, and were very careful excavators, never passing over a thing of value, which is more than can be said of all the white men in our employ. Some of them are decidedly handsome, and not at all like negroes except in skin; many of them have a distinctly Arab cast of countenance, and with their peculiar rows of tufts on the top of their heads looked *en profil* like the figures one sees on Egyptian tombs. There is certainly a Semite drop of blood in their veins; whence it comes will probably never be known, but it is marked both on their countenances and in their customs. In religion they are monotheists—that is to say, they believe in a supreme being called Muali, between whom and them their ancestors, or *mozimos*, to whom they sacrifice, act as intercessors. They lay out food for their dead; they have a day of rest during the ploughing season, which they call Muali's Day; they have dynastic names for their chiefs, like the Pharaohs of old; they sacrifice a goat to ward off pestilence and famine; circumcision is practised amongst some of them. We have also the pillows or head rests, the strigil, the iron sceptres of the chiefs, the iron industry, all with parallels from the north. Then, again, their musical instruments, their games, and their *totems* point distinctly to an Arabian influence, which has been handed down from generation to generation long after the Arabians have ceased to have any definite intercourse with the country. During the course of these pages numerous minor illustrations will from time to time appear which point in the same direction. It is a curious ethnological problem which it will be hard to unravel. All over the country sour milk is much drunk and called *mast*, as it is in the East, and in parts of this country beer is called *dowra* or *doro*, a term which has come from Abyssinia and Arabia, and the method of making it is the same. The corn is soaked in water and left till it sprouts a little; then it is spread in the sun to dry and mixed with unsprouted grain; then the women pound it in wooden mortars, and the malt obtained from this is boiled and left to stand in a pot for two days, and over night a little malt that has been kept for the purpose is thrown over the liquid to excite fermentation. It will not keep at all, and is sometimes strong and intoxicating. Women are the great brewers in Mashonaland, and a good wife is valued according to her skill in this department.

This Kaffir beer is certainly an old-world drink. There are several classical allusions for what is termed 'barley beer.' Xenophon and the Ten Thousand one evening, on reaching an Armenian village in the mountains of Asia Minor, refreshed themselves with what he describes as 'bowls of barley wine in which the grains are floating.'

The Egyptians too made beer after the same fashion, and used it also in sacrifices. Much that was known in the old world has travelled southwards through Nubia and Abyssinia, and is to be found still amongst the Kaffir races of to-day. Some of the words in common use amongst the Kaffirs in Mashonaland are very curious. Anything small, whether it be a child or to indicate that the price paid for anything is insufficient, they term *piccanini*; the word is universal, and points to intercourse with other continents. The term *Morunko*, or *Molungo*, universally applied to white men, is probably of Zulu origin, and has been connected—with what reason I know not—with *Unkulunkulu*, a term to denote the Supreme Being. At any rate it is distinctly a term of respect, and certainly has nothing to do with the Mashona language, in which *Muali* or *Mali* is used to denote God.

Finally, at long last, after exactly three months to a day of 'trekking' in our ox waggons, the mighty ruins of Zimbabwe were reached on June 6, 1891, and we sat down in the wilderness to commence our operations, with the supreme delight of knowing that for two months our beds would not begin to shake and tumble us about before half our nights were over.

CHAPTER III

CAMP LIFE AND WORK AT ZIMBABWE

Our camp was pitched on slightly rising ground about 200 yards from the large circular ruin at Zimbabwe, and was for the space of two months a busy centre of life and work in the midst of the wilderness. There were our two waggons, in which we slept; hard by was erected what our men called an Indian terrace, a construction of grass and sticks in which we ate, and which my wife decorated with the flowers gathered around us—the brilliant red spokes of the flowering aloes, which grew in magnificent fiery clusters all over the rocks, the yellow everlasting (*Helipterum incanum*), which grew in profusion in a neighbouring swamp, wreaths of the pink bignonia, festoons of which decorated the ruins and the neighbouring kraal. Besides these she had the red flowers of the Indian shot (*Canna indica*), which was found in abundance on the hill fortress, fronds of the *Osmunda regalis* and tree fern, the white silky flowers of the sugar tree (*Protea mellifera*), and many others at her disposal, a wealth of floral decoration which no conservatory at home could supply.

MRS. THEODORE BENT

Our tent was our drawing-room ; and in addition to these places of shelter there were the photographic dark tent, five feet six square, the kitchen, and the white men's sleeping-room, cleverly constructed out of the sails of our waggons, with walls of grass. In the centre was an erection for our cocks and hens, but even from here the jackals occasionally contrived to steal one or two. Around the whole camp ran a *skerm*, or hedge, of grass, which latter adjunct gave a comfortable and concentrated feeling to it all. Outside our circle the native workmen erected for themselves three or four huts, into which they all huddled at night like so many sardines in a tin. Around us in every direction grew the tall, wavy grass of the *veldt*, rapidly approaching the time when it can be burnt. This time was one of imminent peril for our camp; the flames, lashed to fury by the wind, approached within a few yards of us. Men with branches rushed hither and thither, beating the advancing enemy with all their might ; our grass hedge was rapidly pulled down, and we trembled for the safety of our Indian terrace. Suddenly a spark caught the huts of the natives, and in a few moments they were reduced to ashes, and the poor shivering occupants had to spend the night in a cave in the rocks behind. Luckily the strenuous efforts of our men were successful in keeping the flames from our camp, and we were thankful when this business was over. Instead of the tall, wavy grass, reeking with moisture when it rained and rotting in the heat of the sun, we had now around us a black sea of ashes, recalling the appearance of the vicinity of a coal mine; but though less picturesque it was far more healthy, and during the last weeks of our stay at Zimbabwe the attacks of fever were less frequent and less severe.

From Fort Victoria came over during our stay a whole host of visitors to see how we were getting on. Prospecting parties going northwards tarried at Fort Victoria for a rest, and came over to see the wondrous ruins of Zimbabwe. Englishmen, Dutchmen from the Transvaal, Germans, all sorts and conditions of men came to visit us, and as temporary custodians of the ruins we felt it our duty to personally conduct parties over them, thereby hearing all sorts and conditions of opinions as to the origin of the same. One of our friends told us that they reminded him foreibly of the Capitol of Rome; another, of a religious turn of mind, saw in them an exact parallel to the old walls of Jerusalem; and a Dutchman, after seeing over them, told me that he was convinced that they must be just ' one tousand year old, and built in the reign of Queen Shabby.' The names of King Solomon and the Queen of Sheba were on everybody's lips, and have become so distasteful to us that we never expect to hear them again without an involuntary shudder.

Thus our two months' stay at Zimbabwe can in no way be said to have been dull. We had our daily work from eight in the morning till sundown, with an hour at midday for luncheon and repose. Out of the working days we lost nine from rain, a curious soaking misty rain which always came on with a high south-east wind, and always, oddly enough, with a rise in the barometer, very exceptional, we were told, at that season of the year. Over these days I would willingly draw a veil; they were truly miserable and always resulted in fresh outbreaks of fever amongst us. With the exception of these nine days the weather was simply delicious, fresh, balmy, and sunny; after sundown and our evening meal we would sit around our camp fire discussing our finds of the day and indulging in hopes for the morrow. Most of our white men were musical, and beguiled the monotony of the evening hours by a series of camp concerts, which made us intimately acquainted with all the latest music-hall ditties. Occasionally rations of Cape brandy, better known as *dop*, would be sent out to the B.S.A. men in our employ; then the evening's fun became fast and furious, and on two occasions caused us no little anxiety. Luckily these ratious were always consumed on the night of their arrival, and though the following morning revealed a headache or two, and an occasional attack of fever, we always rejoiced to see the bottles empty and to know that the orgy would not be repeated for perhaps a fortnight.

Umgabe is the dynastic name of the petty chief whose territory includes the Zimbabwe ruins; he recognises the suzerainty of Chibi, but is to all intents and purposes a free ruler. He came the day after our arrival to visit us, and then we were intro-

F

duced to the Makalanga custom of hand-clapping. The mysterious meaning attached to this hand-clapping I was afterwards able in a measure to fathom.[1] On the arrival of a chief or grand *induna* the hand-clapping is a serious undertaking, and has to go on incessantly until the great man is seated and bids them stop. Umgabe was glad to see us, he said, and had no intention of interrupting our proposed work, provided only we agreed to one thing, and that was to leave his women alone. As for ourselves and our white men, we answered that he need have no fear, but as for our negro workmen we would not hold ourselves responsible for them, but suggested that, as they would all be his subjects, he must see to them himself.

Umgabe is a huge fat man, tall and dignified, though naked; around his neck he has a string of large white Venetian beads of considerable antiquity, brought doubtless to this country by Arabian traders in the Middle Ages; in his hand he carries his iron sceptre, the badge of a chief, and his battle axe is lavishly decorated with brass wire. Amongst his men we saw many of varied types, some distinctly Arabian in features, and I am bound to say the Kaffir type amongst them was the exception and by no means the rule. Arched noses, thin lips, and a generally refined type of countenance are not, as a rule, prominent features amongst those of pure Kaffir blood, but they are common enough around Zimbabwe.

We made arrangements with Umgabe about our

[1] Chap. X.

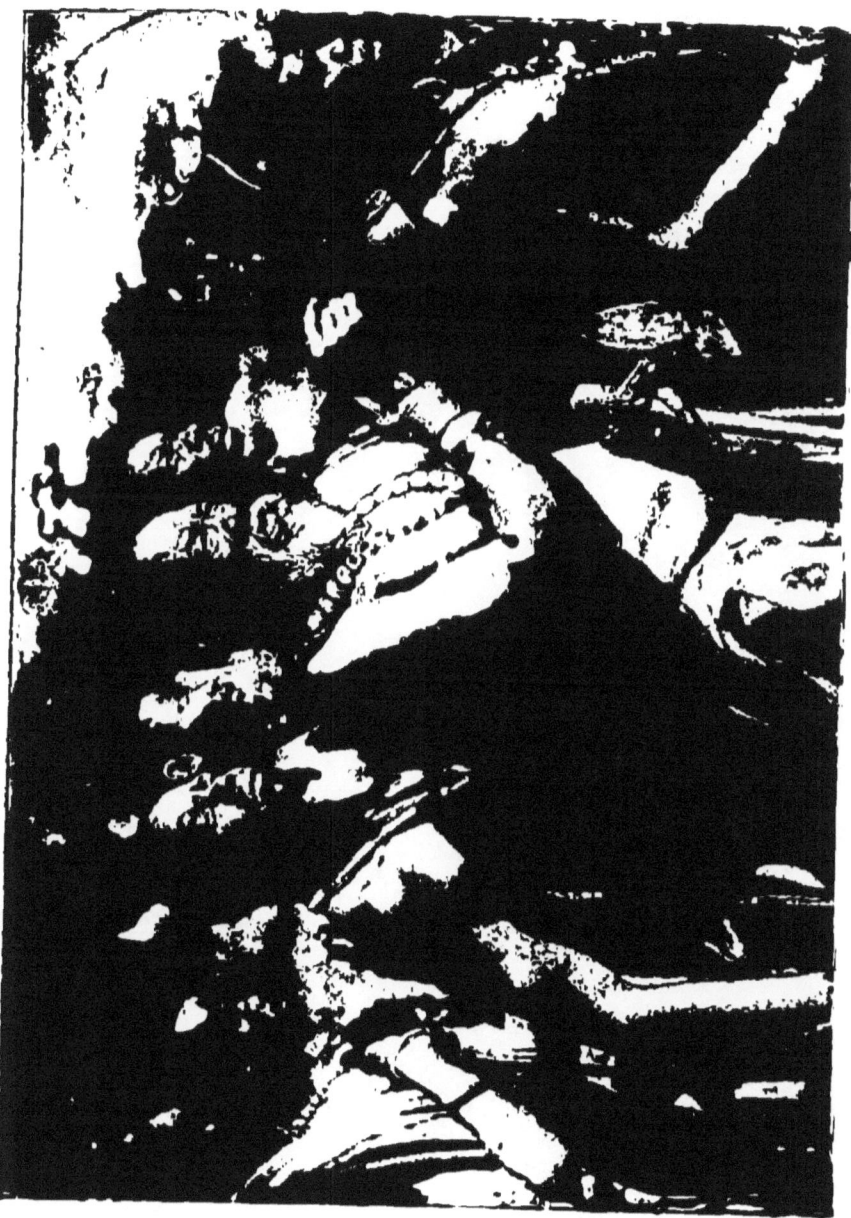
UMGADE AND HIS INDUNAS

work, and collected together a team of thirty individuals who were to do our digging, &c., for the wages of one blanket a month, which blankets cost 4s. 10d. apiece at Fort Tuli, and probably half that in England. For this reward they were to work and also find themselves in everything; it is the present stipulated rate of wages in the country, but I do not expect it will remain so long.

We had great difficulties with them at first. Spades and picks were new to nearly all of them; they were idle; they were afraid of us, and also of the chief on the hill. If it was cold they would sit crouched over small fires of wood, and appear numb and utterly incapable of work. Then they insisted on eating at the inconvenient hour of 10.30 A.M. food brought for them by their women, paste of millet meal and caterpillars; and for every little extra duty they clamoured for a present, or a *parsella*, as they called it. These difficulties gradually disappeared. Some of them became excellent hands with pick and shovel; they got accustomed to us and our hours, and worked with a will, and for a teaspoonful of beads they would do any amount of extra work. Their chief skill was displayed in clearing. I almost despaired of getting rid of the thick jungle which filled the large circular ruin, so that it was almost impossible to stir in it. This they contrived to do for us in three or four days, hacking away at stout trees and branches with their absurd little hatchets, and obtaining the most satisfactory results. Also they were excellent at removing piles of fallen stones, singing as they worked and urging one another on. Altogether we had no cause to complain of our workmen when confidence had been thoroughly established between us. Poor cowardly things that they are, anything like harshness made them run away at once. Our cook, whose temper was exceedingly capricious, one day pursued his native kitchen boy with a hatchet, and he never could get a kitchen boy to stay with him after that; they would poke their fun at him and rouse his ire exceedingly, but always at a respectful distance.

From the many villages on the heights around Zimbabwe came every day crowds of natives, bringing provisions for sale, and we held a regular market in our camp. By this means we got as many cocks and hens as we wanted, eggs, milk, honey, and sweet potatoes; then they would bring us tomatoes, the largest I have ever seen, chillies, capers, rice, and monkey nuts. Some of these, I am told on excellent authority, are distinct products of the New World, the seeds of which must have originally been brought by Dutch, Portuguese, and Spanish traders and given in exchange for the commodities of the country; now they form an integral part of the diet of these people and prove to us how. the ends of the world were brought together long before our time.

HATCHET

These daily markets were times of great excitement for us, for, besides giving us an insight into their ways and life, we found it an excellent time to acquire

CARVED KNIVES

for a few beads their native ornaments. In carving their knives they are particularly ingenious. The sheath of these knives generally ends in a curious conventional double foot; the handle too seems intended to represent a head. Here again it would appear that they take the human form as a favourite basis for a design.

Also their snuff-boxes are many and varied in form; some are made of reeds decorated with black geometrical patterns, some of hollowed-out pieces of wood decorated with patterns and brass wire, also they have their grease-holders similarly decorated, all pointing to a high form of ingenuity.

They were very glad to get good English powder from us; but, nevertheless, before this advent of the white man they made a sort of gunpowder of their own, reddish in colour and not very powerful, specimens of which we acquired. The art must have been learnt from the Portuguese traders and passed up country from one village to another. From a species of cotton plant they produce a very fair equivalent for the genuine article, which they spin on spindles and make into long strings. When the natives found we cared for their ornaments they brought them in large quantities, and our camp was inundated with knives, snuff-boxes, bowls, pottery, and all manner of odd things. They were cunning too in their dealings, bringing one by one into camp small baskets full of meal and other commodities from a large store outside, realising that in this way they got many more

BONE ORNAMENTS

beads and more stretches of *limbo* than if they brought it all at once. As for Umgabe himself, his chief kraal and residence was six miles away, and we saw but little of him after the first excitement of our arrival had worn off; but his brother Ikomo, the *induna* of the kraal on the hill behind the ruins, often came down to see us, and was a constant source of annoyance, seeing that his friendly visits had always some ulterior motive of getting something out of us. On one of these occasions my wife had collected a beautiful bowl of honey; the rascal Ikomo first eyed it with covetousness and then plunged his hand into the very midst thereof, and enjoyed his fingers complacently for some time after, whilst she in disgust had to throw away the best part of her treasure.

Frequently Ikomo would try to interrupt our work, and so frighten our black diggers from other villages that they ran away, and we had to collect a fresh team. On one occasion, whilst digging upon the fortress, we disturbed a large rock, which slipped. On it was perched one of their granaries, which promptly fell to pieces, and the contents were scattered far and wide. In vain we offered to pay for the damage done; almost in no time we were surrounded by a screaming crowd of angry men and women, with Ikomo at their head, brandishing assegais and other terrible weapons of war. For a moment the affair looked serious; all our blacks fled in haste, and we, a small band of white men surrounded by the foe, were doubtful what course to pursue. At length we determined to stand their insults no longer, and seizing whatever was nearest—spade, pick, or shovel—we rushed at them, and forthwith Ikomo and his valiant men fled like sheep before us, clambering up rocks, chattering and screaming like a cageful of monkeys at the Zoo. Sir John Willoughby and one

WOODEN SNUFF-BOXES

or two men from Fort Victoria chanced to come over that day to visit us, and on hearing of our adventure he summoned Ikomo to a palaver, and told him that if such a thing happened again his kraal would be burnt to the ground and his tribe driven from the hill; and the result of this threat was that Ikomo troubled us no more.

Ikomo's kraal occupies a lovely situation on Zimbabwe Hill, with huts nestling in cosy corners amongst the rocks, from the top of which lovely views can be obtained over the distant Bessa and Inyuni ranges on the one side, and over the Livouri range, and Providential Pass on the other, whilst to the south the view extends over a sea of rugged *kopjes* down into the Tokwe valley. From this point the strategical value of the hill is at once grasped, rising as it does sheer out of a well-watered plain, unassailable from all sides, the most commanding position in all the country round. The village is festooned with charming creepers, bignonia and others, then in full flower; rows of granaries decorate the summit, and in the midst are some of those quaint trees which they use as larders, hanging therefrom the produce of their fields neatly tied up in long grass packages, which look like colossal German sausages growing from the branches.

On one of the few flat spaces in the village is kept the village drum, or 'tom-tom,' constantly in use for dances. One day we found the women of the village hard at work enjoying themselves round this drum, dancing a sort of war dance of their own. It was a queer sight to see these women, with deep furrows on their naked stomachs, rushing to and fro, stooping, kneeling, shouting, brandishing battle axes and assegais, and going through all the pantomime of war, until at last one of these Amazons fell into hysterics, and the dance was over. On another occasion, whilst visiting some ruins in a lovely dale about eight miles from Zimbabwe, we were treated to another sort of dance by the women of a neighbouring village. The chief feature in the performance was a grotesque one, and consisted of smacking their furrowed stomachs and long hanging breasts in measured cadence with the movements of their feet, so that the air resounded with the noise produced.

As for the men, they are for ever dancing, either a beer drink, the new moon, or simple, unfeigned joviality being the motive power. Frequently on cold evenings our men would dance round the camp fire; always the same *indomba,* or war dance; round and round they went, shouting, capering, gesticulating. Now and again scouts would be sent out to reconnoitre, and would engage in fight with an imaginary foe, and return victorious to the circle. If one had not had personal experience of their cowardice, one might almost have been alarmed at their hostile attitudes. On pay-day, when our thirty workmen each received a blanket for their month's work, they treated us to a dance, each man wrapped in his new acquisition. Umgabe, with his sceptre and battle axe, conducted the proceedings; it was a most energetic and ridiculous scene to witness, as the blankets whirled round in the air and the men shouted and yelled with joy. When all was over, each man measured his blanket with his neighbour, to see that he had not been cheated, and, gaily chattering, they wended their way to the village, with their blankets trailing behind them. The novelty of possessing a blanket was an intense joy to these savages. One tottering old man was amongst our workmen, and seeing his incapacity, I was about to discard him, but his longing for a blanket was so piteous—' to sleep in a

BOY BEATING DRUM

blanket once before he died '—that he was allowed to continue and do what he could to earn one.

Dancing is the one great dissipation of the Makalanga's life; he will keep it up for hours without tiring at their great beer-drinking feasts, at weddings —nay, even at funerals. At these latter ceremonies they will not allow a white man to be present, so that what they do is still a mystery; but we heard repeatedly the incident festivities after a death had taken place—the shouting, the dancing, and the hideous din of the 'tom-tom.' One day a native

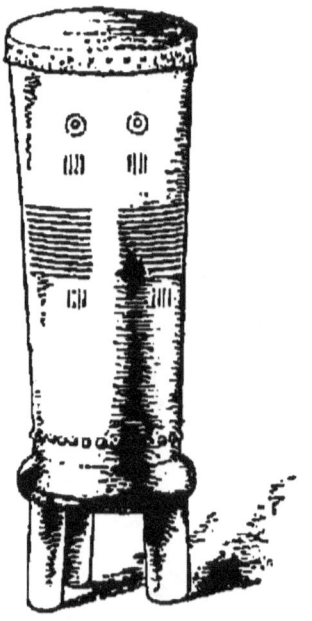

DRUM DECORATED WITH 'BREAST AND FURROW' PATTERN

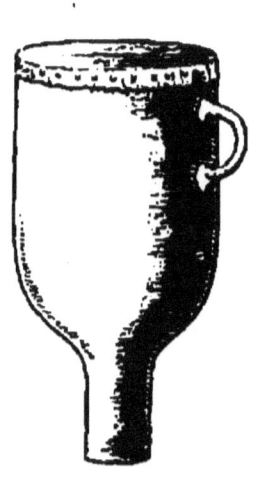

PLAIN DRUM

turned up at our camp with some curious carrot-like roots in his hand. On enquiry as to what he was going to do with them he replied that he was going to a funeral, and that they chewed this root and spat it out—for it is poisonous—at these ceremonies. The natives call this root *amouni*.

In our work at Zimbabwe we unwittingly opened several of their graves amongst the old ruins. The corpse had been laid out on a reed mat—the mat, probably, on which he had slept during life. His bowl and his calabash were placed beside him. One of these graves had been made in a narrow passage in the ancient walls on the fortress. We were rather horrified at what we had done, especially as a man came to complain, and said that it was the grave of his brother, who had died a year before; so we filled up the aperture and resisted the temptation to proceed with our excavations at that spot. After that the old chief Ikomo, whenever we started a fresh place, came and told us a relation of his was buried there. This occurring so often, we began to suspect, and eventually proved, a fraud. So we set sentiment aside and took scientific research as our motto for the future.

In the tomb of a chief it is customary to place a bowl of beer, which is constantly replenished for the refreshment of the spirit, for they are great believers in making themselves agreeable to the departed, and at the annual sacrificial feast in honour of the dead meat and beer are always allotted to the spirits of their ancestors.

One day as we were digging in a cave we came across the skeleton of a goat tied on to a mat with bark string; by its side was the carved knife, with portions of the goat's hair still adhering to it. Here we had an obvious instance of sacrifice, a sacrifice which takes place, I believe, to avert some calamity—famine, war, or pestilence—which at the time threatens the community. The natives were very reticent on the point, but visibly annoyed at our discovery.

There is a good deal of music inherent in the

PLAYING THE PIANO

Makalanga. One man in each village is recognised as the bard. One of our workmen had his piano, which was constantly at work. These pianos are very interesting specimens of primitive musical art; they have thirty or more iron keys, arranged to scale, fixed on to a piece of wood about half a foot square, which is decorated with carving behind. This instrument they generally put into a gourd, with pieces of bone round the edge to increase the sound, which

MAKALANGA PIANO

is decidedly melodious and recalls a spinet. One finds instruments of a similar nature amongst the natives north of the Zambesi. Specimens in the British Museum of almost exactly the same construction come from Southern Egypt and the Congo, pointing to the common and northern origin of most of these African races.

About Zimbabwe we found the natives playing a sort of Jew's harp, made out of a reed and string, giving forth a very faint and ineffective sound. Also they have their cymbals and their drums, which latter they play with elbow and fist in a most energetic manner. Anything, in fact, which makes a noise is pleasing to them. At their dances they tie to their persons small reeds or gourds filled with the seed of the Indian shot, which rattle and add to the prevailing din. They are for ever singing the low, monotonous songs common to primitive races; they encourage one another with song when at work in the fields, or when out on a hunting expedition, and dearly did they love some small musical boxes which we had with us. Music is certainly inherent in them, and one of our men was quite quick at picking up an air, and very angry if his comrades sang out of time or tune.

When time permitted we made several little excursions in the neighbourhood of Zimbabwe. One of these led us to the ruins which they call Little Zimbabwe, about eight miles off. Of all these ruins they have next to no legends, which surprised us greatly. One story, however, they tell, which appears to have obtained universal credence amongst them—that long, long ago white men came and erected these buildings, but the black men poisoned the water and they all died. This story seems to have about as much value in it as the one told us by De Barros, that the natives of his day thought that they had been built by the Devil.

About two miles from our camp there was a long flat granite rock, along which the path passed. On either side of this are two piles of stones, and a line is scratched on the rock between them. Our guides each took a stone, scratched them along the line, and deposited them on the heap opposite. On returning in the evening they did exactly the same thing, and we were told that it is a luck sign, which they do on undertaking a journey to ensure them from danger by the way. It was a very lovely ride, past huge granite boulders, and hills covered with dense foliage, beneath which the women of a village danced for us to the tune of their drum, forming one of the wildest, weirdest pictures we had ever seen. On another occasion we rode to a fortified rock, which had been long since abandoned; but the rude stone walls had been constructed by a more recent race, and compared with certain ruined villages we afterwards saw in Mangwendi's country.[1] On our homeward ride we turned aside to rest in a hut where we found natives busily employed in making beer, a process which they always carry out in the fields, where they have their stores, and in cooking locusts, which we tasted and thought not altogether unlike shrimps.

Thus our time passed at Zimbabwe, actively and pleasantly, and when our second month of work was

[1] Chap. XI.

up, as we had much travelling before us in the country, we reluctantly decided on departure.

We went up to take leave of the *induna* Ikomo at his kraal on the day before our departure. He was seated in front of his hut, eating his red-coloured *sodza*, made of millet meal, and locusts, allowing his head men, who sat around, to take occasional handfuls from his savoury platter. Conversation turned on his tribe. He told us how they had come to Zimbabwe about forty years ago, when he was only eighteen years of age, from the neighbourhood of the Sabi River, where they had lived for many years. No one was then living on Zimbabwe Hill, which was covered, as it is still in parts, with a dense jungle. No one knew anything about the ruins, neither did they seem to care. This is how all tradition is lost among them. The migratory spirit of the people entirely precludes them from having any information of value to give concerning the place in which they may be located; they seldom remain more than one generation in one place, and one place is to them only different from another inasmuch as it affords them refuge from the Matabele and has soil around it which will produce their scanty crops.

On leaving Zimbabwe and our work, we determined on making a tentative trip of a few days, with horses and a donkey, to see how we could manage travelling in the wilds in this country without our waggon home. Moreover, we wished to pay a visit to Umgabe at his kraal, and to take his rival, Cherumbila, on the way back to Fort Victoria.

One lovely morning—the 6th of August—we left our waggons, our cook, and our curios to find their way to Fort Victoria by themselves, and set off. The scenery southwards down the gorge was charming, granite *kopje* after granite *kopje* carrying the eye far away into the blue hazy distance. The foliage was thick and shady, and as we halted at a stream to water our animals we plucked large fronds of *Osmunda regalis* and the tree fern. To our left we passed a huge split rock, just a square block of granite eighty feet high split into four parts, so that narrow paths lead from each side into the heart of it. It was one of the most extraordinary natural stone formations I have ever seen, and the natives call it *Lumbo*. A relation of Umgabe's rules over a fantastic kraal, called Baramazimba, hard by this rock; its huts are situated in such inaccessible corners that you wonder how the inhabitants ever get to them. Huge trees sheltered the entrance to this village, beneath which men were seated on the ground playing *isafuba*, the mysterious game of the Makalangas, with sixty holes in rows in the ground. Ten men can play at this game, and it consists in removing bits of pottery or stones from one hole to the other in an unaccountable manner. We watched it scores of times whilst in the country, and always gave it up as a bad job, deciding that it must be like draughts or chess, learnt by them from the former civilised race who dwelt here. This game is played in different places with different numbers of holes—sometimes only thirty-two holes dug in the ground—always in rows of four. It has a close family relationship to the game called *pullangooly* of India, played in a fish—the sisoo fish, made of wood—which opens like a chess-board, and has fourteen holes in two rows of seven, small beans being employed as counters. The same game hails also from Singapore and from the West Coast of Africa, where it is played with twelve holes and is called *wary*. In short, wherever Arabian influence has been felt this game in some form or other is always found, and forms for us another link in the chain of evidence connecting the Mashonaland ruins with an Arabian influence. The Makalangas are also far superior to other neighbouring Kaffir races in calculating, probably owing to the influence of this very game.

At midday we reached Umgabe's kraal and found our host only just recovering from the effects of drinking too much beer, and he had a relapse in the course of the afternoon to celebrate our arrival. He allotted us two huts, which we proceeded to have cleaned out. My wife and I occupied one, delightfully situated beneath a spreading cork tree; it was about twelve feet in diameter, and in the centre was the fireplace of cement with a raised seat by it on which the cook usually sits when stirring the pot. We spread our rugs where it appeared most level; but during the night, in spite of our candle, the rats careered about us to such an alarming extent that sleep was next to impossible, and we had ample time at our disposal for contemplating our abode.

On one side was a raised place for the family jars, huge earthenware things covered with slabs of stone, containing meal, caterpillars, locusts, and other edibles. On the opposite side was a stable for the calves, which we were able to banish; but we could not so easily control the cocks and hens which came in at all the holes, nor the rats which darted amongst the smoke-begrimed rafters when day dawned. These blackened rafters of the roof the Makalangas use as cupboards, sticking therein their pipes, their weapons, their medicine phials, their tools, and their pillows, and we soon found that this was the place to look for all manner of curios; only the huts are so dark that it is impossible to see anything when there happen to be no holes in the walls. A low door three feet high is the only point for admitting light and air; consequently the huts are not only dark but odoriferous. Besides the walls, the Makalangas construct a primitive sort of cupboard out of the spreading branch of a tree tied round with bark fibre; this contains such things as they fear the rats may spoil. They are very ingenious in making things out of bark—long narrow bags for meal, hen coops in which to carry their poultry about, nets to keep the roofs on their granaries. Bark to them is one of the most useful natural products that they have.

Umgabe's kraal has as lovely a situation as can

well be imagined. It is situated in a glade, buried in trees and vegetation, so that until you are in it you hardly notice the spot. Huge granite mountains rise on either side, completely shutting it in; a rushing stream runs through the glade, supplying the place with delicious water. Here is distinctly a spot where only man is vile; and the great fat chief, seated on the top of a rock, sodden with beer, formed one of the vilest specimens of humanity I ever saw.

The aforesaid stream in its course down the valley, just below the village, runs underneath a vast mass of granite rocks, which form a labyrinth of caves exceedingly difficult to approach. To facilitate the entry the inhabitants have made bridges of trees, and in times of danger from the Matabele they take refuge therein; they take their cattle with them, and pull down the bridges. In the interior they always keep many granaries well filled with grain, in case of accidents. Old Umgabe was most unwilling for us to go in and learn his tribal secret; however, nothing daunted, with the aid of candles we effected an entry, and a queer place it is. Granaries are perched in all sorts of crannies, traces of a late habitation exist all around, and the boiling stream is roaring in the crevices below.

The flat rocks outside were just then covered with locusts drying in the sun; millet meal and other domestic commodities were spread out too.

The rest of that lovely afternoon we spent in wandering about in this paradise, admiring the dense foliage, the creepers, and the euphorbia which towered over the huts, and regretted when the pangs of hunger and the shades of evening obliged us to return to our

HUT AT UMGABE'S KRAAL WITH EUPHORBIA BEHIND

huts to cook our frugal meal and pretend to go to bed.

It was a long ride next day to Cherumbila's kraal, the bitter enemy and hereditary foe of our late host;

we passed many villages and many streams on the way, and had a direful experience at one of the swamps which our path crossed just before reaching our destination. One of our horses disappeared in it, all but his head, another rolled entirely over in it, whilst we stood helpless on the bank and fearful of the result; but at length we managed to drag the wretched animals out, and an hour before sundown we reached Cherumbila's stronghold.

It is quite a different place from Umgabe's, and much larger, with huts running along the backbone of a high granite ridge. The principal kraal, where the chief lives, is fortified with palisades and rough walls, and is entered by a gateway formed of posts leaning against one another; the huts are better, with decorated doors, and the people finer than those of Umgabe's tribe. Many of them have their heads cleanly shaved at the top, with a row of curious tufts of hair tied together and made to look like a lot of black plants sprouting from their skulls.

Cherumbila himself is a lithe, active man, a complete contrast to Umgabe; a man of activity both of mind and body, he is feared and respected by his men, and is consequently one of the strongest chiefs hereabouts, and raids upon his neighbours with great success. Years ago, when he was a boy, he told us, his tribe lived on the top of one of the highest mountains overlooking Providential Pass, when a Matabele raid, or *impi*, fell upon them and drove most of the inhabitants over a steep precipice to their death: the remnant that escaped came here and settled, and have now, under Cherumbila's rule, grown strong. The chief allotted us his own hut for our night's lodging. Nevertheless we had much the same experiences as on the previous night, which

AT CHERUMBILA'S KRAAL.

made us vow that on our prospective trips to the Sabi and northwards we would take our tent and never again expose ourselves to the companionship of rats and other vermin in the native huts.

The following day a lovely ride over the mountains, through dense forests and swarms of locusts, which our black men eagerly collected, brought us back again to Fort Victoria and comparative civilisation, where we made preparations for our more extended expeditions away from the road and our waggons, warned but not discouraged by our discomforts with Umgabe and Cherumbila.

PART II

DEVOTED TO THE ARCHÆOLOGY OF THE RUINED CITIES

CHAPTER IV

DESCRIPTION OF THE VARIOUS RUINS

DURING our stay in Mashonaland we visited and carefully examined the sites of many ruins, a minute description of which I propose to give in this chapter. As a feature in the country they are most remarkable—ancient, massive, mysterious, standing out in startling contrast to the primitive huts of the barbarians who dwell around them and the wilderness of nature. Of course it was impossible in one season, and in the present undeveloped state of the country, to visit them all; but from accounts given of others which we could not visit, and which consequently I shall only briefly allude to here, there is enough evidence to prove that they were all built by the same race, in the same style, and for the same purpose.

From Dr. Emil Holub's work ('Seven Years in South Africa') we learn something about a ruin he saw on the Shashi River, which consisted of a wall protecting a hill and formed ' of blocks of granite laid one upon another, without being fixed by cement of any kind.' Also at Tati he saw another ruin, forming a long line of protection for a hill, roughly put together on the inside, but on the outside, 'probably with some view to symmetry and decoration, there had been inserted double rows of stones, hewn into a kind of tile, and placed obliquely one row at right angles to the other. Each enclosure had an entrance facing north.' He concludes that the ruin was constructed to protect the gold, 'numbers of pits fifty feet deep being found in the vicinity.' This pattern, the construction, and the object undoubtedly connect these ruins with those which I shall presently describe.

Mr. G. Philips, an old hunter in these parts, said at the Royal Geographical Society's meeting, November 24, 1890, of the Zimbabwe ruins, 'They are exactly like others I have seen in the country—the same zigzag patterns and the mortarless walls of small hewn stones. When hunting in the mountains to the west of this I came on a regular line of these ruins, and one must have been a tremendously big place. There were three distinct gateways in the outer wall, which I suppose was at least thirty feet thick at the base, and one of those immense ironwood trees (*hartekol*), that would have taken hundreds of years to grow, had grown up through a crevice in the wall and rent it asunder.' He also described another ruin north-west of Tati. 'The walls are twelve to fifteen feet thick, and it is entered by a passage so arranged as to be commanded by archers from the interior, and it only admits of the passage of one at a time.'

RUIN ON THE LUNDI RIVER

Mr. E. A. Maund, in speaking of the ruins at Tati and on the Impakwe, says, 'As I have said, these ruins are always found near gold workings; they are built in the same way of granite, hewn into small blocks somewhat bigger than a brick, and put together without mortar. In the base of both of these there is the same herring-bone course as at Zimbabwe, though nearer the base of the wall. . . . The remains on the Impakwe are similar in construction and are within fifty yards of the river; it was evidently an octagonal tower.' Mr. Moffat, our political agent in Matabeleland, in speaking to me about this ruin, told me how it had been much demolished during his recollection, owing to the fact that all waggons going up to Matabeleland outspan near it, and the men assist at its demolition.

There is another ruin of a similar character near where the River Elibi flows into the Limpopo, and another further up the Mazoe Valley than the one we visited.[1]

I have alluded to these ruins, which I have not seen, to prove the great area over which they are spread, and I have little doubt that as the country gets opened out a great many more will be brought to light, proving the extensive population which once lived here as a garrison in a hostile country, for the sake of the gold which they extracted from the mines in the quartz reefs between the Zambesi and Limpopo Rivers.

[1] *Vide* Chap. IX.

From personal experience I can speak of the ruins on the Lundi River; of those at and near Zimbabwe; of the chain of forts on the Sabi River, including Metemo, Matindela, Chilouga, and Chiburwe, and the fort in the Mazoe gold fields, all of which belong to the same period, and were built by the same race, and agree in character with those described by Messrs. Philips and Maund on the Tati, Impakwe, and elsewhere, and are quite distinct from the more modern structures in Mangwendi's and Makoni's countries, which we visited towards the end of our tour and which I shall describe in Chapter XI.

The circular ruin erected on a low granite eminence of about five hundred yards from the Lundi River is of exceeding insignificance when compared with those of Zimbabwe and Matindela: it is only fifty-four feet in diameter, and the original wall was only five feet thick; the courses are very regular and neatly put together without mortar, and the stones, of granite, are of a uniform size, broken into blocks about twice the size of an ordinary brick. It had two entrances, one to the north and another to the south-east, the latter being carefully walled up with an inserted structure in which the courses are carried out with a carefulness similar to the walls of the rest of the building. The interesting features of this ruin are the patterns in three tiers beginning at a few feet from the northern entrance, the two lower ones consisting of a herring-bone pattern, formed by the stones being placed obliquely in contrary directions

ACROPOLIS   OUR CAMP   CIRCULAR RUIN

GENERAL VIEW OF ZIMBABWE

in each tier, whilst the upper pattern is produced by regular gaps of two inches being left between the stones in two of the courses. Nearly facing the rising sun at the equinox is a curious bulge, about two feet deep, constructed in the wall. At this bulge the two lower rows of ornamentation terminate, but the upper one is carried on round it as far as the south-eastern entrance. There can be little doubt that these patterns, found on nearly all the Mashonaland ruins, were constructed for a purpose; they only go round a portion of the buildings; they have always the same aspect—namely, south-east—and one cannot dissociate these circular buildings and the patterns from some form of sun worship. 'The circle is a sacred enclosure,' says Major Conder in his 'Heth and Moab,' 'without which the Arab still stands with his face to the rising sun.' Into this question of solstitial orientation in connection with the ruins Mr. Swan will enter at length in the ensuing chapter.

The Lundi ruin had a cement floor, similar to those floors which we afterwards frequently came across in the Zimbabwe buildings; it would appear to have acted the double function of a fortress and a temple, guarding a population settled here on the river's bank, who built their huts around it.

The ruins of the Great Zimbabwe (which name I have applied to them to distinguish them from the numerous minor Zimbabwes scattered over the country) are situated in south latitude 20° 16′ 30″, and east longitude 31° 10′ 10″, on the high plateau of Mashonaland, 3,300 feet above the sea level, and form the capital of a long series of such ruins stretching up the whole length of the western side of the Sabi River. They are built on granite, and of granite, quartz reefs being found at a distance of a few miles.

The prominent features of the Great Zimbabwe ruins, which cover a large area of ground, are, firstly, the large circular ruin with its round tower on the edge of a gentle slope on the plain below; secondly, the mass of ruins in the valley immediately beneath this; and thirdly, the intricate fortress on the granite hill above, acting as the acropolis of the ancient city. These we will now discuss in their order.

When we reached the Great Zimbabwe the circular ruin was on the inside a dense mass of tropical vegetation; creepers and monkey ropes hung in matted confusion to the tall trees, forming a jungle which it was almost impossible to penetrate, and added to the mazy labyrinth of walls a peculiar and almost awe-inspiring mystery.

It was the work of some days to clear this off with the aid of native workmen, whilst at the same time we proceeded with our excavations in the neighbourhood of the tower and other prominent portions of the building.

As for the walls themselves, they were nearly free from vegetation, for, owing to the absence of mortar, no lichen, moss, nor creeper could thrive on them;

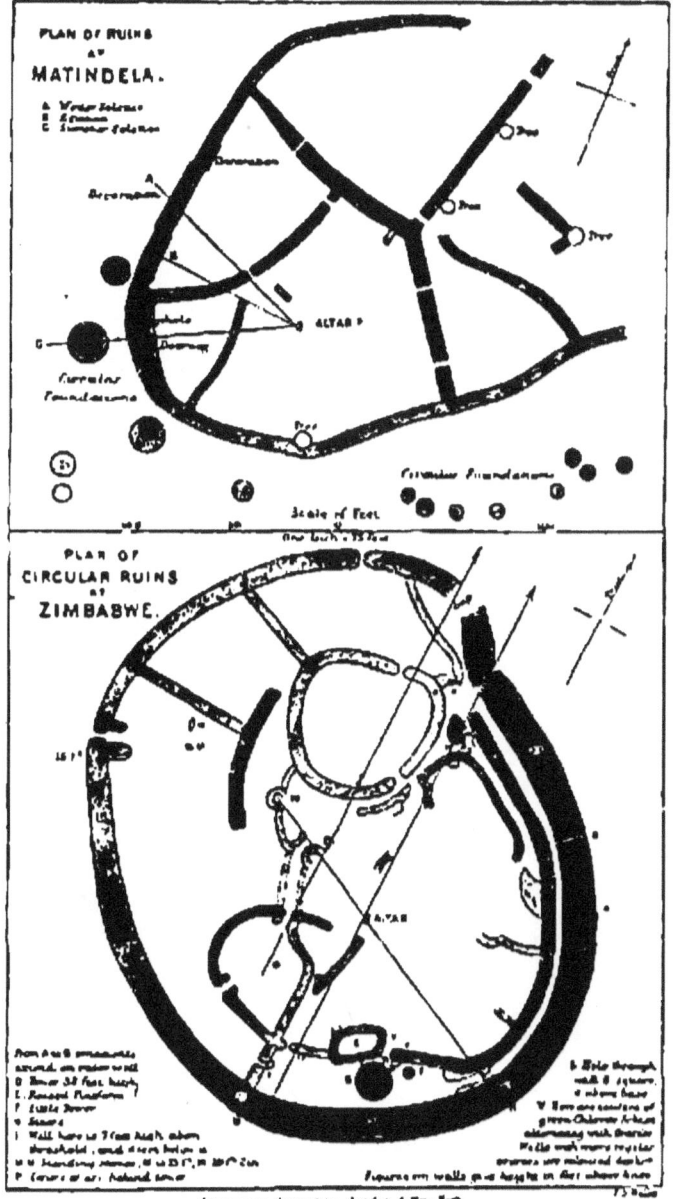

1

and those few things which had penetrated into crevices were of a succulent character, which formed their branches to the shape of the interstices. To this fact is due the wonderful state of preservation in which these ruins are found.

What appeared at first sight to be a true circle eventually proved elliptical—a form of temple found at Marib, the ancient Saba and capital of the Sabæan kingdom in Arabia, and at the Castle of Nakab al Hajar, also in that country.[1] Its greatest length is 280 feet; the wall at its highest point is thirty-five feet above the ground, and fifteen feet at the lowest; its greatest base thickness is sixteen feet two inches, and its thinnest point is about five feet. In the structure of the wall one very noticeable feature is that the portion to the south-east is very much better built, and is both thicker and higher: here the courses are marvellously true, as if built with a levelling line, and the stones, of granite hammered into shape, are exactly the same size, whereas on the north-west side and in some of the interior walls, which are marked in a lighter colour on the plan, the courses begin to get slightly irregular, and the stones of unequal size, suggesting almost a different period of workmanship; but then there is no point where the good definitely ends or the bad begins, except at a short gap on the northern side, where the good wall would seem to have been continued more in a northerly direction, and the

[1] *Encyclop. Brit.*

inferior wall to have been brought round to meet it.

There are three entrances to this circular building. The principal one, only three feet wide, faces the hill fortress and the north. It has an odd curvature in it, constructed evidently true north, whereas all the

MAIN ENTRANCE

other entrances are straight. Below this entrance runs a very substantial substructure wall, and the little space immediately inside it was covered with a thick cement, made out of powdered granite, out of which steps had been formed leading down to the various passages which converge here from the centre of the building. The presence of this concrete in use for

LARGE CIRCULAR RUIN, ZIMBABWE

flooring and steps in buildings constructed without mortar is interesting, showing that dry building was used not from necessity but from choice.

The entrance to the north-west had been walled up, and we had to climb over a heap of stones to gain admittance until it was opened out. It is narrow and straight, and protected by two buttresses on the inside. The wall here is very inferior to what it is at the main entrance. There was also another entrance

PATTERN ON LARGE CIRCULAR RUIN AT ZIMBABWE

between these two, presumably merely a sally-port in the wall, the lintel of which had consisted of wooden beams, which had been burnt, and on their giving way the wall above had also fallen down.

Of the outer wall of the circular building the most interesting portion is decidedly that to the south-east. A few courses below the summit on the outside, from point A to point B on the plan, runs the pattern, formed by two courses having the stones placed chevron-wise, neatly fitted in with smaller stones receding a little, so as to make the pattern at a distance appear as if it stood out in relief, whereas it is really flush with the wall. This pattern coincides with the sacred enclosure inside, terminating at point B exactly where the enclosure terminates, and at the other end at point A about half-way down the narrow passage, forming thus an arc of one and a half right angle. Its connection with the sanctity of the place is obvious, and into its relation to the orientation of the temple Mr. Swan will enter fully in the ensuing chapter. Along this portion of the wall, and on this only, large monoliths were inserted, most of which have fallen away; but those still standing show that they were equidistant. Here too the top of the wall has been neatly paved with slabs of granite, and must have formed a broad promenade, presumably approached by steps from a point near the main entrance. Here one can still walk with ease, whereas on the inferior portion of the wall it is now scarcely possible to scramble.

The labyrinthine character of the interior will be best grasped by a glance at the plan. Entering from the northern portal, we at once plunge into its intricacies. The great and astounding feature is the long narrow passage leading direct from the main entrance to the sacred enclosure, so narrow in parts that two people cannot walk abreast, whilst on either side of you rise the stupendous walls, thirty feet in height, and built with such evenness of courses and symmetry that as a specimen of the dry builder's art it is without a parallel. The large blocks of cut stone used in Egyptian, Greek, and Roman masonry must have been comparatively easy to deal with as compared with these small stones of rough granite built in even courses in a circular wall of immense thickness and height. The idea at once suggests itself that the people who erected these walls had at one time been accustomed to build in bricks, and that in the absence of this material they had perfected a system of stone-building to represent as nearly as possible the appearance of brick; also another reason for the use of small stones may have been to enable them to construct the tower and curves with greater accuracy. The facings of the stones are all uniform, but most of them run back into the wall irregularly, acting in the same way as *throughs* in our dry-built walls at home in preserving the building from falling. In this narrow passage, at point 8, is the remarkable hole, executed with perfect neatness through the thickest part of the wall, about the actual use of which I am able to give no definite theory. It could not have been used for drainage or defence; and in the fortress above there are two similar tunnels equally inexplicable.

The actual approaches to the sacred enclosure are most carefully defended with buttresses on either side, into which a form of portcullis has been fixed, with two grooves, one running down each side, presumably originally intended to receive a wooden door; but at a later period all these entrances have been carefully walled up, for what purpose it is difficult to say. It naturally occurred to us that this had been done at a time of danger for protection, but the neatness with which the blocking-up walls are executed is against this theory.

At point V on the plan there is a remarkable instance of the two periods of building. Here, in front of the sacred enclosure, the wall was decorated with courses of black slate in the older and better wall, whereas they are omitted in the inferior continuation.

At point E there is a raised platform immediately in front of the large round tower, covered with a flooring of thick cement, supported by large stones loosely packed together, into which a monolith had been stuck. This platform was connected with the sacred enclosure by a flight of cement steps, and was presumably used for religious purposes.

In dealing with the two remarkable round towers which stood in the sacred enclosure, one cannot lay too much stress on the symmetry of the courses and the accuracy with which they have been built. They stand in the centre of the sacred enclosure, which was floored with cement. By digging to their foundations we were able to get very accurate measurements of them, and found that the circumference of the smaller one corresponds exactly to the diameter of the big one, and the diameter of the big one is apparently equal to half its original height, and its circumference again is equal to the diameter of the round building on the Lundi River. The battering of

LARGE ROUND TOWER IN CIRCULAR RUIN. ZIMBABWE

the big tower is carried out with mathematical accuracy, the slope of the curve being perfectly regular, and is produced by placing the superincumbent stones in a slightly receding position, so that with the aid of a monkey rope we were able to climb to the top. A few courses below the summit, which would seem to be very much in its original condition except on the south side, where Herr Mauch confesses to have pulled down the stones of several courses, runs a dentelle pattern, marked D on the plan, formed by placing the stones of one course edgeways. This pattern is the same as the lower one given in the illustration of Matindela ruins, p. 157; but unfortunately, owing to the demolition of the upper courses, it is impossible to define its extent. The tower would seem to have been thirty-five feet in height, and the summit to have been a level of about four feet in diameter. By digging below this tower, and pulling out stones from the sides, which we carefully replaced, we demonstrated to our satisfaction that it was solid. It was built on nothing but the soil of the place, and was erected over nothing; the foundations go down for one foot below the floor of cement which covered the enclosure, and it has been preserved to us simply by its solidity, its long through stones, and the way in which the stones have supported one another. We investigated the smaller tower very thoroughly, and found it also solid.

The religious purport of these towers would seem to be conclusively proved by the numerous finds we made in other parts of the ruins of a phallic nature (*vide* Chap. VI.), and I think a quotation from Montfaucon's 'L'Antiquité Expliquée' will give us the keynote of the worship. 'The ancients assure us that all the Arabians worshipped a tower, which they called El Acara or Alquetila, which was built by their patriarch, Ishmael.' 'Maximus of Tyre says they honoured as a great god a great cut stone; this is apparently the same stone resembling Venus, according to Euthymius Zygabenus. When the Saracens were converted to Christianity they were obliged to anathematise this stone, which formerly they worshipped.' This tower doubtless corresponded to the sacred tower of the Midianites, called Penuel, or the 'Face of God,' which Gideon destroyed (Judges viii. 7). Allusions to these towers are constant in the Bible, and the Arabian historian El Masoudi further tells us that this stone or tower was eight cubits high, and was placed in an angle of the temple, which had no roof. Turning to Phœnician temple construction, we have a good parallel to the ruins of the Great Zimbabwe at Byblos; as depicted on the coins, the tower or sacred cone is set up within the temple precincts and shut off in an enclosure (*vide* illustration, p. 150). Similar work is also found in the round temples of the Cabiri, at Hadjar Kem in Malta, and the construction of these buildings bears a remarkable resemblance to that of those at Zimbabwe, and the round towers, or *nuraghs*, found in Sardinia may possibly be of similar significance. MM. Perrot and Chipiez, in their 'History of Art in Sardinia,' speak of these *nuraghs* as forts or temples, around which the primitive inhabitants of the island once lived. They are 'truncated cones, built with stone blocks of different sizes, narrowing to the top. The stones are unhewn as a rule and laid on without mortar.' Here too we have a parallel for our monoliths, menhirs of unhewn stone, and also for the phalli, specimens of which are found carved on stone (p. 57, figs. 49 and 50), and here too the intricate plan of the fortresses suggests at once a parallel to those at Zimbabwe; hence it would appear that the same influence was at work in Sardinia as in South Africa. In Lucian's 'De Syriâ Deâ,' which we shall have occasion again to quote when discussing our finds in Chapter VI., we find a description of a temple at Hierapolis, in Mesopotamia, in the propylæa of which, he tells us (§ 16), 'there stood two very large phalli, about thirty cubits high.' Our tower at Zimbabwe stood apparently twenty cubits high and ten in diameter. He further says (§ 29), 'These phalli are solid, for when a priest had to ascend he had to put a rope round himself and the phallus and walk up.'

Herr Mauch, in his account of Zimbabwe, alludes to a sacrifice which took place here amongst the natives in his day (1871). This ceremony seems to correspond very closely to the sacrifice celebrated elsewhere in this country to the spirits of their ancestors. It is pretty evident that another tribe of Kaffirs dwelt near Zimbabwe at that time, who looked upon the circular building as sacred; whereas the present people do not seem to look upon it with any religious superstition, which will account for the growth of vegetable matter inside only during late years. This was further evidenced by our excavations in this building; we found but little depth of soil, very little *débris*, and indications of a Kaffir occupation of the place up to a very recent date, and no remains like those we afterwards discovered in the fortress.

The rest of the circular building, as the plan shows, is divided off into various smaller enclosures, and in one spot we imagine, by comparison with the temples on the hill, an altar stood; it is now only a heap of rubbish. There are also three remarkable monoliths erected in it, two near the north-western entrance and one behind the altar. They are about 11 feet in height—rough, unhewn blocks of granite, firmly buried in the ground. On the hill fortress, and also, as I have said, on the wall of the circular building, the quantity of monoliths is very marked, and stone-worship seems to have formed an integral feature in the ancient cult of this place. MM. Perrot and Chipiez write (vol. i. p. 58), 'We find the worship of betylæ (βαιτύλια, bethels, *i.e.* sacred stones) in every country reached by Phœnician influence" (*vide* Chap. VI.) Probably we shall be more correct in considering it an even more remote Semitic influence, which continued in vogue amongst the Phœnicians until more recent times. Palgrave in his

Arabian travels also speaks of the many monoliths he saw in Lower Nejed: 'Huge stones, like enormous boulders, placed endways perpendicularly on the soil. They were arranged in a curve, once forming part, it would appear, of a large circle. . . . That the object of these strange constructions was in some measure religious seems to me hardly doubtful . . . in fact, there is little difference between the stone wonder of Kaseem and that of Wiltshire' (Stonehenge).

The valley between the lower circular ruin and the fortress on the hill is a mass of ruins. About a hundred yards from it, and connected by a wall, is a curious angular enclosure, divided into several chambers at different levels; it has three entrances, all of which are straight, like those at the Lundi and Matindela, and not rounded off like those in the circular ruin. The main entrance leads into two narrow passages: the one going to the left is protected by an ambuscade; the other, going to the right, ascends a slope, at the top of which evidently once stood two round towers, the bases of which we excavated, and near them we found several long pillars, presumably fallen monoliths. But here again the Kaffirs had been living until a recent date, and consequently we made no discoveries here. Outside this ruin we opened three kitchen middens, and came across one or two small articles of interest.

Sloping down from this ruin into the valley below a narrow passage conducts one through a perfect labyrinth of ruins. Some of these, notably the large circular erection just outside the big temple, are of very inferior workmanship, and would appear to have been constructed at a much later period; whereas the wall surrounding a large space at the bottom of the valley is as good as the best part of the large circular building. We did not attempt any excavation amongst these, and if we had I expect the results would have been unsatisfactory. All the surface of them has been dug over and over again by generations of Kaffirs for their mealy fields. There is a great growth of brushwood, and probably a considerable depth of soil, which our limited appliances and inexperienced workmen would have found it hard to deal with.

Again and again these circular ruins repeat themselves, always, if possible, occupying a slightly raised ground for about a mile along a low ridge, acting, doubtless, the double purpose of temples and fortresses for separate communities, the inhabitants dwelling in beehive huts of mud around. This, to my mind, is the probable restoration of this ancient African settlement.

Down the valley to the north-west runs a long wall of irregular stones, roughly put together, for a mile or more—such a wall as Kaffirs would erect to-day to protect themselves from the advance of an enemy. This I do not connect with the more ancient and regularly built edifices, but it probably owes its erection to a period when Zulu hordes

swept down on the more peaceful and effeminate descendants of the Monomatapa.

Many were the miles we walked in every direction, around and on the hill fortress, to the east, west, north, and south, intent on one object—namely, that of finding indications of a cemetery, which the ancient inhabitants of these ruins might have used—but our searches were always in vain. Kaffir remains we found in abundance, and a small cemetery of some twenty graves of rough stone piled over the bodies, about ten miles from Zimbabwe, also Kaffir, but nothing else. Consequently we came to the conclusion that the ancient inhabitants, who formed but a garrison in this country, were in the habit of removing their dead to some safer place. This plan seems to have a parallel in Arabia in antiquity, a notable instance of which is to be found on the Bahrein Islands, in the Persian Gulf, where acres and acres of mounds contain thousands of tombs, and no vestige of a town is to be found anywhere near them. The custom still prevails amongst the Mohammedans of Persia, who transport their dead to such places as Kerbela, Meshed, and Kum, to rest in the vicinity of some sacred shrine; and the absence of any burial place near Zimbabwe would seem to point to the same custom having prevailed here.

Having failed to bring to light any definite records of the past during the first fortnight of our work, we naturally cast our eyes around for the most likely spot to carry on our work, and our choice fell on the south-western portion of the hill fortress. Here were certain indications which struck us as favourable, and furthermore it occurred to us that a spot situated on the shady side of the hill behind the great rock might possibly be free from Kaffir desecration; and the results of our excavations on this spot proved this to be the case, for here, and here only, did we come across relics of the past in our digging. In fact, the ancient builders seemed to have originally chosen the most shady spots for their buildings. Undoubtedly the oldest portions of the Zimbabwe ruins are those running along the sunless side of the hill fortress; on the other side, where now the Kaffir village is, we found hardly any trace of ancient structures. Our difficulty was to get the shivering Kaffirs to work there, for whenever our backs were turned they would hurry off to bask in the rays of their beloved sun.

I will now proceed to describe the hill fortress, approaching it from the valley below. The labyrinthine nature of this fortress will best be realised by a glance at the accompanying plan. The *kopje* itself is of great natural strength, being protected on one side by gigantic granite boulders, and on the south by a precipice from seventy to ninety feet in height, and on the only accessible side the ancient inhabitants constructed a wall of massive thickness, like those of the ruins below. This wall is thirteen feet thick on the summit, with a batter of one foot in six; it is thirty feet high in parts, and the flat causeway on the top was decorated on the outside edge by a succession of small round towers alternating with tall monoliths; seven round towers in all we made out, about three feet in diameter, and several others had been destroyed by the fall of a portion of the wall. This system of round towers and monoliths

ROUND TOWER AND MONOLITH DECORATION ON THE FORTRESS

produces one of the most peculiar and unique forms of decoration I have ever seen.

To open out the approach to this fortress town was a work of considerable time and labour; it will easily be seen by the plan how intricate it is, protected at every turn with traverses and ambuscades, and there commences at the bottom of the precipice a flight of steps leading up the steep ascent. The architects availed themselves of a narrow slit in the granite boulder, up which the steps led, the passage being exceedingly narrow; then the path divided into two, one path turning abruptly to the right, and at the turning a pretty little bit of wall with the stones placed pointways for about a yard relieved the monotony and formed a sort of dentelle pattern; then it led along a narrow ledge over the precipice, and in spite of the impossibility of attack at such a point it was nevertheless protected by traverses even here. In fact, the redundancy of fortification all over this mountain, the useless repetition of walls over a precipice itself inaccessible, the care with which every hole in the boulders through which an arrow could pass is closed, prove that the occupants were in constant dread of attack, and lived like a garrison in the heart of an enemy's country.

At the summit of the mountain are huge boulders about fifty feet high. Immediately below the highest is a curious little plateau which had been decorated by the ancient occupiers; it is approached by narrow passages and steps on either side, and a curious passage through the wall below, covered with huge beams of granite to support the superincumbent weight. The steps on one side were made of the same strong cement, and the wall to the left was decorated with the same design of stones, placed edgeways for six rows, that we had

APPROACH TO THE ACROPOLIS

found at the angle of the approach. The little plateau itself was adorned with huge monoliths and decorated pillars of soapstone, the patterns on which were chiefly of a geometric character, and one of which was eleven and a half feet in height. Here too we unearthed many stones of natural but curious

THE PLATFORM WITH MONOLITHS, ETC., ON THE FORTRESS

forms, to which I shall have again occasion to refer in Chapter VI.

The large semicircular space below this platform was a dense jungle when we started to work upon it, consisting of nettles of extraordinary pricking powers and other obnoxious plants, which our natives cleared away with marvellous dexterity. In the centre of this building stood an altar covered with a thick coating of cement, and several large blocks of cement were lying about. In a wall in this enclosure was another of those curious holes pierced through its thickness, and there was plenty of evidence to show that this had once been a most prominent point in the ancient structure, forming, as it does, by far the largest available level space on the fortress, and must probably have been used as an agora, where from the platform an assembled crowd could have been addressed, and for religious celebrations on a large scale. The view from it is extensive and magnificent over the Livouri and Bessa ranges, and situated, as it is, far above the level of the marshy ground below, it would be healthy and habitable during all seasons of the year.

The labyrinthine nature of the buildings now before us baffles description. In one place is a narrow sloping gully, four feet across, ascending between two boulders, and protected, for no conceivable reason, by six alternate buttresses and a wall at the upper end, forming a zigzag passage narrowed in one place to ten inches. Walls of huge size shut off separate chambers. In all directions everything is tortuous; every inch of ground is protected with buttresses and traverses. Here too, as in the large circular building below, all the entrances are rounded off, and I imagine that here we have quite the oldest portion of the ruins, built at a time when defence was the main object. When they were able to do so with safety, they next constructed the circular temple below, and as time went on they erected the more carelessly put together buildings around, which I have described.

The south-western end of this line of ruins was obviously a temple; it has been lately used as a cattle pen by the chief, but the soil has not been disturbed. On removing the soil we came across a level cement floor, supported on an elaborate system of under-walls filled up with large stones on which the cement floor rested, as was the case in the raised platform in the circular temple below. In the centre stood the altar, an angular structure of small granite blocks, which fell to pieces a short time after exposure to the air; when we removed the soil which had buried this altar, around it we found the phalli, the birds or soapstone pillars, and fragments of soapstone bowls, which I shall subsequently describe more in detail.

On a portion of the wall outside, as in the circular building below, ran a pattern—a dentelle pattern formed by placing the stones edgeways, with exactly the same aspect as the pattern below. To the north of the temple a steep ascent, constructed on supporting walls, led through the granite boulders to a hollow space walled in on one side, and protected by the rocks on the other three; a rounded buttress guarded the entrance, and in the centre stood two tall monoliths of slate firmly fixed into the cement floor and the stones beneath; from this spot a slope led up to the top of the rock, on which a terrace had been constructed overlooking the temple and facing the rising sun. Another gully between two boulders, only wide enough for one man to pass at a time, led out of the temple to the side where the modern Kaffir village is. This had also been anciently strongly protected.

The temple was approached from the lower ridge above the precipice by a narrow passage between two high walls gently ascending to a flight of steps. This passage ended in a most curious architectural feature —namely, steps were formed leading to the temple on the one side, and apparently only for ornamentation on the other, by continuing the rounded courses of the outer wall so that they produced the effect of two miniature theatres facing one another, and proving almost more than any other point amongst the ruins the high pitch to which the ancient builders had brought their knowledge of keeping even courses in dry building. This point in the architecture proves the especial attention paid by the constructors to curves, and these curves would seem to have been constructed on the same principle as the curves in the large circular building which Mr. Swan will discuss in Chapter V.

Adjoining the temple to the north is another semicircular building, the inner wall of which has six vertical rows, six feet high, let into the construction, as if for beams, with a ledge on the top, as if for a roof. We were unable to form any opinion as to the use of this chamber, and though we emptied it of soil we found nothing in it.

Between two boulders to the north-west of the temple led a narrow passage, tortuously winding, with walls on either side wedged up against the boulders, and every conceivable hole in the rocks was walled up. This passage led to another open space protected on two sides by rocks and on two by walls. This space was also full of wall foundations; but, being open to the sun, it had been occupied and ransacked by the Kaffirs.

To the south of the temple a flight of steps led down to the gold-smelting furnaces and the caves, of which I shall speak more at length in connection with the finds. This corner of the building was the only one in which our excavations were successful, and I entirely attribute this fact to its chilly and shady position—a spot studiously avoided by the succeeding generations of Kaffir tribes for this reason. Below the temple at the bottom of the precipice we commenced work, with great hope of finding the other portions of the bowls, &c., which we had found above. Here there is an enormous mass of fallen stones from the buildings above, but amongst them we found surprisingly little of interest. Perhaps a thorough excavation of this slope would yield further results, as so many of our finds in the temple above are fragmentary, and the presumption is that the other portions were thrown over the precipice; but this will be a gigantic work, entailing an enormous amount of labour and expenditure.

Such is the great fortress of Zimbabwe, the most mysterious and complex structure that it has ever been my fate to look upon. Vainly one tries to realise what it must have been like in the days before ruin fell upon it, with its tortuous and well-guarded approaches, its walls bristling with monoliths and round towers, its temple decorated with tall, weird-looking birds, its huge decorated bowls, and in the innermost recesses its busy gold-producing furnace. What was this life like? Why did the inhabitants so carefully guard themselves against attack? A thousand questions occur to one which one longs in vain to answer. The only parallel sensation that I have had was when viewing the long avenues of menhirs near Carnac, in Brittany, a sensation at once fascinating and vexatious, for one feels the utter hopelessness of knowing all one would wish on the subject. When taken alone this fortress is sufficiently a marvel; but when taken together with the large circular building below, the numerous ruins scattered around, the other ruins of a like nature at a distance, one cannot fail to recognise the vastness and power of this ancient race, their great constructive ingenuity and strategic skill.

About eight miles from Zimbabwe, standing alone in a fertile valley, there is another ruin which we visited, presumably of a later and inferior date, for the courses and stones are irregular and correspond to the later constructions at Zimbabwe. It too stands

APPROACH TO THE FORTRESS BY THE CLEFT. ZIMBABWE

on a flat granite rock, and its structure is equally intricate, as will be seen from the plan. The natives know it by the name of the Little Zimbabwe, but for purposes of investigation into the origin of the constructing race it affords us no special point of value, which is the case also with most of the other ruins which we visited, and nothing need be said about them except to point out their existence. These remarks refer to the ruins which we found at Metemo, Chilondillo, Chiburwe, and in the Mazoe valley, all of which were obviously erected as forts to protect a surrounding population. Some of them are of the best period of workmanship, notably those at Chiburwe and in the Mazoe valley; others are of inferior workmanship, with uneven courses and irregularly shaped blocks of granite, proving that, as we find the two periods side by side at the Great Zimbabwe, also we have them scattered over the country.

The great ruin at Matindela is second only in importance to the Great Zimbabwe itself, and merits a close description.

The circular building at Matindela encloses an area not far short of that enclosed by the large circular building at the Great Zimbabwe; it crowns a low sloping granite *kopje* about 150 feet in height. The place is full of huge baobab trees, two of which in their growth have pushed down and grown up in the walls themselves. There are those that tell us about the fabulous age of the baobab, attributing an age of 5,000 years to the larger ones. The Director of

136   THE ARCHÆOLOGY OF THE DISTRICT

Kew Gardens, Mr. Thiselton Dyer, tells me that this is grossly exaggerated, and that a few centuries is probably all that can be attributed to the very largest. Be this as it may, the baobabs have grown up and arrived at maturity long after the building of the Matindela ruins and their subsequent abandonment.

BAOBAB TREE IN MATINDELA RUINS

The best built portion of the wall has the same aspect as that at the Great Zimbabwe; but the other side, corresponding to the worst built part of the Zimbabwe wall, has never been completed at Matindela; the fact that the south-eastern side has been so strongly built and so much trouble has been spent on its decoration, and that the north side is compara-

DESCRIPTION OF THE VARIOUS RUINS 137

tively open and neglected, and that the hill is equally assailable from both sides, leads one naturally to infer that the idea of a temple is here more prominent than that of a fortress.

The walls at Matindela are nowhere more than fifteen feet in height, nor are the courses nearly as regular as those at the Great Zimbabwe; but the great feature of interest is here the arrangement of the patterns, which establish beyond a doubt that they

WALLED-UP ENTRANCE AND PATTERN ON MATINDELA RUINS

were inserted in the walls for a more complex purpose than mere ornamentation. The arrangement of these patterns is as follows: First to the south-east comes the herring-bone pattern, running over the chief entrance as a lintel for six yards. Here it ends, and two feet below begins the dentelle pattern for the same distance; then the pattern stops altogether on the outside, but there are indications that it was continued on the inside instead. Then it is again inserted for forty feet on the outside, and finally is again put on the inside for the remainder of its extent—namely, thirteen feet. Above the pattern and nearly over the principal entrance a curious loophole is still left standing, and the best portion of the wall has been battlemented, the outside portion being raised in front two or three feet higher than the back. The wall is eleven feet six inches at its thickest, and on the top of it we saw holes in which monoliths evidently once stood, as they did on the wall of the circular building at the Great Zimbabwe.

Another very marked feature at Matindela is that the doorways are all square, like those at the Lundi ruin, and not rounded off, as those at Zimbabwe, and then again all these doorways have been walled up in an uniform fashion, the courses corresponding exactly to those of the rest of the wall. In the original construction of the building certain spaces of seven feet had been left in the wall; two feet on either side had then been built up, thus leaving an entrance of three feet, which entrance in its turn had also been walled up. Here, as at the Great Zimbabwe, the theory at once occurred to me that these places had been walled up at a time of siege; but when one takes into consideration the care with which these apertures have been walled up, and the triple nature of the added wall, this theory seems untenable. The walling up of the pylons in certain Egyptian temples at Karnak, which Prof. Norman Lockyer brought before my notice, seems an apt parallel, though the reasons for so doing do not seem to my mind at present sufficiently proved. It must also be borne in mind that the walling up of the principal entrance at Matindela must have taken place prior to the construction of the pattern which rests upon it.

The interior of this building, as will be seen from the plan, was divided up into chambers, as the other ruins at Zimbabwe, but the walls here are much straighter, and the circular system of construction seems to have been more or less abandoned. I take it that this ruin at Matindela was constructed by the same race at a period of decadence, when the old methods of building had fallen into desuetude.

Outside the walls of the temple or fortress we found many circular foundations, very regularly built of granite blocks, and varying in diameter from six to fifteen feet. They were built in groups at considerable intervals apart, and we counted over forty of them. Some of these circular foundations have a double circle, as if for a step; the probability is that they formed the foundations of stone huts like those found in the Marico district of the Transvaal, and were the homes of the ancient inhabitants under the protecting wing of the temple-fortress. There are no traces of these circular foundations within the walls of the enclosure, but all were found outside within a radius of two hundred yards. There are traces, too, of other buildings about half-way down the slope of the granite hills, two walls parallel to one another, about thirty feet long, with doorways and six circular foundations outside them. There are also two depressions on the eastern side of the hill, now filled up with timber, which were probably the quarries from which the builders obtained the stone for their work.

About twelve miles to the north of Matindela, near a mountain called Chiburwe, on another low granite hill, we found another fort with similar circular foundations on the plain around it. This fort is about forty feet in diameter, and the walls are of the best period, with courses far more even than those of Matindela, and the stones of more uniform size and fitting more closely, corresponding to the best of the buildings at the Great Zimbabwe. Here, too, was another gigantic baobab tree, which had grown up in the wall and knocked it down; and here, too, the south-eastern portion of the wall is much better and thicker than the rest, which has in places either never existed or fallen down; but the destruction here was so complete that it was impossible to tell if there ever had been a pattern on it or not.

CHAPTER V

ON THE ORIENTATION AND MEASUREMENTS OF ZIMBABWE RUINS. BY R. M. W. SWAN.

The form of nature worship which was practised at Zimbabwe found one of its expressions in the worship of the sun, and we have evidence of this cult in some architectural features and decorations of the temples themselves, and in the many images of the solar disc which were found in the temples along with the other symbols of the worship of reproductive power. It was very natural that these two cults should be associated together or merged in one, and it was common to many early peoples to think of the sun in conjunction with moisture as the great creator of all vegetable fertility, for even the most casual observation would show them that in the dark days of winter the vegetable world seemed to sleep, and that it only awoke to activity when the sun's rays had become more powerful and while the soil was still moistened by rain.

All religions have their times and seasons for special ceremonies of worship, and the appropriate time for the greatest of these festivals of solar worship would be at mid-summer, when the sun seemed most brilliant and his rays most energetic. Accordingly we find that at Zimbabwe means had been provided for ascertaining the time of the summer solstice, and that the side of the temple which faced the rising sun at this period of the year was adorned with a decoration symbolical of fertility.

But the temples at Zimbabwe seem also to have served a more directly practical purpose than that of mere worship of the powers of nature, and while regulating the festivals held in honour of natural powers, to have provided the means of observing the passage of the seasons and of fixing the limits of a tropical year, and thus providing the elements of a calendar.

The duration of a day is clearly marked by an apparent revolution of the sun, and from the most remote antiquity a month has been equivalent to the length of a lunation; but there is no equally obvious astronomical phenomenon to enable the length of the year to be fixed; and although the difference between summer and winter is very apparent in most climates, there is nothing which very obviously defines the limits of these seasons, and the periods of spring and autumn are even less marked. But the dates of all festivals in solar worship would have some relation to the seasons; and, besides, the times for agricultural and many other operations would require to be fixed, and it would thus be doubly necessary to find means of marking the progress of the year. By most ancient peoples twelve lunations were considered to be equal

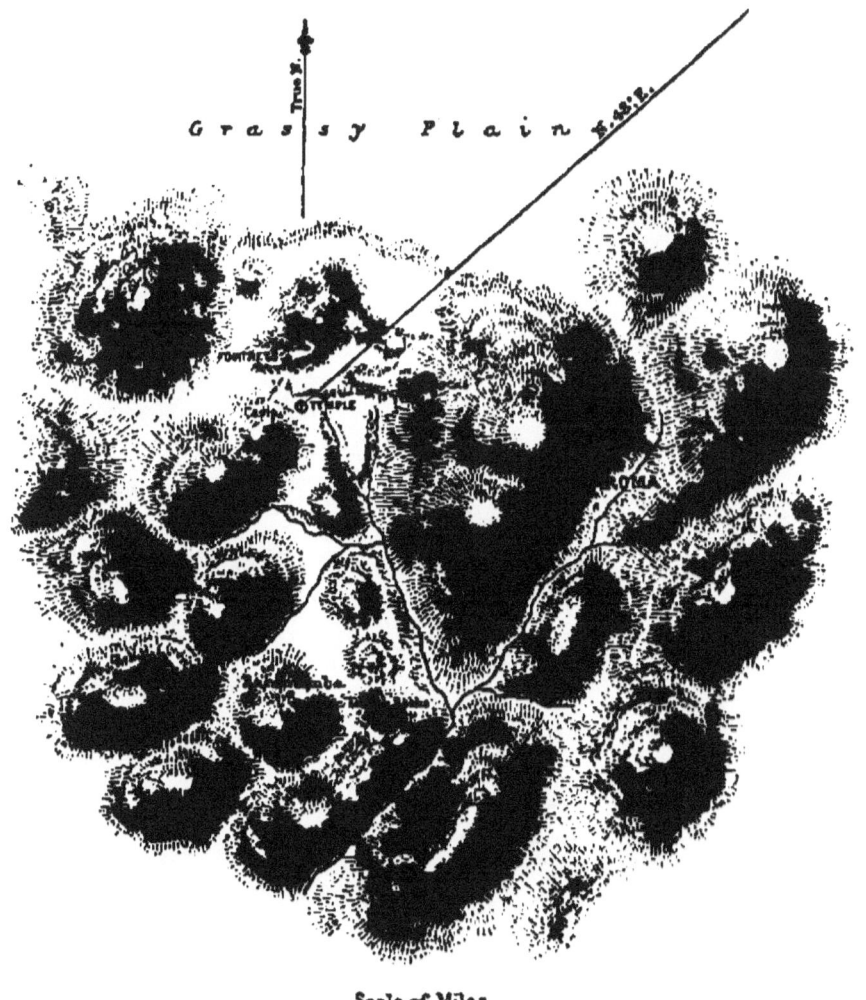

to a tropical year, but it was soon discovered that this was not so, for the several months did not long coincide with their appropriate seasons, and so the history of most ancient calendars tells of devices to make the twelve lunar months of $29\frac{1}{2}$ days each correspond with the tropical year of $365\frac{1}{4}$ days. At Zimbabwe things seem to have been better arranged, unless there, too, as in ancient Egypt, they had their troublesome civil year measured by twelve revolutions of the moon, in addition to their sacred year measured in the temples by an apparent revolution of the sun among the stars.

The simplest way of ascertaining the period of a tropical year is by observing the position of the sun relatively to the equator, or its declination, and this can conveniently be done either when the sun is on the horizon or on the meridian, but most easily with accuracy in the former way, as the angle to be subdivided will generally be greater, and greater accuracy will be attained, because long shadows can more conveniently be used in this way than in the other. Or the right ascension of the sun might also be observed; that is, its place among the stars, or its position in the zodiac. This can be found most readily by observing the heliacal rising of stars, or the meridian passage of stars when the sun is near the horizon. At Zimbabwe all of these methods seem to have been used, and to do so does not necessarily imply more astronomical knowledge than is possessed by the peasantry in any of the more secluded districts of

Europe, where watches are not much used, and where almanacks are not read, but where the people have the habit of telling the time of the day and of the year by the motions of the sun and of the stars; for to an agricultural people the change in position of the sun in summer and winter is as obvious as the seasons themselves, and the variation of the times of rising of the stars with the seasons can as little escape observation. Herodotus tells us that the Greeks used the gnomon to measure the length of shadows, and thus ascertain the position of the sun at midday, or its declination. The Chinese also used it at a very early period, and we have similar arrangements in some of our modern churches. Instances of the observation of the position of the sun on the horizon, except at Zimbabwe, are few and doubtful, although gnomons seem sometimes to have been used for this purpose; but ancient literature contains very many references to the observation of the heliacal risings of stars, and ancient architectural remains illustrate these literary allusions. Hesiod often speaks of the times of different agricultural operations having been fixed by the rising of stars, and Egyptian records tell us that the rising of Sirius was observed at the overflowing of the Nile; also it has recently been found that both Egyptian and Greek temples were generally built so that the rising of some star could be observed from their sanctuaries, and a coincidence has been traced between the date of the great festival proper to each temple and the time of the heliacal rising of the star towards which the axis of the temple was originally directed. The Malays, at the beginning of this present century, had a tradition that their seed-time had in old days been very well fixed by the rising of the Pleiades, but that since they had become Mohammedans the festivals of their religion and its calendar did not so well regulate their seed-time as was done in old times. It has been found that means were provided by the ancient Egyptians for observing the meridian transits of stars; and did we possess detailed and carefully oriented plans of the temples of Chaldæa and Assyria, there is little doubt that we should find that the meridian had been observed there also.

Thus it is evident that the several means which were adopted at Zimbabwe for observing the motions of the heavenly bodies were used in other countries also, and in all cases they seem to have been used for regulating the time of celebration of religious festivals as well as the ordinary affairs of life. Forms of nature worship analogous to that practised at Zimbabwe seem often to have been accompanied in other countries by an observation of the heavenly bodies. It is also worthy of note that the stars which were observed at Zimbabwe seem all to have been northern ones, and the builders of these temples probably acquired the habit of observing these stars in the northern hemisphere. To this we shall refer again.

What El Masoudi says of the temples of the Sabæans of Mesopotamia does not, of course, directly apply to the temples at Zimbabwe; but in the plans of those temples one is reminded of the multiform temples which he describes, and of the mysteries involved in some of their architectural features which he could not fathom, for in these temples of Mashonaland there are some curious evidences of design in plan. A glance at the plan of the great temple suggests that the architects had carelessly drawn a great ellipse on the ground and built round it, getting occasionally out of line and leaving occasional doorways; but when one realises the wonderfully careful nature of the masonry, and the great accuracy with which the comparatively rough stones have been laid in regular courses, and been forced to combine to produce regular forms, and when a careful plan of the whole building has been made, then it is seen that what were regarded as careless irregularities in construction are, in reality, carefully constructed architectural features, which doubtless had some religious significance to the worshippers, but whose meaning remains a mystery to us.

The walls which are lightly shaded in the accompanying plans are much inferior in construction to the more darkly shaded walls, for while the latter are built in most regular courses, and the stones are most carefully packed in the whole thickness of the walls, the former, though sometimes having the exterior courses laid with some regularity, are most carelessly built in their interior, and the stones seem to have been laid in anyhow, and consequently there is a great difference in the durability of these walls; and while it would almost be possible to drive a cart

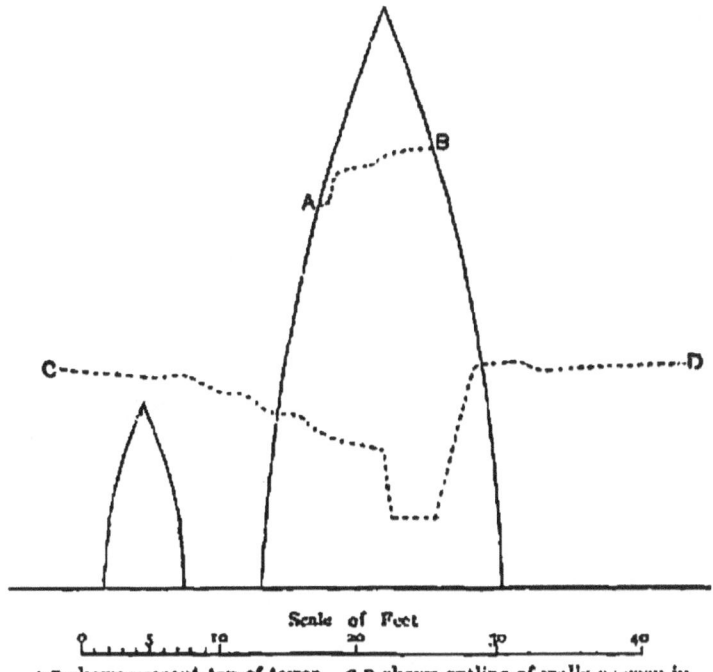

A B shows present top of tower. C D shows outline of walls as seen in illustration, Chap. VI.

THE TWO TOWERS

along the top of the better-built part of the outer wall, one can only creep along the top of the worse-built portion while risking a fall. Besides, the better-built and the worse-built portions of the outer wall do not unite near the great doorway, and the foundation of the well-built walls turns outward, as is shown in the plan. The worse-built walls of all the temples do not show any of the peculiarities of design so characteristic of the better walls, except in two instances, where they seem to be rough reconstructions of older walls. We may, therefore, assume that these poorer

COIN OF BYBLOS SHOWING THE ROUND TOWER

walls are not of the original period, and that they were built by a people who either did not practise solar worship or who did not do so under the original forms. We will, therefore, disregard the poor walls in studying the plans of the temples. It is much to be regretted that we could recover no plan of the western side of the original outer wall, as it might have made clear to us the meaning of many of the features of the eastern wall.

The most important feature in the interior of the temple is, of course, the great tower, which is a marvel of workmanship in rough material, and in the truth of its lines almost as wonderful as the column of a Greek temple. We could at first discover no reason for its being built in its peculiar position. It has not been placed with any reference to the points of the compass nor to the bearing of the sun at the equinoxes, and its position is only indirectly connected with the position of the sun at the solstices. But it is in the middle of the space marked off by the two inner doorways, and the more easterly of these two doorways is at the point where the sun would appear when rising at the summer solstice when regarded from the central altar, as will be shown further on; and the other doorway is at the point where the decoration on the outer wall terminates, and that is at the part of the wall where the sun's rays would be tangential to its curve when rising at the same solstice. The portion of the outer wall behind the above-mentioned sacred enclosure is built in the form of a circular arc with its two extremities at B and K, and its centre at P, and the tower stands midway between these points. Close to the great tower is the little one, and no reason for its position suggests itself; but the relative proportions of the two towers are curious, and seem to offer an explanation of the plan of some other parts of the building—in fact, the diameter of the great tower seems to have represented the unit of measure in the construction of the curves of the outer walls and of all the regularly curved inner walls in the great temple, and in all the well-built temples in Mashonaland. The diameter of the great tower at its base is 17·17 feet or 10 cubits,[1] and this is exactly equal to the circumference of the little tower. This ratio of circumference to diameter and the above measure of 10 cubits seem together to have determined either the length of the radius or diameter, or halves of these, of all the circular curves on which many of the walls are built. For instance, the radius of the curve behind the great tower is 169⅓ feet, and this is equal to the diameter of the great tower multiplied by the square of the ratio of circumference to diameter; or $17·17 \times 3·14^2 = 169·34$. The well-built partly circular enclosure to the north-west of the tower has a diameter of 54 feet, and this is equal to $17·17 \times 3·14$. The curve of the outer wall, from the eastern end of the sacred enclosure (at K) to A is circular, and has its centre at the altar, and its radius is 107⅔ feet. This is equal to twice $17·17 \times 3·14$. This length of 107⅔ feet is also the exact distance between the middle points of the two door-

---

[1] 17·17 feet is equal to 10 cubits of 20·62 inches; and as all parts of the building which we have been able to measure accurately, and all small articles which would probably be made on any scale of measure, apparently have been made in terms of a cubit of this length, it seems probable that this cubit was one of the standards of measure in use.

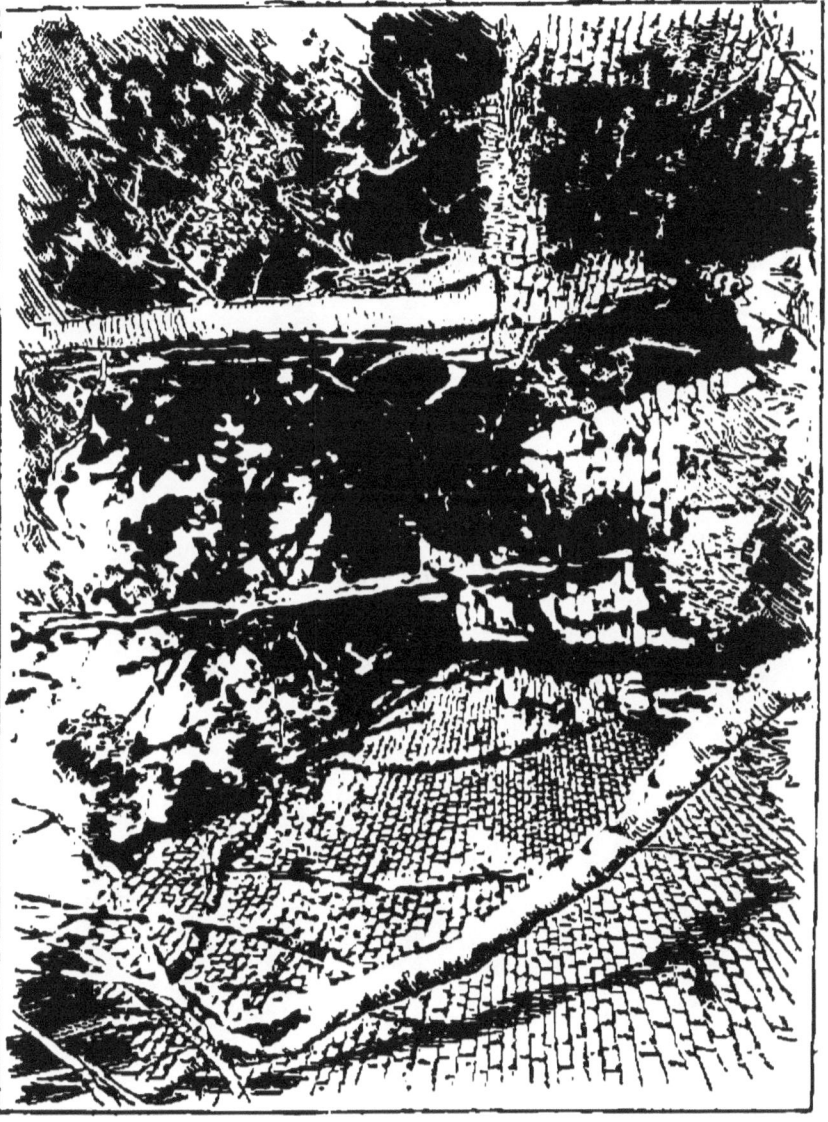

THE TRIPLE WALLS AT ZIMBABWE

ways at either end of the sacred enclosure. The curve of the outer wall from A to the great doorway seems to have a similar radius to the arc behind the tower, namely, $169\frac{1}{3}$ feet, but in our measurements there we hardly fixed a sufficient number of points in the line of the wall to make quite certain of this. The inner long wall is parallel to the outer one until it reaches the sacred enclosure, so it may be considered as combined with the outer wall for our present purpose. Besides these there are no well-built curved walls in the great temple, except the piece of wall near the monoliths at M, and it is too short to allow of the centre of its curve being laid down with certainty of accuracy. It does not, however, seem to belie this system of measurement.

We need hardly expect to find the same measure always applying to the buildings on the hill, for the form of these buildings is often controlled by the nature of the ground. Still they do apply, and the diameter of the curve on which the wall of the eastern temple is built is $84\frac{1}{2}$ feet, which is equal to half of $17\cdot17 \times 3\cdot14^2$. Of the two curved walls on the left hand when entering this temple from the south the diameter of the curve of one is equal to $17\cdot17 \times 3\cdot14$, and the radius of the other is $17\cdot17$ feet. The only other regularly curved wall on the hill is the western great wall with monoliths and round towers, and the diameter of the circle of which the curve of this wall forms a part is 254 feet, and this does not agree with our system of measure.

But this wall and its towers are not well built, and there is good reason to suppose that it is not the original wall, or that the outer portion of it is not original; and, in fact, we discovered the foundation of part of another parallel wall, as is partly shown in plan, six feet west of this wall. If this were the original wall, it would give a diameter of 266 feet for the circle, which is half of 17.17×3.14^3.

At Matindela the only regularly curved piece of wall is that about the principal doorway, but it is so rough in its construction that one hesitates to deal with it, and we can only say that it seems to be built on a curve of $107\frac{1}{4}$ feet radius $= $ twice 17.17×3.14. The whole appearance of this wall and the slight inaccuracies in the orientation of the decorations which it carries, suggest that it is a more recent wall built roughly as a copy of an original wall on the same foundation.

The ruin at the Lundi River is circular in form and well built, and its diameter is fifty-four feet, which is equal to 17.17×3.14.

Of course all the above measurements refer to the outside of the walls at the base, as this is the way in which the tower itself was measured.

The same principle of measurement applies to the curves which determine the shape of the two towers themselves, and this explains why it is that the little tower tapers much more rapidly towards the top than does the great one. If we describe a circular curve with its centre on the same level as the base

of the great tower and its radius equal to twice
17·17 × 3·14 on 107⅜ feet, we find that it exactly fits
the outline of the great tower as it is shown in our
photographs. Also, a curve described in a similar
way but with a radius equal to twice the diameter of
the little tower multiplied by 3·14 (5·45 × 3·14 × 2 =
34·34 feet) will correspond to the outline of that
tower.

The towers when built were doubtless made complete in their mathematical form and were carried up to a point as we see in a coin of Byblos, where we have a similar tower represented with curved outlines. Their heights as determined by these curves would be 42·3 and 13·5 feet respectively, and these numbers also bear the same relation to each other that the circumference of a circle does to its diameter.

We have no explanation to give of the position of the little tower relatively to the great one, but there probably was some meaning in it which might appear had we a plan of the original walls around the towers. It is very doubtful that these walls, which now mark off the sacred enclosure, are of the same period as the towers. They are shaded darkly in our plan because they are fairly well built; but although they are better built than most of the secondary walls, yet they are not equal in point of execution to the great outer wall and the towers, and their lines, too, are not so regular as those of the original walls generally are. It seems probable that they are rough copies of some old walls which had fallen, and are wanting in some

M

of the essential features of their originals. We can only say that the centre of one tower is distant 17·17 feet from the centre of the other, within a limit of error of two inches.

The angular height of both the towers measured from the centres of the curves which determine their forms is the same—namely 23° 1′.

None of the angular values of the arcs seem to have been of any special significance, except perhaps the angle at the altar in the great temple, which is subtended by the arc AK. The value of this angle is about 57°, and is equal to our modern unit of the circular measure of an angle, which is the angle at the centre of any circle that is subtended by an arc equal to the radius. It is hardly likely that it can have had this meaning to the builders of the temple, and the probable cause of the coincidence is that at A they meant to halve the angular distance between K and the doorway. Besides, the sun's rays, when it rises at the summer solstice, do not fall directly on the part of the wall beyond A, and this probably had some connection with their reason for changing the radius of the arc at this point.

There is no evidence that any of the trigonometrical functions were known to the builders of Zimbabwe; not even the chord, which was probably the earliest recognised function of an angle, for the chords of the various arcs bear no simple relation to each other. The only interesting mathematical fact which seems to have been embodied in the architecture of the temples is the ratio of diameter to circumference, and it may have had an occult significance in the peculiar form of nature worship which was practised there. We do not suppose that it was intended to symbolise anything of an astronomical nature, and it is extremely improbable that the builders of Zimbabwe had any notion of mathematical astronomy, for their astronomy was purely empirical, and amounted merely to an observation of the more obvious motions of the heavenly bodies. When the minds of men were first interested in geometry it would at once occur to them that there must be some constant ratio between the circumference of a circle and its diameter, and they would easily discover what this ratio was, and they may have considered this discovery so important and significant that they desired to express it in their architecture. Analogous instances of an embodiment of simple mathematical principles in architectural forms will occur to every one.

The centres of the arcs seem generally to have been important points, and altars were sometimes erected at them from which the culminations or meridian transits of stars could be observed, and on which sacrifices were probably offered to the sun when it was rising or setting at either of the solstices.

Around the outside of the wall of the great temple, between the points marked A and B on plan, there extend two bands of a kind of chevron pattern, formed, as will be seen from the illustrations, by placing stones on their edges. This pattern seems to have been symbolical of fertility, and it extends along the part of the wall which receives directly the rays of the sun when rising at the summer solstice. It reminds one of the Egyptian hieroglyphic symbol for water, and of how naturally the idea of water would be associated with fertility in the mind of a solar worshipper. It also resembles the symbol for the zodiacal sign of Aquarius, and we might suppose that the temple was built when the sun was in this sign of the zodiac at the summer solstice, did such a supposition not carry us back to too remote a period. Besides, the sun is generally believed to have been in Capricornus at the December solstice at the period at which the zodiac was invented, and when its signs received their names.

One hundred and seven and four-fifths feet from A and the same distance from K and from B is the centre of the arc AK, and at this point is some ruined masonry which seems once to have formed an altar. Zimbabwe is in South latitude 20° 16′ 30″, and consequently the sun, when rising there at the summer solstice, would bear East 25° South were the horizon level. But Mount Varoma interposes itself between the temple and the rising sun at this time, so that the sun attains an altitude of 5° before its rays reach the temple. Then its amplitude will be more nearly 24°, and a line produced in this direction from the altar will pass across the doorway of the sacred enclosure, where the curve of the wall changes its radius, and, roughly speaking, through the middle of the chevron pattern. The same line drawn in an opposite direction for seventy-three feet would fall on a tall monolith which we there found lying by its well-built foundation. Where the pattern ends at A and B the rays of the sun are nearly tangential to the wall, so that all parts of the wall, and those parts only, which receive the direct rays of the sun when rising at the summer solstice are decorated by this symbolical pattern.

The sun's rays would not fall on the altar at this time, and it seems strange to have an altar devoted to solar worship under the shadow of a wall; but the same objection would apply to every part of the interior of the temple, and we can hardly suppose that the priests at Zimbabwe performed their ceremonies of worship outside of the temple, as some tribes of Arabs do with some stone circles at the present day, neither is there any sign of such ceremonies having been performed on the top of the broad wall. The monolith, seventy-three feet from the altar, was sufficiently tall to receive the rays of the sun when it rose over Mount Varoma, and the shadow of a monolith erected on the wall at K would fall on it at the same time, thus marking with great accuracy the occurrence of the solstice. Monoliths had been erected at intervals along the decorated part, and only on this part, of the wall, and these may have served to indicate other periods of the year in a similar way.

Near the top of the great tower, which at present

stands thirty-two feet high, there is a dentelle pattern, which may be described as a chevron pattern laid on its side, and which resembles a common Egyptian pattern. This extends partly round the tower, but it is impossible to determine its aspect with accuracy as so much of it has fallen away. It seems, however, to have faced the setting sun at the winter solstice.

At the temple at the east end of the fortress on the hill similar means are provided for observing the summer solstice. Only a small part of the decorated wall remains, the middle part, which was of great height, having fallen, so that we do not know how far the decoration may have extended towards the south. On the other side it terminates at the doorway, which is placed close to the high cliff which forms the northern side of the temple. We discovered the altar, with several phalli and many little terracotta images of the solar disc lying near it, and some among the stones of the altar. This altar is not at the centre of the arc, but is placed ten feet nearer the rising sun at the solstice, and its position seems to be due to the position of the break in the cliff, which is true north of the altar, so that the meridian can be observed through this passage from the altar in its actual position, and it could not have been observed from the altar were it placed at the centre of the arc. It was impossible to describe the arc with the altar as its centre owing to the position of some rocks which would have interfered with the building of the wall. At the summer solstice the sun rises here on a level horizon and bears East 25° South, and a line drawn from the altar in this direction passes through the pattern, and continued for ten feet in the opposite direction it would fall on the centre of the arc.

The great curved wall at the western end of the fortress, which is surmounted by little round towers and erect monoliths, faces the setting sun at the winter solstice. If we suppose the altar was placed here, we have on an eminence marked A, fifty feet true north of the altar, a tall monolith which would enable the meridian transits of northern stars to be observed from the altar, and a line drawn from this altar towards the setting sun at the winter solstice would seem to have passed through the middle of the line of towers and monoliths. This great wall is not so well built as the walls at the eastern temple, and it seems probable that it is a restoration of an old wall which was originally parallel to this, and whose foundations we discovered as already mentioned. Possibly on the original wall the round towers and monoliths were aligned between the altar and the setting sun at certain definite periods of the year. At present they do not seem to mark any important periods, but the position of the setting sun at the summer solstice is well marked by a round tower on the wall overhanging the high cliff, and this is undoubtedly a wall of the best period.

At this western end of the fortress we have two instances of parts of walls which faced the setting sun at the winter solstice being decorated by a dentelle pattern.

The disposition of the ornamental patterns on the little round ruin at the Lundi River is interesting. It faces the rising sun at the winter solstice, but the place had been inhabited by Kaffirs, and all vestige of an altar, if it ever existed, had been destroyed. The nature of the patterns here is different from that of those at Zimbabwe. The one near the top of the wall is composed of two rows of little squares alternating with blank spaces, and a little way below this are two rows of a herring-bone pattern. There is a curious rounded protuberance on the outside of the wall, and the herring-bone pattern stops at this point, but the other extends right round to the south-eastern doorway.

This temple is similar in many ways to the partly circular one north-west of the great tower at Zimbabwe. They have both the same diameter and they each have two doorways which are in somewhat similar positions, although the temple at the Lundi is oriented towards the rising sun at the winter solstice, and the other, if it ever had a pattern, would have had it facing the setting sun at this solstice.

The dentelle pattern on the great tower seems to have been oriented towards the setting sun at the winter solstice, and the centre of the partly circular temple at G is roughly in a line between the centre of the tower and the sun at this time. When the sun is rising at the summer solstice G will be behind the tower and in the middle of its shadow, in a position analogous to that of the altar behind the arc AK. The direction of the wall at the north-eastern extremity of the arc of which G is the centre is towards the rising sun at the winter solstice, and its inner side points past the centre of the arc AK[1] towards the point of the outer wall which is in a straight line between the altar and the sun when it rises at this solstice. The wall at the other extremity of the arc points to the rising sun at the other solstice.

It is perhaps worthy of remark that the centre of the great tower is distant the length of its own height (42·3 feet) from the solstitial line MK, while the centre of the little tower would be the same distance from a parallel solstitial line drawn from the south-eastern extremity of the arc of which G is the centre; and also that the centres of the great tower and the centres of the arcs AK and KB lie in one straight line.

At Matindela the general aspect of the decorated part of the building is towards the setting sun, but the masonry is so rough in its construction that we need expect little accuracy in orientation. The whole appearance of the place suggests that what exists at present is merely a rough rebuilding of an older structure. What remains of the internal arrangements of the building is very fragmentary, and we could find no trace of an altar. Over the doorway there is a herring-bone pattern facing the setting sun at the summer solstice, and adjoining this on its north

[1] This is not very accurately shown in the small scale plan.

side there is a band of ornament of the dentelle kind with a similar aspect. Above this dentelle pattern there is a loophole in the wall which may have served to pass a ray of light from the setting sun to an altar at some festival. Farther along the wall there is another pattern facing the setting sun at the winter solstice, and on the inside of the wall yet another looking towards the rising sun at the summer solstice. The construction of the doorways at Matindela is remarkable. They have been originally made of considerable width, and then been narrowed very much by square masses of masonry which were built at both sides. The direction of the doorways also seems to have some meaning, for three of them look East 25° North, and four East 25° South, thus corresponding to the direction of the sun rising and setting at the solstices.

At the Mazoe Valley, and to the north-east of Matindela, near Mount Chiburwe, there are well-built ruins of the best period of this style of architecture, but, unfortunately, too little of them remains to allow us to understand their plans. They are both very small, and are not circular, like the Lundi River ruin, but their walls seem to have been built on a series of curves like the wall of the great temple. A very extraordinary thing regarding all the older ruins in Mashonaland is the way in which the stones which once composed the walls have disappeared. They have not been covered up by soil, and there is no trace of them in the surrounding country, and yet in these two ruins not one-twentieth part of the stones remain, and all that do remain are in their original places in the walls.

When the western wall was rebuilt at the great temple at Zimbabwe there was apparently a want of stones, and the rebuilders were too lazy to procure more, so they probably shortened the wall by decreasing the size of the temple, and also economised stones by making the new wall much less thick.

The place marked A near the western end of Zimbabwe Hill is remarkable. It is a natural eminence, the height of which has been increased by building. To the south of it is a great mass of masonry which is pierced by several roofed passages, and over which a winding stairway leads from the eastern buildings to the eminence, while a similar staircase leads from the eminence towards the buildings lying northward. To the eastward of the eminence tower great granite boulders, the termination at this end of that line of boulders which caps the hill along its whole length, and which protects the fortress on the north side. At the highest point of the eminence is erected the great monolith before referred to, which seems to have marked the meridian for the altar at R. Close to this monolith stood another made of soapstone. We found its base in its place, and its other fragments, shown in the illustration, were all discovered near. This monolith was decorated with bands of the chevron pattern running halfway round, with images of the sun and other geometrical patterns placed between the bands. It seems probable that it served as a gnomon, and that means had been provided for measuring the length of its shadow at midday. The foundation of the monolith is twenty-five feet higher than the site of the altar, and the monolith itself was ten feet long, so that we have a total height for its summit of thirty-five feet above the base of the altar, and it stood fifty feet true north of the altar. At Zimbabwe the altitude of the upper limb of the sun at midday, at the winter solstice, is about $46\frac{1}{2}°$, so that the top of the monolith would then throw its shadow in the direction of the altar, and to within about seventeen feet of its centre. Probably some arrangement had been made near the altar for observing the length of its shadow; and were the shadow received on an inclined plane or staircase, as seems to have been done with the dial of Ahaz, mentioned in the Old Testament, it might be lengthened to any extent and its variations in length increased in magnitude; and so the change in declination of the sun could be observed with considerable accuracy. The sun is little more than three degrees south of Zimbabwe at midsummer, and it would be difficult to measure with accuracy the short shadows then cast, and we do not find anything to show that they had been observed, and the means provided in the two other temples for observing the position of the sun on the horizon would be much more effectual for fixing this solstice.

The positions of the doorways relatively to the

altars or the centres of the arcs is of interest; and we find that every important doorway in walls of the original period, with the exception of the south-eastern doorway in the temple at the Lundi, and the south-western one in the partly circular interior temple at Zimbabwe, is placed true north of the centre of an arc or of an altar, and the centre of every arc has had a doorway or some other means of marking out the meridian placed north of it. True north of the centre of the tower itself we have a doorway in the wall of the sacred enclosure, and although the wall in which this doorway is made was probably not built at the original period, yet there probably was a doorway in a similar position in the wall which it has replaced. The part of the great outer wall north of the tower seems also to have been marked, for about this point we found a great step constructed on its top about five feet high.

Above the temple at the east end of the fortress on the hill, a cliff rises perpendicularly for fifty feet, and poised on its top there stands a most remarkable great rock which may once have been an object of veneration to the worshippers in the temple beneath it. It forms one of the highest points on the hill. A line drawn true south from this rock and produced 680 yards would pass through the doorway in the great temple and fall on the altar in the centre of the decorated arc. Until this line suggested itself we were puzzled to account for the peculiar character of the doorway. It passes through a wall sixteen feet thick, and is itself only three feet wide, and it does not pass through the wall at right angles, but cuts it somewhat obliquely, so that its axis is roughly parallel to the meridian line.

A line drawn true north from the centre of the arc at G will pass through the doorway of the small temple and the centre of the arc KB at P. This line points through the outer wall where the gap occurs, and it is probable that the opening which was made in the outer wall to allow of observation along this line, determined its fall at this point. This meridian line is thirty-six feet distant from the other from the centre of the arc AK, and it must have pointed to the same great stone. But if both these lines point to the middle of this stone, which is 680 yards distant, they will incline towards each other about one degree, and the time of the transit of a star over the stone observed by one line will differ four minutes from that observed by the other. This inaccuracy would be so obvious to the observers that we cannot suppose they would have worked in this way. The great stone measures nearly, if not quite, thirty-two feet across, and were the lines directed, not both to its centre, but one to either side, they would be parallel to each other and would both give the same time for a transit of a star. This would imply that stars were observed, not passing over the stone, but disappearing and reappearing behind it, and a star observed at the altar to disappear would at the same instant reappear to an observer at G and

WITHIN THE DOUBLE WALLS, ZIMBABWE.

P; or if the rock were less than thirty-two feet wide the star would reappear at G and P before it disappeared at the altar. We have thus a sort of double observation of the same meridian transit.

If we admit that these meridian lines were used for the observation of stars in this way, and if we can determine what star or stars were observed, the time that has elapsed since they were observed admits of calculation. The apparent altitude of the middle of the stone as seen from the centres of the arcs is $7\frac{1}{2}°$, and the latitude of Zimbabwe is $20° 16' 30''$, so that we want stars having a north polar distance of about $28°$. Owing to the changing direction of the pole of the earth, which produces the phenomenon of the precession of the equinoxes, the declinations and right ascensions of all the stars are undergoing a slow but regular change; but there are no stars of the first magnitude which have had approximately this polar distance since any probable date of the foundation of Zimbabwe. Of stars of the second magnitude there are four, and of the third magnitude many more, which may have been used, and they would all serve for widely different periods. In order to enable us to select the proper star from this number we must have its right ascension, and this we may yet hope to get when we have the date of some important yearly festival at Zimbabwe, and the hour at which the star would be wanted on the meridian on the night of this festival.

There are two other places where the meridian

transits of stars have been watched at Zimbabwe, and in these cases it is still the same portion of the heavens which has been observed. The altar in the eastern temple in the fortress has been placed ten feet E.S.E. of the centre of the arc, in order to permit of the meridian being observed through the gap in the rock which formed the northern doorway. Here the line laid off is much shorter than that between the rock and the great temple, but still fairly accurate observations could be made. To the north of the centre of the arc of the great wall of the western temple there is, as we have already shown, a great monolith erected, and at one side of this the stars might be observed at their culminations. As seen from the altar this monolith would mark out an angular distance of 0° of the meridian.

It is remarkable that only stars of the northern hemisphere seem to have been observed at Zimbabwe, for in the great temple itself the culminations of southern stars could quite as easily have been observed as those of northern ones, and in the fortress all view of the northern sky is almost completely shut off by the cliffs and huge boulders which form its northern line of defence; yet every point from which northern stars could have been observed has been used for this purpose, and there is no temple there from which northern stars were not observed, while at the same time the openly displayed southern sky has been left unregarded. This, of course, points to a northern origin for the people, and suggests that before they came to Zimbabwe they had acquired the habit of observing certain stars—a habit so strong that it led them to disregard the use of the southern constellations, though they must have known that they would equally well have served to regulate their calendar; it even seems to indicate that they attached ideas of veneration to certain stars, and rendered them worship. It seems a plausible supposition that while the great temple itself was devoted to solar and analogous forms of worship, the little circular, or partly circular, temples within its walls, of which we found one fairly well preserved and fragmentary remains of several others, were dedicated to the cult of particular stars.

There is no sign in the temples of any observation of anything external to the temples themselves, unless of the heavenly bodies; and no features of the surrounding country, such as prominent mountain-peaks or great isolated rocks, of which there are many striking instances near the temples, have had any regard at all paid to them. The outer walls, with the exception of the decoration towards the solstices, are featureless and blank, and the doorways, where one might expect ornament, are extremely narrow and entirely plain. When one is within the great temple one realises how fitting a place it is in which to observe the starry sky, for the high walls around exclude all view of the landscape, and the only objects which attract one's attention are the heavenly bodies above one; and at night-time one feels how easily the thoughts of a star-worshipper could be concentrated on their proper object.

It is incredible that such a style of architecture as we have described, and such a civilisation as it signifies, could have originated and developed in South Africa, for such a development would have required a very long time, and would have implied at least a long and peaceful settlement in the country; and although the builders of Zimbabwe may have long possessed the place, yet it is apparent that they never considered the country was their own. This is clear from the nature of their defences and the strength of their fortifications. Had they lived long enough in the land to alter or develop any of their arts independently of their mother country, they would have left a deeper mark on their surroundings than they have; besides, living as they must have lived, they could not have increased in civilisation, nor developed any of its arts, and we may assume that they had their architecture as well as their religion in common with their mother country. The balance of probabilities seems to be in favour of that country being South Arabia; and when it and Abyssinia, with which it was so long associated, are better known, we may find temples which are built of similar small stones and with similar mathematical and other peculiarities in their construction. Our information of these countries is meagre, but some of those buildings which are known in Yemen, which seem to combine temple and fortress in one, as on Zimbabwe Hill, may have been built by the same race that constructed Zimbabwe; and the elliptic temples at Marib and Sirwah, and the one at Nakab al Hajar, with its north and south doorways seeming to indicate an observation of the meridian, may embody some of the mathematical principles illustrated by the ruins of Mashonaland.

When the original builders of Zimbabwe have been traced to their home, it will remain to discover who were their successors in Mashonaland that rebuilt the western wall of the great temple and some portions of other buildings, for this certainly was not done by any of the present negro races.

There is nothing to show that even these walls do not belong to a now far distant time; for although they would not long remain in this country, yet at Zimbabwe they might endure for an indefinite period, for there, in a clear atmosphere free from dust, and a tropical climate with its yearly torrential rains, no soil can accumulate among the stones to support vegetation which would destroy the walls. The few small plants which grow even on the oldest walls are of species which do not require much mineral matter for their growth, and whose roots are so soft that they mould themselves to the shape of the interstices in the walls, but do not press asunder the stones. Besides, the present inhabitants of the country do not use stone in any of their constructions, and never trouble themselves to remove stones from any existing walls, so that more stones have probably been disturbed during the two years of British occupation of the country than the Kaffirs would disturb in as many centuries; and under the old conditions the walls might endure for an indefinite time.¹

> ¹ There are many astronomical points in these buildings still to be considered, and the results of further investigation will be published later.

CHAPTER VI

THE FINDS AT THE GREAT ZIMBABWE RUINS

In this chapter I propose to discuss all the objects discovered during our excavations in the ruins as apart from the buildings themselves, and to analyse the light that they throw on the original constructors and their cult. All these objects were found, with a few minor exceptions, in the eastern temple on the fortress As I have said, traces of a recent Kaffir habitation will account for the absence of objects in the lower buildings, but the upper ruin, sheltered from the sun and hidden by trees and lofty boulders, was a spot repugnant to the warmth-loving Kaffir, and to this fact we owe the preservation of so many objects of interest belonging to the ancient inhabitants. The most remarkable feature in connection with the finds is that everything of a decorative nature is made of a steatitic schist or soapstone. This stone is found in the country, and is still employed by natives farther south in making pipes for smoking dokha or hemp; it lends itself easily to the tool of the artist, and is very durable.

First, let us take the birds perched on tall soapstone columns, which, from the position in which we found most of them, would appear to have decorated the outer wall of the semicircular temple on the hill. These birds are all conventional in design. The tallest stood 5 feet 4 inches in height, the smallest about half a foot lower. We have six large ones and two small ones in all, and probably, from the number of soapstone pedestals with the tops broken off which we found in the temple, there were several more. Though they are all different in execution, they would appear to have been intended to represent the same bird; from the only one in which the beak[1] is preserved to us intact, we undoubtedly recognise that they must have been intended to represent hawks or vultures. The thick neck and legs, the long talons and the nature of the plumage point more distinctly to the vulture; the decorations on some of them, namely, the dentelle pattern at the edge of the wings, the necklace with a brooch in front and continued

SOAPSTONE BIRD ON PEDESTAL

[1] *Vide* illustration, p. 181.

SOAPSTONE BIRDS ON PEDESTALS, ZIMBABWE

1

down the back, the raised rosette-shaped eyes, and the pattern down the back, point to a high degree of conventionality, evolved out of some sacred symbolism of which these birds were the embodiment, the nature of which symbolism it is now our object to arrive at. Two of the birds, similar in character,

FRONT AND BACK OF A BROKEN SOAPSTONE BIRD ON PEDESTAL

with straight legs and fan-shaped tails different from the others, are represented as perched on zones or cesti; two others have only indications of the cestus beneath their feet; a fifth, with nothing beneath its feet, has two circles carved under it and two on the wings[1]; a sixth is perched on a chevron pattern

[1] *Vide* Illustration, p. 181.

184   THE ARCHÆOLOGY OF THE DISTRICT

similar to that which decorates the large circular temple; hence there is a sort of similarity of symbolism connecting them all.

We have now to look around for comparisons

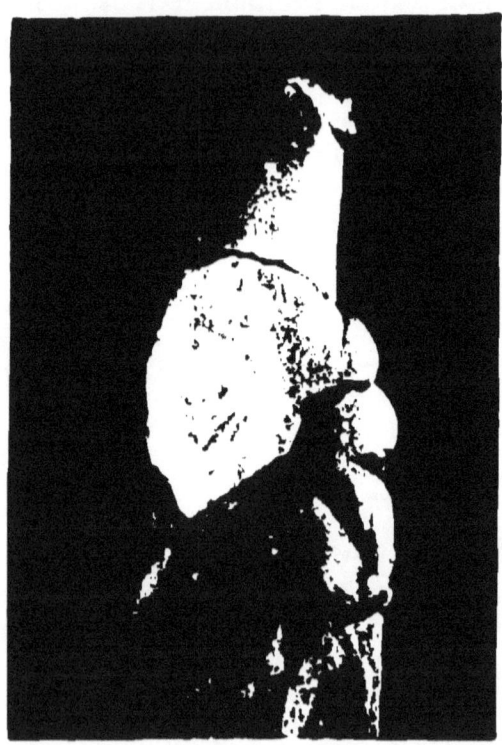

BIRD ON PEDESTAL

by which we may hope to identify the origin of our birds, and I have little doubt in stating that they are closely akin to the Assyrian Astarte or Venus, and represent the female element in creation. Similar birds were sacred to Astarte amongst the Phœnicians and are often represented as perched on her shrines.

Of the maternal aspect in which the ancient Egyptians held the vulture we have ample evidence. Horapollo tells us (I. 11) that the vulture was emblematic of 'Urania, a year, a mother,' whilst Ælian goes so far as to suppose that all vultures were females, to account for their character as emblems of maternity. The cesti and the circles point obviously to this, and these birds in connection with phallic worship are interesting as emblems, signifying incubation. Let us now consult Lucian, who in his work 'De Syriâ Deâ' describes a temple at Hierapolis, near the Euphrates, which, as we have seen, has much in common with these temples at Zimbabwe. In § 33, p. 479, he mentions a curious pediment, of no distinctive shape, called by the Assyrians 'the symbol,' on the top of which is perched a bird. Amongst some of Dr. Schliemann's discoveries at Mycene, there are also images surmounted by birds which differ from the ξόανον in the 'De Syriâ Deâ' solely in the fact that they are not shapeless, but represent a nude female figure. The goddess of this shrine was evidently Astarte, and wore a cestus, 'with which none but Urania is adorned.'[1]

BIRD ON PEDESTAL FROM THE ZODIAC OF DENDERAH

[1] Lucian, *De Syriâ Deâ*, p. 477.

On a Phœnician coin found in Cyprus we have the dove on the betyle or pedestal as the central object.[1] In Egyptian archæology we also come across the bird on the pedestal, more particularly in the curious zodiac of Denderah, where a bird perched on a pillar, and with the crown of Upper Egypt on its head, is, as Mr. Norman Lockyer tells me, used to indicate the commencement of the year; also from the Soudan we have a bird on a pedestal carved on some rude stone fragments now in the Ashmolean Museum. It is just possible that the birds at Zimbabwe had some solstitial meaning, but as their exact position on the temple walls is lost, it is impossible to speak on this point with anything like certainty. Also in the difficult question of early Arabian cult, which was closely bound up with that of Egypt, Assyria, and Phœnicia, we find the vulture as the *totem* of a Southern Arabian tribe at the time of the Himyaritic supremacy, and it was worshipped there as the god Nasr, and is mysteriously alluded to in Himyaritic inscriptions as 'the vulture of the East and the vulture of the West,' which also would seem to point to a solstitial use of the emblem.[2]

The religious symbolism of these birds is further attested by our finding two tiny representations of the larger emblems; they, too, represented birds on pillars, the longest of which is only three and a half inches, and it is perched on the pillar more as the

---

[1] Perrot and Chipiez's *Phœnicia*, p. 281.
[2] Kremer, *Akademie der Wissenschaft*. Wien.

THE FINDS AT THE GREAT ZIMBABWE RUINS 187

bird is represented in the zodiac of Denderah. Evidently these things were used as amulets or votive offerings in the temple. Lucian alludes to the phalli used as amulets by the Greeks with a human

MINIATURE BIRDS ON PEDESTALS

figure on the end, and he connects them with the tower thirty cubits in height.

In the centre of the temple on the hill stood an altar, into the stones of which were inserted and also scattered around a large number of soapstone objects representing the phallus either realistically or conventionally, but always with anatomical accuracy which unmistakably conveys their meaning, and proves in addition that circumcision was practised by this primitive race; 'its origin both amongst the Egyptians and Ethiopians,' says Herodotus, ii. 37, 104, 'may be traced to the most remote antiquity.' We have seen in the previous description of the tower the parallel to Lucian's description of the phalli in the temple at Hierapolis. Here, in the upper temple, we found no less than thirty-eight miniature representations of the larger emblem; one is a highly ornate object, with apparently a representation of a winged sun on its side, or perchance the winged Egyptian vulture, suggesting a distinct Semitic influence. There is a small marble column in the Louvre, twenty-six inches in height, of Phœnician origin, with a winged symbol on the shaft like the one

PHŒNICIAN COLUMN IN THE LOUVRE

ORNATE PHALLUS. ZIMBABWE

before us; it is crowned by an ornament made of four petalled flowers. This winged globe is met with in many Phœnician objects, and MM. Perrot and Chipiez, in their work on Phœnicia, thus speak of it as 'a sort of trade-mark by which we can recognise as Phœnician all such objects as bear it, whether they come from Etruria or Sardinia, from Africa or Syria.' And of the stele in the Louvre the same authors say, 'We may say that it is signed.' A carefully executed rosette with seven petals forms the summit of our object found in the temple. Now the rosette is also another distinctly Phœnician symbol used by them to indicate the sun. We have the rosette on Phœnician sepulchral stelæ in the British Museum in conjunction with the half-moon to indicate the heavenly luminaries, and here at Zimbabwe we have this object surmounted by a rosette, rosettes carved on the decorated pillars, and the eyes of the birds, as before mentioned, are made in the form of rosettes. The fact of finding these objects all in close juxtaposition around the altar and in the vicinity of the birds on pillars is sufficient proof of the nature of the objects and their religious symbolism. Thus we have in both cases the larger emblems and their miniature representatives, the tower and the smaller phalli, the large birds and the tiny amulets, proving to us that the ancient inhabitants of the ruins worshipped a combination of the two deities, which together represented the creative powers of mankind.

A curious confirmation of this is found in the

LONG DECORATED SOAPSTONE BEAM IN TWO PIECES

pages of Herodotus, who tells us [1] : 'The Arabians of all the gods only worshipped Dionysus, whom they called Ourotalt, and Urania;' that is to say, they worshipped the two deities which, in the mind of the father of history, represented in themselves all that was known of the mysteries of creation, pointing to the very earliest period of Arabian cult, prior to the more refined religious development of the Sabæo-Himyaritic dynasty, when Sun-worship, veneration for the great luminary which regenerated all animal and vegetable life, superseded the grosser forms of nature-worship, to be itself somewhat superseded or rather incorporated in a worship of all the heavenly lumi-

[1] *Herod.* Bk. III. § 8.

THE FINDS AT THE GREAT ZIMBABWE RUINS

naries, which developed as a knowledge of astronomy was acquired.

We have already discussed the round towers and the numerous monoliths which decorated the walls and other parts of the Zimbabwe ruins; excavation yielded further examples of the veneration for stones amongst the early inhabitants. One of these was a tall decorated soapstone pillar 11 feet 6 inches in height, which stood on the platform already alluded to, and acted as a centre to a group of monoliths; the base of this pillar we found *in situ*, the rest had been broken off and appropriated by a Kaffir to decorate a wall; it was worked with bands of geometric patterns around it, each different from the other and divided into compartments by circular patterns, one of which is the chevron pattern found on the circular

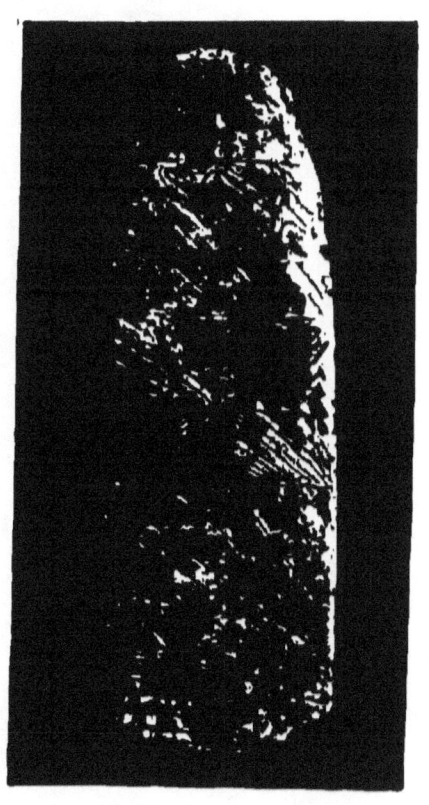

DECORATED SOAPSTONE BEAM

192 THE ARCHÆOLOGY OF THE DISTRICT

ruin below; it only runs round a portion of the pillar; and may possibly have been used to orient it towards the setting sun. Besides this tall pillar we found two

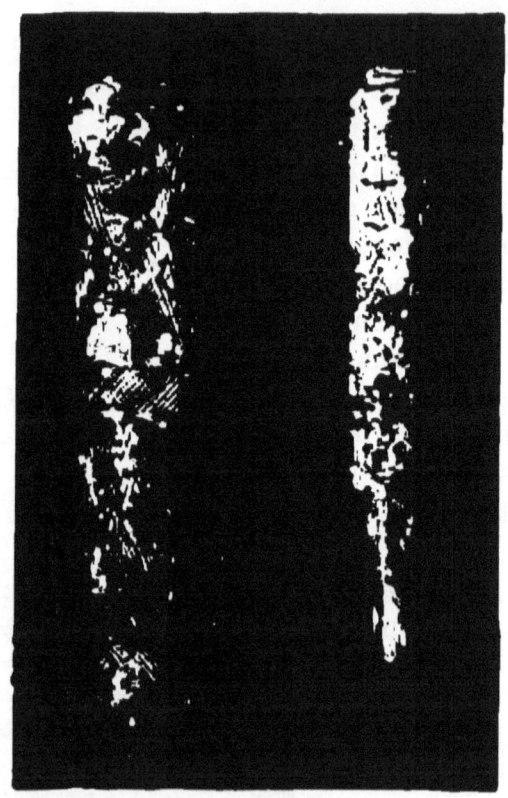

DECORATED SOAPSTONE BEAMS

fragments of other similar pillars decorated one with geometric patterns and the other with an extraordinary and entirely inexplicable decoration. On these pillars the rosette is frequently depicted, and it

THE FINDS AT THE GREAT ZIMBABWE RUINS 193

would seem that they all came from the same place, namely, the platform decorated with monoliths. Here also we found several stones of a curious nature

COLLECTION OF STRANGE STONES

and entirely foreign to the place. Two of them are stones with even bands of an asbestiform substance, a serpentine with veins of chrysolite, the grooves being caused by the natural erosion of the fibrous bands. Another stone is an irregular polygonal pillar-like object of coarse-grained basalt, the smooth faces of which are natural points, the whole being a portion of a rough column or prism. Another, again, is a fragment of schistose rock, apparently hornblendic; also we found several round blocks of diorite in this place. The collection here of so many strange geological fragments cannot be accidental, and points to a veneration of curious-shaped stones amongst the

FRAGMENT OF BOWL WITH PROCESSION OF BULLS

earlier inhabitants of the ruins, which were collected here on the platform, a spot which, I am convinced, will compare with the βαιτύλια or betyles of the Phœnicians, and of this stone cult we have ample evidence from Arabia. El Masoudi alludes to the ancient stone-worship of Arabia, and leads us to believe that at one time this gross fetichism formed a part of the natural religion of the Semitic races. Marinus of Tyre says they honoured as a god a great cut stone. Euthymius Zygabenus further tells us that apparently 'this stone was the head of Aphrodite, which the Ishmaelites formerly worshipped, and it is called Bakka Ismak;' also, he adds, 'they have certain stone statues erected in the centre of their houses, round which they danced till they fell from giddiness; but when the Saracens were converted to Christianity they were obliged to anathematise this stone, which formerly they worshipped.'[1] Herr Kremer, in his account of the ancient cult of Arabia, makes frequent allusions to the stone-worship. In the town of Taif a great unformed stone block was worshipped, identical with the goddess which Herodotus calls Urania; and one must imagine that the Kaaba stone at Mecca resembles the black schistose block which we found at Zimbabwe; it is an exceedingly old-world worship, dating back to the most primitive ages of mankind.

The next series of finds to be discussed are the numerous frag-

FRAGMENT OF BOWL WITH HUNTING SCENE

[1] *Akademie der Wissenschaft.* Wien, 1890.

ments of decorated and plain soapstone bowls which we found, most of them deeply buried in the immediate vicinity of the temple on the fortress; and these bring us to consider more closely the artistic capacities of the race who originally inhabited these ruins. The work displayed in executing these bowls, the careful rounding of the edges, the exact execution of the circle, the fine pointed tool-marks, and the subjects they chose to depict, point to the race having been far advanced in artistic skill—a skill arrived at, doubtless, by commercial in-

BOWL WITH ZEBRAS

tercourse with the more civilised races of mankind. Seven of these bowls were of exactly the same size, and were 19·2 inches in diameter,[1] which measurements we ascertained by taking the radii of the several fragments. The most elaborate of these fragments is a bowl which had depicted around its outer edge a hunting scene; it is very well worked, and bears in several points a remarkable similarity to objects of art produced by the Phœnicians. There is here, as we have in all Phœnician pat-

[1] Equal to two Egyptian spans of 0·58 inches.

terns, the straight procession of animals, to break the continuity of which a little man is introduced shooting a zebra with one hand and holding in the other an animal by a leash. To fill up a vacant space, a bird is introduced flying, all of which points are characteristic of Phœnician work. Then the Phœnician workmen always had a great power of adaptability, taking their lessons in art from their immediate surroundings, which is noticeable all over the world, whether in Greece, Egypt, Africa, or Italy.

Here we have the same characteristic, namely, a procession of native African animals treated in a Phœnician style— three zebras, two hippopotami, and the sportsman in the centre is obviously a Hottentot. The details

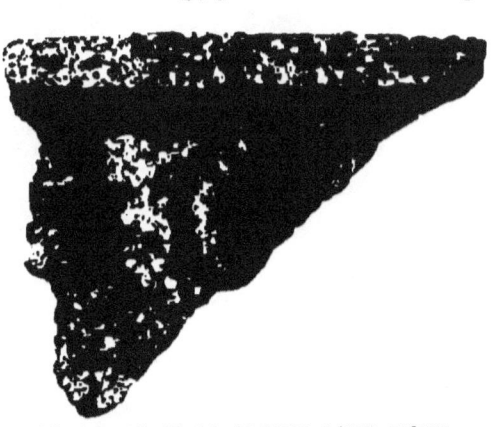

FRAGMENT OF SOAPSTONE BOWL WITH PROCESSION

in this bowl are carefully brought out, even the breath of the animals is depicted by three strokes at the mouth. There is also a fragment of another bowl with zebras on it similarly treated, though somewhat higher and coarser. The fragments of a large bowl, which had a procession of bulls round it, is also Phœnician in character.[1] The most noticeable feature in the treatment of these bulls is that the three pairs of horns we have preserved to us are all different.

There are three fragments of three very large bowls, which are all of a special interest, and if the bowls could have been recovered intact they would have formed very valuable evidence. Search, however, as we would, we never found more of these bowls,

FRAGMENT OF SOAPSTONE BOWL WITH EAR OF CORN

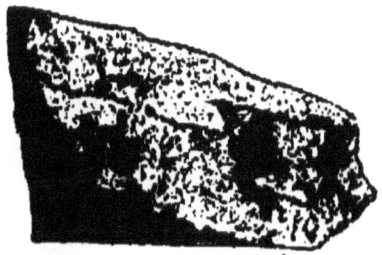
FRAGMENT WITH LETTERING ON IT

and therefore must be content with what we have. The first of these represents on its side a small portion of what must have been a religious procession; of this we have only a hand holding a pot or censer containing an offering in it, and an arm of another figure with a portion of the back of the head with the hair drawn off it in folds. Representations of a similar nature are to be found in the religious functions of many Semitic races, and it is much to be regretted that we have not more of it for our study.

[1] *Vide* illustration, p. 104.

The second fragment has an elaborate design upon it, taken from the vegetable world, probably an ear of corn; it was evidently around the lip of the bowl and not at the side; it is a very good piece of workmanship, and of a soapstone of brighter green than that

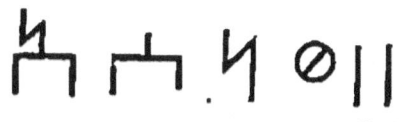

LETTERS FROM PROTO-ARABIAN ALPHABET

employed in the other articles. The third fragment is perhaps the most tantalising of all; it is a fragment of the lip of another large bowl which must have been more than two feet in diameter, and around which apparently an inscription ran. The lettering is pro-

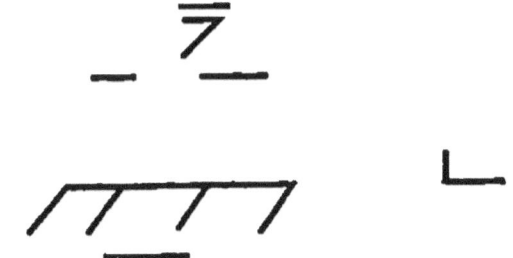

LETTERS ON A ROCK IN BECHUANALAND, COPIED BY MR. A. A. ANDERSON

vokingly fragmentary, but still there can be no doubt that it is an attempt at writing in some form: the straight line down the middle, the sloping lines on either side recall some system of tally, and the straightness of the lettering compares curiously with the proto-Arabian type of lettering used in the earlier Sabæan inscriptions, specimens of which I here give, and also with some curious rock carvings found by Mr. A. A. Anderson in Bechuanaland. It was common in Phœnician and early Greek vases to have an

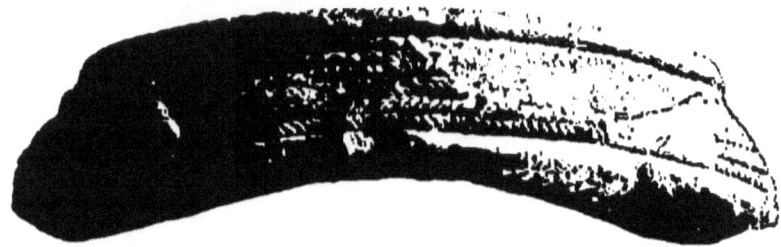

SOAPSTONE BOWL WITH CORD PATTERN

inscription or dedication round the lip; *vide*, for example, a *lebes* in the British Museum from a temple at Naucratis with a dedication to Apollo on the rim, and used, like the one before us, in temple service. The circles on the birds also appear to have

FRAGMENT OF SOAPSTONE BOWL

a line across, like the fourth letter given as illustrating the early Arabian alphabet.

Of the other fragments of bowls we found, one has a well-executed cord-pattern running round it, another a herring-bone pattern alternating with what would appear to be a representation of the round tower; and besides these there are several fragments of

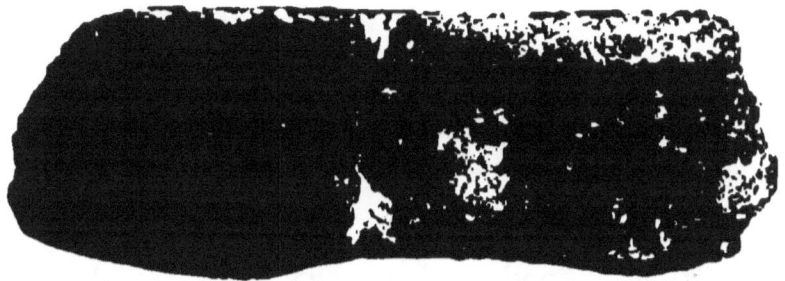

PLAIN SOAPSTONE BOWL WITH HOLE

what have been perfectly plain bowls, notably one large one, the diameter of which is outside 2 feet and

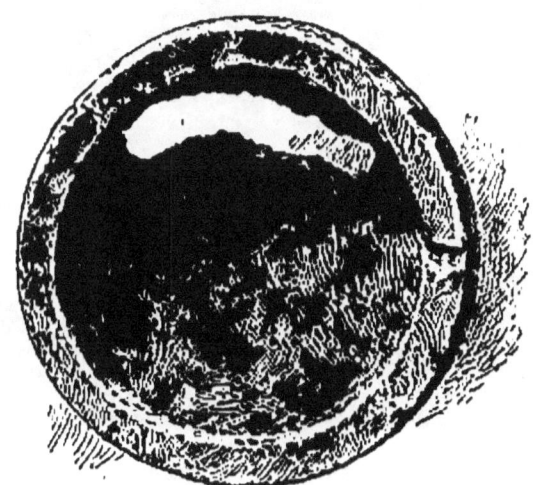

PLAIN SOAPSTONE BOWL

inside 1 foot 8 inches. The edges of this bowl are very carefully bevelled and the bottom rounded, and it is a very fine specimen of workmanship, the whole of which we were able to recover saving a portion of

FRAGMENT OF BOWL WITH KNOBS

the bottom. Another plain bowl has a round hole pierced through its side, and another fragment is

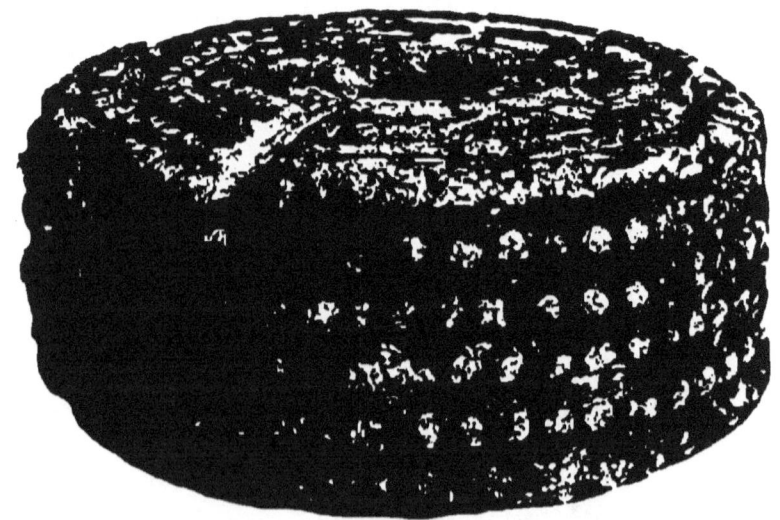

SOAPSTONE CYLINDER FROM ZIMBABWE

made of a reddish sort of soapstone with oxide of iron in it. The tool marks on these bowls point to very fine instruments having been used in carving.

them. Altogether these bowls are amongst the most conspicuous of our finds, and the fact they all came from the proximity of the temple would undoubtedly seem to prove that they were used in temple service, broken by subsequent occupants of the ruins, and the fragments thrown outside.

The next find from Zimbabwe which we will

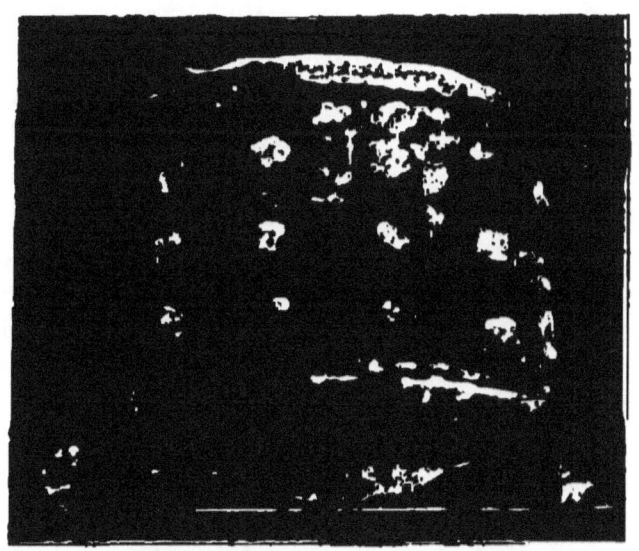

OBJECT FROM TEMPLE OF PAPHOS, CYPRUS

discuss is the circular soapstone object with a hole in the centre, which at first is suggestive of a quern; but being of such friable material such could not have been the case. It is decorated round the side and on the top with rings of knobs, four on the side and four on the top; from the central hole a groove has been cut to the side, and the whole is very well finished off. This thing is 2 feet 2 inches in circumference. We also found portions of a smaller bowl with the same knob pattern thereon. The use of this extraordinary soapstone find is very obscure. Mr. Hogarth calls my attention to the fact that in the excavations at Paphos, in Cyprus, they found a similar object, similarly decorated, which they put down as Phœnician. It is now in the Fitzwilliam Museum at Cambridge, and is a cylindrical object of coarse white marble six inches in diameter and about four and three-quarter inches high. It is studded with round projecting studs left in relief on the marble, resembling in general disposition those on our soapstone find, and there is no question about the similarity of the two objects. They remind one of Herodian's description of the sacred cone in the great Phœnician temple of the sun at Emesa, in Syria (Herodian, bk. v. § 5), which was adorned with certain 'knobs or protuberances,' a pattern supposed by him to represent the sun, and common in phallic decorations.

In the vicinity of the temple we also came across some minor objects very near the surface, which did not do more than establish the world-wide commerce carried on at the Great Zimbabwe at a much more recent date, and still by the Arabians—namely, a few fragments of Celadon pottery from China, of Persian ware, an undoubted specimen of Arabian glass, and beads of doubtful provenance, though one of them may be considered as Egyptian of the

Ptolemaic period. Glass beads almost of precisely the same character—namely, black with white encircling lines—have come from ancient tombs at Thebes, in Bœotia, and are to be found in almost every collection of Egyptian curiosities.

The pottery objects must have been brought here

GLASS BEADS, CELADON POTTERY, PERSIAN POTTERY, AND ARABIAN GLASS

by Arabian traders during the middle ages, probably when the Monomatapa chiefs ruled over this district and carried on trade with the Arabians for gold, as European traders do now with objects of bright appearance and beads. Similar fragments have been found by Sir John Kirk in the neighbourhood of Quiloa, where in mediæval times was a settlement of

P

Arabs who came from the Persian Gulf, forming an hereditary intercourse between the Arabs and the east coast of Africa until the Portuguese found them there and drove them away three centuries ago. It is impossible that a collection of things such as these could have been brought together by any but a

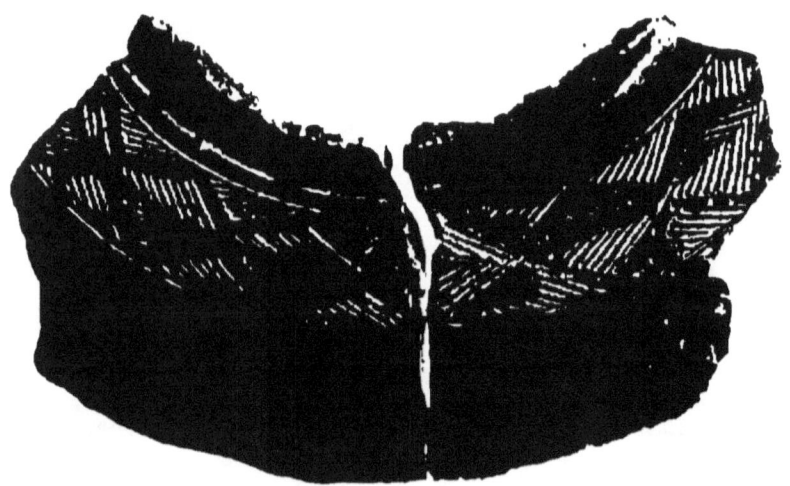

FRAGMENT OF BOWL OF GLAZED POTTERY

highly commercial race during the middle ages, and the Arabians alone had this character at the time in question.

Considering the large quantity of soapstone fragments, bowls, and other things, the finds of pottery of a good period at Zimbabwe were not many. Noticeably one piece of pottery is exceedingly excellent, worthy of a good period of classic Greek ware. The pattern round it is evidently stamped on, being done with such absolute accuracy. It is geometric, as all the patterns on the pottery are. It is not handmade pottery, for on the back of it are distinct signs of a wheel. Then there are some black fragments with an excellent glaze and bevel, also fragments of pottery lids, and a pottery stopper, pointing to the fact that the old inhabitants of Zimbabwe had reached an

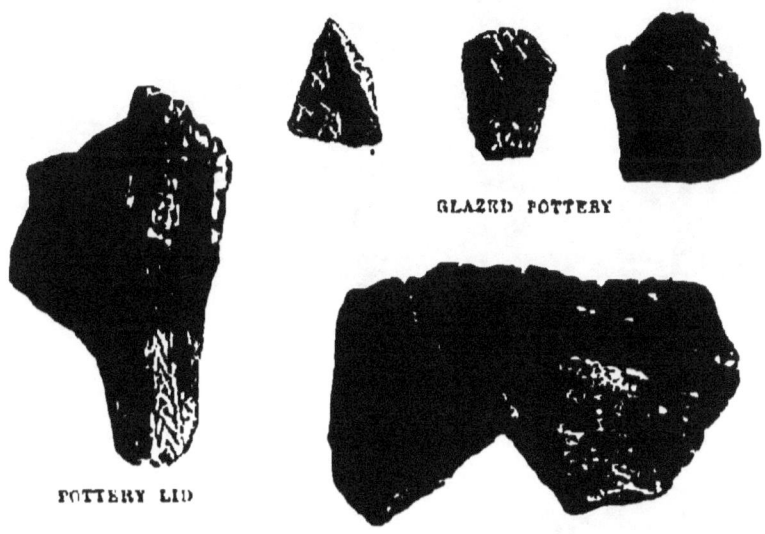

GLAZED POTTERY

POTTERY LID

DECORATED FRAGMENT OF POTTERY

advanced state of proficiency in ceramic art. Fragments of one pot with holes neatly bored round the neck remind one of water-coolers still found in the East. Besides the fragments of pots, we found an enormous number of small circular objects of pottery, which may have been used as spindle-whorls, though most of them show no signs of wear, and some of them having rude decorations thereon. The only fragment which shows an attempt at the use of pot-

TOP OF POTTERY BOWL

tery for other than domestic purposes is a sow which we found in a kitchen midden just outside the large

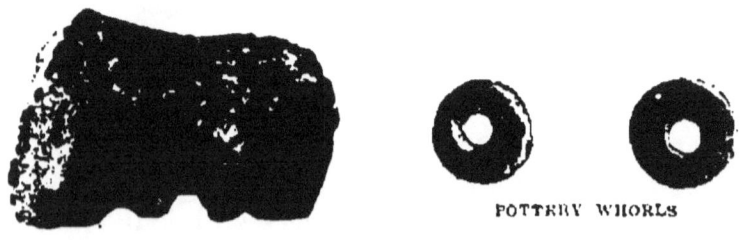

POTTERY SOW

POTTERY WHORLS

circular building on the plain, with two phalli near it. This animal compares well with the rude

THE FINDS AT THE GREAT ZIMBABWE RUINS   209

attempts to depict animal life found in prehistoric excavations on the Mediterranean. Whether it has any religious significance or not is, of course, only conjecture, but it is curious that Ælian tells us that the Egyptians 'sacrifice a sow to the moon once a year;' and Herodotus says 'the only deities to whom the Egyptians are permitted to offer a pig are the moon

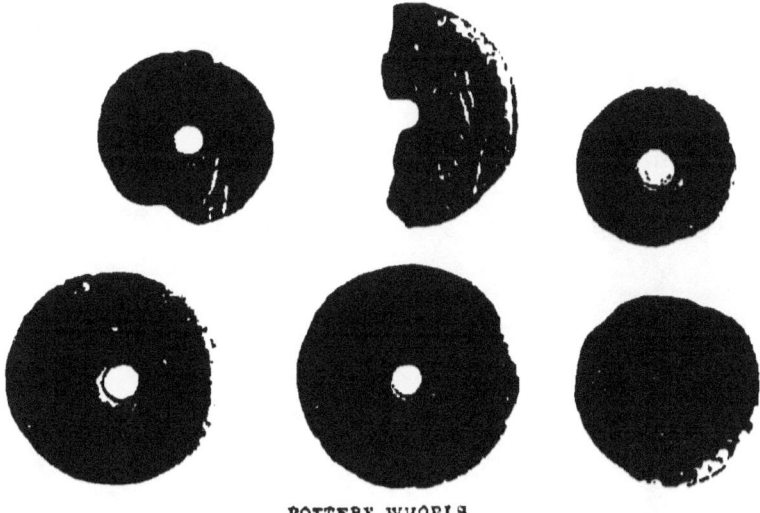

POTTERY WHORLS

and Bacchus.' All that the pottery proves to us is that the ancient inhabitants of Zimbabwe had reached a high state of excellence in the manufacture of it, corresponding to a state of ceramic art known only to the rest of the world in classical times.

Concerning the bronze and iron weapons and implements which we found at Zimbabwe it is very difficult to say anything definite. In the first place, these ruins have been overrun for centuries by Kaffir races with a knowledge of iron-smelting, who would at once utilise fragments of iron which they found for

WEAPONS

their own purposes; secondly, the shapes and sizes of arrows and spear-heads correspond very closely to those in use amongst the natives now. As against this it must be said that there are many iron objects amongst

THE FINDS AT THE GREAT ZIMBABWE RUINS 211

our finds which are quite unlike anything which ever came out of a Kaffir workshop, and the patterns of the assegai, or spear-head, and arrow are probably of great antiquity, handed down from generation to

IRON BELL

generation to the present day. Amongst the most curious of our iron finds at Zimbabwe certainly are the double iron bells, of which we found three in the neighbourhood of the temple on the fortress. Similar bells are found now on the Congo. There are some in the British Museum, and also in the Geographical Society's Museum at Lisbon, which came from San Salvador, on the Congo, and are called Chingongo,

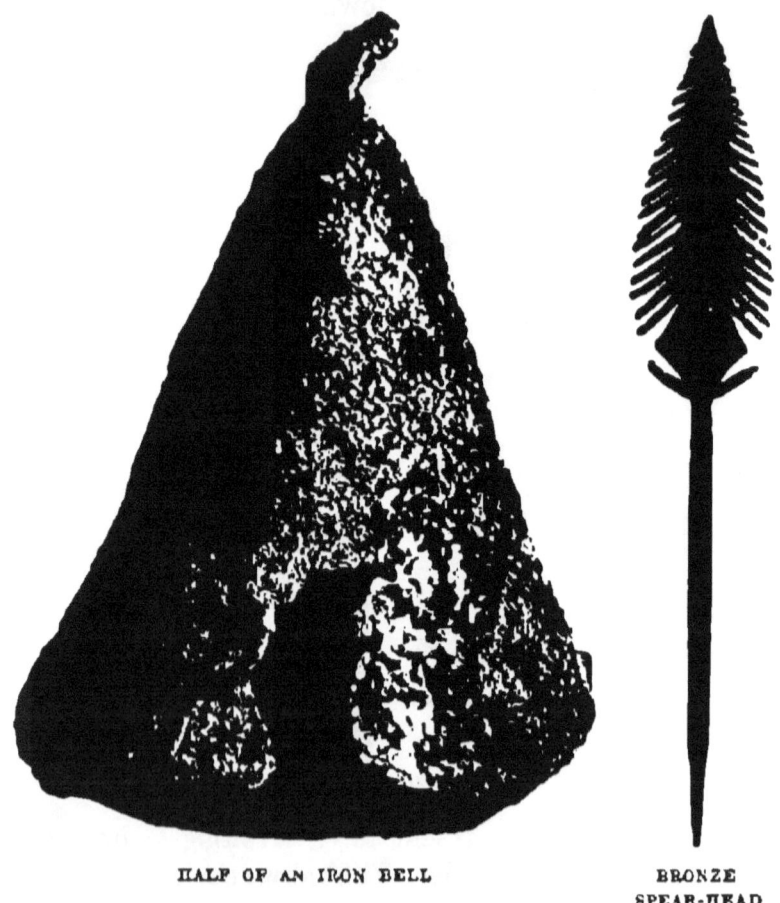

HALF OF AN IRON BELL   BRONZE SPEAR-HEAD

whereas amongst the present race inhabiting Mashonaland the knowledge of this bell does not exist, nor did it presumably exist in Dos Santos' days, who

THE FINDS AT THE GREAT ZIMBABWE RUINS 213

enumerates all the Kaffir instruments which he saw; and he would assuredly have mentioned these bells had they existed there in his days 300 years ago. We must, therefore, conclude that either these bells are ancient, and were used by the old inhabitants of these ruins, the

BATTLE-AXE AND ARROWS

traditional form of which has been continued amongst the negroes of the Congo, or that some northern race closely allied to the Congo races swept over this country at some time or another, and have left this trace of their occupation. The barbed bronze spear-head we found under a mass of fallen rock close to the entrance to the fortress. This again finds a parallel in weapons which come from much farther north in Nubia, though its execution is finer than any of that class which has come before my notice. The shape of this weapon

BATTLE-AXE

is exactly the same as that of the unbarbed spearhead, which has a coating of gold on it,[1] and shows the same peculiarity of make as the assegai-heads still made by the natives—namely, the fluting which

[1] *Vide* illustration, p. 216.

THE FINDS AT THE GREAT ZIMBABWE RUINS 215

runs down the centre being reversed on either side. Then there are the tools—chisels, an adze, pincers, spades, &c., which are quite unknown to the Kaffir races which now inhabit this country. Still it is possible that all these things may have been made during the time of the Monomatapa, who evidently had reached a higher pitch of civilisation than that existing to-day; so that I am inclined to set aside the iron implements as pertaining to a more recent occupation, though at the same time there is no actual reason for not assigning to them a remoter antiquity.

The finds in the fortress of Zimbabwe which touch upon, perhaps, the most interesting topic of all are those which refer to the manufacture of gold. Close underneath the temple in the fortress stood a gold-smelting furnace made of very hard cement of powdered granite, with a chimney of the same material, and with neatly bevelled edges. Hard by, in a chasm between two boulders, lay all the rejected casings from which the gold-bearing quartz had been extracted by exposure to heat prior to the crushing, proving beyond a doubt that these mines, though not immediately on a gold reef, formed the capital of a gold-producing people who had chosen this hill fortress with its granite boulders for their capital owing to its peculiar strategic advantages. Gold reefs and old workings have been lately discovered about twelve miles from Zimbabwe, and it was from these that their auriferous quartz was doubtless obtained.

Near the above-mentioned furnace we found many

216 THE ARCHÆOLOGY OF THE DISTRICT

little crucibles, of a composition of clay, which had been used for smelting the gold, and in nearly all of them still exist small specks of gold adhering to the glaze formed by the heat of the process. Also we found several water-worn stones, which had been used as burnishers, which was evidenced by the quantity of gold still adhering to them; and in the adjoining cave we dug up an ingot mould of soapstone of a curious shape, corresponding almost exactly to an ingot of tin found in Falmouth Harbour, which is now in the Truro Museum, and a cast of which may be seen at the School of Mines in Jermyn Street. This ingot of tin was undoubtedly made by Phœnician workmen, for it bears a punch mark thereon like those usually employed by workmen of that period; and Sir Henry James, in his pamphlet describing it, draws attention to the statement of Diodorus, that in ancient Britain ingots of tin were made ἀστραγάλων ῥυθμοὺς, or of the shape of astragali or knuckle-bones; and the form of both the ingots is such that the astragalus may easily be used as a rough simile to describe them. Probably this shape of ingot was common in the ancient world, for Sir John Evans, K.C.B., has called my attention to an ingot mould somewhat similar in form, found in Dalmatia, and the Kaffirs far north of the Zambesi

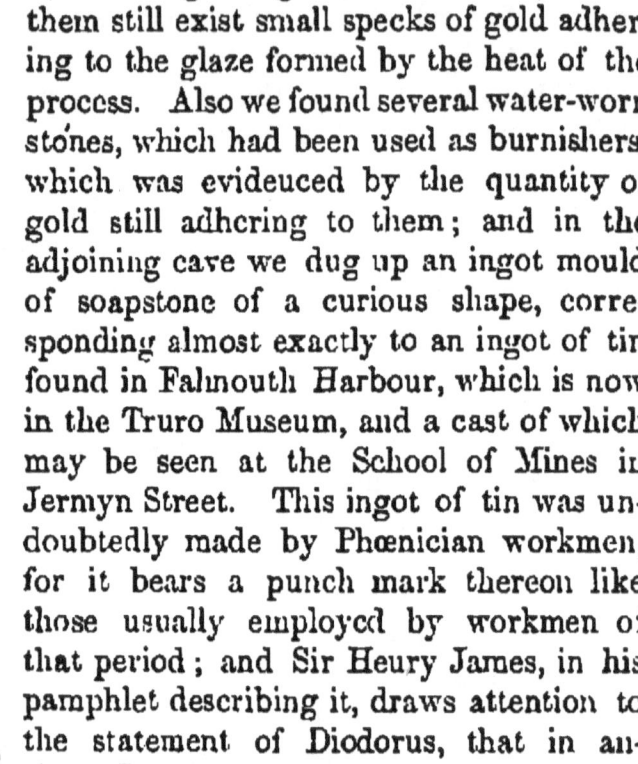

GILT SPEAR-HEAD

THE FINDS AT THE GREAT ZIMBABWE RUINS

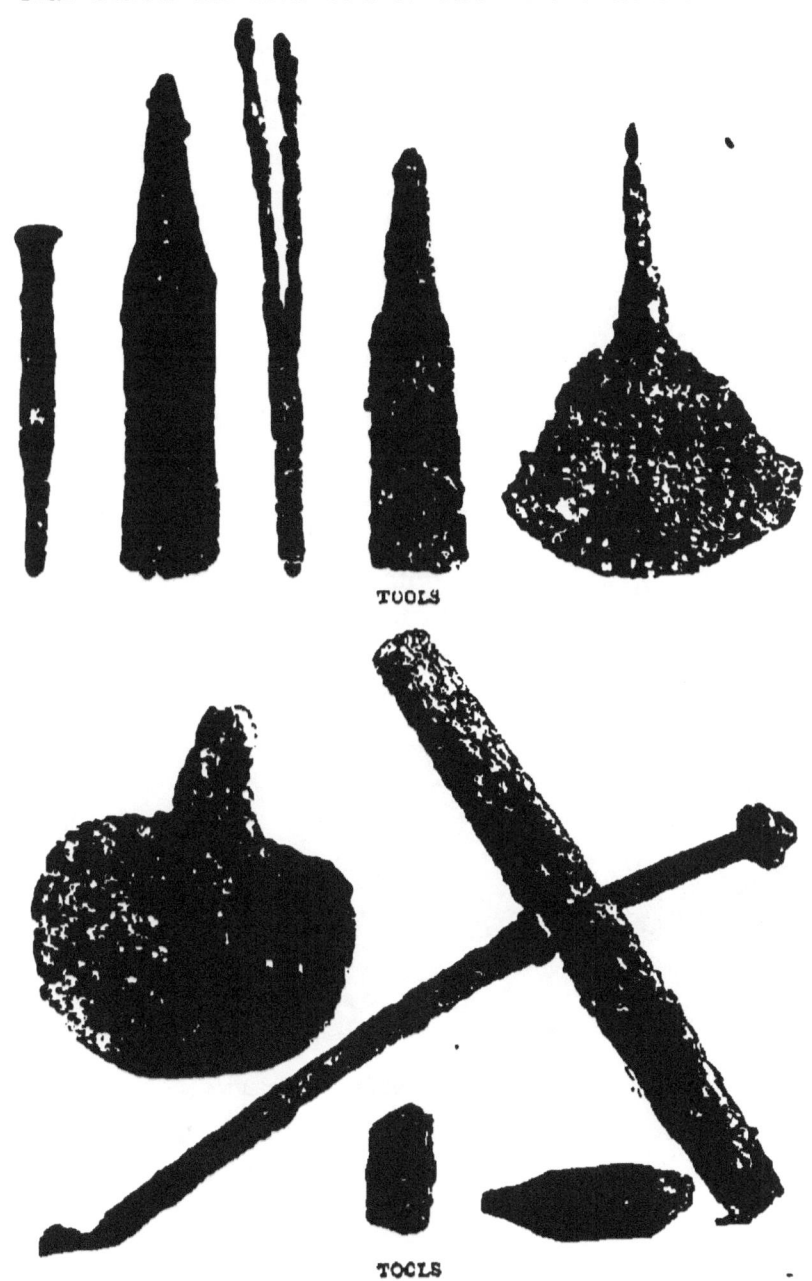

TOOLS

TOOLS

218 THE ARCHEOLOGY OF THE DISTRICT

now make ingots of iron of a shape which might easily be supposed to have been derived from the astragalus; but at the same time the finding of two ingots in two remote places where Phœnician influence has been proved to be so strong is very good presumptive evidence to establish the fact that the gold workers of ancient Zimbabwe worked for the Phœnician market. A small soapstone object with a hole in the centre would appear to have been a sort of tool used for beating gold.

ANCIENT SPADE

An interesting parallel to the ancient gold workings in Mashonaland is to be found by studying the account of the ancient gold workings at the Egyptian gold mines in Wadi Allaga, also given us by Diodorus.

SOAPSTONE INGOT MOULD. ZIMBABWE

There, too, the gold was extracted from the quartz by a process of crushing and washing, as we can see from the process depicted in the paintings on the Egyptian tombs; and in any gold-producing quarter of Masho-

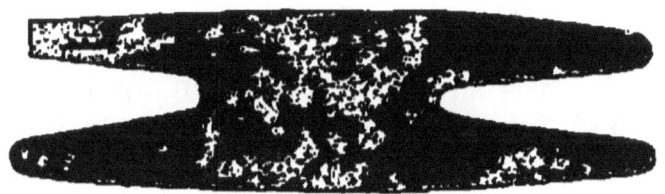

INGOT OF TIN FOUND IN FALMOUTH HARBOUR.

naland, near old shafts and by the side of streams, innumerable crushing-stones are still to be seen, used anciently for a like purpose, when slave labour was employed. Diodorus tells us of the gangs of slaves employed, of the long dark shaft into which they descended, of which a countless number are scattered still over Mashonaland; and after describing the process of washing and crushing he concludes: 'They then put the gold into earthen

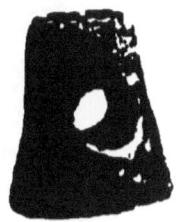

SOAPSTONE OBJECT

crucibles well closed with clay, and leave it in a furnace for five successive days and nights, after which it is suffered to cool. The crucibles are then opened, and nothing is found in them but the pure gold a little diminished in quantity.' Hence it is obvious that the process employed by the ancient Egyptians for crushing, smelting, and forming into ingots was exactly the same as that employed by the ancient inhabitants of Zimbabwe; which fact, when taken in conjunction with the vast amount of evidence of ancient cult, ancient construction, and ancient art, is, I think, conclusive that the gold-fields of Mashonaland formed one at least of the sources from which came the gold of Arabia, and that the forts and towns which ran up the whole length of this gold-producing country were made to protect their men engaged in this industry. The

BEVELLED EDGE OF GOLD-SMELTING FURNACE

cumulative evidence is greatly in favour of the gold diggers being of Arabian origin, before the Sabæo-Himyaritic period in all probability, who did work for and were brought closely into contact with both Egypt and Phœnicia, penetrating to many countries unknown to the rest of the world. The Bible is full of allusions to the wealth of Arabia in gold and other things. Ezekiel tells us that the Sabæans were merchants in gold for the markets of Tyre. Aristeas

THE FINDS AT THE GREAT ZIMBABWE RUINS 221

tells us that a large quantity of spices, precious stones, and gold was brought to Rome διὰ τῶν Ἀράβων, not from Arabia, but by the Arabians. The testimony of all travellers in Arabia is to the effect that little or no gold could have come from the Arabian peninsula itself; it is, therefore, almost certain that the country round Zimbabwe formed one at least of the spots from which the ' *Thesaurus*

CRUCIBLES FOR SMELTING GOLD FOUND AT ZIMBABWE

Arabum' came. Egyptian monuments also point to the wealth of the people of Punt, and the ingots of gold which they sent as tribute to Queen Hatasou. No one, of course, is prepared to say exactly where the kingdom of Punt was; the consensus of opinion is that it was Yemen, in the south of Arabia. But suppose it to be there, or suppose it to be on the coast of Africa, opposite Arabia, or even suppose it to be Zimbabwe itself, the question is the same:

where did they get the large supply of gold from, which they poured into Egypt and the then known world? In Mashonaland we seem to have a direct answer to this question. It would seem to be evident that a prehistoric race built the ruins in this country, a race like the mythical Pelasgi who inhabited the shores of Greece and Asia Minor, a race

FRAGMENTS OF POTTERY BLOW-PIPES FROM FURNACE

like the mythical inhabitants of Great Britain and France who built Stonehenge and Carnac, a race which continued in possession down to the earliest dawnings of history, which provided gold for the merchants of Phœnicia and Arabia, and which eventually became influenced by and perhaps absorbed in the more powerful and wealthier organisations of the Semite.

CHAPTER VII

THE GEOGRAPHY AND ETHNOLOGY OF THE MASHONALAND RUINS

THE ancient geography of the east coast of Africa is a subject fraught with difficulties on all sides. To begin with, our authorities are not only meagre, but they are men who had no practical knowledge of the subject, and who knew next to nothing of the vast extent of commercial operations which were going on outside the limits of the Red Sea. The written accounts come to us from either an Alexandrian or Roman source, whereas the practical knowledge possessed by the Arabs themselves of these outer waters is lost to us for ever. It was probably the monopolising policy of the Semitic nations which induced them to conceal from other countries the whereabouts of their commercial relations, which on the one hand extended outside the pillars of Hercules to the Canaries and Great Britain, and on the other hand outside the Straits of Bab-el-Mandeb to India, China, and the east coast of Africa. Of these two directions the voyage to

Great Britain was undoubtedly the most adventurous, the navigation of the Indian Ocean with a knowledge of the monsoons, which the Arabian who lived on it must have had from time immemorial, presenting far less difficulty. Hippalus has the credit of introducing the monsoons to Western civilisation, but surely a seafaring race like the Arabians, who lived on the spot, must have known all about them long before his day; and just as they were reticent on the subject of their voyages, so were they reticent on the subject of the localities from which their merchandise came. The knowledge given us by Marinus of Tyre, by the anonymous author of the 'Periplus of the Red Sea,' by Ptolemy, by Pliny, and others, was obviously not the knowledge possessed by the traders of the world, for they do not even attempt to elucidate the question of where the precious commodities came from which they enumerate.

Ptolemy's information is provokingly vague, and he candidly admits in his first chapter that it was obtained from a merchant of Arabia Felix; he gives us such names as Cape Aromata, supposed to be Guardafui, outside the straits, the inland province of Azania and Rhapta. The only thing we gather from him is that they were trade emporia, and therefore places of considerable importance.

The 'Periplus' enters into further details, and mentions that the Arab settlement at Rhapta was subject to the sovereign of Maphartes, a dependency of Sabæa or Yemen. Dean Vincent imagines Rhapta to have been 10° south of the equator, that is to say, near Quiloa, where again an Arab settlement continued right down into the middle ages. The 'Periplus' further tells how Muza, Aden, and other points near the mouth of the Red Sea were emporia for the goods brought from outside by the Arabians and then transferred to Egyptian and Phœnician trading vessels.

Further south the 'Periplus' mentions Prasum as the farthest point known to the author; and here he says 'an ocean curves towards sunset and, stretching along the southern extremities of Ethiopia, Libya, and Africa, amalgamates with the western sea.' All this probably the author of the 'Periplus' got from the Arabs, just as the Portuguese got all their information from the same source thirteen centuries later, and just as Herodotus got his vague story of the circumnavigation of Africa six centuries before, when he tells us how the Phœnicians in the service of Pharaoh Necho, B.C. 600, 'as they sailed round Africa had the sun on their right hand.'

From these and other statements in Marinus of Tyre, Pliny, and others, it is obvious that the waters of East Africa were known only to the Greeks and Romans vaguely through a Phœnician and Arabian source. The early legendary stories of Greece tell of a voyage fraught with every danger in search of gold. The celebrated Argonautic expedition has given commentators an immense amount of trouble to reconcile its conflicting statements—namely, that it went to the extremities of the Euxine, entered the great stream ocean that went round the world, and returned by the Nile and Libya. It certainly appears to me simple to suppose that it is merely the mutilation of some early Phœnician story made to suit the existing circumstances of the people to whom the story was narrated. The Bible gives us the account of King Solomon's expedition undertaken under Phœnician auspices; in fact, the civilised world was full of accounts of such voyages, told us, unfortunately, in the vaguest way, owing doubtless to the fact that those who undertook them guarded carefully their secret.

From an Egyptian source also certain knowledge may be gained, though the Egyptians themselves would appear never to have carried their commerce outside the Straits of Bab-el-Mandeb, but to have met at the port of Adule, at the south of the Red Sea, Arabian merchants who did so. Now in the reign of Queen Hatasou, of the eighteenth dynasty, in the seventeenth century B.C., the land of Punt was conquered by an Egyptian expedition, and on the monuments of Deir-el-Bahari the conquered people of Punt are depicted as sending tribute, which included ebony, ostrich feathers, leopard skins, giraffes, lions, living leopards, cynocephalous apes, elephants' tusks, and ingots of gold, all products of South-eastern Africa. When compared with the Biblical account of King Solomon's expedition about seven centuries later, the productions of both show a very remarkable analogy. Gold was the most important of the objects brought, gold in ingots such as the mould would produce which we found at Zimbabwe, and the gold of Arabia in antiquity was proverbial. During the height of the prosperity of Rome gold was sent thither by the Arabians, as we have seen from Aristeas. Horace bears testimony to this in his line, 'Thesauris Arabum et divitis Indiæ.' Agatharcides, in B.C. 120, speaks in glowing terms of the wealth of the Sabæans; allusions to it are common in the Bible, and the connection between Phœnicia and Arabia is borne testimony to by Ezekiel in his denunciation of Tyre: 'Arabia and all the princes of Kedar, they occupied with thee in lambs, and rams, and goats: in these were they thy merchants. The merchants of Sheba and Raamah, they were thy merchants: they occupied in thy fairs with chief of all spices, and with all precious stones, and gold.'[1] Probably community of origin, the inherent commercial instinct common to the Semitic races, brought about this intimate relationship between Phœnicia and Sabæa. Another testimony to the wealth of gold in Arabia is given us by the Assyrian inscriptions, on which Tiglath Pileser II., B.C. 733, is mentioned as receiving tribute from that country in gold, silver, and much incense; and Sargon in his annals also mentions the tribute of Shamsi, Queen of Arabia, as paid in gold and spices. There was little, if any, gold to be found in Arabia itself; on this point all travellers who have

[1] Ezek. xxvii. 21. 22.

penetrated this country are agreed. Here, near the east coast of Africa, far nearer to Arabia than India and China and other places, which they were accustomed to visit, not only is there evidence of the extensive production of gold, but also evidence of a cult known to Arabia and Phœnicia alike, temples built on accurate mathematical principles, containing kindred objects of art, methods of producing gold known to have been employed in the ancient world, and evidence of a vast population devoted to the mining of gold.

As to the vexed question of the land of Ophir, I do not feel that it is necessary to go into the arguments for and against here. Mashonaland may have been the land of Ophir or it may not; it may have been the land of Punt or it may not; Ophir and Punt may be identical, and both situated here, or they may be both elsewhere. There is not enough evidence, as far as I can see, to build up any theory on these points which will satisfy the more critical investigation to which subjects of this kind are submitted in the present day. All that we can satisfactorily establish is that from this country the ancient Arabians got a great deal of gold; but as gold was in common use in prehistoric times, and lavishly used many centuries before our era, there is no doubt that the supply must have been enormous, and must have been obtained from more places than one. 'Tyre heaped up silver as the dust, and fine gold as the mire of the streets,' Zechariah tells us (ix. 3), and the subject could be flooded with evidence from sculptural and classical sources; and though the output from the old workings in Mashonaland is seen to have been immense, yet it can hardly have supplied the demand that antiquity made upon it. The study of Arabian and Phœnician enterprise outside the Red Sea is only now in its infancy—we have only as yet enough evidence to prove its extent, and that the ruins in Mashonaland owe their origin to it.

After the commencement of the Christian era there is a great gap in our geographical knowledge of these parts; and as far as Western civilisation is concerned, this corner of the world had to be discovered anew. It was not so, however, with the Arabians, who, though probably banished from the interior many centuries before by the incursions of savage tribes, still held to the coast, and exchanged with the natives their cloth and their beads for gold which they brought down. Of Arab extension in Africa we have also other evidence. The 'Periplus' tells us that the Sabæan King Kharabit in A.D. 85 was in possession of the east coast of Africa to an indefinite extent. The Greek inscription from Axume in Abyssinia, copied by Mr. Salt in his travels there, further confirms this. It was a dedication to Mars of one golden statue, one silver, and three of brass in honour of a victory gained by 'Aizanes, king of the Axomites, of the Homerites (given us by Eratosthenes as one of the Arabian tribes), of the Æthiopians, and of the Sabæans.' Three cities of the name of Sabæ are mentioned as connected with this kingdom, two in Arabia and one in Æthiopia; and now we have the river which doubtless in those days formed the great outlet for the population between the Zambesi and the Limpopo, still bearing the name of Sabæ or Sabi, and in the Æthiopian tongue the word Saba is still used for 'a man.' Herr Eduard Glaser, the Arabian traveller and decipherer of Himyaritic inscriptions, states in his work: 'So much is absolutely certain, that Himyar (Arabia) then possessed almost the whole of East Africa. Such a possession, however, was not won in a night, but rather presupposes, in those old times, without cannon and without powder, centuries of exertion.'

Arabian writers of the ninth and tenth centuries A.D. frequently allude to the gold of Sofala; but to the Western world this country was a blank until Portuguese enterprise again opened it out. John II. of Portugal sent Pedro de Covilham and Alfonso de Payva in 1487 to Cairo to gather information concerning a route to India by the Cape. It is not at all unlikely that Covilham heard from the Arabs reports concerning the gold country behind Sofala; but sufficient evidence to this effect is not forthcoming. He died in Abyssinia, and never returned to Portugal to tell in person his experiences. At any rate, ten years later the Cape was rounded by the Portuguese, and Vasco da Gama in all the ports he called at on the east coast of Africa found Arab traders established, who told him about the gold. The next expedition, under Alvarez de Cahal in 1505, found Sofala, and in its harbour two Arab dhows laden with gold.

The Portuguese commander, Pedro de Nhaya, took possession of the town of Sofala in the name of the King of Portugal and garrisoned the old Arab fort there, and with this act began the modern history of this country, about which a veil of mystery had hung from the very beginning of time. That the Arabs were confined to the coast at this period is evident from Duarte Barbosa's remarks, who wrote in 1514: 'The merchants bring to Sofala the gold which they sell to the Moors (the name applied to the Arabs by the Portuguese), without weighing it, for coloured stuffs, and beads of Cambay.'

Before discussing the Portuguese accounts of this country, let us linger a little longer amongst the Arabs, and see what we can get from them about the inhabitants of this district and the irruption of the wild Zindj tribes over it, which probably caused the destruction of the earlier civilisation. Zaneddin Omar ibn l' Wardi' gives us an account of these Zindj. He wrote in the 336th year of the Hegira, and tells us that ' their habitations extend from the extremity of the gulf to the low land of gold, Sofala 't il Dhab,' and remarks on a peculiarity of theirs, namely, that ' they sharpen their teeth and polish them to a point.' He goes on to say: 'Sofala 't il Dhab adjoins the eastern borders of the Zindj . . . the most remarkable produce of this country is its quantity of native gold, that is found in pieces of two or three *meskalla*, in spite of which the natives generally adorn their persons with ornaments of brass.' He also states that iron is found in this country and that the natives have skill in working it, and adds that 'ships come from India to fetch it.' This shows us the origin of the skill still possessed by the natives in smelting iron, which has been handed down from generation to generation.

El Masoudi, who has been called the Herodotus of Arabia, gives us still further details about the race, speaking of Sofala as a place to which the Arabs of his time went habitually to obtain gold and precious stones from the natives. He is more explicit about the descent from the north of the Zindj tribes, which took place not long before his day; and unless there was a previous wave of barbarians, concerning whom we have no account, it may be supposed that it was owing to their advent that the gold settlements up country were finally abandoned, and the Arab traders restricted to the coast. Describing the natives of the land behind Sofala, he speaks of them as negroes naked except for panther skins; they filed their teeth and were cannibals; they fought with long lances, and had ambuscades for game. They hunted for elephants, but never used for their own purposes the ivory or gold in which their country abounded. From this picture it is easy to see that in those days the inhabitants were just as they are now, an uncultured wild race of savages. We get another testimony to this in the voyage of two Arabs who went to China in 851 A.D., and returned by the east coast of Africa. M. Renaudot has translated their experiences, in which they describe the Zindj as follows: 'Among them are preachers who harangue them, clad in a leopard skin. One of these men, with a staff in his hand, shall present himself before them, and having gathered a multitude of people about him, preach all the day to them. He speaks of God and recites the actions of their countrymen who are gone before them.' In this account we easily recognise the witch-doctor and ancestor worship, the Mozimos and Muali of the present race. Abou Zeyd's evidence is also to the same effect. He thus speaks of the Zindj: 'Religious discourses are pronounced before this people, and one never finds elsewhere such constant preachers. There are men devoted to this life who cover themselves with panther and monkey skins. They have a staff in their hands, and go from place to place.' Quite an accurate description of the South African witch-doctor. Consequently, from this mass of evidence we may affirm with absolute certainty that for a thousand years at least there has been no change in the condition of this country and its inhabitants. Further testimony to the same effect is given us by Edrisi in his geography, who alludes to the Zendj tribes as inhabiting this country, and occupying the coast towns Dendema and Siorma, ' which latter is situated on a gulf where foreign vessels come to anchor.' He speaks, too, of the iron trade which the Zendj carried on with the Indians, and of the abundance of gold in the mountains behind Sofala, adding, 'nevertheless, the inhabitants prefer brass, making their ornaments of the latter metal.'

The simple Arabian stories of Sindbad the sailor and Aladdin are quite as credible as some of the stories which the first Portuguese travellers who visited the east coast of Africa tell us about the great Emperor Monomatapa and the wealth of gold in his dominions. When they first appeared on the scenes the Monomatapa was a big Kaffir chief, like Cetewayo or Lobengulu, who ruled over the gold district in which the Zimbabwe ruins are situated; nevertheless they burden their accounts with stories of the gilded halls in which he lived, of nuggets of the precious metal as big as a man's head, and which with their force raised the roots of trees. Needless to say these are the fabrications of their own brains, written to attract attention to the country they had discovered.

That this big Kaffir chief, Monomatapa, lived at his Zimbabwe or head kraal is, however, pretty clear, not necessarily at the place where the ruins are, because the whole of this country is scattered with Zimbabwes. Each petty chief now calls his head kraal by this name, and this fact, not thoroughly recognised, has brought about endless confusion in topography. The derivation for this name which to my mind appears the most satisfactory is of Abantu origin, and came from the north, where it is generally used to denote the head kraal of any chief. *Zi* is the Abantu root for a village, *umzi* being in Zulu the term for a collection of kraals. *Zimbab* would signify somewhat the same, or rather 'the great kraal,' and *we* is the terminal denoting an exclamation, so that Zimbabwe would mean, 'here is the great kraal.'

Again, another source of confusion arises from the fact that Monomatapa—or, as it ought to be written, *Muene*, or lord of Matapa—is a dynastic name, just as every petty chief in Mashonaland to-day has his dynastic name, which he takes on succeeding to the chiefdom. So did the lords of Matapa. In various Portuguese treaties we have the names of different Monomatapa's: one is called Manuza, another Lucere, and so forth, right down to the days of Livingstone, when the Monomatapa he mentions was a petty chief near the Zambesi.

When the Portuguese arrived at Sofala they got a lot of information from the Arab traders they found there concerning the wonders of the country, the great chief and the great ruins; and as Zimbabwe was the name of the chief's residence and the name given by the inhabitants to the ruins, it is not to be wondered at that some confusion arose.

Now these Arab traders were particularly and not unnaturally jealous of the arrival of the Portuguese, perhaps not unlike the Portuguese are now of the British arrival. They made all the mischief they could between the Portuguese and the natives, they represented the Portuguese Jesuit Father Silveira, who nearly managed to convert the Monomatapa to Christianity, as a spy, and conduced to his martyrdom in 1561. In fact, one of the great obstacles to the success of the Portuguese was Arab jealousy, which was at the bottom of the failure of all their expeditions up country.

Of all the Portuguese travellers who wrote about this country, Father dos Santos is the most reliable. Though he did not travel far up country, nevertheless he told no lies; and anyone who has been amongst the inhabitants as they are now will recognise in his narrative a faithful and accurate account of the people, proving how little they have altered in the lapse of between three and four centuries. A few extracts will show this: 'They beat their palms, which is their mode of courtesy.'[1] 'They smelt iron and make mattocks, arrows, assegai-points, spears, little axes, and they have more iron than is necessary, and of copper they make bracelets, and both men and women use them for their legs and arms.' He describes their indistinct idea of a Supreme Being, their feasts in honour of their ancestors, their curious pianos, 'with bars of iron enclosed in a pumpkin,' their 'wine of millet, which the Portuguese could not bear, but were obliged to drink and make festivity, for fear of quarrelling.' 'They have an infinity of fowls, like those of Portugal;' and also he describes the days on which they are not to work, appointed by the king, unknown to them, when they make

[1] *Vide* Chap. III.

feasts and call these days *Mozimos,* or days of the holy already dead.¹ In fact, this narrative is so truthful in all its details, that we may safely take from it his account of the disintegration of the Monomatapa chiefdom, as it accounts for many things which otherwise would be obscure. He tells us that a Monomatapa sent three sons to govern in three provinces, Quiteve, Sedanda, and Chicanga; on their father's death they refused to give up to the heir their respective territories, and the country became divided into four. Since then it has been subdivided again and again; each petty chief fought with his neighbour, union was impossible, and in their turn they have fallen an easy prey to the powerful Zulu organisation under Umzilikatze and his successor Lobengulu. This I take to be, in a few words, the history of the country and its people during modern times, and as much probably as will ever be known of them.

Dos Santos calls these people Mocarangas, and in this too, I think, he is right, for the reasons I have previously given.² They are now, as we have seen, a miserable race of outcasts, fleeing to the mountain fastnesses on the approach of a Zulu raid, hounded and robbed until there is no more spirit in them. Monteiro mentions a Monomotapa, or emperor of Chidima, very decayed, but respectable, with a territory to the west of the Zambesi, near Zumbo. This is probably the same that Livingstone alludes to. An interesting fact that Monteiro also gives us is the

¹ *Vide* Chap. XI.   ² Chap. II.

number of Zimbabwes north of the Zambesi, as the head kraals of chiefs, showing the northern origin of the name.

Having considered the people in whose country the Great Zimbabwe ruins are, let us now proceed to cull what we can from a Portuguese source concerning the ruins themselves.

De Barros[1] gives us the fullest account of the ruins. Let us take it and see what it is worth: 'In the midst of the plains in the kingdom of Batua, in the country of Toroe, nearest the oldest gold mines, stands a fortress, square, admirably built, inside and out, of hard stone. The blocks of which the walls consist are put together without mortar and are of marvellous size. The walls are twenty-five spans in thickness; their height is not so considerable compared with their breadth. Over the gate of the building is an inscription, which neither the Moorish traders (the Arabs of the coast) who were there, nor others learned in inscriptions, could read, nor does anyone know in what character it is written. On the heights around the edifice stand others in like manner built of masonry without mortar; among them a tower of more than twelve bracas (yards) in height. All those buildings are called by the natives *Zimbahe* —that is, the royal residence or court, as are all royal dwellings in Monomotapa. Their guardian, a man of noble birth, has here the chief command, and is called Symbacao; under his care are some of the

[1] De Barros, *De Aria*. Lisbon, 1552.

wives of Monomotapa, who constantly reside here. When and by whom these buildings were erected is unknown to the natives, who have no written characters. They merely say they are the work of the Devil (supernatural), because they are beyond their powers to execute. Besides these, there is to be found no other mason work, ancient or modern, in that region, seeing that all the dwellings of the barbarians are of wood and rushes.'

De Barros further states that when the Portuguese Governor of Sofala, Captain Vicento Pegado, pointed to the masonry of the fort there, with a view to comparison with the buildings up country, the Moors (Arabs) who had been at the ruins observed that the latter structure was of such absolute perfection that nothing could be compared to it; and they gave their opinion that the buildings were very ancient, and erected for the protection of the neighbouring gold mines. From this, De Barros inferred that the ruins must be the Agizymba of Ptolemy,[1] and founded by some ancient ruler of the gold country, who was unable to hold his ground, as in the case of the city of Axume, in Abyssinia.

In criticising this account, it is at once apparent that it was written by a person who had never seen the ruins; the fortress is round, not square; the blocks of stone are all small and not of 'marvellous size;' the

[1] According to Ptolemy, the Romans penetrated from the north through the heart of Africa to a nation called Agizymba, south of the equator.

tower is wrongly placed on the heights above instead of in the ruin on the plain. But at the same time De Barros is candid, and as good as tells us that his account was gathered from 'the Moorish traders who were there.' That is to say, all the wonders of the upper country we get second hand from an Arabian source. Legends of inscriptions on stone are common to all mysterious ruins in every country. Possibly the decorated soapstone pillar gave rise to it, as it did to the subsequent account of the 'Zimbabwe cryptogram,' which ran through the papers shortly after the visit of the first pioneers of the Chartered Company. At all events, now there is no sign of anything over any gateway or any trace of such a stone having been removed.

Alvarez gives us an account even vaguer than De Barros. The following is Pory's translation, published in London in 1600: 'For here in Toroa and in divers places of Monomatapa are till this day remaining manie huge and ancient buildings of timber, lime and stone being singular workmanship, the like whereof are not to be found in all the provinces thereabout. Heere is also a mightie wall of five-and-twenty spannes thick, which the people ascribe to the workmanship of the divell, being accounted from Sofala 510 miles the nearest way.'

Pigafetta copies this account in pretty much the same strain, as also does *Dapper*, whose account of this country is a tissue of exaggerations. He says: 'In this country, far to the inland on a plain in the middle of many iron mills, stands a famous structure called *Simbaœ*, built square like a castle with hewn stone, but the height is not answerable. Above the gate appears an inscription which cannot be read or understood, nor could any that have seen it know what people used such letters. . . . The inhabitants report it the work of the devil, themselves only building in wood, and aver that for strength it exceeds the fort of the Portuguese at the seashore, about 150 miles from hence.'

We could quote several other allusions to the ruins from Portuguese, Dutch, and English sources, copied one from the other, and all bearing the stamp of having come from the same fountain-head, namely, the Arabians, who told the Portuguese about them when they first arrived at Sofala. Our examination of the ruins confirms this in every respect. In our excavations we found Celadon pottery, Persian pottery, and Arabian glass, similar to the things found at Quiloa, where the Arabs also had a settlement. These objects represent the trading goods brought by the Arabians and exchanged with the inhabitants who lived in and around these ruins in the middle ages; but at the same time we found no trace whatsoever of the Portuguese, which would have been the case, as in other places occupied by them in Arabia and the Persian Gulf, had they ever been there. From these facts I think it is certain that we may remove from the Portuguese the honour claimed by them of being the modern discoverers of the ruins, an honour only claimed in the face of recent events, for De Barros is candid enough in telling us that his information came 'from the Arabs who were there.' Clearly to settle this question it is only necessary to quote a letter which I saw in the library at Lisbon, dated April 17, 1721, from the Governor of Goa, Antonio Rodrigue da Costa, to the king. East Africa was included then in the province of India, and the governor wrote as follows :—

'(1) There is a report that in the interior of these countries many affirm there is in the court of the Monomatapa a tower or edifice of worked masonry which appears evidently not to be the work of black natives of the country, but of some powerful and political nations such as the Greeks, Romans, Persians, Egyptians, or Hebrews ; and they say that this tower or edifice is called by the natives Simbabóe, and that in it is an inscription of unknown letters, and because there is much foundation for the belief that this land is Ophir, and that Solomon sent his fleets in company with the Phœnicians; and this opinion could be indubitably established if this inscription could be cleared up, and there is no one there who can read it. If it were in Greek, Persian, or Hebrew, it would be necessary to command that an impression be made in wax or some other material which retains letters or figures, commanding that the original inscription be well cleaned.

'(2) At the same time it would be suitable to examine whether in that land is a range of mountains called Ofura, what distance it is from the coast or seaport, and whether it contains mines of gold or silver.

'(3) In the same way it would be as well to inquire into the most notable names of those parts, mountains, chiefdoms, and rivers.

'(4) To learn if the lands of Sofala are high or low, or marshy, or if they have any mountain ranges.'

Hence it will be seen that, even as late as 1721, it was only rumoured that there were ruins, and that the Portuguese sphere of influence went very little inland. Needless to say, the expedition was never sent, and that the reports were of the vaguest and most contradictory character. Bocarro and Corvo both testify to the fact[1] that the Portuguese, after the disastrous campaigns of Baretto, advanced but little into the country, and were confined almost exclusively to the littoral. Taking the map of this district, and looking at the spelling of the names, it is easy to see how far Portuguese influence extended. They spell the common prefix *Inya* with an *h* instead of a *y*: for example, they write it Inhambane. Also they spell the name Gungunyama, Gungunhama; other nations spell such names with a *y*, for example, Inyagowe. Hence the *h* for *y* clearly marks the Portuguese sphere of influence.

These reports of an Eldorado northwards continued, and produced periodical excitements amongst

[1] Chap. IX.

the young colonists of South Africa. The Boers were everlastingly getting up *treks* with a view to reach it; the vague mystery about King Solomon's mines existing there, and the palace of the Queen of Sheba, whetted their appetites when they heard these rumours; but still nothing was definitely done until a German traveller of more than ordinary energy penetrated as far as the Zimbabwe ruins in the year 1871. This man was Karl Mauch: he examined them carefully and wrote an accurate account of them, but, unfortunately, he ventured on a speculation as to their origin which at once cast discredit on his discoveries in the eyes of unbelieving archæologists. He maintained that the fortress on the hill was a copy of King Solomon's temple on Mount Moriah, that the lower ruins were a copy of the palace which the Queen of Sheba inhabited during her stay of several years in Jerusalem, and that the trees in the middle of it were undoubtedly almug trees.

The result of this was that the subject of Zimbabwe ruins was in abeyance for nearly twenty years after Mauch's visit, and was rather accredited as a traveller's tale until the British Chartered Company took possession of the country and enabled research to be satisfactorily made. Nevertheless to Karl Mauch is distinctly due the honour of being the first to investigate the ruins in modern times.

PART III

EXPLORATION JOURNEYS IN MASHONALAND

CHAPTER VIII

DOWN TO THE SABI RIVER AND MATINDELA RUINS

It was the report of extensive ruins, 'larger,' said a native, 'than those of Zimbabwe,' which induced us to make an expedition involving considerable hardships and unknown risks down in the direction of the Sabi River. Our waggons, of course, could not go, as our way would be by the narrow native paths. Previous experience had warned us against depending on the native huts, so for the transport of our tents, bedding, and provisions we had to make considerable preparations.

At Fort Victoria we borrowed seven donkeys from the Chartered Company, and we engaged a few natives of reputed respectability under the command of a man called Mashah, quite the most brilliant specimen of the Makalanga race we came across during our sojourn in the country. He, his father and his mother and his wife, a sister of our old friend Umgabe, had been captured some years ago by the Matabele and spent several years in servitude, during which time he had learnt the Zulu tongue and the more energetic habits of this stronger race. Eventually, after the death of his father and mother, he and his wife had escaped and returned to Umgabe's kraal, and on the arrival of the Chartered Company's pioneer force Mashah placed his services at their disposal. He greatly distinguished himself by saving the lives of a band of the pioneers when on a wild prospecting trip, for which service he received a present of a Martini-Henry rifle, of which he was naturally very proud.

Mashah's Makalanga brethren call him 'the white man's slave,' from his devotion to the new race, and he constantly affirmed that if ever the white man left this country he would go with them, for he was heartily sick of the petty jealousies and constant squabbles of his countrymen. He was a strange object to look upon with his tawny B.S.A. hat with an ostrich feather in it, his shirt with a girdle round his waist, and bare legs. He never once grumbled at anything he had to do, he was never tired, and kept our other Kaffirs in excellent order. As for the rest of them, they were as naked as God made them, save for the insignificant loin-cloth. A man called Metzwandira was told off as our body-servant, to wash the cups and plates and spoons, which latter treasures he counted carefully over to us after every meal. We got greatly attached to this individual, his manners were so gentle and courteous and his voice so soft and silvery. One and all of them were delighted to become possessed of our rejected milk tins, &c., with which

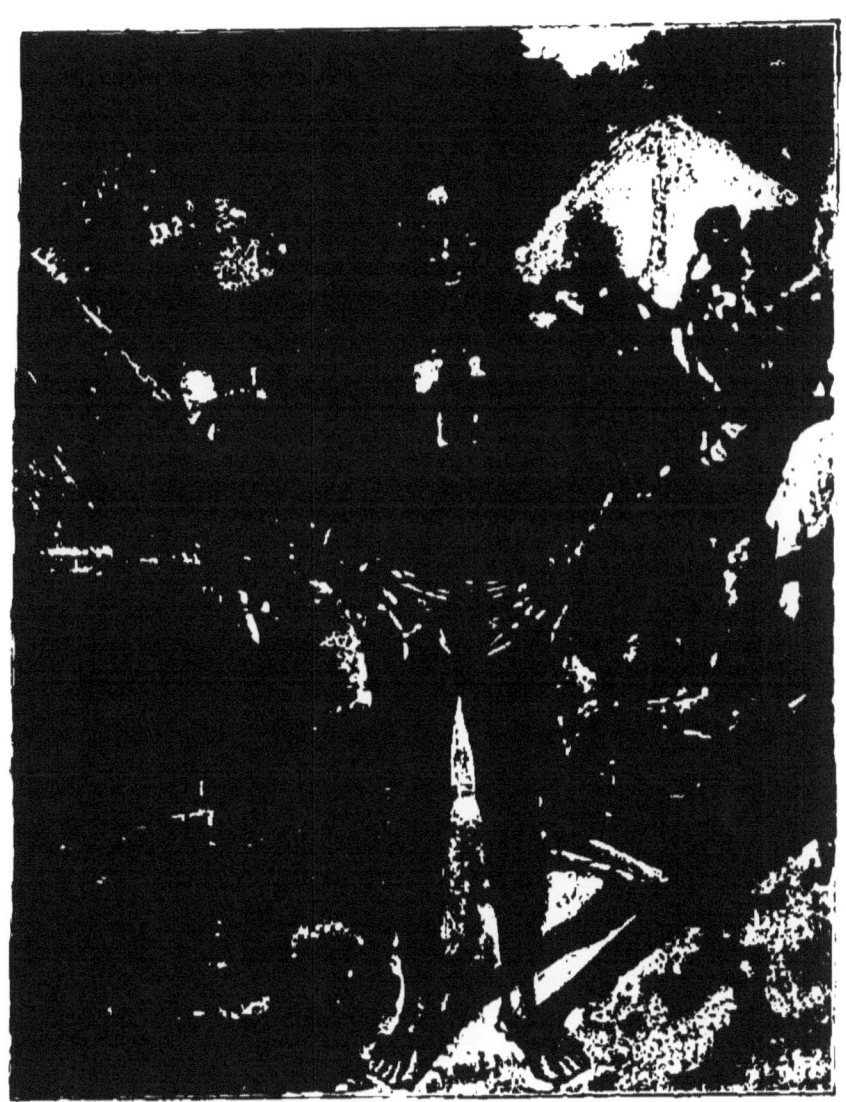

MKTZWANDIRA

they made bracelets, seven inches wide, by cutting off the two ends of the tin and drilling holes along the edge. One man tied the lid of a 'bully beef' tin round his neck, another fastened the round bottom of a milk tin in a jaunty fashion on to his black hair. Every tin we opened and finished was eagerly picked up by our followers and carried in net bags all the way, with a view to making some object of ornament out of them. Even when given an old pair of boots, the recipient only took out the brass hooks and eyes to fasten as ornaments in his loin-cloth, and cast the rest away.

On leaving Fort Victoria we followed the Chartered Company's road for forty miles northwards with our waggons to Makori post station. One day we were encamped near the two large villages of Umfanipatza and Sibibabira built on two rocks, but now, with the confidence inspired by the presence of the Chartered Company, the inhabitants are beginning to build huts on the flat space around. We paid a visit to them both, and admired the tall euphorbia which grew in them and the rich entanglement of begonia and other creepers then in flower. In one hut we found a man weaving a bark blanket very neatly with no loom, only platting it with his fingers. It was done with a kind of pink twine made of some bark.

At Makori post station, under the shade of wide-spreading trees, and in close proximity to some fantastic granite rocks, which rose like gigantic menhirs out of the plain and were covered with an almost scarlet lichen, we passed several busy days, preparing cruppers, girths, and breast-bands for our seven pack-donkeys; bags for our coffee, sugar, and tea; cobbling our boots and overhauling our clothes, and nursing four fever patients, for there had been two days of chilly drizzling rain, the inevitable result of which was fever for some of our party. The post station lay about one mile from our camping-ground; the two huts where the B.S.A. men lived were situated on a rocky *kopje* full of caves, in one of which their horse was stabled, and from the top of the rock an extensive view was gained over the high plateau, well wooded just here and studded with rocks of fantastic shape. Here and there thick volumes of smoke rose from the grass fires common all over the country at this season of the year, which looked for all the world like distant manufacturing towns, and suggested the comparison of a view from a spur of the Derbyshire hills over the plain of Cheshire, with Stockport, Manchester, and other centres of industry belching forth their dense volumes of smoke.

On August 14 we started on our journey. It was a lovely morning, and our progress was very slow, for our cavalcade was so heterogeneous—my wife and I on horseback, Messrs. Swan and King with a horse between them, three white men to look after the donkeys, and Mashah and his Makalangas to carry what the donkeys could not. We straggled terribly at first, for the donkeys were obstinate and their pack-saddles unsteady, the natives were fresh and anxious to get along, so we had to call for frequent halts to readjust ourselves, which gave us ample opportunity for looking around. The country here is sown broadcast with strange granite rocks; one group had formed themselves into an extraordinary doorway, two columns on either side about sixty feet high, with a gigantic boulder resting on the top of them for the lintel. Like the structures of a giant race, these strange rocks rise out of the thick vegetation in all directions. Presently, as we were experiencing some little difficulty in getting our raw cavalcade across a stream, a Makalanga joined us who had been born without hands. To his left stump had been attached, by means of a leather thong, the claw of a bird; with the assistance of this he ate some food we gave him with marvellous dexterity, and fired his gun. He was a bright cheery individual, evidently greatly respected by his more gifted comrades.

IRON RAZOR
4 INCHES LONG

CHIEF'S IRON SCEPTRE
3½ FEET LONG

We only accomplished seven miles this first day, owing to the difficulties of progression, and in the afternoon found ourselves encamped by a wretched village called Chekatu. Here they had no cattle and no milk to sell us owing to Matabele raids. The chief, Matzaire by name, came to visit us with his iron

ROCK NEAR MAKORI POST STATION

sceptre in his hand, which made us think of the rods of iron with which certain Israelitish kings are stated to have ruled. We climbed amongst the huts before sundown and came across an old hag busily engaged in shaving the heads of her younger sisters, cutting their woolly locks into all sorts of odd shapes as fancy or fashion suggested. She refused our most tempting offers to part with her razor, and it was not till some time afterwards that we were able to obtain a specimen of this Makalanga ironcraft.

Next day we crossed two rivers, tributaries of the Tokwe, and after a prosperous ride of ten miles reached Sindito's kraal, called Sekatu, the inhabitants of which took us for a Matabele *impi*, and would not come down till Mashah had screamed to them that we were no rogues, but honest men. We gave the chief a cup of tea, which he detested, and as soon as politeness permitted he said he had had enough. He returned the compliment by giving us a calabash of good beer, which we drank with pleasure. Sekatu was rather a nice village, on a hill covered with thick jungle, amongst which grew in profusion cucumbers, about six inches long, of a rich orange colour, with thorns outside and with a delicious bright green pulp inside. They are the *Cucumis metuliferus*, specimens

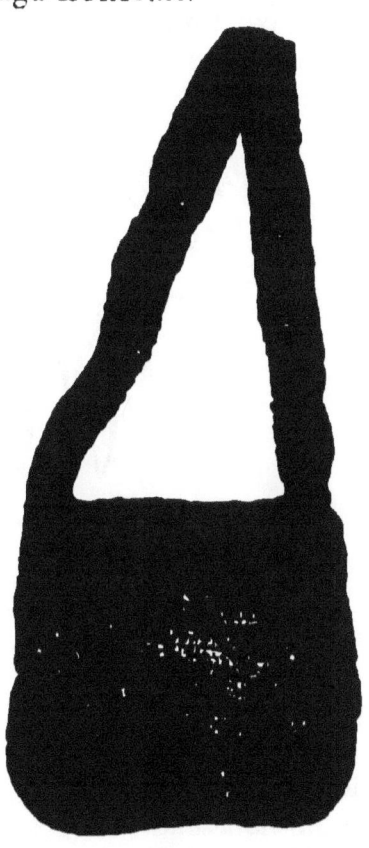

KNITTED BAG

of which may be seen in the museum at Kew Gardens. We had seen these before, and looked upon them as poisonous, until our natives partook of them and gave us confidence. Ever afterwards, as long as they were in season, we indulged freely in this de-

LARDER TREE

licious fruit, and voted it the best we had come across in Mashonaland.

The next day we halted for half an hour at a village called Imiridzi, where we acquired a bag of bark fibre, made by knitting the twine with two sticks for knitting-needles. These articles seemed very popular in this village, and nearly everyone was en-

DOWN TO SABI RIVER AND MATINDELA RUINS 257

gaged in their production. Midday found us at a very large kraal, the chief place in the dominions of a powerful Makalanga chief called Gutu. Gona is the

REED SNUFF-BOXES AND GREASE-HOLDER

name of the kraal, and it is completely buried between two high granite *kopjes*. At the entrance to it some tall trees are completely hung with provisions packed away in their long sausage-like bundles—bags of locusts, caterpillars, sweet potatoes, and other delicacies. These trees we henceforth called 'larder trees,' and found them at nearly every village. The inhabitants of Gona were unusually rich in savage ornaments, and we annexed many snuff-boxes, knives, and other oddments. The chief was unfortunately away, but his representative brought us fine pots of beer and milk, and we made a hearty meal despite the dense and rather unsavoury mass of natives which surrounded us during its consumption. They have a plentiful growth of tobacco plants near Gutu's kraal, and large fields of rice, in which the women were just then busily engaged in making the broad furrows; they have very prettily carved doors to their huts, and many of the men wear sandals on their feet. Altogether Gona struck us as one of the most prosperous kraals we had seen in the country.

As we journeyed eastwards the appearance of the people was certainly wilder. We here saw their heads decorated with curious erections of woven grass, fastened into their hair and reaching an elevation of a foot, like miniature Eiffel towers on their heads;[1] and at a village called Muchienda we acquired two quaint-shaped straw hats with ostrich feathers sticking in the top, quite different to anything we had seen elsewhere. As we approached this village a long string of natives passed us on their way to hunt; on their heads they carried bark cases full of nets,

[1] *Vide* Illustration, p. 262.

which they stretch across the valleys and drive the game into them. Muchienda was a lovely village by a rushing stream full of rocks, which formed a little waterfall; the stream was shaded by magnificent timber, and a background of lovely mountains made us think Muchienda an ideal spot, at which we would willingly have tarried longer.

Every day, as we approached the Sabi Valley, the scenery became grander; the dreary high plateau gave place to deep valleys and high rugged mountains; the vegetation was much more luxuriant and the atmosphere many degrees hotter, so hot that during our midday halts we did not care to wander very far

DECORATED HUT DOOR.

from our camp, especially as we had a good deal of manual labour to perform apart from the actual travelling, in tent pitching, bed making, and cooking, for our white men were generally so tired with driving and packing the donkeys that we could not ask them to do anything after the march was over.

We soon got accustomed to sleeping on the ground. When it was unusually rugged, for the grass grows here in tufts like the hair on the niggers' heads, we got grass cut on which to lay our rugs; occasionally we found it necessary to encamp on

STRAW HAT

spots over which a grass fire had passed, and then we got hopelessly black, and lived like sweeps until we reached a stream, where we could wash ourselves and our clothes.

Lutilo, with the village of Luti perched upon one of its lower precipices, is quite a grand mountain, almost Alpine in character, with exquisite views over the distant Sabi and Manica Mountains. Here we tarried for almost a whole day to visit an insignificant set of ruins a few miles distant, called Metemo, but which formed a link in the great chain of forts stretching northwards. It had been built in three circles of very rough stone, somewhat ingeniously put together on the top of a rounded granite hill, but hopelessly ruined. So we only tarried there a while to make a plan, and to rest, and enjoy the lovely view.

The country around here is very thickly wooded, and on our return to our camp a herd of deer passed close to us, a species known to the Dutch as *Swartvit-pens*, or 'swarthy white paunches,' but we failed to get one, a matter of considerable regret from a commissariat point of view, for meat is scarce in the villages about here, and our tinned supplies were getting low.

We struck our camp at Lutilo rather late in the afternoon, and only got as far as a river called the 'Nyatzetse, the crossing of which involved the unloading of our animals. On the way we passed through two villages, where the inhabitants were busily engaged in building huts, for it was evidently a new encampment, and in making beer, which was too new to drink; the land around was being freshly turned up for their fields, after the approved Makalanga fashion. First they clear a space of jungle, leaving the larger trees, and pile up the brushwood round the roots, then they set fire to the heaps, and when it is consumed the tree is killed, and more easy to cut down.

The next day brought us at a very early hour to the site of the Matindela ruins, which was to be our halting-

DECORATED HEADS

place for a few days. The ruins certainly are fine, but far inferior to those of Zimbabwe; they are perched on the top of a bare granite rock about 150 feet high, a most admirable strategical position.[1] In the centre of them we pitched our tents for our welcome halt of three days, and made ourselves as comfortable as rain would permit, for it fell in torrents here even though it was the dry season. The

[1] For description of ruins, *vide* Chap. IV.

term 'Matindela' means 'guinea-fowl,' quantities of which birds are found around here, as indeed they are in most parts of this country.

We were now only twenty miles from the Sabi River, and the country around was almost deserted, ruined villages crowned most of the heights, and the deserted fields and devastation in every direction were lamentable to behold. There were evidences, too, of a fairly recent raid, in which the poor Makalangas had been driven out of their homes and probably carried into slavery. By common consent the two great Zulu chiefs, Lobengula and Gungunyana, whose embassy visited England last year, consider the Sabi as their respective boundary for marauding expeditions. On this occasion I believe Gungunyana and his Shaugans were to blame, who, finding that Lobengula was cut off by the Chartered Company from this part of his district, had made bold to cross the Sabi and raid on the western side, bringing destruction into the Makalanga homes, which in former years had here been thought very secure, being, as they were, far from Lobengula and just out of Gungunyana's recognised district.

The Makalangas have the greatest horror of the Shangaus, who dwell across the Sabi, and do Gungunyana's bidding. One day at Matindela we brought home a specimen of a curious fruit which hangs from the trees, eighteen inches to two feet long, like thick German sausages; it has beans inside, and we asked Mashah if it was good to eat : 'No Makalangas eat *umvebe*,' as he called it, 'only the Shangans and baboons.'

Whilst at Matindela we sampled several kinds of strange fruit: firstly the Kaffir orange, a kind of strychnia, which is a hard fruit with yellow pulp inside around seeds, and of which every traveller should beware of eating if not quite ripe—an error into which several of our party fell; it is apt to produce violent sickness under those conditions, and at best it is painfully astringent, causing horrible facial contortions when you eat it, as most of the fruits about here do. Amongst other things, they brought to our camp at Matindela large quantities of the delicious cucumbers, monkey-nuts, sweet potatoes, and a sweet fruit which you chew and spit out like sugar-cane, which they call *matoko*. From the gigantic trees around us, the far-famed baobab trees, we gathered the nuts with the refreshing cream of tartar pulp inside. The baobab is the great feature of Matindela Hill; there are a dozen of them on it, huge giants, which in their growth have knocked down large portions of the walls. Though probably these trees are not as old as report says, nevertheless their presence here proves that these ruins have been utterly abandoned for many centuries. It is another problem to prove how their thick roots find sustenance for so huge a vegetable growth, perched as they are on an almost soil-less granite rock. Doubtless these roots follow the fissures in the granite and obtain the required moisture from some considerable distance. The effect, however, is exceedingly odd to see these colossal trees growing in no depth of soil on the top of a granite rock.

I had always been sceptical about the honey-bird until its virtues were properly proved to us when at Matindela. An insignificant little bird, with a significant chirp, led our men over rocks and through jungle till they actually found honey, so that we could no longer indulge in doubts as to this mysterious gift, which, like the water-finding divining rods, I will leave to others to explain.

Traces of recent life around Matindela were numerous: the valleys had all at one time been ploughed: ruined huts, constructed high up in the trees, had served as outlooks for the agriculturists, bark beehives were in the trees, but the villages were all blackened and burnt, the granaries knocked down and the inhabitants gone, no one knows where. Never during any camp of lengthened duration were we visited by so few natives as at Matindela. About here game is very plentiful; we sighted fresh elephant and giraffe '*spoor*,' and we personally made the acquaintance of zebras, kudu, and other kinds of antelope. Across the valley below was an old and now disused stockade for catching game, and hunting-parties in this locality have been numerous. These parties are arranged by the Makalangas on a small or large scale; sometimes, when they have an elaborate system of stockades, they just drive the game towards a *cul de sac* or a narrow gap where men are hidden in the grass; sometimes they have great parties forming two half-moons; one of these stations itself behind a *kopje*, whilst the other, with dogs and shouting, drives the game to them.

Their game laws give rise to frequent squabbles amongst the chiefs; it is generally understood that, if a man wounds a buck and another kills it, the wounder claims the carcass, but the killer is entitled to take whichever limb he wishes. There is a tribe near Zimbabwe who will not eat a buck unless it has had its throat cut, and so they endeavour first to wound it, and then proceed to cut its throat. For small buck, hares, &c., they make traps across the narrow paths with a beam which falls when the animal treads on the plank below, being fixed on the path between two sloping rows of stakes.

Our course from Matindela was north-east—not the most direct route to the Sabi, which is only about twenty miles due east, but we had nobody with us who knew the way, and we had to go to a village for a guide. After a ride of seven miles we reached a curious lofty mountain called Chiburwe, close on 1,000 feet above the plain; it is almost round, and its flanks are decorated with huge granite boulders rising out of euphorbia, baobabs, and rank tropical vegetation. On the side we first reached this mountain the vegetation was too dense to allow us to ascend, so we had to ride to the northern side and go up by a slippery slope of black granite, the ordinary approach used by the natives, whose bare feet cling readily to the rocks, but which was horrible for feet encased in European boots. The summit is flat and grassy like a Brighton down, being covered with a soft small stagshorn moss, delightful to lie upon. This spot is the happy playground of two native villages, which are placed on either side of the mountain; here they are sublimely safe and free from the raids of their enemies, and Chiburwe forms a sort of Makalanga outpost in the direction of the Sabi. Amongst other names mentioned by Portuguese writers which are still retained in the locality we find Chiburga as a stronghold, where the Monomatapa's wives were kept. I think it highly probable that this is the spot. On the summit we found several sets of holes for the Isafuba game, and the inhabitants we came across seemed more than usually timid. Our view was indescribably lovely, with Lutilo and the spots we knew well behind us, and the mysterious blue mountains of Manica before us.

In a rocky crevice we found one of the miserable villages of Chiburwe, with no beer, no milk, no fowls and no eggs to be had; it appeared to be solely inhabited by two women grinding millet, who were much afraid of us, and retired into the darkest recesses of their huts. Their ingenuity in utilising bark is exemplified up here, where mud is scarce, for they make their granaries of the bark of the baobab, only covering the edges with mud, and binding them round with withes.

For two days after leaving Chiburwe we wandered

through trackless forests, guided only by a notion of the direction we wished to go, for we could not annex a native guide. A mile or two from Chiburwe we found a ruined fort of the best period of Zimbabwe work, with courses of great regularity, but much of the wall had been knocked down by the baobab trees which had grown up in it. Nobody could give us a name for this ruin in the wilderness, so we called it Chiburwe, measured it, took notes on it, and rode on.

The forest scenery was grand and impressive in its solitude; sometimes we had great difficulty in getting our animals through the thick undergrowth; the trees were rich in colour, red and light green, equal to any of our autumnal tints, out of which now and again rose granite boulders. The crossing of the River Mwairari, a fine tributary of the Sabi, gave us a little trouble; it has a fine volume of water with occasional rapids, waterfalls, and high rocks, and we had to follow its right bank for several miles before we could get our animals across; the river bed was luxuriant in tall pampas grass and patches of papyrus.

On the second afternoon after leaving Chiburwe we sighted the Sabi River, having gone miles out of our way; it is a really magnificent stream even here so far inland, and is navigable now for canoes very little below where we struck it. In ancient times it must have been navigable for larger craft, for all African rivers are silting up. There is little doubt but that the ancient builders of the ruins in Mashonaland, the forts and towns between the Zambesi and the Limpopo, utilised this stream as their road to and from the coast; and as the country again is opened out it may still be found useful as a waterway for small craft. Where we struck the Sabi it is a rapid river, flowing through a gorge and with a rocky bed; there are no marshes here, but fertile-looking slopes leading down to it, which appeared to us to promise well for the future agriculturists who settle on its banks, though the rainfall, which takes place only in summer, and for the space of only four months, will be a drawback to cereals. Now these slopes are entirely deserted, and about here we saw no villages, nor natives, nor paths, for days, doubtless owing to the raids of Gungunyana and his Shangans from across the stream. There is no doubt about it, the world is not full yet. In Mashonaland there exist tens of thousands of acres of fertile land entirely unoccupied. Thanks probably to the Matabele raids, the population is here exceedingly scanty, and when one travels through the long-deserted stretches of country, healthy, well watered, and capable of growing anything, which still exist between the Zambesi and the Limpopo, one cannot help thinking that those who complain of the world being too full, and that there is no opening for colonisation, are a century or two before their time.

Everybody revelled in the waters of the Sabi that evening—bathing and washing clothes occupied most of our time until it was dark; but, alas, our camp was pitched on ground over which a grass fire had passed, and the good effects of our Sabi wash were more than obliterated. We again plunged into the trackless wilderness, and it was not till the second day after leaving the river that we once more joyfully found ourselves in a native path leading in the direction which we ought to go; but we followed it for over thirty miles before we came across a village. This was called Zamopera, on the banks of a pleasant stream. We were so pleased to see people again and to have a chance of replenishing our stock of provisions that we tarried there for the best part of a day, and pitched our camp beneath the shadow of a friendly rock. Crowds of men and women from Zamopera came to visit us; wild-looking people they were—the men with long matted hair hanging like a fringe over their faces, and hung with beads and cowrie-shells, whilst the women here cut off all their hair except a circle in the middle, which is short and threaded with beads in seven rows, four of white outside and three of red in the centre, looking exactly like round bead mats on the top of their heads. We were now in the country of another great Makalanga chief, called Gambidji, whose kraal, perched on a lofty rock, we sighted in the distance, but had not time to visit.

In the villages about here, which are numerous and flourishing, we saw many curious objects, some of which we acquired, others we could not strike a bargain for: a native razor, bone dollasses, and quaint-shaped battle-axes were added to our collection.

Mafusaire's village is perched amongst odd-shaped boulders, fantastic as the rocks in Dovedale, ever varying in form. The inhabitants were a very friendly lot, and were almost beside themselves with delight when my wife took down her hair and showed them its length. They greatly prized a gift of a few of these long hairs, which they will doubtless keep as a memento of the first white lady who ever came amongst them.

The fear of the Makalanga of horses is most curious; even our own men would not touch them, and the villagers were quite awestruck when we mounted. They generally followed us in crowds for a little distance from the village, and screamed with delight when we trotted, scampering and capering by our sides.

We passed by the tomb of a chief on the afternoon after leaving Mafusaire's; it consisted of a mound with a circular construction of stones on the top of it, over which is a thatched roof standing on posts; on the top of the stones stood a pot, in which beer is periodically put, for the delectation of the deceased.

CHIEF'S TOMB

We were now in the immediate neighbourhood

of Mount Wedza, the highest point in Mashonaland, with an elevation of over 6,000 feet above sea level. It is for the most part a dark forest-clad ridge, and it is from here that the natives of Gambidji's country get the iron ore which they smelt in their furnaces and convert into tools and weapons. The villages in this district are entirely given up to the smelting business, and outside the kraals usually are erected two or more furnaces. They are still in the Stone Age here, using for anvils and hammers pieces of hard diorite. One of these villages where we halted for a while was, to our astonishment, called Smet. Not believing our ears, we asked again and again, and got the same reply. The only solution to this strange nomenclature seems to be, that they either got the name from some Dutch trader or from some enterprising Makalanga who had been down to work in the Kimberley mines. For long these natives have been in the habit of doing this, tramping all the way from the Zambesi to the diamond-fields, and not returning thence until they have acquired enough wealth to buy a wife or two and settle themselves in life.

A man from Smet, who was going to 'Mtigeza's kraal, volunteered to act as our guide. He carried with him three large iron hoes which he had made, and for which he expected to get a goat at the kraal. Gambidji's country is very extensive, extending nominally from the Sabi to a ridge which we crossed before reaching 'Mtigeza's, and most of the iron-smelting villages recognise his sovereignty.

Two chiefs of the name of 'Mtigeza live around Mount Wedza, both claiming to be the descendants of the old 'Mtigeza stock. Our 'Mtigeza was a queer little old man, almost in his dotage, but considered very powerful by his neighbours, and this was evidenced by the villages being more in the open, and not seeking protection from rocky heights. His fortress is a curious one, situated on an extensive plateau 4,800 feet above the sea level, with disjointed low masses of rocks dotted about. Around the central mass of rocks is 'Mtigeza's head kraal, surrounded by palisades, and the rock itself is strongly fortified, with all the approaches walled up, and for us Europeans it was by no means easy to reach the summit by means of holes through which we could hardly squeeze, and slits in the rock through which we could only pass sideways. On the top is a circular fort built of rough stones and mortar, and the boast of the people here is that the Matabele have never been able to take their stronghold. From the fort we had a good bird's-eye view over 'Mtigeza's realm; there are a number of encircling villages built on similar masses of rock, about half a mile or more distant. These are governed by the old man's sons.

We sent the old chief a blanket, and he presently came to pay us a visit. According to our custom, we showed him our things, in which he did not manifest much interest until my wife produced a burning-glass, and showed off its wonderful fire-producing qualities on his skin. Then in a weak little voice the old chief murmured, 'I, 'Mtigeza, want it,' and she promptly presented it to him, also a little salt. As we lunched he sat and watched us, but would partake of nothing we offered him, until we threw some well-picked chicken bones to our men; these he coveted and got.

'Mtigeza held an *indaba* or palaver of his in-

INTERIOR OF A HUT

aunas in a shady nook before his kraal, the result of which was that a goat was to be presented to us by quite a lengthy process. First of all it was presented to Mashah, who humbly received it with hat off and head bowed, making all the necessary compliments for us. Mashah then presented it to our white men, and they finally presented it to us, and it formed a valuable addition to our larder.

We were surprised to find little evidence of wealth in 'Mtigeza's kraal. Their knives and snuff-boxes were decidedly inferior in workmanship to those we had seen elsewhere, and this we found as we travelled on to be invariably the case where the Matabele or Zulu influence has been least felt. The Zulu is the most ingenious of the Abantu races, and has imparted his ingenuity to the Makalanga, over whom he has raided and many of whom have been his slaves.

HOUSEHOLD STORE FOR GRAIN, WITH NATIVE DRAWINGS

There were two as yet roofless but substantial huts being built in the kraal entirely of mud, which is a new departure for the Makalanga. The insides of these were decorated with squares of black and white, like those one sees in Bechuanaland. Undoubtedly foreign influence is being felt here from its proximity to Fort Charter, and very soon the architectural features of Makalangaland will change with the rapidity that all things change in Kaffirdom. Inside the huts were big household granaries for the domestic stores, also made of mud and decorated curiously with rims, and rude paintings in white of deer, birds,

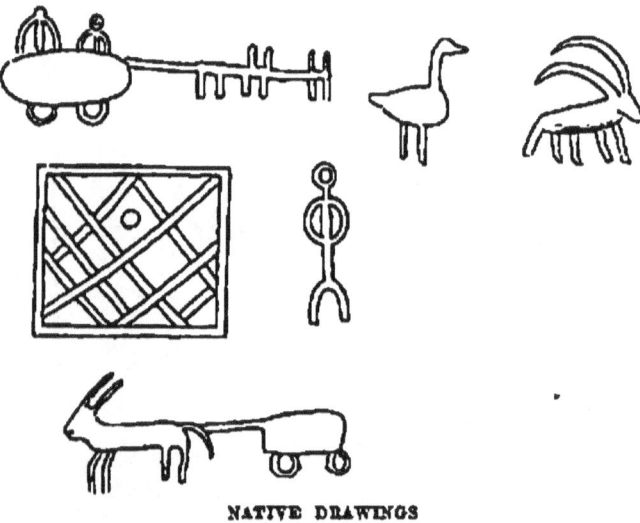

NATIVE DRAWINGS

and men. One represents a waggon with a span of six oxen and a man driving it. The artistic skill is, of course, of a low order, but it shows the influence of the Morunko, or white man, and how his approach has been the theme of their wonder and excited their imagination. I doubt not but those who follow after us will find attempts made to illustrate on their granaries a Morunko lady with long flowing hair trotting on that strange animal, the horse.

'Mtigeza and his kraal pleased us so much that we did not leave till quite late in the afternoon. We passed through quantities of rice-fields, which spoke of prosperity; and this Makalanga rice is truly excellent, being larger, more glutinous, and of a pinker hue than our Indian rice, which to our minds tasted very insipid after it. It was almost dark when we reached Matimbi's kraal, and pitched our tents close to the tomb of another chief. Matimbi came down to see us; he is the handsomest of all the chiefs we had yet seen, with quite a European-shaped face, long hair and long beard, both rarities in this country, and a splendid knife, carved and decorated with brass wire, which we coveted but could not obtain.

On the following day, September 2, a long ride brought us to Fort Charter and our waggons in time for our midday meal. Thoroughly did we enjoy our tables, our chairs, and our waggon-beds after nearly three weeks' intimate acquaintance with mother earth. Until the experience of greater privations farther north came upon us, we thought we enjoyed the food, the soup, the bully beef, the bread, and the jam which our cook placed before our hungry eyes to the utmost extent that man could do.

Here we regretfully parted with our friend Mashah and most of our Makalangas; two only of enterprising mind elected to follow us and earn more blankets, and they served us with unswerving fidelity till we reached the coast at Beira. Mashanani was the name of one of them, whose only fault was a too great attachment to Kaffir beer; Iguzu was the name of the other, the most industrious man I ever saw. When not working for us, he would sit on a rock for ever patching a ragged old shirt that had been presented to him, until there was little of the original fabric left, or else turning old jam tins into ornaments or threading beads.

CHAPTER IX

FORT SALISBURY AND THE OLD WORKINGS AND RUINS OF THE MAZOE VALLEY

A FEW remarks on the future capital of the Mashonaland gold-fields may not be amiss, by way of sharp contrast, in a work more especially devoted to the study of the past. The same motive, namely, the thirst for gold, created the hoary walls of Zimbabwe and the daub huts of Fort Salisbury, probably the oldest and the youngest buildings erected for the purpose by mankind, ever keen after that precious metal which has had so remarkable an influence on generation after generation of human atoms. These remarks on Fort Salisbury will, moreover, have a certain amount of historical value in years to come, when it has its railway, its town hall, and its cathedral, for we were there on the day on which its first birthday was kept, the anniversary of the planting of the British flag by the pioneers on the dreary upland waste of Mashonaland. It seemed to us a very creditable development, too, for so young a place, when it is taken into consideration that Fort Salisbury, unlike the mushroom towns of the Western Hemisphere, has grown up at a distance of 800 miles from a railway, without telegraphic communication, and for months during the rainy season without intercourse of any kind with the outer world, handicapped by fever, famine, and an unparalleled continuation of rain.

In the space of twelve months three distinct townships had grown up. One was under the low hill or *kopje* devoted to business men, where indications of brick houses succeeding daub huts had already manifested themselves; solicitors, auctioneers, and a washerwoman had already established themselves there; bars, restaurants, and a so-called hotel had been constructed. Fort Salisbury had already started its mass meetings and revolutionary elements, for it seems that in all new communities the spirit of evil must always come in advance of the good. An enterprising individual had produced a paper called the *Mashonaland Times and Zambesia Herald*, and two men had brought billiard-tables with them, one of which was hopelessly smashed on the journey, ensuring for the other a successful and paying monopoly. About half a mile from this busy quarter was the military centre, the fort and the Government stores surmounted by Her Majesty's flag, forming a little village in itself. A quarter of a mile farther were the huts devoted to the civil administration; and farther off still were the hospital huts superintended by some charming Benedictine sisters and a Jesuit Father. Around all this was the wide open *veldt* of Mashonaland, studded just then by lovely flowers, and grazed upon by many lean, worn-out oxen, the sole survivors of many well-appointed teams which had struggled up the same interminable road that we had, leaving by the roadside the carcasses of so many comrades, which, in process of decay, had caused us many an unpleasant sensation.

On September 12, the anniversary of the arrival of the pioneers, a grand dinner was given to about eighty individuals at the hotel to celebrate the event: representatives of the military, civil, and business communities were bidden; gold prospectors, mining experts, men of established and questionable reputations—all were there, and the promoters underwent superhuman difficulties in catering for so many guests, and gave fabulous prices for a sufficiency of wine, spirits, and victuals properly to celebrate the occasion. It was in its initiative ostensibly a social gathering to celebrate an ostensibly auspicious occasion; but one after-dinner speech became more intemperate than the other: the authorities were loudly abused for faults committed by them, real or imaginary; well-known names, when pronounced, were hooted and hissed; and the social gathering developed, as the evening went on, into a wild demonstration of discontent.

At the bottom of all this ill-feeling was the question of supplies. The previous rainy season had been passed by the pioneers in abject misery; there was no food to eat, and no medicine to administer to the overwhelming number of fever patients. The rainy season was now fast approaching again, when for months the place would be cut off by the rivers from the outer world, and the 400 waggon-loads of provisions promised by the company had not yet arrived. Lucky were those who had anything to sell in those days: a bottle of brandy fetched 3*l*. 10*s*.; champagne was bought at the rate of 30*l*. a dozen; ham was 4*s*. 6*d*. a lb.; tins of jam 5*s*. 6*d*.; butter, tinned meats, and luxuries were impossible to obtain; and yet when, after a few weeks, the 400 waggons did come, there was a glut in the market of all these things; plenty was ensured for the coming wet season, and there were no more mass meetings or abuse of the authorities.

Probably few cases have occurred in the world's history of greater difficulty in catering than that which presented itself to the Chartered Company during the first year of Fort Salisbury's existence. Very little could be obtained from a native source, for the inhabitants here are few. Hungry, impecunious gold prospectors were flocking into the place; the usual tribe of adventurers, who always appear as impediments to a new and presumably prosperous undertaking, were here by the score. Eight hundred miles lay between Fort Salisbury and the food supply, which had to be traversed by the tedious process of bullock waggons. The Pungwe route, which had been confidently looked to as a more rapid means of communication, had so far proved a *fiasco*, and hundreds of pounds' worth of provisions were rotting on the other side of the fly belt at Mapanda's and Beira; so no wonder discontent was rife at the prospect of famine and death during the ensuing wet months, and no wonder just then that the administrators were at their wits' end, for, though firmly believing that the waggons would come, they could not be sure, for there was no telegraphic communication in those days. One morning we saw Mr. Selous hurriedly despatched to bring up the waggons at any cost. A few weeks later we heard that they had arrived, and the danger which had threatened the infant Fort Salisbury was averted.

At an elevation of 5,000 feet above the sea level, and barely 18° south of the equator, the air of Fort Salisbury is naturally delicious, and it will probably be the healthiest place in the world when the swamps in its vicinity are properly drained, from which, during the rainy season, malarious vapours proceed and cause fever. The question of drainage was exercising the minds of the authorities when we were there, and much probably has now been done in that direction. Searching winds and clouds of dust were about the only discomforts we personally experienced whilst encamped there; these, however, caused us no little inconvenience, as we were preparing our belongings for various destinations, a matter of no small difficulty after seven months of waggon life. We were told to sell everything we could, including our waggons and oxen, as it would only be possible to perform the rest of the journeys before us with horses and donkeys and bearers, necessitating the reduction of our impedimenta to the smallest possible quantity. What promised to be a very interesting expedition was in store for us—namely, to take a present of 40*l*. worth of goods from the Chartered Company to a chief, 'Mtoko by name, who lived about 120 miles north-east of Fort Salisbury. His country had as yet been hardly visited by white men, and was reported to be replete with anthropological interests. Then we were to make our way down to Makoni's country, where the existence of ruins was brought before our notice, and so on to Umtali and the coast. This prospective trip would take us many weeks, and would lead us through much country hitherto unexplored, so that ample preparations and a careful adjustment of our belongings were necessary. The best interpreter to be had was kindly placed at our disposal by the Chartered Company, as the language in those parts differs essentially from that spoken at Zimbabwe and the Sabi, a certain portion of which had by this time penetrated into our brains. The interpreter in question was just then absent from Fort Salisbury, so to occupy our time we decided on a trip to the Mazoe Valley, and the old gold workings which exist there.

Having despatched three donkeys with bedding and provisions the night before, we left Fort Salisbury one lovely morning, September 15, and rode through country as uninteresting as one could well imagine until we reached Mount Hampden. Somehow or another we had formed impressions of this mountain of a wholly erroneous character. It has an historic interest as a landmark, named after one of the first explorers of Mashonaland, but beyond this it is miserably disappointing. Instead of the fine mountain which our imaginations had painted for us, we saw only a miserable round elevation above the surrounding plain, which might possibly be as high as Box Hill, certainly no higher. It is covered with trees of stunted growth; it is absolutely featureless; and is alone interesting from its isolation, and the vast area of flat *veldt* which its summit commands.

Soon after leaving Mount Hampden the views grew very much finer, and as we descended into the valley of the Tatagora, a tributary of the Mazoe, we entered into a distinctly new class of scenery. Here everything is rich and green; the rounded hills and wooded heights were an immense relief to us after the continuous though fantastic granite *kopjes* which we had travelled amongst during the whole of our sojourn in Mashonaland. The delicate green leaves of the machabel tree, on which, I am told, elephants delight to feed, were just now at their best, and take the place of the mimosa, mapani, and other trees, of which we had grown somewhat weary. The soil, too, is here of a reddish colour, and we enjoyed all the pleasurable sensations of getting into an entirely new formation, after the eye had been accustomed to one style of colouring for months.

As we proceeded down the valley the hills closed in and became higher; occasional rugged peaks stood up out of gentle wooded slopes; and if one had ignored the trivial detail of foliage, one might have imagined that we were plunging into a pretty Norwegian valley with a stream rushing down its midst.

Presently we came upon a nest of native kraals, and alighted to inspect them. There are those who say that these people are the real Mashonas, who have given their name to the whole country. This I much doubt; at any rate they are very different from the Makalangas, with whom we had hitherto been entirely associated, and have been here only for a few years. When Mr. Selous first visited this valley on one of his hunting expeditions in 1883, he found it quite uninhabited, whereas now there are many villages, an apt illustration of the migratory tendencies of these

NATIVE BOWL FROM THE MAZOE VALLEY

tribes. They are quite different in type to the Makalangas, and, I should say, distinctly inferior in physique. They build their huts differently, with long eaves coming right down to the ground. Their granaries are fatter and lower, and made of branches instead of mud, these two facts pointing distinctly to a tribal variation. They wear their hair in long strings over their face, one on each side of the nose, and the others hanging on their cheeks, giving them quite a sphinx-like appearance. These strings are adorned with beads and cowrie-shells, and must form the most uncomfortable style of *coiffure* that ever was invented. They have magnificent bowls of handmade pottery, decorated with chevron patterns in red and black, which colours they obtain from hematite and plumbago; and on all advantageous spots near the villages are platforms raised on stakes for drying grain.

Undoubtedly this race, whoever they may be, have a northern origin, for they call beer *Doorah* or *Doro*, the same word used for the same material in Abyssinia and Nubia. This word is also used in M'toko's and Makoni's country. Curiously enough, Edrisi, in his geography, when speaking of the Zindj inhabitants near Sofala, makes this statement: 'Dowrah is very scarce amongst them,' pointing to the Arabian origin of the word; whereas in Manicaland beer is called *Wa-wa*, and in Mashonaland, south of Fort Salisbury, it is called '*Mtwala*, a word of Zulu origin.

Four miles beyond these villages the valley gets

very narrow and the scenery very fine; and the shades of evening found us comfortably located in the huts of Mr. Fleming, a gold prospector, at a distance of twenty-five miles from Fort Salisbury and in the vicinity of the ancient mines. Immediately opposite to us rose a fine rocky mountain in which are caves where the natives hide themselves and their cattle during Matabele raids. It was a lovely warm evening, and as we sat contemplating the scene and resting after the labours of the day, we felt the soothing influence upon us of scenery more congenial to our taste than any we had yet seen in Mashonaland.

The first set of old workings which we visited was only a few hundred yards from Mr. Fleming's huts, and consisted of rows of vertical shafts, now filled up with rubbish, sunk along the edge of the auriferous reef, and presumably, from instances we saw later, communicating with one another by horizontal shafts below. We saw also several instances of sloping and horizontal shafts, all pointing to considerable engineering skill. It must have been ages since these shafts were worked, for they are all filled nearly to the surface with *débris*, and huge machabel-trees, the largest in the vicinity, are growing out of them. We then proceeded to visit some old workings about a mile and a half off on the hill slopes. One vertical shaft had been cleared out by Mr. Fleming's workmen, and it was fifty-five feet deep. Down this we went with considerable difficulty, and saw for ourselves the ancient tool marks and the smaller horizontal shafts which connected the various holes bored into the gold-bearing quartz.

I am told that near Hartley Hills some of these old workings go down even to a greater depth, and that one has been cleared out to the depth of eighty feet, proving incontestably that the ancient workers of these mines were not content with mere surface work, and followed the reef with the skill of a modern miner.

All about here the ground is honeycombed with old shafts of a similar nature, indicated now by small round depressions in straight lines along the reef where different shafts had been sunk; in fact, the output of gold in centuries long gone by must have been enormous.

Since the modern invasion of this gold-producing district a considerable amount of prospecting has been done, but of necessity time has not allowed of a thorough investigation of the country. Wherever the gold prospector has been, he finds instances of ancient working, and these old shafts extend all up the country wherever the gold-bearing quartz is to be found. There are ruins similar to those at Zimbabwe and the old workings in the Tati district. The old workings and ruins extend for miles and miles up the Mazoe Valley. Numerous old shafts are to be found at Hartley Hills, and on the 'Mswezwe River. Near Fort Victoria and in the immediate vicinity of Zimbabwe the prospectors have lately brought to light the same features; everywhere, in short, where the pioneer prospectors have as yet penetrated overwhelming proof of the extent of the ancient industry is brought to light. Mr. E. A. Maund thus speaks of the old workings in the 'Mswczwe district:[1] 'On all sides there was testimony of the enormous amount of work that had been done by the ancients for the production of gold. Here, as on the Mazoe and at Umtali, tens of thousands of slaves must have been at work taking out the softer parts of the casing of the reefs, and millions of tons have been overturned in their search for gold.'

In all these places, too, as in the Mazoe Valley, especially down by the streams, are found crushing-stones, some in long rows, suggesting the idea that the gold had been worked by gangs of slaves chained together in rows, after the fashion depicted on the Egyptian monuments and described by Diodorus; and near Mr. Fleming's camp we were shown traces of a cement smelting furnace similar to the one we discovered in the fortress of Zimbabwe, showing that all the various processes of gold production, crushing, washing, and smelting, were carried on on the spot.

As we proceeded up the Mazoe Valley we saw plenty of traces of the juvenile enterprise at work on the old hunting-ground; and a little below Mr. Fleming's camp the Taragona and Mazoe Rivers join, the latter coming down from a valley of higher level, by a *Poort* or gorge. Established on the old workings along here were numerous settlements bearing

---

[1] Lecture before the Colonial Institute, April 12, 1892.

modern names—Rothschild's, Cherry's, Lockner's, and others—and soon probably a little township will spring up around the mining commissioner's hut, where the Mazoe River is lined by fine timber, including lemon-trees, the fruit of which was just then ripe, and deliciously refreshing after our hot morning's work. These lemon-trees are alluded to by Dos Santos as existing in these parts in his day three hundred years ago.

The mining commissioner, Mr. Nesbit, entertained us most hospitably for our midday repast, and directed us on our way to the Yellow Jacket Mine, near which we were to see more old workings and an ancient ruined fort. By another narrow gorge or *Poort*, rich in vegetation, and lovely to look upon, we reached the higher valley, and when darkness had already set in, by the aid of the distant glimmering light of a camp fire we made our way to the tents of the Yellow Jacket prospectors, whose abode we had nearly missed in the gloaming. The kindly prospectors hastened to prepare for us an excellent supper of eland steak, for they had shot one of these fine beasts a day or two before, a wonderfully good stroke of luck for us, as we were without meat. The eland is the best beast you can kill in Mashonaland, for not only is it large, but around its heart it has a considerable amount of fat, so that its flesh can be properly served up, and not reduced to lumps of leather for want of grease. They had also shot a fine lion here not long before, and proudly showed us the skin.

The country about here is very thickly wooded, and we had a glorious ride next morning to the ruins we wished to visit, about five miles distant, across rushing streams overhung with verdure, and in which alluvial gold is still found in small quantities. Here we saw specimens of those curious birds with long tail-like feathers at the end of their wings, which can only fly for a short distance, and seem overweighted by nature for some peculiar freak of her own. There are, too, all up this country many varieties of small birds with tail feathers four or five times their own length, which droop as they fly. These birds seem to me to resemble closely the one depicted on the temple of Deir-el-Bahari in the representation of a village in Punt (Mariette's ' Deir-el-Bahari,' plate v.), identified as the *Cinnyris metallica*, and found all along the east coast of Africa.

We reached the ruin in good time, and halted by it for a couple of hours. It is a small ancient fort, built, as usual, on a granite *kopje*, and constructed with courses of wonderful regularity, equal to what we term the best period of Zimbabwe architecture. Not much of the wall was standing; enough, however, to show us that the fort had been almost twenty feet in diameter, and to cause us to wonder where the remaining stones could have gone to, as there are no buildings or Kaffir kraals anywhere near it. This is another of the many mysteries attached to the Mashoualand

FORT SALISBURY AND THE MAZOE VALLEY

ruins; where the walls are ruined the stones would seem to have entirely disappeared. This difficulty confronted us at several places, and I am utterly at a loss to account for it.

The fort, as it stands now, is exceedingly picturesque, in a green glade with mountains shutting it in

RUIN IN MAZOE VALLEY

on all sides; fine timber grows inside it and large boulders are enclosed within the walls. It was obviously erected as a fort to protect the miners of the district, and is a link in the chain of evidence which connects the Zimbabwe ruins with the old workings scattered over the country.

On our homeward journey we visited a lot more

ancient workings, some of which are being opened by the present occupiers, who seemed tolerably well satisfied with their properties, despite the strictures which had been passed by experts, that the gold reefs in the Mazoe Valley 'pinched out' and did other disagreeable things which they ought not to do. From a picturesque point of view the Mazoe Valley is certainly one of the pet places in Mashonaland: the views in every direction are exquisite, water is abundant everywhere, and verdure rich; and if the prospectors are disappointed in their search for gold, and find that the ancients have exhausted the place, they will have, at any rate, valuable properties from an agricultural point of view.

Owing to our previous arrangements we were obliged to return to Fort Salisbury the next day, regretting much that we had not time to proceed farther up the Mazoe Valley, where, about forty miles farther on, is another great centre of ancient industry. I was told of another ruin there, probably built for the same defensive purpose; it is near a Kaffir village called Chipadzi's. About twenty-five miles farther up the valley from the commissioner's is Mapandera's kraal on the Sangwe River, a tributary of the Mazoe or Mazowe. Here, on the Inyota Mountain, gold is said to be plentiful and old workings very numerous, as many as seventy-five crushing-stones having been counted on one single claim. Twenty miles southeast of Mapandera's is Chipadzi's kraal, and a few miles from here in the mountains is another ruin, described to me as being a circular wall round a *kopje* from 150 to 200 feet in diameter. This wall is in a very ruined condition, being not more than four feet in height, but the courses are reported to be quite as regular as those of Zimbabwe, which appears to be the crucial test in classifying these remains of ancient workmanship. It has no entrance, and the natives thereabouts did not appear to know anything about it or attach any special interest to it.

The Mazoe Valley is frequently alluded to in early Portuguese enterprise, being easily approachable from the Zambesi, and the river is, I am told, navigable about eighty miles below where we struck it.

Couto, the Portuguese writer, thus speaks of the gold mines here in his quaint legendary style: 'The richest mines of all are those of Massapa, where they show the Abyssinian mine from which the Queen of Sheba took the greater part of the gold which she went to offer to the Temple of Solomon, and it is Ophir, for the Kaffirs called it *Fur* and the Moors *Afur* . . . the veins of gold are so big, that they expand with so much force, that they raise the roots of trees two feet.' He fixes the spot which he here alludes to farther on when speaking about the three markets held by the Portuguese in these parts: '(1) *Luanhe*, thirty-five leagues from Tete South, between two small rivers, which join and are called Masouvo; (2) *Bacoto*, forty leagues from Tete; and (3) *Massapa*, fifty leagues from Tete up the said River Masouvo.' Now the Mazoe, which, doubtless, in the native tongue, is the

Maswe, like the Pungwe, Zimbabwe, &c., joins the Zambesi just below Tete.

Further evidences of this Portuguese enterprise will doubtless come to light as the Mazoe Valley is further explored. In the vicinity of a new mine called the Jumbo, fragments of old Delft pottery have been found, a few of which were shown to me when at Fort Salisbury. Nankin china is also reported from the same district, an indubitable proof of Portuguese presence; and no doubt many of the large Venetian beads, centuries old, which we saw and obtained specimens of from the Makalangas in the neighbourhood of Zimbabwe, were barter goods given by the traders of those days to the subjects of the Monomatapa, who brought them gold in quills to the three above-named depôts, collected from the alluvial beds of the Mazoe and other streams. It is rumoured amongst the inhabitants of the Mazoe and Manica that long ago, in the days of their ancestors, white men worked gold and built themselves houses here. This rumour most probably refers to the Portuguese, who at the three above-mentioned places had churches and forts, faint traces of which are still to be found in the district.

Corvo, in his work 'As Provincias ultramarinas,' speaks at considerable length about the early Portuguese enterprise and the jealousy of the Arab merchants at their advent, and how these men excited the suspicion of the Monomatapa and brought about the subsequent martyrdom of the Jesuit missionary

FORT SALISBURY AND THE MAZOE VALLEY 297

Silveira and the entire destruction of the Portuguese mission, which had nearly converted the Monomatapa

THREE VENETIAN BEADS; ONE COPPER BEAD; THREE OLD WHITE VENETIAN BEADS; BONE WHORL, MEDICINE PHIALS, AND BONE ORNAMENTS

in 1561. He concludes his remarks on this subject as follows:—

'The early Portuguese did nothing more than substitute themselves for the Moors, as they called them, in the ports that those occupied on the coast; and their influence extended to the interior very little; unless, indeed, through some acts of violence, or through some ephemeral alliance of no value whatever, and through missions without any practical or lasting results. It is easy to see, by looking at the map, where the Portuguese influence extended to, and that they never left a good navigable river as a basis of operation. They went up the Zambesi, and up the Mazoe as far as they could, where they established the three fairs for trading purposes, and up the Pungwe and Buzi Rivers, establishing themselves in the same way at Massi-Kessi and Bandiri; and beyond this their influence did not extend at all during what may be called the most flourishing epoch of their colonial existence.'

From the Yellow Jacket tents we had a long ride before us of thirty miles back to Fort Salisbury. We arose betimes and found it very cold, with a thin coating of ice on the water-cans, almost the only time we saw ice during our 'winter' in Mashonaland, although occasionally the wind was cold and the nights very fresh. Winter in these parts is delightful, with brilliant sun by day; but as evening approaches a coat is necessary, and during our two nights at the Yellow Jacket huts we had to remove rugs, which were sorely wanted below, to procure the necessary warmth above.

One more breakfast off that excellent eland fortified us for our ride, and the sun was not high in the heavens when we bade farewell to our hospitable entertainers. About three hours' ride brought us to the Mazoe again just before it enters the Poort on its way to the lower valley. At the extremity of the valley we were riding down, just before the hills are ascended to reach the level plateau, there is another nest of Kaffir villages; one of these had incurred the enmity of the officers of the Chartered Company for refusing to recognise its authority by restoring stolen cattle.

A fine of cattle had been imposed on the chief, accompanied by a threat that if the fine was not paid by a certain day the kraal would be burnt down. The fine was not paid, and Major Forbes, with a band of men, rode out to execute the orders, borrowing two of our horses for the occasion. As we passed through the village the ashes of huts and granaries were still smouldering, broken pots and household goods lay around in wild confusion, and all the inhabitants had taken refuge at one of the neighbouring villages. As we passed by this it is needless to say we did not meet with an altogether cordial reception; we dismounted and went amongst them, asking in vain for beer, eggs, and fowls.

'The Morunko had taken them all,' they said, and they received our overtures of friendship with silent, and we thought rather ominous, contempt. Accordingly we remounted and rode off, and I think all parties were relieved when we had put a little distance between us and the village. Since then I hear a solitary white man has been murdered in the Mazoe Valley. Luckily our force amounted to three, a number sufficient to overawe any Mashonaland village.

There are some nice-looking farms just started on the slopes of the hills here. Near there we met a wondrous long string of natives in single file, who avoided us and looked askance at us and our animals. Some day or another, when Fort Salisbury becomes a big place, and food supplies are needed, those who have pegged out farms in the Mazoe district will reap a fine profit from their agricultural produce, if I am not much mistaken.

CHAPTER X

OUR EMBASSY TO THE CHIEF 'MTOKO

THERE is always a charm to us connected with the investigation of a country the name of which conveys nothing to anybody, and which is a blank on the map. This, I think, was one of the chief incentives to us to accept the diplomatic post of presenting a gift of forty pounds' worth of goods from the Chartered Company to the chief 'Mtoko.

We gathered that 'Mtoko was a powerful chief, dreaded by the natives, whose country lay about 120 miles to the north-east of Fort Salisbury; that he ruled over a large and almost unknown district reaching on the west to the territories under the influence of the Portuguese satellite Gouveia; and that his father, who had lately died, had entered into a treaty with the Chartered Company which gave them paramount influence, but that the present chief and his subjects, who were reported to have customs of an exceedingly primitive order, had as yet had no official dealings with the Company. This was about all the information we could gather.

The following is an exact copy of my credentials:—

To the Chief Matoko

The British South Africa Company, Salisbury.
September 21, 1891.

My Friend,—Mr. Selous has told Mr. Rhodes, the Big Induna of all white men in this country, all about you, and he has sent his friend Mr. Bent to see you and your people, and to give you some presents from him; and also to tell you that you are now under the Great White Queen, and that the Portuguese will not trouble you any more.

You and your people will now live in peace and security.
I am, your Friend,
F. RUTHERFOORD HARRIS,
Secretary.

We certainly felt somewhat adventurous when we left Fort Salisbury, on September 23, on this journey of uncertain length and uncertain results. We could take hardly any comforts with us except our tent, and the smallest possible allowance of bedclothes, and only just enough food to keep us from starvation for a week, for the donkeys of this country carry very little weight, and the only bearers we could get were our two faithful Makalangas, Mashanani and Iguzo. These, together with our three white men, who looked after the eleven donkeys, formed our only staff, for the interpreter had not yet come in, and was to be sent after us. The only fixed idea of time that we had was that a steamer was supposed to leave Port Beira for the Cape on November 18, and this at all hazards we had to catch; the intervening space of time was to us a maze of delightful uncertainty, only to be unravelled as that time went by.

After a comfortable breakfast at the civilian mess hut, and farewells to our kind friends at Fort Salisbury, my wife, Mr. Swan, and I started on our three horses in pursuit of our donkeys, which had started along the Manica road about an hour before. These we soon caught up, and after a hot dusty ride of about ten miles we pitched our tents about one hundred yards from a large Kaffir village on a flat space, hidden away amongst a sea of small granite boulders. Here the women wore pretty chaplets of red and white beads sewn on to snake-skins, and aprons and necklets gaily decorated with the same; the chief had a splendid crop of long black hair. Beyond this the village presented nothing fresh to our notice until night fell, when our rest was disturbed for hours by a series of hideous noises: drums were beaten, dogs were barking, men were howling like wild beasts, and when they ceased the women would take up their refrain, guns were periodically let off, and everything conceivable was done to render night hideous. On rising next morning and inquiring the cause of this nightmare, we were informed that a death had taken place in the village, and that the inhabitants were indulging in their accustomed wailing. I was also told that in these parts they carefully tie up the limbs of a dead man, his toes and his fingers each separately, in cloths, prior to burial, whereas a woman is only tied up in a skin, and her grave is of no account.

At the village of Karadi we left the Manica road

TATTOOED WOMEN FROM CHIBI'S, GAMBIDJI'S, AND KUNZI'S COUNTRIES

and entered a very populous district with numerous villages perched on the rocky heights, the inhabitants of which were greatly excited at the sight of us, and followed us for miles. This, we learnt, was Musungaikwa's country. The women here had a distinct tattoo mark of their own—namely, the lizard pattern, which we have seen on the dollasses or divining-tablets [1]—done in dots on their stomachs. Some of the men, too, have the same device tattooed on them on their chests and backs. This is the third distinctive tattoo mark we have seen in Mashonaland—namely, the furrow pattern around Zimbabwe, the dots in squares in Gambidji's country, and here the lizard pattern, all of which are raised marks on the skin made by the insertion of some drug. They are evidently connected with some charm, but what the nature of it is I was never able to discover.

At Musungaikwa's, necessity for the first time made us acquainted with red millet-meal porridge, called respectively *sodza* and *ufa* in different parts of the country. With milk and sugar it is quite palatable but gritty; the natives like it best very thick, eating it with a stick and dipping it into water before consumption; they appear almost to live upon it, and dispose of surprising quantities. Much rice is grown about here in the swampy ground, sometimes in round holes, sometimes in wide furrows, which are surprisingly straight for Kaffirs, who seem to have the greatest difficulty in

WOODEN BOWL FROM MUSUNGAIKWA'S KRAAL

[1] Chap. II.

producing a straight line. Their paths, though very accurate in direction, represent to the eye a long wavy line, and they are aggravatingly narrow for a European, who turns his toes out, to walk in, for the Kaffirs always go in single file, and always put their feet down straight.

The natives about here followed us with bags of bark fibre full of figs of a rich brown colour, which we purchased, and found excellent when they were not inhabited, as was generally the case, by hundreds of little ants.

At about thirty miles from Fort Salisbury we reached a nest of seven or eight kraals ruled over by a chief called Kunzi. Here we elected to stay and wait for the interpreter, and as he did not join us for two days we had a pleasant time for rest and for studying the inhabitants. Kuñzi, the paramount chief of this community, is a young and enterprising individual; he corresponds to the *nouveau riche* of Kaffirdom, being spoken of as 'a chief of the assegai' in contradistinction to the old hereditary chiefs around. He came originally from 'Mtigeza's country, got together a band of followers, and won for himself with his assegai the territory he now occupies. To a chief of this description all the youth and prowess of the country flock, hence he had a remarkably fine set of followers, and these he rules with marvellous strictness. We had an example of his power, for we wanted to get bearers from him. He brought the men in person, and would not allow them to go with us until we had paid the stipulated quantity of cloth in advance and deposited it with him. This arrangement did not please me at all, knowing well the tendency paid bearers have to run away, but it was inevitable. The men served us extremely well, accompanied us for a fortnight until we reached the spot arranged upon with the chief, and when I offered them more to go farther they refused, saying that they dare not do so without the consent of their chief.

Kunzi is an ambitious man, and talks of becoming king of Mashonaland, but as he was driven back during his last attack on his neighbour Mangwendi, and as the Chartered Company may have something to say to it, this eventuality seems at present in the dim future. Kunzi is, however, a man of promise, and if he had been born a little earlier he might have been in a position to resuscitate the fallen glories of the race.

Outside Kunzi's kraal is a fine iron smelting furnace, decorated with the breast and furrow pattern, and with a large quantity of newly made blow-pipes of dried mud, and decorated with a spiral pattern, lying in heaps outside. We watched the process here at our leisure. First they crush the ore obtained from the neighbouring mountains, which has a large quantity of manganese in it, and spread it on the rocks; the forge is heated with charcoal and kindled by two men with four bellows, each worked by one hand; the nozzles are inserted into the blow-pipes, and the blow-pipes into the charcoal; they press the bellows with their hands by means of a wooden handle, and work with great vigour, singing and perspiring freely as they work. Around the furnace is a hedge of tall grass, and at night time, when the ore is cool, they remove it from the furnace and afterwards weld it into the required shapes with stone hammers. This time-honoured handicraft interested us much, mentioned as it is by Dos Santos three hundred years ago, and

MAKALANGA IRON SMELTING FURNACE

by the Arabian writers close upon a thousand years ago, as a speciality of the country.

One of the neighbouring kraals is ruled over by Kunzi's brother Gwadeli, who, in his anxiety to be hospitable, gave us warm beer to drink, which nearly had the effect of an emetic. A rock rises out of the centre of this kraal, where is an *induna's* grave walled into the rock, with four pots of beer before it, and hedged off by a rope of bark.

The following morning we watched with some

interest a trader from Fort Salisbury selling goods to the natives. Beads, gunpowder, and salt were the favourite commodities he had to offer, in return for which he rapidly acquired a fine lot of pumpkins, maize, potatoes, and other vegetables; whilst for blankets and rifles he obtained cattle which I am sure would bring him in a handsome profit when he reached the capital. We ourselves got a

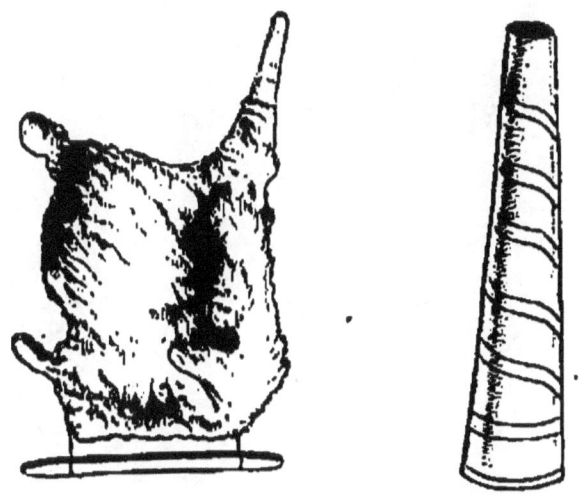

GOATSKIN BELLOWS AND BLOW-PIPE FOR IRON SMELTING

few interesting things at Kunzi's, including a quill with gold in it which the natives had found in the 'Nyagowe River, and a dexterously wrought garment for a young lady, about half the size of a freemason's apron; it is made of bark fibre, with geometrical patterns of excellent design worked into it, a species of textile with which we were to become better acquainted in 'Mtoko's country. Here, too, we saw sticks set up in the ground with the bark peeled off and bound round the top—a sort of fetich, which they call their *Maklosi* or luck sign. They set these things up whenever they come to a new country; also, on similar occasions, they kneel before a tree and burn snuff, saying as they do so: 'Muali!' (the

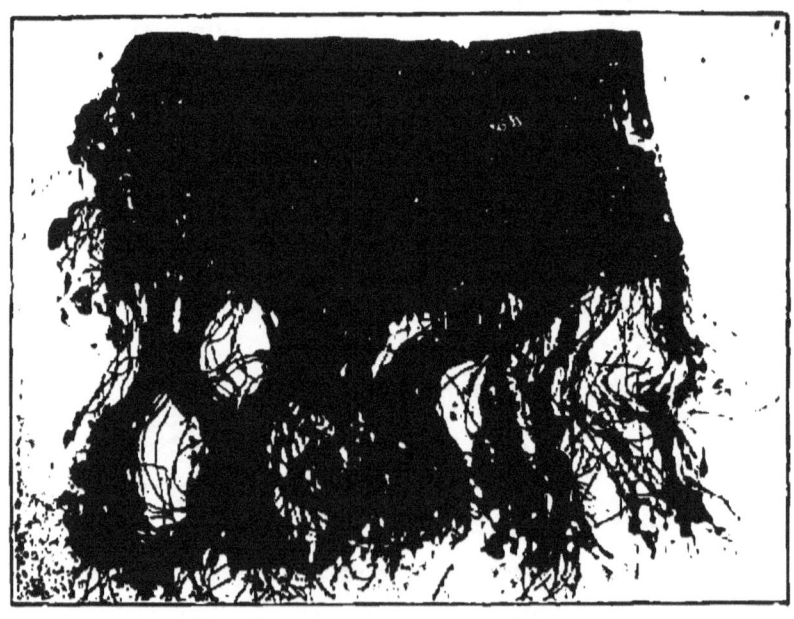

WOMAN'S DRESS OF WOVEN BARK FIBRE

native name for God) 'we have brought knives, give us meat.' Then they do the same at another tree, asking the same petition for their children.

A delicious stream for bathing and washing clothes flowed a few yards below our camp, which gave us sufficient employment for what would otherwise have been an idle afternoon. At midnight our interpreter arrived, and the following morning we commenced our journey in real earnest.

At a village where we halted for a while we were introduced to a young girl, who was shortly to become chief Kunzi's eleventh wife—the state wife, to be presented to him by his tribe, whose son will be heir to the chiefdom, to the exclusion of the children by his other purchased wives. This marriage is usually recommended and seen to by the tribe when the chief is getting on towards middle life; and the succession in these parts is carried on in this way. She wore round her neck one of the large white whorls made out of the end of shells, which are common amongst the natives, but a specimen of which I tried ineffectually to get. This, I now learnt, is the sign of betrothal, and is transferred to the neck of the baby when born. Men also wear them for love philtres, and hence their reluctance to part with them.

During this day's march we passed by a pond dug in a hollow which was in process of drying up. These holes are dug by the natives in the dry season with the object of catching fish when the swamps dry up; also for fishing they make use of a thing very like our lobster-pot, which they tie to a fence across a rapid portion of the stream. The love the natives have for salt throughout this saltless country is very marked; for sugar and lollipops, which we offered them, they have a positive aversion; anything of a savoury nature pleases them immensely, and their gestures of delight over the scrapings of tins of anchovy paste were most pleasing to contemplate. Mice, locusts, and caterpillars are their daintiest viands, and if given a lump of salt they will put it straightway into their mouths and consume it with the greatest complacency.

We halted that night at the village of Yandoro, still in Kunzi's country, with a solitary rock in its midst, divided into two parts by a narrow split forming a gully which is bridged over by trees, so that they can retire to the highest point when the Matabele come, and wait there till the *impi* has departed with their cattle and grain.

I learnt here a little more concerning the mysteries of hand-clapping and greetings. One of our bearers from Kunzi's kraal, Girandali by name, had relatives here, and I followed him to their hut, the inmates of which were seated solemnly on the floor and began to clap, whereupon Girandali commenced to relate parenthetically the events of his career since they last met; between each parenthesis the host clapped and said his name. This went on for fully ten minutes, each parenthesis being received with more or less clapping, as it attracted the attention of his hearers. When Girandali had done, there was a general clapping which lasted for some time, and then the formal part of the conversation was over.

The chief of a neighbouring village, Bochiko by name, here paid us a visit. He is a most curious specimen of his race, a veritable pigmy only four feet four inches in height. He has lost all his toes in battle and has had one leg broken and never set; he wore a large brass ring with curious patterns on it on his tiny fingers, and brass bracelets on his tiny arms, both of which we purchased from him. He is said to have five wives and five stalwart children.

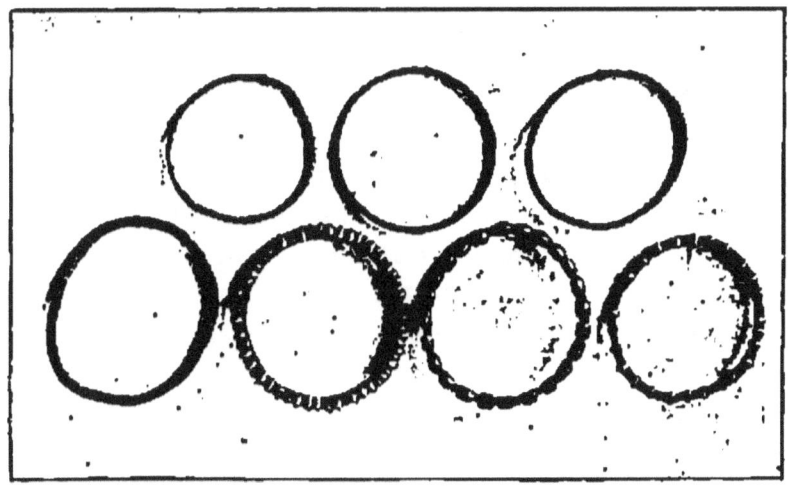

BRACELETS

We were greatly surprised on rising next morning to learn that my mare, an old 'salted horse,' which we had had with us for six months, and ridden hard all the time, had presented us with a foal during the night—unfortunately a dead one. The mare did not seem much the worse for her adventure; in fact, I personally was the only sufferer, for a probably misplaced compassion prompted me to walk instead of ride for the next day's march.

We were now passing through a corner of Mangwendi's country, a chief with whom we were to become better acquainted later on. Gaza, one of his chief *indunas*, has a kraal on an exceedingly high rock by which we passed; in fact, about here the country is very populous, owing to the rocky nature of the ground and the inaccessible eyries in which the natives can plant their huts. We wondered what the meaning of many pots might be which we saw here on high boulders with stones around and on the top. By inquiry we learnt that they were beehives, equivalent to the bark hives we so constantly saw farther south. There is much ceremony about here at the presentation of beer. At Malozo's kraal the chief handed the pot to one of our bearers, who handed it to the interpreter, who handed it to me. Their hair, too, is very wildly dressed, being long and tangled, and when it becomes past endurance by reason of the insects collected therein, they shave it off and hang it to a tree, revealing to the world their bare and greatly disfigured pates.

After this we went through a long stretch of almost uninhabited country, very lovely indeed to look upon, richly wooded, with glimpses through the woods of tree-clad heights, with strange finger-shaped rocks appearing out of them as far as the eye could reach into the blue distance. These granite *kopjes* would be distinctly wearisome were it not for the ever-varying fantastic shapes. The forests themselves are painfully monotonous; at one time you are riding through groves of medlars with coarse large leaves, then you come across a stretch of white-flowered sugar-tree (*Protea mellifera*), which, I think, of all trees is the most aggravating, from the dull monotony of its leaves and generally scraggy appearance of its branches. Its flower is very pretty, being like a soft silvery white chrysanthemum, three inches in diameter; it is very attractive to butterflies and pretty sun-beetles, with which the flower is sometimes quite covered. About here we passed a curious granite mountain called Mount Jomvga, rising above all the rest like a gigantic silver thimble. Mount Jomvga haunted us for days and days, and we never lost sight of it during the whole of our stay in 'Mtoko's country.

We were now rapidly approaching 'Mtoko's country, but the nearer we approached our goal the more difficulty we had in obtaining information as to where the chief actually lived. Some said he lived at the village of Lutzi, a few miles across the border, others said he lived about six miles farther on; consequently we were somewhat perplexed, and ended by stopping near Lutzi for a while, whilst our interpreter rode on to make further inquiries.

Amongst other embarrassing things that a son inherits with the chiefdom are his father's wives. Of course a man is not expected to marry his own mother, but his stepmothers are different, especially if, as often happens, they are young and comely. At Lutzi we were told that the new 'Mtoko had

WOODEN PLATTER FROM LUTZI

deposited several of his father's widows, presumably the old and ugly ones, whom he did not admire. Certainly some of the customs of this country are exceedingly strange, and we should not have believed them had we not again and again asked the same questions from different individuals and always got the same reply. One of these is sufficiently horrible, and I hope the influence of the Chartered Company will soon work for its suppression. If a woman gives birth to twins they are immediately destroyed. This they consider an unnatural freak on the part of a woman, and is supposed to indicate famine or some other calamity. In this custom they differ essentially from their Matabele neighbours, where Lobengula, like our Queen, honours a prolific mother with a special gift. In 'Mtoko's country the unfortunate twins are put into one of their big pots, with a stone on the top, and left to their fate.

In their marauding transactions there is a curious code of honour amongst them. Suppose a woman to be stolen from a tribe, the injured individuals lie in wait for the oxen of the thieves, and when captured take them to the chief, who allots them as follows: 1. One is slaughtered for general consumption and joviality. 2. The rightful owner of the stolen woman is next indemnified. 3. The rest of the tribe are questioned as to whether they have any grievance to be rectified. 4. If there are any oxen over they are scrupulously returned to their owners. Their code of morality is far below the standard amongst the Zulus in Matabeleland.

Many of the customs have a curious Eastern tinge; for example, hired labour is unknown, and if a man wants assistance in his fields he brews a quantity of beer, bids his neighbours come, and the better the beer the more labourers he will get. This custom is still common in Asia Minor and the East, where wine is the substitute for beer.

Lutzi did not interest us much; it is a scattered and poor-looking kraal on a bleak hill, with large stone semicircles, where the men of the village can sit and smoke sheltered from the wind; so on hearing that the 'Mtoko's kraal was really about six miles off, we set out for it about ten o'clock on the following morning.

There is much that is different in this country

from what we had seen elsewhere in Mashonaland, enough almost to point to a difference of race; the language, too, we found so different that we could understand but little of it ourselves, though the ordinary Makalanga terms for commodities such as *mazai* for eggs, *makaka* for milk, &c., were still in vogue. Probably the different circumstances of life will account for the difference in character. The people do not live in kraals huddled together on the top of rocks, but in small scattered kraals of from six to twenty huts dotted all over the country, where agriculture may take them, arguing a degree of prosperity and security to property which we had not seen elsewhere in Mashonaland. In these little kraals there is generally a hut raised on poles in the midst, which acts as a kind of watch-tower. They told us that the Matabele never penetrate as far as this, and that the only enemy they fear is the Portuguese half-caste Gouveia, whose territory lies over the mountains to the east; but his attacks were successfully repulsed by the old 'Mtoko, who had thereby established such a reputation for valour that none of his neighbours durst interfere with him.

The result of this condition of affairs was that in 'Mtoko's country we saw more cattle than we had seen elsewhere, but all of the same calibre. The characteristic of all domestic animals in Mashonaland is their small size. The cows are less than our Guernsey breed, and give very little milk; the sheep and goats are diminutive and unhealthy looking; the hens are ridiculous little things, and their eggs not much bigger than pigeons' eggs at home. As for the dogs, they are the most contemptible specimens of the canine race I have ever seen in any of my wanderings. This does not look well for the prospects of the agriculturists, but probably the diminution in physique amongst the Mashonaland cattle is rather due to the coarse grass and swampy land and the want of proper care than to any other cause.

Up a narrowing valley, with a gorge or *kloof* at the end of it, under the shadow of a rocky mountain, and almost hidden by a dense mass of timber, lies 'Mtoko's kraal, also, after the fashion of the country, a small one. In our innocence we advanced right up to the kraal; and despite the expostulation of an angry crowd of natives, who screamed and yelled at us, we commenced to pitch our tents close by the shady trees in a spot which looked very inviting for a few days' rest. Suddenly it dawned upon us that we had been guilty of some breach of savage etiquette, so I immediately despatched our interpreter to see the chief, with a portion of the present as a foretaste of better things to come. We seated ourselves rather disconsolately beneath the trees awaiting his return, watching the inhabitants, who swarmed around us.

The women of 'Mtoko's country are quite the most decent of their sex that we had seen since entering Mashonaland. Out of bark fibre they weave for themselves quite massive dresses, two yards long

320 EXPLORATION JOURNEYS IN MASHONALAND

and one yard wide, which they decorate with pretty raised geometric patterns like one sees on old-fashioned 'Marsella' quilts at home; these they gird round their loins and fasten on with a girdle of bark netting, and consequently they present an air of decency to which their sisters in other parts of this country are strangers, with their tiny leather aprons scarce worthy of the name of clothing. Nevertheless, when in their huts the women of this country take off this heavy and somewhat awkward garment, and one day, having crawled into a hut, I was somewhat startled to find myself in the presence of two dusky ladies dressed like Eve in the Garden of Eden. Most of the

EARRING.   STUD FOR THE LIP.

BATTLE-AXE.

people about here have their upper and lower lips bored, and insert in them either a nail-like object, somewhat after the fashion of the Nubians, or a bead or ring, or a plain bit of stick. . Their front teeth of both upper and lower jaws are filed, an ancient custom to which both Dos Santos and El Masoudi, the Arabian historian, allude. There is evidently a strong Zambesi influence in 'Mtoko's country; their battle-axes, their assegais, and their powder-horns are far more elaborately carved and decorated with brass wire than those we had seen farther south, and bear a close resemblance to those which the tribes on the Zambesi produce. In their hair they wear combs

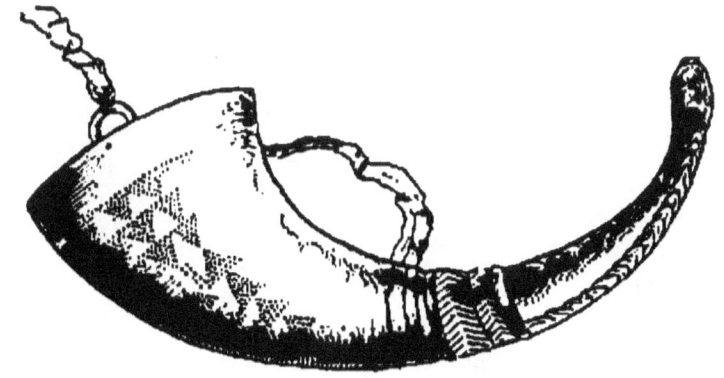

POWDER-HORN

inlaid with different-coloured straws, and their bracelets also are very elaborate.

Our emissary came back with a long face. The 'Mtoko, despite the offering we had sent him, was indignant at our invasion of his privacy; in fact, to avoid seeing a white *induna* without taking counsel with his head men, he had been obliged to take refuge in a cave. His father, he said, would not allow a white man to encamp within eight miles of his kraal. This happened to Mr. Selous, the only white man who had as yet visited the country in an official capacity, when he came to get the old 'Mtoko to sign the treaty a few months before. However, he said he would consent to our pitching our tents at a spot indicated about a mile away, and would come and visit us and receive the rest of his gifts on the morrow.

A COLLECTION OF COMBS

Somewhat crestfallen and highly indignant at our treatment, we packed up our things again and hurried off as fast as we could, so that we might get our tents pitched before night came on.

The following day was advancing rapidly, and still no signs of 'Mtoko's visit. We were much annoyed at the loss of time and the supposed insult, so we collected our presents together, and determined to take them and get them given, come what might. We set off and marched behind the gift, which was carried on the heads of many bearers. We had scarcely gone two hundred yards on our way, when men came running to us, announcing the advent of his majesty; so we went back again to prepare our rugs for the reception, and sat in state.

Through the trees we saw him coming, with a following of about fifty men armed with battle-axes and assegais. About two hundred yards from our camp they all seated themselves, and held a council which we thought would never end. The result of this was an envoy sent to state it as the monarch's opinion that the white lady had bewitched the presents, for she had been seen going to a stream and sprinkling the things with water which she had fetched from thence; that he would nevertheless graciously receive the presents, but that he would not keep them but give them at once to his uncle. Whilst we were making up our minds whether we should be annoyed or amused at this message, the chief and his men moved one hundred yards nearer to us, so we determined to await the progress of events. Here again they stopped for another *indaba*. This time the message, that the chief would like us to send him the presents to the spot where he was, was accompanied by a present to us of a kid and twenty pounds of meal. This somewhat pacified us. Nevertheless we sent a message back that if the chief wished for the things he must come and fetch them in person. To the *indunas* who brought the message we gave a few articles for themselves.

The result of this last message was instantaneous. His majesty came forthwith, but he refused to sit on the rug prepared for him. He refused to shake hands, nay, even look at the white lady, and during the whole of the interview he trembled so violently, and looked so nervous, that we felt quite sorry for him.

'Mtoko is a fine specimen of his race, lithe and supple of limb, but more like a timid wild animal than a man. As he sat before us he nervously peeled a sweet potato with his battle-axe, and looked ill at ease. Gradually, as the presents came out, his sinister face relaxed, and in spite of himself became wreathed with smiles. Spread out before him was an entire uniform of the Cape Yeomanry, helmet and all, with two horsehair plumes. Then there were knives, and looking-glasses, and handkerchiefs, and shirts, and beads, and yards of limbo; wealth, doubtless, of which he had scarce dreamt, was now his. The impression made on him was great. He was overcome with gratitude, and after stepping aside for a few moments' talk with his head men, he told us that, as a return present, a whole live bullock should be ours. Permission was given to us to come and encamp under his kraal if we liked. His apologies were profuse, and he even ventured to touch the white lady's hand; and thus ended this strange interview.

Not wishing to uproot ourselves again, we thanked him for his offer, and said we preferred to remain where we were, but would come up and visit him on the morrow.

Afterwards we learnt the cause of all 'Mtoko's nervousness. His father had died shortly after Mr. Selous's visit. The common belief was that he had been bewitched; naturally he thought that the white lady had been sent purposely to cast a glamour over him. He had been told how these white men are ruled over by a woman, and he thought Queen Victoria had sent a humble representative of her sex to bring about the same state of affairs in his country. Her name was of course asked at the interview, and feeling the flatness with which her English appellative would be received, our interpreter promptly called her 'Msinyate, 'the Home of the Buffaloes,' to which high-sounding name she answered for the rest of her stay in 'Mtoko's country.

The day was far spent when the chief left us, and we took a stroll in the cool of the evening to a tiny kraal, consisting only of three huts, about half a mile from our camp. There was an air of prosperity about the place which pleased us. The huts are better built than elsewhere, and have porches. Their granaries are wattled, and have very well thatched roofs, and our reception was most cordial. They spread mats for us to sit on. They brought us monkey-nuts, tamarind, and other vegetables to eat, and seemed to think themselves greatly honoured by a visit from the white *indunas* who had brought their chief such a fine present.

Next morning we walked up to visit 'Mtoko in his kraal. The twenty huts which compose it are girt around with a strong palisade. Each hut is large, and has a porch. 'Mtoko and his head men were seated on a rock in the midst of it with a wood fire for lighting their pipes. One of the *indunas* had just decorated his hair in splendid fashion, tying up his black tufts with beads, and covering the whole with a thick coating of grease, which soaked into his matted hair before our eyes under the strong influence of the sun. Into this circle we were all invited, for the dread of the white lady seemed to have passed away. She presented the monarch with some English needles, and his delight in receiving these treasures exceeded even that which he showed on receipt of the Chartered Company's gifts, for in 'Mtokoland they are accustomed to use strong sharp blades of grass for needles, on which ours were a distinct improvement.

Our object to-day was to inquire into the politics of the country, and to verify the strange stories we had heard about the priest of the lion god, the Mondoro, who is reported to be even stronger than the chief. We wanted to learn more concerning the cult of the lion, and where the Zimbabwe of 'Mtokoland was, where the annual sacrifices take place to the king of beasts.

The question was a delicate one, and had to be tenderly approached, knowing as we did by this time the extreme reluctance of the Kaffirs to disclose to white men the secrets of their religion. A man called Benoula seemed to take the lead in everything. The 'Mtoko hardly spoke, and looked very uncomfortable whilst the catechising was going on. The results of our investigations were vague. The Mondoro, or lion priest, was uncle to the chief, and he resided at Lutzi, the village by which we had passed. The old 'Mtoko on his death-mat had left his son and heir somehow or another in tutelage to this mysterious priest-uncle of his. When asked where the Zimbabwe was, he replied reluctantly: 'The Mondoro may tell you if he likes; I dare not.' Finally, after 'the Home of the Buffaloes'' hair had been taken down by his majesty's special request, we made arrangements for Benoula to accompany us to Lutzi on the morrow and introduce us to the priest, whom we had been so near without knowing it when we first entered the country.

We took a look round the kraal before taking our leave. The cattle are all housed in the centre of it. There was the pigeon-cote, a feature in all the villages about here, consisting of a mud box with holes, raised on poles. Hard by dwelt a hideous black sow with a litter of young ones in a grass sty. There was a hut for the calves and a hut for the goats, a scene of bucolic prosperity which we had come across nowhere else in Mashonaland.

The following morning, after breakfast, we set off for Lutzi once more, armed with presents for the lion priest, and exceedingly curious about him.

Benoula was there before us, and everyone was expecting our arrival. Presently we were ushered into a large but rather dilapidated hut, where sat a venerable-looking old man, who received us and our presents with great cordiality. We seated ourselves on the ground, forming a curious assemblage: the Mondoro and his son, 'Mkateo, his enormously fat daughter Tourla, Benoula, and one or two *indunas*, our three selves, and our interpreter. 'I am the 'Mtoko,' was almost the first thing the old man said, explaining how he considered himself the rightful heir to the chiefdom. 'Next year, when the crops are gathered in, I shall return to the kraal where my brother died, and assume the command of the country.' We soon saw the state of things, which explained many points that had previously been mysterious. 'Mtokoland was threatened with a grave political quarrel, and all the elements of civil war were present. The elders of the country all recognise the Mondoro as their chief; whilst younger men, with everything to gain and little to lose, affect to follow the chief whose kraal we had visited, and whom they speak of as Bedapera at Lutzi, his own name, as distinguished from the dynastic name of 'Mtoko.

WOODEN SPOON.
LUTZI

In his position as religious head of the community lies the Mondoro's strength. 'Here is the Zimbabwe of our land, here the annual sacrifice to the Maklosi of our ancestors now takes place;' that is to say, wherever the chief lives, and wherever the annual sacrifice takes place, there is the Zimbabwe of the chiefdom.

Then we questioned him about the lion god, and he gave us to understand that the Mondoro or lion god of 'Mtoko's country is a sort of spiritual lion which only appears in time of danger, and fights for the men of 'Mtoko; all good men of the tribe, when they die, pass into the lion form and reappear to fight for their friends. It is quite clear that these savages entertain a firm belief in an after-life and a spiritual world, and worship their ancestors as spiritual intercessors between them and the vague Muali or God who lives in Heaven.

The lion of 'Mtoko is the totem of the tribe. We asked the old priest if we should get into trouble if we shot a lion whilst in his country. 'If a lion attacks you,' he replied, 'you may shoot it, for it could not be one of ours; our lions will do the white man no harm, for they are our friends.' There was a charming amount of dignity and sophistry about the old Mondoro. We felt that he was a far better man to rule the country than his nervous, superstitious nephew. Once a year this old Moudoro (the name Mondoro is common in this country both to the sacred lions and the priest) sacrifices a bullock and a goat to the Maklosi or luck spirit of their ancestors. Formerly this ceremony took place at the residence of the old chief, and now here at Lutzi; much beer is drunk on the occasion, and it takes place in February, about the same time as the Matabele war-dance.

There is much more of the old spirit of the race about the Mondoro. He gave us the names of three generations of 'Mtokos who had ruled here before his brother—a rare instance of pedigree in this country; but the royal residence, Lutzi, is a miserable place, consisting of two little kraals crowning the two summits of a bare granite hill. One tree of sickly growth stood there, decorated, for what reason I could not discover, with part of a woman's bark dress, grass roots, hair, and other oddments. Doubtless they were luck signs too, but we could gain no information on this point. Evidence of festivities was also present in the shape of drums and long chains of grass cases for beads, which they hang round their calves to rattle at the dances. On a hill opposite stood a single hut, where an outlaw had lived till quite recently, they told us.

Before we took our leave the Mondoro presented us with a goat, regretting that, owing to the bad times, he could not give us a handsomer present. We now understood several points which had been a mystery to us before—the constant and rather deferential way in which the 'Mtoko had spoken of his uncle, and the reason why, in the first instance, our guides had told us that the 'Mtoko dwelt at Lutzi. Also we now seemed thoroughly to grasp the strange cult of the lion god, a cult probably carrying us back to the far-distant ages, when the Arabian tribes invented the system of totems, and called the stars by their names.[1]

Monteiro and Gamitto, two Portuguese travellers, who went to Cazembe in 1831-32, throw some light on the worship of the lion. They relate how the negroes near the Zambesi, ' being Munyaes, subjects of Monomatapa, revere royal lions of great corpulence as containing the souls of their ancestors. When the Munyaes discover the lions eating their prey, they go on their knees at a distance, and creep, clapping their hands and begging them with humility to remember their slaves, who are hungry, and that when they were men they were always generous; so that the lions may retire and the negroes profit by what they leave behind.' This is again another link connecting these people with the Zambesi and lands farther north. We were also told a story of how, during the old 'Mtokos' struggles with the Portuguese, lions had been seen to attack the enemy, whilst they left the natives alone. Doubtless a faith of this kind is very conducive to valour, and may account for the superiority of the men of 'Mtoko over their neighbours.

The two above-quoted Portuguese travellers mention many Zimbabwes on their route northwards to Cazembe, and in another part of their work they often make mention of the Monomatapa, especially

---

[1] Kremer, *Akademie der Wissenschaft*.

the Monomatapa of Chidima, whom they speak of as 'a much decayed person, but still respectable.' His territory commences at Tete and goes on to Zumbo, 'and when one dies all make civil war, until one gets possession, and sends to the governor of Tete to confirm his title.'

BUSHMAN DRAWING NEAR 'MTOKO'S KRAAL

From what I can make out of the older Portuguese accounts, the district of Chidima was formerly in the mountains to the north of 'Mtoko's. This was the district where the famous silver mines were supposed to be, in searching for which several Portuguese expeditions came to grief. In fact, it would appear that 'Mtoko, Mangwendi, Makoni, and the chiefs in this part of the country are the modern representatives of the broken-up Monomatapa empire, who, fortunate in the possession of a rugged and mountainous country, escaped the visitation of the Zulu hordes, who on their way southwards probably passed by the more open high plateau of Mashonaland.

OUR EMBASSY TO THE CHIEF 'MTOKO

Next morning, whilst we were packing for our start from 'Mtoko's, I was informed of the existence of some Bushman drawings under an overhanging rock

BUSHMAN DRAWING NEAR 'MTOKO'S KRAAL

about half a mile from our camp. I hurried thither and took some hasty sketches of them. The rock is

BUSHMAN DRAWING NEAR 'MTOKO'S KRAAL

literally covered with these drawings in colours of red, yellow, and black, which had evidently eaten into the granite, so that the figures are preserved to us. They represent all sorts of wild animals such as elephants, kudus, and cynocephalous apes; these are wonderfully well executed; the figures of warriors with poised spears and quivers of arrows are, however, grotesque. The most curious fact about them is finding these drawings so far north, and a close examination of this district will probably bring to light many more. The people who made these drawings inhabited all this district and down into Manicaland. Specimens, too, are found near Fort Salisbury; oddly enough, during our wanderings near Zimbabwe and the Sabi, we never saw any or heard of their existence.

After a ride of eight miles we reached the kraal of Kalimazondo, another son of the late 'Mtoko. It is just a circular collection of wattled huts, all joined together by a stockade. We alighted for a while here and sat in a hut, with a view to putting some leading questions to the chief concerning the state of the country. He told us that, in his opinion, his uncle the Mondoro was the rightful heir to the chiefdom, for his father, the old 'Mtoko, had wished it, but that his brother Bedapera had said: 'I am a man, I wish to be chief.' All the old *indunas* and the head men of the country were on the Mondoro's side, and he had little doubt but that he would succeed in establishing his claim.

When approached on the subject of religion, Kalimazondo grew vague and uncommunicative. We let him know that we had seen the Mondoro, and knew a great deal. To all this he replied: 'I dare not tell you anything, or I should become deaf. I like my gun, and if I was to tell you anything it would be taken away, and I should be no man.' Kalimazondo is a cunning man in his generation, and we saw that we should learn no more about this strange and primitive community than it had pleased the priest of the lion god to tell us.

Close to Kalimazondo's kraal we passed the remains of the hedges or *skerms* which Mr. Selous and his followers had erected to protect their camp when on their visit to the old 'Mtoko, and we congratulated ourselves that it had not been our fate to be driven thus far from headquarters.

Next day we rode through an uninteresting waterless country, and encamped for the night by a stream which formed the southern border of 'Mtoko's country.

CHAPTER XI

THE RUINED CITIES IN MANGWENDI'S, CHIPUNZA'S, AND MAKONI'S COUNTRIES

WE were now once more in the country of Mangwendi, a chief of considerable power, so nearly equal to 'Mtoko, they told me, that the two neighbours, like well-matched dogs, growl but do not come to close quarters.

The noticeable characteristic of this part of the country and all the way down to Manicaland is the number of ruined fortified kraals which one comes across, culminating, as if to a central head, at Chipunza's. These spots have been long deserted and are now overgrown with jungle. We visited one of these just after entering Mangwendi's territories; there is something about them which recalls the Great Zimbabwe—the triple line of fortifications, the entrances slightly rounded; but then the stonework is uneven, the walls being built of shapeless stones, roughly put together with mortar. Here we see none of the even courses, the massive workmanship, and the evidences of years of toil displayed in the more ancient ruins;

the walls are low, narrow, and uneven. Are we to suppose an intermediate race between the inhabitants of Zimbabwe and the present race, who built these ruins? or are we to imagine them to be the work of the Makalangas themselves in the more flourishing days of the Monomatapa rule? I am decidedly myself of the latter opinion. No one who had carefully studied the Great Zimbabwe ruins could for a moment suppose them to be the work of the same people; yet they are just the sort of buildings an uncivilised race would produce, who took as their copy the gigantic ruins they found in their midst. For the next few weeks we were constantly coming across these ruins, and the study of them interested us much.

Mount Masunsgwe was a conspicuous landmark for us for several days about here. It is a massive granite *kopje,* placed as a sort of spur to the range of hills which surrounds 'Mtoko's country. It is also covered with similar ruined stone walls belonging to a considerable town long since abandoned. The next day we crossed a stream near a village, called the Inyagurukwe, where the natives were busily engaged in washing the alluvial soil in search of gold. We halted for the night by another stream, under the impression that Mangwendi's was only about four miles off, and that an easy day was in store for us. But the fates willed otherwise. Shortly after passing a large village, where the inhabitants were more than usually importunate to see my wife's hair, screaming 'Voudzi! voudzi!'—Hair! hair!—as they scampered by our side until she gratified their curiosity, we all lost our way in an intricate maze of Kaffir paths. Our interpreter was ahead and took one way; my wife and I on horseback, in attempting to follow him, took another; Mr. Swan on foot took another; and what happened to the men with the donkeys we never knew, for they did not reach Mangwendi's till late in the after-

MANGWENDI'S KRAAL.

noon, complaining bitterly of their wanderings. We thought we were making straight for our goal, when, lo and behold! we found ourselves at the top of a hill near one of the deserted towns, tenanted only by a tribe of baboons. Our position was critical—we did not know which way to turn, when luckily we espied two little Kaffir boys, who guided us to Mangwendi's; and, worn out with our long hot ride, we made a frugal meal by the side of a stream before ascending to the kraal.

Mangwendi's kraal is a large one, and situated curiously on the top of a lofty ridge. On turning to a Portuguese writer, Antonio Bocarro, who gives, in his thirteenth decade of his chronicle of India, an interesting account of the empire of Monomatapa, he says: The 'Monomatapa are of the Mocaranga race, a free race who do not have defensive arms, nor fortresses, nor surrounded cities.' This seems at first sight rather against the theory that the Monomatapa erected these hill fortresses, but then we must bear in mind that the Portuguese penetrated but little into these districts; and, furthermore, we found at Chipunza's kraal, a few days' journey off, the natives actually constructing similar walls around their chief kraal, evidently a heritage of stone building retained by them from some higher form of civilisation.

Bocarro gives us further information concerning the Monomatapa. He enumerates the chief officers of the kingdom, and amongst others he mentions 'Manguendi' as the chief wizard, or witch-doctor; he also mentions 'Makoni, king of Maungo,' as a vassal of the Monomatapa; and on inquiry at Makoni's we learnt that his country is still called Unga, and the tribal name is Maunga, just as Mangwendi's is called Noia and the tribe Manoia. Furthermore, he mentions one Chiburga as the majordomo of a large town where the chief's wives were kept, probably the lofty hill we visited near the Sabi.[1] Thus Bocarro furnishes us with almost positive proof that the same people dwell here now as dwelt here under the rule of the Monomatapa, the only difference being that the Mocaranga race has split up into numerous branches. Over two of these Mangwendi and Makoni still exercise sway, still retaining their old dynastic names, and still inhabiting what once was the heart of the Monomatapa country. For these reasons I feel pretty confident in asserting that the series of ruined cities amongst which we had now entered is what remains to us of the once powerful chiefdom of Monomatapa.

In Mangwendi's country, as in 'Mtoko's, the great worship is sacrificing to ancestors, called here Bondoro, a name remarkably like the lion god Mondoro. The Bondoro are supposed to intercede for them with Muali, or God, and to get for them long life and prosperity. In Mangwendi's country, however, it is the head of each family who performs the sacrifice, with the help of a man called Nanza, the witch-doctor, one of the chief's family, but by no means having the same power as the Mondoro in 'Mtoko's country. They go to the ruined town which we had accidentally visited, where probably the tribe lived in former days. Here the bullock or goat is sacrificed, everyone present is sprinkled with the blood, and they put out portions of the meat, together with some beer, for the consumption of the Bondoro, and eat the rest themselves.

[1] Chap. VIII.

On the anniversary of the death of the last Mangwendi they assemble from all the country round and hold a great feast in honour of the late chief, at which the present chief conducts the sacrifice. Dos Santos, in his 'De Asia,' describes almost the same thing as taking place amongst the Mocarangas in his day: 'Obsequies are made every year to defunct kings; every year, in the month of September, when the first moon appears, the king makes grand obsequies for his predecessors, who are all buried there on a high rock where he lives, called Zimbaohe.' This hill-set village, where the people of Mangwendi now sacrifice, is still called by them their Zimbabwe. Dos Santos describes the eating, drinking, and dancing just as it might be done now.

Another curious custom to which Dos Santos also alludes is continued amongst them to-day. At Mangwendi's, during the ploughing season, they only work for five consecutive days; they observe the sixth, and call it Muali's day, and rest in their huts and drink beer. The chief always announces this day of rest publicly to his tribe. Dos Santos gives the following account of it: 'There are days on which they are not to work, appointed by the king, unknown to them, when they make feasts, and they call these days Mozimos, or the days of the holy who are already dead.' The term Mozimo for the spirits of ancestors is still used in many parts of the country, and has been compared with the term *molimo*, used by the Bechuana for the Supreme Being. Alvarez mentions the *muzimo* as the god of the Monomatapa, and Gravenbroek (A.D. 1695) also states: 'Divinitatem aliquam Messimo dictam in lucis summo cultu venerantur.' This day of rest is observed during the ploughing season only; it may possibly be of Semite origin, but more probably has been suggested by the obvious necessity and advantage of intervening days of rest during a period of hard work.

Mangwendi's kraal is a very fine one, quite a long climb from the spot where we were encamped. It is surrounded by palisades, and at the entrance is a tree filled with trophies of the chase, the antlers of many deer, and the skins of many wild beasts, which present quite an imposing appearance. The chief was seated on a rock outside, chatting with his *indunas*, when we arrived. He took us into the village and had beer fetched for our delectation. He is an extremely courteous, gentlemanly man, and seems most friendly to the white men who come in his way; and as his kraal is not very far from the new road into Manicaland, and as this district is very populous, he is constantly visited by traders and others.

Mangwendi has ten wives, and two young girls, whom he has bought but not yet married, and his family consists of ten sons and ten daughters, one of whom, a bright-looking girl of about fifteen, came down to our camp to sell us meal and beer. Unfortunately we could get little else, for the traders had bought up all the available provisions, and from this point until we reached Umtali we suffered more from starvation than during any part of our journeyings in Mashonaland. 'Mtoko's bullock was done; we could get no meat at any of the kraals, or game along our road; our coffee, sugar, and jams were all done, and our meals, with rare exceptions, reduced themselves to millet-meal porridge, rice, and tea, none of which were very palatable without the ingredients of milk and sugar; and the provoking thing about Kaffir meal is that it will not bind to make bread, so that for the staff of life cold rice made into a shape was our only substitute. We generally kept our pockets full of the ground-nuts (*arachis*), commonly called 'monkey-nuts,' which are excellent when roasted in the embers, and capital assistants in warding off hunger.

On leaving Mangwendi's we had regretfully to part with our bearers, who had accompanied us all the way from Kunzi's, and engage fresh ones in their place. One of these, to our surprise, chose to take his wife with him, but as she had to carry her baby on her back and food for herself and her husband, she, poor thing, was so done up after our first day's march of seventeen miles, that her husband sent her back again.

Our first camp after leaving Mangwendi's was at a very interesting spot—an isolated granite *kopje* called Nyanger, rising about two hundred feet above the surrounding plain. It was entirely covered with old walls, irregular in shape, and similar to those above mentioned, and evidently in former years a place of great strength. It had been long abandoned, for there were no signs of habitation thereon, and the approaches were full of *débris*. To the north-east of this *kopje* is a very curious grotto, or domed cave, entirely covered with Bushman drawings. A kudu and a buffalo are excellently drawn, almost worthy of a Landseer, and in their drawings one can distinctly trace three different periods of execution: (1) Crude and now faint representations of unknown forms of animal life. (2) Deeper in colour, and admirably executed, partly on the top of the latter, are the animals of the best period of this art in red and yellow. (3) Inartistic representations of human beings, which evidently belong to a period of decadence in the execution of this work.

The colours are invariably red, yellow, and black. I am told that the two former are obtained from certain coprolites found in these parts, which, when broken open, have a yellow dust inside.

In this curiously decorated cave we found also many graves formed by plastering up holes in the rock with a hard kind of cement. We opened one of them, and found that the corpse had been wrapped in skins and placed here. In the centre of the cave is a large semicircular wall, entered in the middle by a rounded entrance; behind this is a sort of palisade of grass matting placed against poles, to protect it from the wind, and behind this are similar cement-covered graves. Now the present race do not bury in this way, but evidently come here at certain times to keep the place in order, and doubtless venerate the spot as the resting-place of remote ancestors. There are also several other graves on the flat space around Nyanger rock, piles of stones placed around a crescent-shaped wall, which is evidently a sort of rudimentary temple in which the sacrifices take place.

On our march that day we passed several of these cemeteries in the open *veldt* far from any trace of

BUSHMAN DRAWINGS FROM NYANGER ROCK

habitation. They are generally placed on slightly rising ground, and always have the semicircular structure, which reminded us of the stones placed at the village of Lutzi, where the inhabitants collected to smoke and talk, protected from the wind. These spots are evidently still venerated, and form another of the many problems connected with the past in this district of Africa. I think they are the places to which Dos Santos alludes in the following paragraph, where he refers to the chiefs who 'make grand obsequies to their predecessors, who are all buried there.' In a memoir written by Signor Farao, governor of Senna in 1820, there is a curious testimony to this theory. He writes: 'The mountains of Magonio (Makoni?), in Quiteve, were noted as the burial-places of the kings and queens of Quiteve, Gembe and Dombo. The remains were carried in procession to the caves, where they were deposited alongside the bones of former kings, and some of the most esteemed women of the deceased, or his secretary, and some of the great people, were sacrificed at the ceremony.'

Most of the granite *kopjes* in this district have been similarly fortified to Nyanger rock. Time would not permit of our visiting many of them, but I am certain that a careful investigation of this district would produce many valuable additions to the already large collections of Bushman drawings. The fortifications of these rocks are generally in rows of walls in terraces with narrow rounded entrances; they are all constructed in a rough manner, with irregular-shaped stones joined together with cement.

Near the river Chimbi, which we crossed shortly before reaching Chipunza's kraal, there is a particularly interesting specimen of this class of ruin. The rocky *kopje* is fortified with walls, all the nooks and crannies being carefully walled up, and below this is a curious half-underground passage which evidently connected the fortress with its water supply; it has a wall on either side of it—one four feet thick, and the other eight feet thick; and the passage is roofed over with large slabs of stone, some four and some five feet long. This passage can now be traced for about fifty feet; it is nearly choked up with rubbish, but the object for which it was originally constructed is obvious, as it leads down to low swampy ground, where water could be obtained.

A mile or two beyond this we alighted for a short time at a pretty village called Makonyora, which had been surrounded by a palisade which had taken root and grown into shady trees of considerable size. The inhabitants seemed numerous and well to do. In this village there are many instances of walls constructed like those we had seen in the ruined villages; the foundations for the huts and granaries also are of stone, so that the air may pass underneath, forming neatly executed stone circles. The various gullies between the rocks are carefully walled up, and you pass from one collection of huts to the other through low entrances in these walls. There is no doubt about it, that these people here possess an inherited knowledge of stone building which exists nowhere else in Kaffirland, unless it be amongst the Basutos, who, I am told, are skilled in stone building, and who, at a not very remote period, are believed to have migrated from this very country. It seems to me hardly possible that the gigantic buildings of Zimbabwe and places in this country can have existed in their midst without the inhabitants making some attempt to copy them; and here we have an imitation, though a poor one, in the heart of what was the strongest chiefdom of the country.

The aspect of the country is here very curious, the high level plateau (it is about 5,000 feet above sea level) is, as it were, closely sown for miles around with rugged granite *kopjes*, some only fifty feet high, whilst others reach an elevation of several hundred feet. They are very evenly arranged, too, as if they were the pieces for a cyclopean game of chess. Through this region we passed, and at the eastern end of it we reached our destination, Chipunza's kraal, where we proposed to halt for a day or two. Chipunza's is a very large village, built on a gentle rise on the right bank of the Rusapi River, with huts packed away into all sorts of snug corners amongst the rocks. Immediately below these, and within easy reach of the river, we pitched our tents. It was a great disappointment to us to be able to get no meat here. Our meals, which were composed entirely of things farinaceous, were growing exceedingly monotonous, and we almost hated the sight of the porridge-pot, which turned up with unvarying regularity. As against this, the air at Chipunza's was the finest I have ever breathed, exhilarating like draughts of champagne.

When we reached the village we found the ladies of Chipunza with their bark blankets tied tight around them, for it was chilly, seated in picturesque and strange groups amongst the rocks, busily engaged in a still stranger occupation. They were burning little

CHIFUNZA'S KRAAL

heaps of cowdung, and then spreading the results on the rocks to cool. Not understanding what they were about we approached them, when, to our surprise, an old crone picked up a lump of this delectable material, put it into her mouth and consumed it with evident satisfaction, muttering, as she saw our unfeigned surprise, 'Salt, salt; good, good!' and then we realised that here they use the extract of nitre from the ash as their substitute for salt, the commodity of life for which they have the greatest craving, but which it is hardest to obtain.

In the afternoon we went to pay a visit to the chief, who received us in a sort of inner fortress surrounded by a wall, through an opening in which, about three feet high, and covered with large slabs of stone, we had to creep. He is a grey-haired, refined-looking man, with manners very like, and not the least inferior to, an Arab sheikh. He sat surrounded by his councillors, and we all set to work to clap hands vigorously. By this time my wife had learnt to clap hands in the female fashion, namely, crosswise, whereas previously she had disgraced herself by clapping like a man, with the fingers straight upon one another; but, of course, the intricacies of savage etiquette can only be acquired by practice.

After a little conversation had passed between us, a woman, one of the chief's wives, made her appearance, bending her body humbly, and carrying a large pot full of *wa-wa*, as they term beer in this part of the country. This she presented to her lord and master on bended knee, after having previously drunk a little herself, to convince us that there was no poison in it; then the chief took a drink, then his councillors, and finally it was handed to us. We found it was lovely beer, very potent, and after our long abstinence from anything so intoxicating, as exhilarating as the air.

We were much struck by the courteous manners of the natives here. One man, on receiving a present, bowed low and scraped the ground with his feet. There is something about these people which points distinctly to a higher form of civilisation having existed amongst them at a former time; and when one reads Dos Santos's account of the Mocarangas of Monomatapa of his day, one cannot help feeling that they are the remnant of that higher civilisation about which the early Portuguese travellers tell us so much.

'The Portuguese,' says Dos Santos, 'did not enter the king's presence, like the Kaffirs, with deep obeisance, only with bare feet;' and in a curious old treaty published in the Portuguese Yellow-book, and purporting to have been made between the Monomatapa chief Manuza and Manuel Gomes Serrao in 1629, the following stipulation is inserted:—

'The ambassadors who shall come to speak with him shall enter his Zimbahe covered and shod (with boots on their feet) and with their arms at their sides, as if they were before the King of Portugal. He shall give them chairs upon which to sit, and they shall not be submitted to the ceremony of the clapping of hands.'

Chipunza has another name, Chipadzi. The exact relation between these two names we were unable to ascertain; Chipadzi, however, I believe to be the old dynastic name of the chief. His Zimbabwe, or place of sacrifice, is about a mile from the present village, at a spot called Chittakette, or the Chipadzi's old town. To this place we were to be taken on the morrow. We found it an interesting old spot, buried in trees and with tomatoes and tobacco plants all amongst the ruined walls. It evidently had had a wooden palisade around it, which had sprouted and produced the venerable trees, and it had an inner fortress with walls encircling it, and low gateways through, with large stone slabs over them. It is an excellent specimen of this rough style of fortress: the walls are from six to eight feet thick, with loopholes out of which to shoot, built with no attempt at keeping even courses, and with mortar. Within the fortress are the remains of huts and granaries, as if the place had not been abandoned for very many years.

Just outside is Chipadzi's tomb, with a tall stone erected over it, and the surrounding ground is covered with tombs. This spot is called the Zimbabwe by the natives, where they sacrifice annually to the Maklosi of their ancestors.

We spent two days wandering amongst the granite rocks around Chipunza's kraal, and we found evidence of a vast population having lived here at some period. Nearly every one of the granite *kopjes* is fortified with walls, and on some of them we found graves of cement similar to those we saw at Nyanger rock; and on the hill just behind Chipunza's kraal a tall stone is erected on a pile of stones, the object of which nobody seemed inclined to tell us.

How long ago it is since these walled towns were inhabited, and who inhabited them, is, of course, a mystery. There is, however, no evidence of any great antiquity about them; the mortar may have stood for a few centuries, but not more; and from the evidence given us by the Portuguese, above quoted, from the continuity of certain names and many customs, and from the fact that the present inhabitants still retain a certain knowledge of stone building, I think it is a very reasonable assumption that this was one of the great centres of the so-called Monomatapa Empire.

After leaving Chipunza's kraal, and crossing the River Rusapi, a ride of two hours brought us to Makoni's kraal. Makoni, chief of the Maunga tribe, is still one of the most powerful potentates in this district. He, too, calls his town Zimbabwe, and it is doubtless the same spot occupied by Makoni, chief of the Maungo, one of the great vassals of the Monomatapa that Antonio Bocarro tells us about three centuries ago.

It is probably the highest inhabited spot in Mashonaland, being 5,200 feet above the level of the sea, just at the edge of the high plateau, where it breaks into the serrated ridges of Manicaland. The town covers a very large area of ground, being a conglomerate mass of huts and granaries surrounded by a palisade. We spent about an hour resting there at a sort of public meeting-place surrounded by a wall, where the inhabitants collected in crowds to stare at us. Most of the men had very large holes pierced in the lobes of their ears, into which they would insert snuff-boxes of reeds, decorated with black geometric patterns, and other articles. The women are all girt with the same bark-fibre garments which we had seen worn in 'Mtoko's country. Accompanied by a swarthy rabble, we climbed a rock behind the town, from which we got an exquisite view down into the valleys of Manica, bearing eastwards—a view of rugged mountains tumbled together, of deep valleys and running streams—a view such as one would get when descending from the Alps into the plain of Italy. Chief Makoni never came to see us, and as our time was limited we had to hurry away without making his acquaintance.

Almost immediately on leaving Makoni's our road began to descend, and we entered upon a series of richly wooded gorges, flanked by gigantic granite cliffs. On one of these pinnacles, about the height of Makoni's own kraal, is perched Chigono's village, occupying a most wonderful position. How they ever manage to drag up here a sufficiency of water and the necessaries of life is a marvel. One thing they have in perfection is climate. We found it hot and stuffy in the valleys, but in their mountain eyries the Kaffirs enjoy the most perfect air that it is possible to breathe.

On the third day after leaving Chipunza's, one of our men had the good luck to shoot an antelope, an event which was hailed with delight by all in our camp. We had never in our lives been so long without meat, and the want of it was beginning to be felt by all. On the fourth day we crossed the Odzi River, the boundary between Mashonaland and Manicaland. It is a fine stream even here, with a good body of water even at the end of the dry season, on its way to join the Sabi River, just where we touched it a few weeks before. At the point where we crossed the Odzi the stream was sixty feet across, and the bed is at least one hundred yards wide, and when the rains are on it must be a terrible obstacle. Even as it was we had to unload the donkeys and carry their burdens across, which means, when the afternoon is advancing, a halt for the night.

A ride of twelve miles brought us next day to the kraal of 'Mtasa, the most powerful of all the Manica chiefs. He is the paramount lord of the Nica tribe, which gives its name to the country, and dwells in the heart of the most mountainous district we had as yet traversed. A mass of mountains, known to the natives as Mount Yenya, occupies the heart of his country. 'Mtasa's kraal itself is over 4,000 feet above the sea level, and above this the rocky mountains tower 2,000 feet at least. Here, though not actually as high as Makoni's, you feel much higher, looking down into the deep valleys below, and seeing no high plateau behind you. Amongst these mountains lie numerous scattered kraals, excellent grazing-ground for cattle, and from marauding neighbours 'Mtasa is free. Nevertheless, during the last two years poor 'Mtasa has had rather a bad time of it, being the bone of contention between the Portuguese and English chartered companies. Early in 1891, in the very centre of this kraal, a small English contingent captured Andrade, Gouveia, and the representatives of the Mozambique Company, and now the British flag floats over it.

'Mtasa's kraal is quite one of the most extraordinary ones we had yet visited, being a nest of separate villages, each surrounded by its own stockade, hidden away amongst granite boulders beneath the shade of a lofty mountain. It is almost impossible to form any idea of the exact extent of this place, so hidden away is it amongst trees and rocks, and so intricate are its approaches; but, if report tells truly, which it does not always do in South Africa, it is one of the largest native centres in the country. We wandered up to a village the first afternoon, a considerable climb from our camp. Little groups of natives sat chattering under the shade of open huts, or just roofs on piles, the rudimentary form of the café or the club: there were pigeon-cotes on piles in all directions, and at every turn we found ourselves blocked by palisades, which caused us to retrace our steps; so, as we intended to stay another day here, we contented ourselves with gazing at the magnificent view, the peaked heights of the Yenya range, the deep wooded valley below with its dashing stream, and far away in the horizon the distant blue Manica mountains. Certainly no kraal we had as yet visited enjoys such excellent views as 'Mtasa's. The huts here are large and roomy, at the side they have two tall decorated posts to support shelves for their domestic produce; most of them have two doors, and with the dense shade of many trees above them they are exceedingly picturesque.

On our second visit to the kraals we met 'Mtasa's son, who regretted that his aged father was ill just then, and had gone away for change of air. We took leave of him, and climbed up through rocks and through palisade after palisade, shutting off the various kraals from one another; one of these we entered by a curious gateway made by swinging beams, and penetrated into the headquarters of the old chief. By this time we noticed that the people began to glare at us unpleasantly and audibly to grumble. Seated in rows on the rocks, they chattered to us like angry monkeys, but we went on without heeding them. One man, with a bayonet fixed on to his rifle, followed unpleasantly close behind us; and then, as we were about to penetrate into what I suppose formed

DECORATED POST

their innermost recesses, 'Mtasa's son, who, by the way, had had more beer than was good for him, came up to us in hot haste, and peremptorily commanded us to depart. Again he reiterated the statement that his father was away, and during his absence none could see the royal kraal; so, somewhat crestfallen, we turned back again and saw no more. Afterwards we were informed that the old 'Mtasa was there all the time, but, as he had suffered so much lately from the conflicting interests of England and Portugal, he thought it best not to see us, for fear we might make him sign some new treaty against his will.

Of all the natives we had met during our wanderings, those of 'Mtasa's pleased us least; they appeared to us to be completely wanting in all delicacy of feeling, and had to be driven by force from our tents. They seemed to us to be an ill-bred, impudent race, and though their home was so lovely we left it without regret. Somehow, too, our visit to 'Mtasa's kraal was altogether unsatisfactory; we left it with the consciousness that there were mysteries in it which we had not yet explored. At the very last moment, just as we were packing up our things, I chanced to see on a rock close by our camp some more of the Bushman drawings, grotesque figures of men with bows and arrows and deer grazing, in the usual colours of red and yellow. I feel confident that in the massive mountain behind the kraal some more fortunate travellers will find objects of interest which will well repay investigation. We have distinctly unpleasant recollections of the place, as we have also of a certain dangerous slippery drift or ford across the River Odzani, which we found about half way between 'Mtasa's and the B.S.A. camp at Umtali. We had to take off our shoes and stockings and lead our horses across the slippery rocks; they, poor things, slipped at every step and trembled with fright. As for our donkeys, they subsided altogether, and had to be unloaded and almost carried across.

CHAPTER XII

THE JOURNEY TO THE COAST

We reached Umtali on October 24, just a month after leaving Fort Salisbury. We were distinctly weary and wayworn, and having had but little food of late we partook of the refreshments kindly set before us by the officers of the Chartered Company with, to us, unparalleled heartiness. At Umtali we pitched our tents near a stream with every intention, as time would permit, of taking a few days of rest and retrospect before starting on the arduous journey down to the coast.

We had now travelled through the greater part of Mashonaland, as, I suppose, the new country must inevitably be called; we had studied the archæology and anthropology of the districts through which we had passed with all the diligence that hard travelling and hard work would allow. Mr. Swan had constructed a map of the route from observations and bearings taken at every possible opportunity by day and by night; and at the same time we had formed opinions on the country from our own point of view, perhaps all the more unbiassed because we were not in search of gold, neither had we pegged out any claims for future development.

That the country is a magnificent one, apart from gold, I have no hesitation in saying. Any country in such a latitude, and at such an elevation, well watered, with prolific soil, healthy and bracing, if ordinary comforts are attainable, could not fail to be. The scenery is in many parts, as I have previously described, very fine; there is abundance of timber, excellent prospects for cereals, and many kinds of ore exist which will come in for future development; and gold is there too. On that point I am perfectly satisfied; whether in large or small quantities, whether payable or unpayable, is a matter which can only be decided by years of careful prospecting and sinking of shafts, not by hasty scratching on the surface or the verdict of so-called 'experts' after a hurried visit. That gold was there in very large quantities is also certain, from the vast acres of alluvial soil, turned over, and the countless shafts sunk in remote antiquity.

To carry out what is necessary for this possible future development, or, perhaps, to speak more correctly, resuscitation of this country, an easy access is indispensable, and the great check to this progress hitherto has been the absence of railways in South Africa on the eastern seaboard, the natural and easiest entrance to the country being in the hands of the listless Portuguese. Progress is impossible with Kimberley as a base of operations and a thousand miles *trek* over difficult and swampy roads before the scene of action is reached. In Western America the railway is the first thing, development comes next; and inasmuch as the Chartered Company have tried the converse of this—to put the cart before the horse, to use a familiar simile—they have met with innumerable difficulties at the very outset.

Having entered the country by the weary waggon-road through Bechuanaland, and having left it by the now somewhat arduous Pungwe route, I can confidently affirm that this latter is the only possible route; and I now propose to describe it as it at present exists, feeling sure that in years to come, when the railway hurries the traveller up to Umtali, when the venomous tsetse-fly no longer destroys all transport animals, when lions cease to roar at night, and the game has retired to a respectful distance, a back glimpse at the early days of this route will be historically interesting.

Umtali is the natural land terminus of this route, as Beira is its legitimate port. Umtali, so called from a rivulet which flows below it, was, when we were there, a scattered community of huts, now brought together in a 'township' at a more favourable spot, about five miles distant from the former site, which township the British South Africa Company hope to call Manica, and to make it the capital of that portion of Manicaland which they so dexterously, to use an Africander term, 'jumped' from the Portuguese. Of all their camps Umtali was the most favourably situated that we visited, enjoying delicious air, an immunity from swamps and fevers, lovely views, and many flowers. On the ridge, where the camp huts stood exposed to the violent and prevailing blasts of the south-east winds, which descend in furious gusts from the surrounding mountains, stood also the guns taken from the Portuguese, nine in all, and presenting a formidable enough appearance, until we learnt that they were useless then, for the pins were abstracted before capture. Far away on the hill slopes were the huts of the original settlers; the bishop's palace likewise, a daub hut standing in the midst of a goodly mission farm. The hospital, with the sisters' huts, crowned another eminence, and the newly made fort stood on the highest point, from which glorious views could be obtained over the sea of Manica mountains, the rich red soil and green vegetation, so pleasant a change to the eye after the everlasting grey granite *kopjes* of Mashonaland and its uniform vegetation.

Of ancient Portuguese remains there are several in the neighbourhood of Umtali fort, where centuries ago the pioneers held their own for awhile against native aggression. To-day, if you dine at the officers' mess at Umtali, you find evidences of Portugal of another nature. You sit on Portuguese chairs and feed off Portuguese plates obtained from the loot at Massi-Kessi; and when the governor of that district came to pay an amicable visit to the governor of Umtali, they had nothing to seat him on save his own chairs, nothing to feed him off save his own plates, and nothing to give him to eat save his own tinned meats. But Portuguese politeness rose to the occasion, and no remarks were made.

Crossing a stream below the fort, we found ourselves amidst a collection of circular daub huts and stores, on either side of what a facetious butcher, who dealt largely in tough old transport oxen, had termed in his advertisement 'Main Street.' Here you might pay enormous prices for the barest necessities of life, and drink at old Angus's bar a glass of whisky at the same price you could get a bottle for in England. Scotch is the prevailing accent here, and I think the greatest gainers out of Mashonaland, in the first year of its existence, were those canny traders who loaded waggons with jams and drink, and sold them at fabulous prices to hungry troopers and thirsty prospectors. Old Angus was a typical specimen of this class, a sandy-haired little Scotchman, well up in colonial ways, who kept two huts, in one of which eating, drinking, and gossip were always to be found; whilst the other was divided into three bare cells, and called an hotel.

Such was the first Umtali, primitive and fascinating in its rawness. Now these huts are abandoned to the rats and the rain, and a new Umtali of doubtful expansion has been built five miles away.

Our journey from Umtali to Beira was one which required much forethought. First, we had much luggage, which we did not wish to leave behind or bury on the way, as others had been obliged to do; secondly, my wife did not feel inclined to do the one

B B

hundred and eighty miles on foot, through heat and swamp, in tropical Africa; and thirdly, the Kaffir bearers were scarce, and especially—at that season of the year, when their fields wanted ploughing—apt to run away at awkward moments. So the services of the homely ass were brought into requisition. The ass would die of the fly-bite, everyone told us, but not until it had deposited us safely in Beira. Consequently our eleven asses were retained in our service and considered in the light of the railway tickets of the future, to be used and thrown away. It seemed horribly cruel, I must admit, to condemn eleven asses to certain death; but then, what are animals made for but to lay down their lives to satisfy the requirements of man in his dire emergencies?

A cart was constructed on two firm wheels, the wonder of its day. Eight donkeys were harnessed therein, with gear made out of every imaginable scrap. Three donkeys trotted gaily by its side, to be brought into requisition in case of sore backs and other disasters; and one wet evening we despatched our hopeful cart with our blessing on its road to the coast. It would take three or four days getting by the waggon-road to Massi-Kessi, whilst we could cross the mountains in one. So next morning, we on foot and my wife on horseback, started by the mountain road for Massi-Kessi, and got there as evening was coming on. A good walk in any of the mountainous districts of the British Isles would have been just the same. A drenching mist obscured every vision, the paths were slippery and uneven; occasionally a glimpse at a stream with bananas waving in the mist, or at a Kaffir kraal, would dispel the homelike illusion, and bring us back to Africa again. Towards evening the aggravating mist cleared away, and gave us a splendid panorama of the surrounding mountains as we approached Massi-Kessi and entered the valley of the River Revwe. Just here we walked for miles over ground which had been worked for alluvial gold in the olden days, the soil being honeycombed with low holes, and presenting the appearance of a ploughed field with circular furrows.

Certainly the Portuguese, or rather the Mozambique Company, are to be congratulated on the possession of such a paradise as this Revwe Valley—fertile in soil, rich in water, glorious in its views over forest-clad mountains; and it is not to be wondered at that they keenly resented the temporary appropriation of it. Massi-Kessi and its neighbourhood are rich in reminiscences of the Portuguese past; the new fort, where the new company has its store, was built out of the remains of an old Portuguese fort, around which you may still pick up fragments of Nankin porcelain, relics of those days, now long since gone by, when the Portuguese of Africa, India, and the Persian Gulf lived in the lap of luxury, and fed off porcelain brought by their trading-ships from China. Higher up in the mountain valleys are forts and roads of this occupation. As in the Persian Gulf, as in Goa and elsewhere, the Portuguese influence vanished in East Africa after her union with Spain and the consequent drafting off of her soldiers to the wars in Flanders; barely a phantom of her former power remained to her in the province of Mozambique. A few futile expeditions under Barretto, Fernandez, and others were destroyed either by the natives or by fever, during one of which the legend is still told that the defenders of this fort of Massi-Kessi were obliged to cast bullets out of gold nuggets when cheaper material came to an end. After this the inland country was practically abandoned to the savages. Old treaties existed but were not renewed; lethargy seemed to have taken entire possession of the few remaining Portuguese who were left here, a lethargy from which they were rudely awakened by the advent of the Chartered Company. What better argument do we want for the reoccupation of this country by a more enterprising race than these forts abandoned and in ruins, and the treaties with savage chiefs long since neglected—consigned to the national archives? The little episode of Massi-Kessi is certainly one which deserves to be engraven on our national records, though it arose from a mistake, and the ground gained had ultimately to be abandoned; nevertheless these facts do in no way detract from the bravery of the Chartered Company's men.

Forty Englishmen of troop A, under the command of Captain Hayman, were stationed about 1,500 yards from the fort at one o'clock on the day of the fight. Messengers were sent from the Portuguese bidding them retire, but Captain Hayman said his orders were to the contrary, and he could not. Thereupon the Portuguese force, mustering 150 white men and 300 blacks, advanced, and the action began. At five o'clock they retreated, with many killed and wounded, but not one single Englishman suffered. Next morning our troops were surprised to find that the Portuguese flag was not up, and on marching to the fort they found it abandoned. Here it was that they took the guns we had seen at Umtali and 110,000 rounds of ammunition. The victorious troops pushed on as far as Chimoia's, and would have driven the Portuguese out of the country had they not then been met by orders to retreat. Massi-Kessi was also eventually abandoned, and by the recent treaty is included in the dominions of the Portuguese Chartered Company. In the store, however, one of the B.S.A. troopers carved the following memento of his visit before taking his departure:—

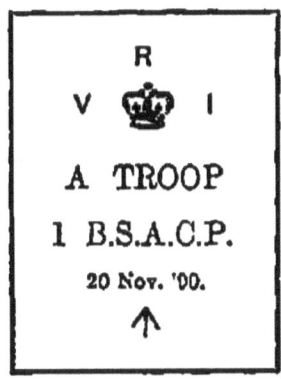

The tradition of good living is still maintained by the Portuguese officials at Massi-Kessi. Never saw I a greater contrast in seventeen miles than that offered by the fare provided at the British camp at Umtali, and that placed before us by the kind Portuguese commandant at Massi-Kessi; here we had six courses of meat and excellent wines, and other, to us, unwonted luxuries. They have farms for vegetables, and many head of cattle around; they have their natives under complete control, and make them work; they build large roomy huts, but the commandant's apologies because we had to sit on wooden boxes, not on chairs, made us blush, for we knew that the said chairs were there once, but now were gracing the British mess-room at Umtali.

When speaking of roughing it in the interior, the want of food and the necessaries of life, Commandant Béthencourt was slightly sarcastic. 'What strange people you English are to do such things!' he said. 'We Portuguese might, perhaps, do them for our country, but for a Company—never!'

Now we started in good earnest for the coast, refreshed by our three days' rest at Massi-Kessi under the kind roof of the Portuguese; our cart had arrived, and our eleven donkeys and men looked fit, despite the evil road they had had to traverse.

Two roads from here were open to us to Beira— one by the Pungwe, the other by the Buzi River. We hesitated somewhat in our choice, for the latter, we were told, was less swampy, and the fertile district of Umliwan would have interested us—where they grow the best tobacco in these parts, and the prospects of which for agricultural purposes, they said, are brilliant; but, as the season was growing late, and the rains might come on any day, we decided on taking the quicker and more frequented route. Moreover, we were anxious to witness for ourselves the calamities which had befallen Messrs. Heany and Johnson on their pioneer route, and to form our own opinion as to its possibility for the future.

Our first halt was at the Mineni River, a tributary of the Revwe, which we reached after an easy journey, marked only by the upsetting of our cart when we least expected it, an accident which occurred for the first and only time. The Mineni is a rapid stream, flanked by rich tropical vegetation, with graceful bamboos and lovely ferns overhanging the water; it supplied a deficiency we had long felt in Mashonaland scenery, namely, water in conjunction with mountains and rich vegetation. The greens are peculiarly vivid here, and the red young leaves of some of the trees give the appearance of autumnal tints, and form a feature peculiar to African landscape. In its rocky bed we dared to bathe without fear of crocodiles, an ever-present terror to those who venture into the sluggish sandy pools of Eastern Africa.

Messrs. Heany and Johnson undoubtedly did good work in preparing their road, for which work we probably are the only people who are devoutly thankful, for ours is the only wheeled vehicle which has traversed it in its entirety since the single pioneer coach went up to Umtali, after infinite difficulty and weeks of disaster, with such sorry tales of fever, fly, and swamp, that no waggons have since ventured to repeat the experiment. The trees which they had cut down, and the culverts which they had made over the *dongas*, assisted us materially, and we stepped along our road right merrily.

The farther we went the more reason we had to be thankful for our frail cart and homely asses. Others we passed in dire distress whose bearers had deserted them, and who could not find more: we overtook one party holding solemn conclave as to what they should throw away, what they should bury, and what they could possibly manage to take on. Boxes, containing liquor, clothes, and other commodities which could be dispensed with, are frequently found on the road, telling their tale of desertion by bearers and acute misery of the possessors.

He who first started the evil plan of paying these dark bearers in advance ought for ever to be held up to public obloquy. The Kaffir, doubtless, has been often cheated by the white man, for many unscrupulous individuals have traversed this road from Umtali to Beira, and the black man was wise in his generation when he insisted on payment before undertaking the journey; but now he has too dangerous an opportunity for retaliation, of which he takes frequent advantage, and many are the cases of desertion at awkward points. A white man, stricken with fever, had to pay his bearers over and over again before he could persuade them to go on; the Sisters on their way to Umtali were deserted at Chimoia; and at the season of the year when the fields are to be ploughed they develop a still greater tendency to this unscrupulous behaviour.

The Portuguese manage their affairs far better than we do. Troops of so-called convicts are shipped from their West African provinces to those on the east coast, and *vice versâ*, so that in both places they have ready-made slaves to carry their baggage and their *mashilas*, or travelling hammocks. The Portuguese word is law with their black subjects, whereas the unfortunate Englishman has to pay 25s. or 2l. for a bearer, who will carry sixty pounds, but will desert when the fancy takes him. Furthermore, the Englishman dare not treat his nigger as he deserves; if he did, he would be had up at once before the Portuguese magistrates, and be sure to get the worst of it. Before the Pungwe route can be made available, even for the lightest traffic, this order of things must cease. The native bearer is undoubtedly a fine specimen of humanity. He will carry on his head weights of surprising size, which it requires two men to lift up to its exalted position; he runs along at a rapid pace, and does his twenty-five to thirty miles a day with infinite ease; and if the desertion and payment question were settled, there would not be so many thousands of pounds' worth of valuable stuff spoiling at Beira, and much wanted at Umtali. Each chief ought to be compelled to supply a fixed number of bearers at a fixed tariff, and cases of desertion should be severely punished. But the way to do this is not clear as yet, for the Portuguese do not wish it, and to the British mind this form of compulsory labour might savour too much of slavery.

With our cart we did eighteen and twenty miles a day; quite far enough for the pedestrian in this warm climate. The first hour's walk, from 6 to 7 A.M., was always delicious, before the full power of the sun was felt; the rest of the day was atrociously hot, especially when our road led us through steaming tropical forests and rank vegetation. Luckily for us at this season of the year the long grass in the open *veldt* was all burnt, and the stifling experience of walking through eight or ten feet of grass and getting no view whatsoever was spared us.

Shade for our midday halts was always precarious. African trees have the character of giving as little shade as possible, and this we found to be invariably the case. Luckily, water is everywhere abundant, and we could assuage our thirst with copious draughts of tea.

The native kraals on this road are highly uninteresting; the inhabitants are wanting altogether in that artistic tendency displayed in Mashonaland, which showed itself in carved knives, snuff-boxes, and weapons. A chief named Bandula occupies a commanding position on a high range which we passed on our left, at the foot of which flows a stream called the Lopodzi, which delighted us with its views over the Nyangombwe Mountains, and offended us with its swampy banks, where the frogs croaked as loud as the caw of the rooks in our woods at home.

Chimoia's kraal is a sort of half-way halt, where all waggons are now left before entering the much-dreaded 'fly belt;' and here my wife parted reluctantly with her horse, and transferred herself and her saddle to the back of one of the three loose asses which accompanied our cart. Most people seem to have two or three asses in their train, for fear of being utterly helpless in case of the desertion of their blacks, and all are prepared for their ultimate demise, either by the violence of the lion or the bite of the fly. One ass at Chimoia's distinguished itself by seizing its master's sugar-bag, and consuming it and its contents with all the greater avidity when the master and his stick turned up. All laughed; but all who had experienced the great calamity of being without sugar in this land felt deep compassion for the victim.

Chimoia's is a scattered kraal, poor and destitute: clusters of round huts with low eaves, and doors through which one has to crawl on hands and knees.

We could get no meal here, as everyone had told us we should, and when talking over our supplies the faces of our men grew long and anxious; and if it had not been for the kindness of other white men whom we met on our way down, famine would have been added to our other discomforts; but good fellowship and spontaneous liberality are the characteristics of all those Englishmen who have been up country, and at one time or another known what it is to be without food. At Chimoia's ends the pleasant traffic in beads and cloth, which for months past had kept our money in our pockets. Here a rupee is asked for every commodity; and some day surprising hoards of these coins will be found in the Kaffir kraals near the coast, for they never spend them, neither do they wear them as ornaments, and it is a marvel to all what they do with them. The vegetation is very fine around Chimoia's, and the land appears wonderfully fertile. On the top of a strangely serrated ridge of mountains behind the village is a deserted Portuguese fort, and a flagstaff with nothing floating therefrom.

Beyond Chimoia's the streams grow more sluggish, and emit more foetid odours, suggestive of fevers. Ragged-leaved bananas, bamboos, and tree-ferns luxuriate in all these streams, which work their way in deep channels, or *dongas*, across the level country.

The fall is now scarcely perceptible, and the long flat belt which girdles Africa is entered, the much-dreaded low *veldt*, teeming with swamps, game, and tsetse-fly. At one time you are walking through a forest of bamboos, making graceful arches overhead with their long canes, and recalling pictures of Japan;

at another time you go through palm forests, and then comes a stretch of burning open country; and at night-time, for the first time, we heard the lions roar. We lighted huge camp-fires and trembled for the safety of our eleven donkeys, for which animals lions are supposed to have a particular predilection.

Mandigo's kraal is twenty-four miles from Chimoia's, and to us was equally uninteresting and equally unproductive of the much-needed supplies. Some say the fly only begins here, and certainly we saw none ourselves till after Mandigo's; and from here to Sarmento we saw plenty of it. The tsetse-fly is grey, about the size of an ordinary horse-fly, with overlapping wings. Our donkeys, poor things, got many bites, and we felt grieved at their prospective deaths. We provided them with the only remedy of which we could hear, namely, a handful of salt every night; but how this is supposed to act in counteracting the bite of the fly I am at a loss to imagine.

Certainly this fly has many peculiarities. All domesticated quadrupeds—horses, oxen, and dogs—die from it when brought up country; whereas zebras, buffaloes, and native curs flourish amongst it with impunity, and its bite has not so much effect upon human beings as that of a common midge.

Ample evidence of the ravages of this venomous insect are visible on the roadside. Dozens of waggons lie rotting in the *veldt*, bearing melancholy testimony to the failure of Messrs. Heany and

Johnson's pioneer scheme. Everywhere lie the bleaching bones of the oxen which dragged them; and at Maudigo's is an abandoned hut filled to overflowing with the skins of these animals, awaiting the further development of the Pungwe traffic to be converted into ropes, or *reims*, as they are usually termed in South Africa. Fully 2,000*l*. worth of waggons, we calculated, as we passed by on one day's march, lies in the *veldt*, ghostlike, as after a battle.

Then there are Scotch carts of more or less value, and a handsome Cape cart, which Mr. Rhodes had to abandon on his way up to Mashonaland, containing in the box-seat a bottle labelled 'Anti-fly mixture,' a parody on the situation.

But the greatest parody of all is at Sarmento itself, a Portuguese settlement on the banks of the Pungwe. Here two handsome coaches, made expressly in New Hampshire, in America, for the occasion, lie deserted near the Portuguese huts. They are richly painted with arabesques and pictures on the panels; 'Pungwe route to Mashonaland' is written thereon in letters of gold. The comfortable cushions inside are being moth-eaten, and the approaching rains will complete the ruin of these handsome but ill-fated vehicles. Meanwhile the Portuguese stand by and laugh at the discomfiture of their British rivals in the thirst for gold. Even the signboard, with 'To Mashonaland,' is in its place; and all this elaborate preparation for the pioneer route has been rendered abortive by that venomous little insect the tsetse-fly. In his zeal to carry out his contract, Major Johnson committed a great error and entailed an enormous amount of misery when he telegraphed that the Pungwe route was open, and circulated advertisements to that effect, giving dates and hours which were never carried out.

Heaps of people, for the most part poor and impecunious, flocked to this entrance to their Eldorado, and after waiting without anything and in abject misery at Chimoia's had to return to Mapanda's, where the condition of affairs was desperate—people dying of fever, the doctor himself ill, and no food, for the Portuguese governor of Neves Ferreira, Colonel Madera, boycotted the English and forbade the natives to bring them provisions. Assistance was brought to them by Dr. Todd, of the *Magicienne*; but many died, and the rest, disappointed and penniless, had to return to Capetown.

The River Pungwe is imposing at Sarmento, its bed being nearly two hundred yards across, and the view of the reaches up and down from the verandah where the Portuguese governor has his meals *al fresco* is fairly striking. But the Pungwe is imposing nowhere else where we saw it, being a filthy, muddy stream, flowing between mangrove swamps, relieved occasionally by a tall palm and villages on piles; the surroundings are perfectly flat, and its repulsive waters were until lately plied only by the tree canoes of the natives. Crocodiles and hippopotami revel in its muddy waters, and on its banks game is abundant enough to satisfy the most ardent sportsman. Deer of every conceivable species are to be seen still quietly grazing within shot of the road; buffaloes, zebras, lions, hyenas, wild pigs, nay, even the elephant, may be found in this corner of the world. Disappointed as the sportsman may have been with the results of his exploits in Mashonaland and the high *veldt*, he will be amply rewarded for the fatigues of his journey to Beira by finding himself in a country which would appear to produce all the kinds of wild animals that came to Adam for their names. One herd of zebra, numbering about fifty, stood staring at us so long, at a distance of not more than a hundred yards, that we were able to photograph them twice. The flesh of the zebra is eatable, and we, with our limited larder, greatly enjoyed a zebra steak when one was shot. A little farther on a *gnu*, or blue *hartebeest*, as the Dutchmen call it, stood and contemplated us with almost as much curiosity as we manifested in seeing him so near our path. But, for my part, no amount of game or quaint tropical sights would compensate for the agonies of the walk from Sarmento to Mapanda's across the shadeless burning plain, beneath a torrid, scorching sun. Now and again we got shelter from the burning rays beneath the wild date-palms, a very pleasing feature in the landscape, varied by the fan-palms, with their green feather-like leaves and bright orange stalks, covered with similarly coloured fruit. When ripe the fruit becomes dark brown, like the cultivated date; and though we ate quantities, we did not get very considerable satisfaction from the consumption. Then a few delightful moments of repose would be passed by a sluggish stream, almost hidden by its rich jungle of shade; but on these last days of our long tramp we did not care to delay, but pushed on eagerly to reach the corrugated iron palaces of Mapanda, where we should find the river and the steamer.

Mapanda's is, indeed, a sorry place: not a tree to give one shade, only a store or two, built of that unsightly corrugated iron so much beloved by the early colonists of South Africa, and a few daub huts. It is a paradise only for those who arrive weary and worn from the interior, and for the sportsman, affording him a *pied-à-terre* in the very midst of the land where 'the deer and the antelope roam.' It has, however, certain points on which it justly prides itself. Firstly, it is the only spot for miles around which is not under water when the floods are out, for the banks of the Pungwe are fairly high here. Secondly, the river is navigable up to here for small steamers, even in the driest season; and, uninviting though it is at present, Mapanda may have a future before it.

We had three days to wait at Mapanda's before the little steamer *Agnes* would come up to take us away, and these three days were not without their excitements.

Three lions penetrated one night into the heart of the camp, and partially consumed three donkeys

—not ours, we are thankful to say, but those of a wicked Polish Jew, who had given infinite trouble to the English there, by causing an innocent Briton to be arrested by the Portuguese on a charge of theft; on which account he (the Jew) was well ducked in the Pungwe, and no one was sorry when the discriminating lions chose his donkeys for their meal; nay, many expressed a wish that the owner himself had formed part of the banquet. The next night the three lions, which had been lurking during the day in the jungle by the river, came to visit us again, with a view to demolishing what they and the vultures had left of the Hebrew's donkeys. One of the three visitors was shot, but he got away, and we heard no more of them.

Opposite the British colony at Mapanda is a large island forty miles long by twenty at its widest; this island is formed by the Pungwe and a branch of the same known by the Kaffir name of Dingwe-Dingwe. The island is perfectly flat, covered with low brushwood here and there, and long grass. It abounds in game; and on it the chief Mapanda has his kraal, having removed thither when the English came to settle at his old one on the banks of the river. One day we devoted to visiting this kraal, performing part of the journey in a native canoe which we borrowed—just the hollow stem of a large tree—which oscillated so much under our inexperienced hands that we momentarily expected it to upset and hand us over to the crocodiles; so we effected a hasty landing in the swampy jungle and proceeded on foot.

Mapanda's own village consists of only eight bamboo huts, built close to a tall palm-tree; in the centre of the huts is a raised platform, on which the grass-woven granaries of the community are kept. Beneath, in the shade, lay idle inhabitants, and from it were hung the grass petticoats and jangling beads which they use in their dances. I entered one of the huts on all-fours for inspection, and as I was engaged in so doing a terrified woman inside tore down the frail wall and made a hurried exit at the other side. I am told by those outside that the effect was most ludicrous. No wonder these dusky beauties are somewhat afraid of the white man, as hitherto they have dealt only with the Portuguese, who pride themselves on amalgamating well with the natives. In choosing a wife the Portuguese is not at all particular as to colour, nor is he a monogamist, as he would have to be in his far-off country. This we discovered for ourselves at Neves Ferreira, the Portuguese settlement on the Pungwe, about six miles below Mapanda's, where, beneath tall bananas and refreshing shade, the authorities of that nation pass a life of Oriental luxury which somewhat scandalises the strait-laced Briton.

There are several little kraals on the island belonging to the sons and relatives of Mapanda, all built on the same lines, and in visiting which we made ourselves insufferably thirsty, so that a good drink of Kaffir beer, or, as the Portuguese call it, 'millet wine,' was highly acceptable. It is much more potent than the beer they make up country, and if it were not for the husks therein, and general nature of fermented porridge it presents, one might fancy it champagne. Here, too, they make palm wine, tapping all the neighbouring palm-trees for the sap, which is highly intoxicating, and of by no means a disagreeable flavour. At Mapanda's we bade farewell to our donkeys and our cart and our conductor, Meredith, who had been with us and served us faithfully ever since we left Kimberley, ten long months before. He returned to Fort Salisbury with the cart, and wrote to inform us of the miseries of his journey owing to the rains, which brought fever, and the demise of the donkeys before the end of the journey.

The voyage from Mapanda's to the sea at Beira would be indescribably monotonous were it not for a few interesting features afforded by the stream itself. The tide here comes up with a remarkably strong bore, or wall-like wave, reminding one of the same phenomenon in the Severn at home. We heard it murmuring in the distance like the soughing of a rising wind; as it approached us the roar grew very loud, and finally the wave floated our stranded steamer almost in an instant.

Sandbanks are the bane of the navigator of this stream. On his last voyage our captain had been detained for three days on one, and we passed a Portuguese gunboat which looked as if it would remain there till the end of time. Our fate was a mild one:

we were only on a bank for a few hours, until the bore came up. These sandbanks are constantly shifting, and the captain never knows where they may next appear; consequently slow speed and constant soundings are the only safeguards. Crocodiles innumerable bask on these sandbanks, and in the stream itself hippopotami raise their black heads and stare at the strange animal which has come, and which will shortly cause the extermination of their species in the Pungwe.

Beira itself is the Portuguese word for a spit of sand, and is a horror of corrugated-iron domiciles on a bare shadeless sandspit at the mouth of the Pungwe. There is no drinkable water to be got within three miles of the place, and we paid half-a-crown a bucket for a very questionable quality of the precious fluid. Nobody washes himself or his clothes in anything but the sea during the dry season. On the last day of our stay at Beira (November 23) the heavens were opened and rain fell in torrents. Never was rain more welcome; pot, pan, and bucket were placed in every direction, and the extortionate water vendors had to retire from the field.

Where the eye does not rest on sea or sand it wanders from Beira over miles of flat mangrove swamps. The heat was scorching; when you walked you sank ankle-deep in sand at each step. Of all places Beira is the most horrible. When a Portuguese merchant goes to his office he is borne by four tottering negroes in his *mashila*; the Englishman walks and does most of his own work for himself, for the very good reason that he can get nobody to do it for him. This labour question is one of vital importance in Beira, and if ever it is to be a port of note the present order of things must be altered.

Yet, in spite of the fever, the heat, and the sand, Beira must go ahead, as nature has provided it with an excellent harbour, a rarity on the east coast of Africa. This is the only harbour for the proposed railway to the interior, which is to have its terminus on the opposite side of the harbour to Beira, nearer to the mouth of the Buzi, and will run along the flats between that river and the Pungwe. Until this line is made, I think few of those who have come down this road will care to return and face the discomforts of another foot journey through the fly country and the swamps. Perhaps it will be two years before this line is completed, and it must be done by the co-operation of the two interested companies, the British South Africa and the Mozambique. Between Massi-Kessi and Umtali it will cost a considerable amount of capital if the hills are to be tunnelled. On the flats the swamps will cause difficulties: fevers will play havoc with the labourers, and the rivers and the *dongas* will have to be bridged.

When this line is completed, I feel confident that Mashonaland will rapidly go ahead. There are in it all the elements of prosperity; and we may yet live to see the glories of the ancient ruins revived under other auspices, for long centuries have not altered the love of gold inherent in mankind.

APPENDICES

APPENDIX A

Notes on the Geography and Meteorology of Mashonaland

By ROBERT M. W. SWAN, Esq.

CENTRAL MASHONALAND consists of elevated granite plateaux, varying in height between 3,000 and 5,000 feet. Through the surface of these plains rise groups of isolated little granite hills which are most remarkable and varied in form, and which sometimes attain an elevation of 1,000 feet above their base, but more frequently they are about 400 feet high. Generally they are composed of enormous broken blocks of granite, but often they are dome-shaped and of one unbroken mass of rock, and suggest the idea of huge bubbles on the surface of a molten mass. The summits of the latter kind of hills are, of course, quite inaccessible. They are not hills left in relief by the denudation of the surrounding country, but, judging from exposed sections of some that I have seen, they have been elevated by a force acting at a comparatively small distance below the present surface, and they are older than the stratified rocks of the country.

On the granite plateaux one meets with patches of stratified rock—of quartzites and schists, and rarely some crystalline limestone. Magnesia, too, is sometimes present, notably at Umtali, and in the steatite which occurs near the Great Zimbabwe, of which many of the objects foond in the excavations were made. The strike of the strata is generally east and west, and the various patches arrange themselves in several fairly continuous lines running across the country in the same direction as the strike. These semi-continuous deposits or belts of stratified rock are generally two or three miles wide, and in them occur the gold-bearing quartz reefs. The most southerly belt that I know of in Mashonaland proper passes by Fort Victoria, and probably crosses the Sabi River about latitude 20°. The next large one passes by Umtali and the 'Mfuli River, where it crosses the waggon-road, and so on to Hartley Hill. This belt includes Mount Wodsa, the highest mountain in Mashonaland. Next in order comes the Mazoe deposit, which perhaps also includes the Kaiser Wilhelm gold-field. These deposits are all fairly similar in nature, but no fossils have been found in them, and their age has not been determined. They probably represent a contiouous sheet of stratified rock, all of which has been denuded away except the above-mentioned belts. They generally present a rugged surface, elovated in mountain ranges, which often rise 1,500 and 2,000 feet above their base, and, although they are nearly always steep, they are rarely precipitous. These monntains are regular and beautiful in outline, and refresh the eye after it has grown wearied of the grotesque forms of the granite hills. The soil on the stratified rocks is more fertile than it is on the granite, and the vegetation is more charming; the very coarse grasses of the granite soils being replaced by many flowering plants.

The ruins which have just been described are all built on granite, but are generally within a short distance of the quartz formation; and the ruins at Zimbabwe are situated four miles from the southern edge of the quartz belt. At Zimbabwe we found little clay crucibles in which gold had been melted, and an accumulation of quartzite rock which had been obtained from the casing of a quartz reef. I carefully tested this rock for gold, but could only find a very minute trace; so I conclude that it had been rejected as too poor for treatment. While at Zimbabwe, whenever I could spare time from the excavations, I made excursions to the quartz belt, and searched for old workings and gold reefs. I found one reef carrying a small quantity of gold, but no old workings. Since then, however, rich gold reefs have been discovered about twenty miles to the north-west of Zimbabwe, and from these probably the ancients obtained their quartz. The quartz formation near the little ruin at the Mazoe River has been much worked for gold, and the Manica belt seems to have been even more exploited. Where the high plateau breaks down at Massi-Kessi an enormous amount of alluvial has been worked. The old people must have obtained, from both the alluvial and the reefs, a great quantity of gold to repay them for the work that they did, and there is no reason to suppose that they have exhausted the reefs; indeed, I have seen at the bottom of old workings the reef continuing and carrying visible gold.

Besides gold reefs, these quartz belts contain much iron ore and some manganese. In two isolated patches of the quartzite formation at the Doroba Mountains, near the Sabi River, I found great masses of rich magnotite and hematite, and on the top of Mount 'Nyaguzwe, near Fort Victoria, there is also a mass of magnetite; in fact, so very abundant is iron ore, that compass bearings can rarely be taken with safety from hills in the quartz formation. Along the right bank of the Sabi River, near Mount Wedsa, are many native villages, whose one industry is iron smelting. They obtain the ore from Mount Wedsa, which is renowned far and wide in Kaffirland as an iron-producing mountain. The mineral they select is not very rich, and is consequently more easily smelted, and it contains some manganese. The iron they produce is very pure, and is consequently soft and easily fashioned into weapons and tools. Their anvils are simple blocks of hard diorite, on which they hammer with another smaller block.

The tributaries of the Sabi River flowing near Zimbabwe have been ill-defined on previous maps. The 'Mpopotekwe joins the 'Mtelekwe and the 'Mshagashe flows into the united stream a short distance south of Zimbabwe. This river, under the name of the 'Mtelekwe, then flows into the Lunde, and not to the Sabi direct. The Tokwe joins the Lunde farther north. The most interesting geographical work that we did was on our expedition to the Sabi River, and on that from Fort Salisbury to 'Mtoko's, and down by Mangwendi's and Makoni's country to Umtali. On our journey to the Sabi we crossed a great many of its western tributaries; and as the same streams rose near the waggon-road, and we crossed them pretty far down their courses, we were able to lay down their direction for a considerable distance with certainty. The Sabi River itself, in latitude 19° 15′, we found was placed twenty miles too far west in former maps; and from the information which I gathered from the natives, in the latitude of Zimbabwe, it must be about fifty miles farther east than it is placed in these maps. This river, where we struck it, was a considerable stream flowing rapidly over a rocky bed. It had fallen about 1,800 feet from its source near Fort Charter, and had 2,700 feet more to fall before it reached the sea. When it has received all the tributaries we crossed it must be a very big river.

Going from Fort Salisbury to 'Mtoko's we crossed many tributaries of the Mazoe River, which were either not shown at all in former maps, or were most inaccurately placed. We recrossed these streams again farther up returning from 'Mtoko's to Mangwendi's. I also got excellent views of them from the various mountains which I ascended so that I was able to lay them down in my map with certainty. To the eastward of 'Mtoko's we could see the high *veldt* breaking into mountain ranges as it descended towards Gouveia's country.

Approaching Mangwondi's, and also going between Mangwendi's and Chipunza's, our way lay along a very high watershed, on the western side of which rose some of the eastern tributaries of the Sabi River, the most important of which was the 'Msheke. At Makoni's we reached the highest part of the plateau, and this is, with the exception of some villages on Mount Yenya, the highest inhabited part of Mashonaland. From Makoni's to Mount Yenya the country is broken; and the descent is very rapid, but on the east of our route the descent is still more rapid and the mountains more imposing. On the north side of Mount Yenya flows the Odzi River, which is there a very considerable stream. Mount Yenya is a most imposing mountain and the highest in Mashonaland, with the exception of Mount Wedsa. It rises to a height of 5,800 feet above sea level, and within 300 feet of its summit are several villages which own a considerable number of cattle. It probably represents the Mount Doe which the Portuguese place on their maps about this part, and which they say is 7,900 feet high, for certainly there is no mountain near Mount Yenya of equal height. Between Umtali and Massi-Kessi the country is extremely mountainous, and the scenery is the grandest that we saw in Mashonaland. We lost 1,400 feet in height between these two places. A short distance after leaving Massi-Kessi we crossed the Revwe River, and our way lay along a watershed about 2,000 feet high. This watershed is thickly wooded, and is traversed sometimes by deep ravines. On the left hand the streams flow to the Pungwe River, and on the right to the Revwe and the Muda and Mutachiri Rivers.

Approaching Sarmento, the country falls rapidly to nearly sea level; and thence to the coast we traversed a flat alluvial country through which the Pungwe River sluggishly flows. This swampy level country swarms with game, especially towards the end of the dry season, but the vegetation is not nearly so luxuriant as one would expect, and some parts of this country are quite bare.

I have been careful throughout to spell the native names in accordance with the rules laid down by the Royal Geographical Society. The sound of the Bushman clicks which occurs so often in the names of places and in the names of tribes derived from the names of places, but most frequently of all in the names of rivers, is slurred over by the present tribes, and represented by a combination of letters. As I know of no rule for the spelling of these sounds, I have represented them by an inverted comma and the consonant nearest in sound. In maps of Africa north of the Zambesi these clicks are generally spelt in this way, although the comma has often dropped out, as in words like 'Nyanza,' 'Mpwapwa,' 'Mvumi;' but south of that river cartographers have been less accurate, and have often used various vowels instead of the comma. I have used such mis-spellings of the native names only when they have been long established and passed into constant use: as 'Umtali' and 'Inhambane.'

A point of interest in the remote history of the country and of the ruins which we examined—for the old people doubtless entered the country by this coast—is the growth of the land at the mouth of the Pungwe River and around Sofala. From about Sarmento down to Beira one passes over a low alluvial country which has been slowly encroaching on the sea for ages. I am sorry that in the rush to the coast I did not have time to collect data to enable me to form any idea of the quantity of mud deposited from the waters of the Pungwe in a given time, but its waters hold in suspension a great quantity of fine clay derived from the decomposition of the granite in its basin, and this is deposited where the river enters the sea. The distance from Sarmento to Beira as the crow flies is sixty-five miles, so that at some period the road to the interior must have been shortened by this amount, and even in early historical times some part of the journey across the low fever belt would have been saved. The site of ancient seaports will now be far inland, so it need not surprise us that remains of these ports have not yet been found.

Owing to frequent absence from camp, I was unable to read the thermometer and barometer as continuously and regularly as I could have wished, but the readings which I did take give us some idea of what the climate at Zimbabwe was in June and July last year. We arrived there on June 6, after a week of south-east winds, high barometer, and rain and mist. The wind then gradually fell and the barometer with it, and we had three weeks of fine calm weather. The barometer reached its minimum on June 27, and at the same time the difference of the readings of the wet and dry bulb thermometers was at its maximum. The air was then very dry and the sky clear, with light north winds which were evidently local in origin, and the temperature at night fell below freezing-point, so that in the morning we saw a light deposit of hoar-frost. Immediately after this the barometer began to rise, there were light south-east winds, the atmosphere became moister, and on July 4 the south-east wind had increased considerably in strength, and some rain fell. From this time until the end of our stay at Zimbabwe, on August 2, the barometer slowly rose and fell, its range being limited to about three-tenths of an inch; and whenever the south-east winds blew at all strongly the barometer rose and we had mist and rain. We had during this period generally about a half-day of rain each week.

At first sight it seems surprising that we should have windy wet weather with a high barometer, but we must remember that the only winds which can bring rain to Zimbabwe, at least in winter, are the south-easterly winds, and these, like all other winds blowing towards the equator, increase the atmospheric pressure. Zimbabwe is situated on the edge of a plateau about 3,400 feet above sea level. The country breaks down gradually towards the south and east and more rapidly towards the west, while towards the north it rises gently until after about 100 miles it attains an altitude of nearly 5,000 feet. The west winds, if they do blow, have to traverse the continent and the high country about the sources of the Limpopo before they reach Zimbabwe, so that they will deposit their excess of moisture for the altitude of Zimbabwe before reaching that place; and the northerly winds will tend to increase in temperature, and consequently in dryness, after falling from the high country towards the north; so that westerly and northerly winds will not part with moisture at Zimbabwe. The predominant winds in this latitude are the south-east trades, and they, carrying their moisture from the Indian Ocean, are forced to rise as they pass over this country, and they consequently expand and are lowered in temperature and so deposit much of their moisture on this edge of the high plateau. A similar winter climate seems to prevail in most parts of Mashonaland, the edges of the plateaux receiving most of the moisture. Manica is situated much nearer the sea than Zimbabwe, and the country there falls much more rapidly towards the east (it falls 1,400 feet in ten miles near Umtali), and consequently the rainfall there is heavier. Fort Salisbury is better situated for a dry winter, for it is in the middle of a high plateau, and the south-east winds will have parted with most of their surplus moisture for that altitude before they reach it. The driest time of the year in Mashonaland is from August to November. I may mention that the greatest difference I observed in the readings of the wet and dry bulb thermometers was 24° F. at the 'Mshabetsi River, at an altitude of 2,140 feet, on May 13 at 2 P.M.; the readings being 64° and 88° respectively. At Zimbabwe during June and July the difference in readings varied from 0° to 20° F., and the dew point sometimes fell to 32° F. at midday. The extreme range of shade temperature in the two months was 46° F.

APPENDIX B

List of Stations in Mashonaland Astronomically Observed, with Altitudes

By ROBERT M. W. SWAN, Esq.

Stations	Latitude ° ′ ″	Longitude ° ′ ″	Heights[1] feet
Mafeking	25 51 1	25 41 0	—
Ramathlabama River	25 37 57	—	—
At Pan	25 30 13	25 8 15	—
Kanye, 11 miles S.S.E of	25 7 2	25 8 15	8580
Kanye	24 58 30	25 10 0	8760
Molopolole	24 25 30	25 21 0	4020
Molopolole, 4 miles N. of	24 21 30	25 21 30	8872
Klippan, ¼ mile N. of	24 17 12	—	4020
Knrumurwa	24 8 33	—	8570
Khemi	23 50 8	—	8490
Boatlenama, 15 miles S.E. of	23 42 20	25 35 30	8540
Boatlanama	23 32 30	—	8400
S. of Selinia Pan	23 27 11	—	3120
N. of Selinia Pan	23 20 51	26 8 15	8050
Near Hataloklu Vley	23 15 4	26 10 53	8140
S. of Shoshong	23 8 47	26 19 30	3160
Near Shoshong	23 4 0	26 29 0	3310
At stream	23 1 57	26 41 30	3260
Near Mahalapsi River	22 57 41	26 51 15	3240
Chuloan Vley	22 46 0	27 6 30	3010
Palapwe	22 37 30	27 18 0	3150
At Lotsani River	22 32 45	27 21 30	2740
At Lotsani River	22 33 58	27 34 0	2460
At Lotsani River	22 32 37	27 46 45	2450
Near Elibi Fort	22 32 55	—	2800
Near Elibi Fort	—	—	2250
At Muralla Vley	22 32 55	28 10 30	2290
Makwonje River	22 26 53	28 21 30	2275
Pakwe River	22 15 20	28 24 15	2400

[1] The heights have been obtained with aneroid and boiling-point thermometers, and with the exception of that of Zimbabwe, where we stayed some time, are only approximate.

List of Stations in Mashonaland Astronomically Observed, with Altitudes—continued

Stations	Latitude ° ′ ″	Longitude ° ′ ″	Heights feet
Marapong River	22 7 88	28 31 0	2230
Matlapntla River	22 3 39	—	—
Maklutsi Camp	22 0 42	28 88 15	2010
Maklutsi River	21 58 20	28 41 0	1870
Metsimoshokwan River	21 49 55	28 52 0	1920
Semalali	21 53 2	29 0 40	2080
Baobab Spruit	21 53 17	29 14 0	—
Fort Tuli	21 55 20	29 20 15	—
Ipagi River	21 51 59	29 36 15	—
Sigabi River	21 43 53	29 42 30	—
'Msingwan River	21 89 7	29 49 15	1720
'Mshabetsi River	21 26 22	29 57 15	2140
Mount Yanda	21 21 57	30 6 15	2330
Bubye River	21 20 80	80 14 0	2090
'Nyamanda	21 11 84	30 23 15	—
Mount Hoat	21 9 10	30 80 20	2250
Near Nwanetsi River	21 5 16	30 88 80	1910
Near Nwanesti River	20 50 23	30 41 0	1880
Near Mount Ibonda	20 49 40	80 42 0	2180
Lunde River	20 41 0	80 44 45	1970
Near Naka Mountains	20 85 54	30 45 0	2130
'Mlala	20 27 9	80 47 80	2580
Tokwe River	20 23 5	30 58 80	2380
Providential Pass	20 11 11	30 57 45	8090
Fort Victoria	20 7 58	31 0 0	3350
Zimbabwe	20 16 80	31 7 80	3840
'Mshagashe River	20 8 40	—	3200
Makori	19 88 29	80 58 30	4200
Chekatu	19 88 40	31 8 0	4100
Gona	19 36 52	—	4350
'Msingana	19 81 80	—	8050
Kutimasinga's	19 88 19	31 37 0	8250
Lutile	19 84 12	—	8700
Matindela	19 30 28	81 51 45	8850
Near Mount Wizinde	19 17 0	—	3250
Near Mwairari River	19 14 50	82 2 45	2900
Mukubu River	19 8 45	82 4 15	2700
Sabi River	19 7 40	82 1 30	2900
Ampsai River	19 6 41	—	2950
Zamopera	19 0 17	81 39 15	8660
Mafusaire's	18 50 25	—	8950
East of Smet's Kraal	18 51 25	—	—
West of Kwendo's Kraal	18 48 25	81 25 45	4220

List of Stations in Mashonaland Astronomically Observed, with Altitudes—continued

Stations	Latitude	Longitude	Heights
	° ′ ″	° ′ ″	feet
'Mtigesa's	18 43 30	31 10 45	4570
Fort Charter	18 85 40	31 9 45	4408
'Mfuli River	18 18 85	31 5 30	4080
Near stream	18 10 15	31 10 15	—
S. of Hanyani River	18 0 22	31 3 15	4800
Fort Salisbury	17 49 80	31 4 15	4820
Fleming's Camp, Mazoe River	17 32 48	30 56 0	—
Yellow Jacket Mine, ditto	17 28 32	31 4 15	4030
Madelsywa's	17 48 80	31 12 0	—
Musungaikwa's	17 52 33	31 20 15	5010
Nora River	17 55 18	31 20 0	4470
Kunzi's	17 58 40	31 33 0	4400
Yandoro's	17 47 0	31 41 45	4720
Bambabashla's	17 40 30	31 43 0	4410
Mahume River	17 31 0	31 57 45	3420
Near Lutsa	17 25 30	32 0 0	3450
Near 'Mtoko's	17 28 50	32 14 0	3900
'Nyandea River	17 32 5	32 8 30	3600
'Nyamashupa River	17 39 22	32 2 15	8900
Near Mount Masunsgwai	17 50 12	31 54 15	4350
Yaungurukwe River	17 59 25	31 45 45	4700
Mangwendi's P.S.	18 0 42	31 39 30	4870
Nyanger Mountain	18 15 20	31 46 0	4850
Chikamondi River	18 21 6	31 56 30	4810
Mount Ruanda	18 22 80	32 7 30	4830
Chipunza's	18 27 30	32 10 15	4450
Near Chigono's	18 33 50	32 17 0	4450
Near Yenya Mountains	18 45 0	32 22 45	5020
Odzi River drift	18 48 50	—	8420
'Mtasa's	18 44 30	32 20 0	4170
Umtali, our camp	18 53 80	32 32 45	3600
Massi-Kessi (Portuguese camp)	18 53 45	32 44 30	2200
Mineni River	18 56 0	32 50 80	2140
Lusika River	18 59 27	33 2 0	2000
Vundusi River trib.	18 59 10	33 13 0	2300
Near Chimoia's	18 59 0	33 20 0	2140
Zombana River	18 57 15	—	1930
Maknmbese River	19 2 10	—	120
Vley	19 8 85	—·	100
Mutuchiri River	19 16 40	—	50
'Mpanda's	19 23 80	34 32 30	20

APPENDIX C

Addenda to Chapter V

By R. M. W. Swan, Esq.

Since writing the preceding pages (Chapter V.) it has been found to be possible from the measurements made at Zimbabwe to determine the radius of another curve of the outer wall of the great temple. This part of the wall extends from B in a north-westerly direction for 111 feet, to a point which we shall call C. The radius of its curve is 133 feet, so that the diameter of the circle of which it is a part is equal to one half of $17·17 \times 3·14^2$, and the centre of the curve (which we shall call W) is situated on the meridian line from the altar through the main doorway. The middle point of this arc B C, the S.S.E. doorway of the arc G, the centres G and W, all lie in one and the same straight line. This line cuts the meridian at an angle of 30°, and when produced will pass over the outer wall at a point which is marked by a step which is built across the top of the wall. A line drawn in a similar way from the middle of the arc K B through the centre of the great tower, the altar, and F, also cuts the meridian at an angle of 30°, but from its other side. As the original wall no longer exists at the point where this line would pass we cannot say if its position was marked on the wall.

These lines of sight seem to have been used, like the meridian lines, for the observation of stars, but of stars off the meridian. It could hardly have served any useful purpose to observe several stars crossing these lines unless they all had the same polar distance; for stars with different polar distances would cross the lines at different lengths of time before and after their culminations. Nor, in the latitude of Zimbabwe, would any individual star cross the lines at any important time in its daily circuit. But if we suppose that this temple is built on the model of one in the parent country in the northern hemisphere, it is easy to imagine a useful purpose which these lines may have served. In the latitude of Southern Arabia, for instance, an observer facing north would see the North Pole elevated about 15° above the horizon. If we compare the northern portion of the sky to a watch dial, the stars will represent the moving hands, the pole the centre of the dial, the meridian the XII. and VI. hour-points, and the III. and IX. hours will be marked by a horizontal line passing through the pole east and west. When stars cross this line they may be said to be at their east or west elongation. Now it seems probable that the two lines in question would be used in the parent country to observe a star having a north polar distance of 30° when it was at its east and west elongations and six hours from the meridian.

We have before remarked that none of our trigonometrical functions seem to have been recognised by the builders of Zimbabwe, and that the angular values of the arcs are of no special importance when measured in our way. But they must have been of importance to the builders of the temples. The locating of the centres of the arcs on the several meridian lines, supposing the meridian lines were first laid down in planning the temples (as the central one undoubtedly was in the great temple), does not really determine the intersecting points of the arcs; for, were the centre moved along the meridian lines in either direction, the points of intersection would change their positions and the lengths of the arcs would be altered.

ADDENDA TO CHAPTER V

The lengths of the arcs seem to have been determined by the intersections of circles of radii different from those of the arcs themselves, but the lengths of whose radii were determined by the same system as those of the arcs. The centres of the intersecting circles are situated on the radius of the arc which lies midway between its extremities, and the distance between the arc and the intersecting circle measured on the same radius produced is equal to the diameter of one of the towers.

The arc AK is built on a curve of 107·8 feet radius; and if a circle be drawn as described with a radius of 169·3 feet, it will determine the length of the chord of the arc at 107 feet, and the distance between the two arcs measured on the middle radius will be 5·45, which is equal to the diameter of the little tower.

The arc KB treated in the same way, with a curve of 84·6 feet, and with a distance of 17·17 feet (the diameter of the great tower) between the intersecting circle and the arc, has the length of its chord fixed at 129½ feet. These two lengths of 107 and 129½ feet agree to within six inches with our actual measurement of the wall itself.

If we apply our system to the arc BC in an exactly similar manner, but with the distance between the circle and the arc made equal to the radius of the great tower, we find that the length of its chord should be 111 feet; and this also agrees closely with our measurements.

The arc of the eastern temple on the hill has a radius of 42·8 feet, and if a circle of 169·3 feet be applied to it with a distance of 17·17 feet between the circle and the arc, we find that the length of its chord should be 72 feet;. and this is exactly what we make it on our plan. This also explains the hitherto inexplicable position of the eastern doorway.

In a similar way we determine the length of the chord of the great wall in the western temple to be 140 feet; but as the ends of this wall are in a ruinous condition, and as the present outer face is not of the original period, we cannot say whether this was the actual measurement or not.

With two exceptions, there are no other arcs which are sufficiently complete to allow us to ascertain their original measurements. These exceptions are the arc in the little temple at G, and that from the doorway to A. In the former case, the length of the arc is fixed by the two doorways; and as one of these is placed north of the centre in order to permit of observation along the meridian line, and the other is made to serve the same purpose for the line GW, it is obvious why the length of this arc was not determined in the same way. In the latter case, as one end of the arc is at a northern doorway, and as we are not quite certain of the length of the radius of the arc itself, we have not attempted to determine the length of its chord.

It is much to be desired that more of the plan of the original temple should be recovered, and this can only be done by careful excavation conducted by some one of experience in the art; for an inexperienced or careless workman could easily and unwittingly remove any of the remaining mortarless foundations without ever discovering that he had done so.

APPENDIX D.

The following notes have been kindly supplied by the Secretary of the British South Africa Company:—

Progress in Mashonaland summarised from November 1891 to May 1893.

HEALTH.

The rainy season of 1891 to 1892 found the settlers in Mashonaland well housed and with an abundance of provisions; in consequence, a wonderful improvement was manifested in the health of the community, proving that the insufficiency of food and shelter, necessarily associated with the initial occupation of a wild country so many hundreds of miles from a base of supply, was mainly responsible for the sickness of the rainy season of 1890–1891.

The Senior Medical Officer of the British South Africa Company reported early in 1892 that not a single case of fever had arisen among the inhabitants of Salisbury during the worst part of the wet season; in every case the patient had contracted his fever elsewhere, and there had been no deaths at all from climatic causes in Salisbury or its district. He adds: 'Good food, good clothing, shelter from inclement weather and the sun, an abundant supply of medicines and invalid necessaries and a milder season have wrought an enormous improvement in the general health of the people.

and Mashonaland of 1892 is not recognisable as Mashonaland of 1891.'

The general health has been equally good in the rainy season of 1892–3, and the experience of the last two years has shown that perfect health may be enjoyed by anyone who will avoid undue exposure and will observe a few simple precautions.

TOWNSHIPS

Progress in the townships of Salisbury, Victoria, and Umtali has been rapid.

At Salisbury 1,800 stands have been surveyed and mapped out; at Victoria 572 stands, and at Umtali 300. In July 1892 a sale of stands was held at the three places mentioned above, 70 at Salisbury being sold for 2,250*l*., 150 at Victoria for 6,107*l*., and 44 at Umtali for 1,396*l*., the total sum realised being nearly 10,000*l*. for 264 stands. It is intended to hold another sale in July of this year, where competition no doubt will be keen, as the attention of capitalists in England, as well as those on the spot, is being directed to the matter.

The public buildings at Salisbury, such as the Administrator's Offices, the Standard Bank Offices, the Police Station, Magazine, Court House, Survey, Mines, Post and Telegraph Offices, are already completed or on the verge of completion. All the material required for these buildings has been drawn from the district itself, with the exception of wood for doors, skirting, and architraves.

A Sanitary Board has been formed at Salisbury to manage the affairs of the township with a revenue derived from one-half the stand-rents (10*s*. per month) and other fees, such as market dues.

A branch of the Standard Bank was opened at Salisbury on July 20, 1892, and is doing a very good business. A printed newspaper, the *Rhodesia Herald*, is also published there weekly.

The Mining Commissioner for Victoria reported on September 24, 1892, as follows:—

'The township of Victoria is growing very fast, and very good buildings are being erected, the majority being composed of brick and iron or brick and thatch; they are far superior to those erected at Kimberley, Barberton, or Johannesburg. The town has only been surveyed a few months, and progress made is very good. This shows that the people have every confidence in the mining and general prospects of Mashonaland.'

Victoria also possesses a newspaper, the *Mashonaland Times and Mining Chronicle*.

As regards hotels, there are several most substantial buildings of brick and iron offering excellent accommodation at Salisbury, and between Victoria and Salisbury there are wayside hotels at the various post-stations. Victoria itself possesses two, and others are to be found every 20 miles or so along the 200 miles of road connecting Victoria with Tuli. At the latter place there is an excellent hotel, conducted by the Tuli Hotel Company.

On the Salisbury-Umtali Road and at Umtali wayside houses and hotels have been established, and their number will no doubt be augmented on the completion of the Beira Railway.

ROADS.

The existing roads have been kept up and improved, and under Mr. Selous's superintendence new ones have been made in many directions connecting Fort Salisbury with the various gold-fields and with the main road to the Pungwe.

During 1892 Mr. Selous constructed an excellent road from Umtali to Chimoio, a distance of over 70 miles, to meet the head of the Beira Railway. The road will be available for heavy waggons at all seasons of the year. Two road-making parties are engaged at the present time in maintaining and improving it.

BEIRA RAILWAY.

Satisfactory progress is being made with the Beira Railway, the first section of which from Fontes Villa, (about 48 miles up the Pungwe from Beira) to Chimoio, a distance of 75 miles, will be opened by the end of July.

The embankments are completed for 65 miles and the permanent way for 50, but the curves in some places, especially in the last few miles, are sharp, owing to the broken and hilly nature of the country. Special rails for these curves have had to be procured from England and are now on their way out. By the time they arrive at the end of June all the earthworks will be finished, and they will then only have to be linked to complete the railway through the fly-belt. It is this fly-belt which has hitherto opposed such an insuperable obstacle to the importation of heavy goods by this otherwise easy, cheap, and convenient route.

It is estimated that the cost of transport of goods from Cape Town to Salisbury will thus be decreased by more than 20*l.* per ton, and it will then be possible to import machinery &c. at rates which compare favourably with those which obtained at the Randt before the recent completion of the line to Johannesburg.

On completion of the first section, the construction of the second section as far as Salisbury will be pressed on with, transport being carried on in the meantime by services of waggons on the Chimoio-Umtali Road, alluded to above.

AGRICULTURE.

The main occupations of settlers have been gold mining and farming.

Favourable reports of the country from an agricultural and pastoral point of view have on several occasions been furnished by deputations of experienced farmers appointed at public meetings, both in the Cape Colony and the Orange Free State, to inspect and report upon the land. As the result of these reports, large 'treks' of farmers from those countries have already proceeded, and will be followed shortly by others, to occupy tracts of land in Mashonaland.

A recent return from the Surveyor-General's Office at Salisbury shows that farms representing a total area of 3,178 square miles or 2,000,000 acres have been granted and located, nearly one-half having been properly surveyed in addition. Grants of land for farms of 3,000 acres in extent at an annual quit rent of 3*l*. were obtainable during 1892, but so many applications were received that these practically free grants have been altogether suspended, and the price of land is fixed for the present at 9*d*. per acre subject to the annual quit rent.

Farming operations in Mashonaland should offer special advantages, owing to the proximity of the various gold-fields, which have always afforded markets at most remunerative rates for all farm produce, and will no doubt continue to do so in the future in an even greater degree.

The most important of the deputations above referred to upon inspection estimated that in the parts of the country visited there were at least 40,000 square miles well adapted for colonising purposes. When it is remembered that the area of Mashonaland and Matabeleland is 125,000 square miles, and that not one-half of this extent of country was seen by the deputation, it will be generally conceded that their estimate, large as it is, admits of considerable amplification.

It may be incidentally mentioned, dealing with quite another part of the British South Africa Company's territories, viz. the sphere north of the Zambesi, which amounts to upwards of 500,000 square miles, that most favourable reports of its mineral and agricultural resources have been furnished by such well-known travellers as Joseph Thomson and Alfred Sharpe.

GOLD.

The attention of the majority of the population has mainly been directed to the exploitation of the gold reefs, and in spite of difficulties arising from want of transport and from ignorance of the country, a great deal of solid development has been achieved.

Owing to various causes, it was not until July 1891 that regular workings were commenced. Since that time prospecting has been carried on in a systematic and efficient manner, resulting in the discovery of the gold-bearing districts of Victoria, Manica, Hartley Hill, Mazoe, and Lo Magondas, having a total area of 27,000 square miles. It is believed that the gold-belt starting from Umtali passes through Victoria, and will in all probability connect with the gold-belt stretching eastward from the Tati gold-fields in the western portion of Matabeleland, and on which considerable development work has been done.

Fresh discoveries on a large scale have recently been made within 15 miles of Salisbury. The latest cable intelligence states that in these new fields the reefs proved to 40 and 60 feet are as rich and as wide as at the surface. Gold-belts have also recently been discovered at Mt. Darwin, about 80 miles north of Mazoe, at points 120 miles north of Umtali (Manica) and 80 miles south of the same place, and on the Tokwe River about 30 miles west of Victoria. The gold formations at the above places are all very extensive, show visible freely, and give very rich pannings, while they cannot be said to have been developed at all up to the present. Another series of reefs, which are described as being phenomenally rich by the British South Africa Company's Administrator, have just been discovered in the commonago at Umtali.

The immense cost of importing even the lightest stamp batteries has, of course, retarded the gold industry to an enormous extent, but the completion of the Beira Railway will work a great change in this respect. What crushings have taken place show very rich results. The average yield from several hundred tons of ore extracted from all reefs in the Victoria district, good and bad together, was 18·3 dwt. per ton, or about 73s. It has, however, been proved in practice that mining operations even under present conditions can be carried on in Mashonaland at a cost not exceeding 20s. per ton, leaving the very handsome profit of 53s. for every ton crushed in the above district.

In a cablegram recently received from the Company's administrator on his return from a tour of inspection of the various mining districts he states that new finds were occurring everywhere daily, and that crushings were everywhere successful; that the reefs were improving with depth, and that wonderful development was proceeding in every district. As regards alluvial gold, that large deposits do exist, and that their discovery is only a question of time, is the opinion of all experienced miners. That this time has now arrived seems probable from a cable message recently received reporting that 50 oz. of alluvial gold had been brought into Salisbury, causing great excitement there. Should, however, alluvial fields, so valuable to a new country from their power of attracting a large mining population, never be discovered, it may not be too much to say—the progress that has been made in so short a time, and the enormous extent and richness of the auriferous reefs being taken into consideration—that the time cannot be far distant when Mashonaland will assume a leading position amongst the principal gold-producing countries of the world.

INDEX

ABANTU charms, 89; origin of the name Zimbabwe, 234

Abyssinia, Mr. Salt's exploration in, 229

Ælian on vultures, 185; on Egyptian sacrifice, 200

Æthiopia, Sabæan city in, 230

Africa, Phœnician circumnavigation, 225; Arab extension in, 229; Arab opposition to Portuguese, 235; Roman penetration through, 239; extent of Portuguese influence in, 243

    East: Greek and Roman knowledge of, 225; ancient gold-mining population, 228; Sabæan possession of, 229; Portuguese enterprise, 230; wild tribes of, 232; Abou Zeyd's description of the Zindj tribes, 233; wealth of gold in, 234; curious birds, 202

    South: British Chartered Company of, expedition assisted by, 4; Dr. Emil Holub's work on, 95

    South-East: ancient products sent as tribute to Egypt, 220

Alvarez, Pory's translation of, 240; on the god of the Monomatapa, 342

Agatharcides on the wealth of the Sabæans, 227

Agizymba, Ptolemy's mention of, 239

Aizanes, King, victory of, 229

Anderson, Mr. A. A., rock carvings discovered in Bechuanaland by, 199, 200

Aphrodite, stone head of, worshipped by the Ismaelites, 195

Arab settlement at Rhapta, 224

Arabia, tower worship in, 116; Himyaritic supremacy in, 186; Herodotus on native worship, 190; Herr Kremer on the ancient cult, 195; Biblical allusions to wealth of, 220, 227; ancient knowledge of monsoons, 224; trading emporia on the Red Sea, 225; exportation of gold to Rome, 227; Horace on wealth of, 227; ancient enterprise, 229; Sabæan cities in, 230; Herr Kremer on tribal system of totems, 331

Argonautic expedition, 223

Ashmolean Museum, stone carvings from the Soudan in, 186

'**Asia, De**,' by M. De Barros, 238

Asia Minor, mythical inhabitants of, 222

Axume, Abyssinia, ancient Greek inscription at, 229

BAC

Bacoto, ancient Portuguese market in Mazoe valley, 205
Bahrein islands, Persian Gulf, tombs in, 121
Ba-kalahari tribe, 14
Bakalanga tribes in Natal, 83
Ba-mangwato tribe at Palapwe, 23; beer-drinking, 25; witch-doctors, ib.; superstition, ib.; women of and civilisation, 27
Bandiri, early Portuguese influence at, 298
Bandala, kraal of, 374
Ba-Ngwatetse tribe, 7; soldiers, 10
Baobab trees, 135
Ba-quaina tribe, 15
Baramazimba, a fantastic kraal near Zimbabwe, 85
Barbosa, Duarte, on the gold trade of Sofala, 231
Baretto, disastrous campaigns of, 248
Ba-rolongs of Mafeking, 7
Barros, De, on the Mashonaland ruins, 233
Basuto skill in stone-building, 347
Batnen, chief of Kanya, 6, 7; under missionary influence, 8; his tribal gatherings, 9; his household, ib.; his slaves and soldiers, 10; his parents, ib.
Bechuanaland, British influence in, 5; Crown colony in, 3; boundaries of, ib.; roads through, ib.; 'Ally Sloper' in, 7; cattle disease, 8; inoculation of oxen, ib.; native justice, 9; native soldiers, 10; funeral of a chief, ib.; music and dancing, 11, 12; marriage and divorce, 13; derivation of name, 15; tribal worship of crocodiles, ib.; produce, 16; gardens and fields, ib.; jungle travel, 17; flora and fauna, 18; cattle stations, 19; tribal

BEI

migration, 21; Border Police at Macloutsie, 22; baboons at Palapwe, 24; drought in, 30; rock carvings discovered by Mr. Anderson, 199, 200
Beira, waste of provisions at, 283; steamer from, to Cape, 302; journey from Umtali to, 365; unhealthy condition of port, 385; proposed railway to the interior, 386
Benoula, in 'Mtoko's kraal, 327; accompanies author on a visit to the lion priest at Lutzi, ib.
Bessa range, as viewed from Zimbabwe, 75
Béthencourt, Portuguese commandant at Massi-Kessi, 370
Bocarro, Antonio, on Portuguese exploration in Africa, 243; on the empire of the Monomatapa, 339
Bochiko, village chief in Kunzi's country, 312; his remarkable appearance, 313; his wives and children, ib.
Bœotia, relics from Thebes, 205
Boer expedition in Mashonaland, 244
Bondoro worship in Mangwendi's country, 340
Britain, ancient, tin ingots found in, 216; mythical inhabitants of, 222
British Association, expedition to Mashonaland assisted by, 4
British Chartered Company of South Africa. See 'Chartered'
British Museum, Egyptian pillow in the, 87; African musical instruments, 81; Phœnician sepulchral stelæ in, 189; lebes from temple at Naucratis, 203; iron bells from the Congo, 311, 312
Brittany, avenues of menhirs near Carnac, 182

BUF

Bufwa mountains, 43
Buzi river, early Portuguese influence on the, 208

CABIRI ruins at Hadjar Kem in Malta, 116
Cabral, Alvarez da, Portuguese explorer, 231; his entry into Sofala harbour, ib.; Arab gold-laden dhows, ib.
Cairo, Portuguese at, 230
Cambridge, cylindrical object from Cyprus in Fitzwilliam Museum at, 204
Carnac, Brittany, avenues of monhirs near, 132; mythical builders of, 222
Charter fort, Makalanga tribes at, 82; arrival of expedition at, 277; parting with native servants, ib.
Chartered Company of South Africa, author's obligations to, 4; pioneers in Mashonaland, 240; difficulty in catering at Fort Salisbury, 282; punishment of Kaffirs by officers of, 290
Chekatu, village of, 254; Matabele raid on, ib.; female barber at, ib.
Cherumbila, native chief, 89; visit to his kraal, 90; description thereof, ib.; his raids upon neighbouring tribes, ib.; interview with, ib.; Matabele raid upon, ib.; his hospitality, 91
Chibi's country, 44; native iron-smelting, 45; pot-making, ib.; granaries, 48; rats and mice, ib.; native costumes, 40
Chiburga, Monomatapa's stronghold for wives, 267
Cluburwe mountain, north of

COR

Matindela, ruins of fort near, 100, 135, 140; gigantic baobab tree, 140; Makalanga outpost, 267; holes for Isafnba game, ib.; miserable villages around, ib.; trackless forests in vicinity, 268; ruin there, ib.
Chidima, the Monomatapa of; Portuguese accounts of, 331, 832; silver-mining at, 832
Chigono village, 355; its wonderful position, ib.
Chilondillo fort, ruins of, 135
Chilonga fort, ruins of, 100
Chimbi river, underground passage near, 846
Chimoia, kraal of, 375; fertility of country, 876; lions in vicinity, 877
China, Celadon pottery from, in Zimbabwe, 204
Chipadzi village in Mazoe valley, 294; ruins near, ib.
Chipiez, M. See Perrot and Chipiez, MM.
Chipunza's village, wall-building in, 839; interesting ruin near, 846; aspect of the country, 848; camping in, ib.; native craving for salt, 349; interview with chief, 351; savage etiquette, ib.; beer and beer-drinking, 851, 852; native courtesy, 852; fortress at, 853; Chipadzi's tomb, ib.
Colonial Institute, Mr. E. A. Maund's lecture at the, on ancient gold-mining in Mashonaland, 290
Conder, Major, on the circular ruin near the Lundi river, 103
Congo river, discovery of iron bells on the, 211
Corvo on Portuguese exploration in Africa, 243; on the ancient gold-mines in Mazoe valley,

E E 2

COU

295; on early Portuguese enterprise in Mashonaland, 290

Couto, Portuguese author, 88

Covilham, Pedro de, Portuguese explorer, 230; his death in Abyssinia, *ib.*

Cyprus, Phœnician coin found in, 186; excavations in, 204

DALMATIA, ingot mould found in, 216

Dapper's description of Mashonaland ruins, 240

Deir-el-Bahari, monuments of, 226

Delft pottery in Mazoe valley, 296

Dendema in occupation of Zendj tribes, 233

Denderah, zodiac of, 186

Diodorus on tin ingots found in ancient Britain, 216; on the Egyptian gold-mines at Wadi Allaga, 218

Dutch nomenclature, 17, 18

Dyer, Mr. Thiselton, Director of Kew Gardens, on the age of the baobab, 185, 186

EDRISI, geographer, on Zendj tribes of East Africa, 233

Egyptian gold-mines in Wadi Allaga, 218; commerce on the Red Sea, 226

Elibi river, ruin near, 99

Emesa, Syria, temple of the sun at, 204

Eratosthenes, historian, on Arabian tribes, 229

Evans, Sir John, on ingot mould found in Dalmatia, 210

Ezekiel's denunciation of Tyre, 227

GRE

FALLOW-PAUNCHES, a wild tribe of the Kalahari desert, 14

Falmouth, ingot of tin found in harbour of, 216; Sir Henry James's pamphlet on, *ib.*

Farao, Signor, governor of Senna, on regal burials at Magonio, 346

Fitzwilliam Museum at Cambridge, cylindrical marble object from Cyprus, 204

Forbes, Major, destruction of Kaffir village by, 299

Francs, mythical inhabitants of, 222

GAMA, Vasco da, Portuguese explorer, 230

Gambidji country, 270; extent of, 272; tattooed women in, 305

Gamitto, Portuguese traveller, on lion worship, 331

Gasetsive, chief of Kanya, 8; death and funeral of, 10; visit to his widow, *ib.*

Gaza, kraal of, 314

Geographical Society, Royal, expedition assisted by, 4; Museum at Lisbon, 212

Girandali, native bearer from Kunzi's kraal, 312

Glaser, Herr Edward, Arabian traveller, 230

Godobgwe stream, 50

Gona, village of, 257; larder trees at, 257, 258; savage ornaments of inhabitants, 258; growth of tobacco, *ib.*; rice-fields, *ib.*; prosperity of kraal, *ib.*

Gouveia, a Portuguese half-caste in 'Mtoko country, 318

Greece, mythical inhabitants of, 222; ancient legends of, 225

Gungunyana, Zulu chief, raids of, 263

Gutu, Makalanga chief of Gona, 257

Hadjar Kem, Malta, Cabiri temple ruins at, 116

Hampden, Mount, isolation of, 285

Harris, Mr. F. R., Secretary of British South Africa Company, his letter to Chief 'Mtoko, 302

Hartley Hills, gold workings near, 289

Hatason, Queen of Egypt, ingots of gold sent from kingdom of Punt to, 221; native expedition in reign of, 220

Hayman, Captain, conquers Portuguese at Massi-Kessi, 868; guns and ammunition captured by troops of, 869

Heany and Johnson, Messrs., pioneer work in Mashonaland, 871; failure of their expedition, 377

Hepburn, Mr., missionary at Palapwe, 24

Herodian's description of the sacred cone in Syrian temple, 204

Herodotus on the origin of the phallus, 188; on the worship of the Arabians, 190; on Egyptian sacrifice, 209; on the circumnavigation of Africa, 225

Hierapolis, Mesopotamia, temple at, 117, 185; phalli in temple at, 188

Himyaritic supremacy in Arabia, 186; inscriptions, 230

Hippalus and his knowledge of monsoons, 224

Hogarth, Mr., and the excavations at Paphos, in Cyprus, 204

Holub, Dr. Emil, 'Seven Years in South Africa' by, 95

Horace on Arabian wealth, 227

Horapollo on the vulture, 185

Icuzu, native servant attached to author's expedition, 278; accompanies author to chief 'Mtoko's country, 302

Ikomo, brother to the chief of Zimbabwe, 73; his kraal on Zimbabwe hill, 75; taking leave of, 84

Imiridzi, village of, 256; knitting industry at, ib.

Impakwe river, Mr. E. A. Maund's description of ruins, 99; Mr. Moffat's account, ib.

Inyagurukwe, native search for gold at, 337

Inyamanda, arrival of expedition at, 34; trade at, ib.; scarcity of meat, 35; human vultures, ib.; flora, ib.; villages, ib.; rock tunnel, ib.; family charms, 39; view from summit of rock, 41

Inyota mountain, ancient goldworkings in, 294

Inyani range, as viewed from Zimbabwe, 75

Isafuba game, holes for, 207

Ishmaelites, fetichism of, 195

James, Sir Henry, on tin ingot found in Falmouth Harbour, 216

John II., King of Portugal, equips an expedition to Africa, 230

Johnson, Mr. See Heany and Johnson, Messrs.

Jomvga, a curious granite

418 INDEX

JOM.

mountain in Kunzi country, 315

Jumbo mine in Mazoe valley, 296

KAABA stone at Mecca, 195

Kaffir beer, 58; language, ib.; cemetery near Zimbabwe, 121; habitation, 179; tribes at Zimbabwe, 210; instruments enumerated by Dos Santos, 212; manufacture of iron ingots, 218; death-wailing in villages, 303

Kalahari desert route, 14

Kalimazondo, kraal of, 334; interview with chief, ib.; camp of Mr. Selous at, 335

Kanya, road to, 7; town of, 9; its inhabitants, ib.; character of scenery, 11

Karnak, Egyptian temples at, 183

Kerbela, Mohammedan burial at, 121

Khama, native chief, 6; cattle disease in country of, 8; migration of his tribe, 21; his reputation, 23; his power and intolerance, 25; his religious enthusiasm, ib.; prohibits beer-drinking among his tribe, 25; his discipline, 26; interview with, 28

Kharabit, Sabæan king, East Africa in possession of, 229

Kimberley, purchases at, 5

Kirk, Sir John, at Quiloa, 205

Kremer, Herr, on the solstitial use of emblems, 186; on the ancient cult of Arabia, 195; his allusions to stone-worship, ib.; on the Arabian system of totems, 331

Kum, Mohammedan burial at, 121

Kunzi country, description of

LUN

chief, 306; iron-smelting furnace in, 307; hospitality of chief's brother Gwadeli, 308; interesting relics obtained by author, 309; woman's dress of woven bark fibre, ib.; fetichism in, 310; bathing and washing, ib.; chief's wives, 311; native fishing, ib.; dainty viands, 312; love of salt, ib.; hand-clapping and greetings, ib.; native bracelets, 313; Mount Jomvga, 315

Limpopo river, ruins near junction with the Elibi, 99; ancient gold-mines in vicinity, ib.

Linchwe, native chief, 6, 11

Lisbon, Geographical Society's Museum at, 212

Livingstone, Dr., at Shoshong, 23

Livouri range, as viewed from Zimbabwe, 75

Lobengula, King of Matabeleland, 6; raids of, 22, 237, 263; and plural births, 316

Lockyer, Prof. Norman, on Egyptian temples at Karnak, 188; on the zodiac of Denderah, 186

Lopodzi river, 375

Lotsani river, crossing the, 29

Louvre, Phœnician column of marble in the, 188; remarks by MM. Perrot and Chipiez, 189

Luanhe, ancient Portuguese market in Mazoe valley, 295

Lucian's 'De Syriâ Deâ,' 117; description of the temple at Hierapolis, 185; allusion to Greek amulets, 187

Lundi river, crossing the, 42; adjacent population, 43; agriculture near, 44; ruins in vicinity, 100; description of

circular fort ruin near, *ib.*;
dimensions of ruin, 156; ornamental patterns on ruined temple, 104

Lnti, village of, 261

Lntilo mountain, 261; deer in vicinity, *ib.*

Lutzi, author's stay at village of, 310; interview with lion priest, 328; festivities at, 330

MACLOUTSIE, Border Police at, 22

Madera, Portuguese Colonel, boycotts English immigrants in Mapanda'e country, 379

Mafeking, stay of expedition at, 5; routes from, 6; Ba-rolong tribe of, 7

Mafusaire, village of, 271; first white lady in, *ib.*; tomb of a chief, *ib.*

Magonio mountains, 346

Makalanga tribes, 32; their vanity, 37; ornaments for head, 38; witchcraft, 39; domestic implements, *ib.*; anklets and necklaces, 40; character, 55; religion, 56; musical instruments, 57; Arabian influence, *ib.*; beer brewing, *ib.*; female brewers, 58; custom of hand-clapping, 66; festivities and funerals, 77; graves at Zimbabwe, 79; sacrificial feasts, *ib.*; playing the piano, 80; songs and music, 82; outdoor games, 85; interior of hut, 86; their ingenuity, 248; a native born without hands, 258; dread of Shangan tribe, 263; fear of horses, 271; architectural features of country, 275; native drawings, 276; rice-fields, 277

Makoni chief, visit to, 284; his village and its inhabitants, 354

Makonyora village, 347

Makori post station, 251

Malozo's kraal, presentation of beer in, 314; hair-dressing in, *ib.*

Malta, temple ruins in, 116

Mandigo, kraal of, 377; teetse pest, *ib.*; abandoned waggons near, *ib.*

Mangwendi's country, ruined villages, 83; journey through, 314; visit to ruins, 330; description of chief's kraal, 339, 342; Bondoro worship in, 340; sacrifice in, *ib.*; ploughing season, 341; wives and children of chief, 342; author's departure from, 343

Manicaland, mountains of, 261, 354; valleys of, 355

Mapanda'e country, waste of provisions in, 298; desperate condition of English immigrants, 379; corrugated iron palaces, 381; camp attacked by lions at night, *ib.*; ducking a Jew in the Pungwe, 382; British colony in, *ib.*; island game on the Pungwe river, *ib.*; island village of chief, 383

Mapandera, village of, 294

Maphartee a Sabæan dependency, 224

Marib, the ancient Saba and capital of the Sabæan kingdom in Arabia, 105; ruins of elliptic temple, 177

Marico district, Transvaal, ruins of stone huts in, 130

Marinus of Tyro on Semitic fetichism, 194; his vagueness of information, 224

Mashah, a Makalanga native engaged by author, 247; his life and adventures, *ib.*

Mashanani, native servant attached to author's expedition,

MAS

278; accompanies author to chief 'Mtoko's country, 302 Mashonaland, departure of expedition for, 5; roads to, 6; cattle disease en route, 8; government, 30; interpreters, 31; pioneers, 32; intercourse with natives, ib.; tribal feuds, 33; Portuguese in, ib.; description of country, 84; granite hills, ib.; native head-rests, 36; skin-polishing, 38; dollasses, or wooden charms, 39; witchcraft, ib.; domestic and other implements, 39, 40; Zulu raids, 43; native agriculture, ib.; iron-smelting, 45; female decoration, 47; quaintness of scenery, 50; quadrupeds diseases, 51; 'salted horses,' ib.; 'drunk sickness' among oxen, ib.; discovery of gold, 52; bridge-building, 53; tree-barking, ib.; caterpillars as food, ib.; sleeping in the forest, 54; forest scenery, ib.; native game pits, 55; beer-brewing, 57; Kaffir language, 58; 'trekking' for three months, 59; camp life and work at Zimbabwe, 60; native gunpowder manufacture, 72; cotton-spinning, ib.; native war-dance, 75; festivities and funerals, 77; native pianos, 80; travelling in the wilds, 84; extraordinary block of granite near Zimbabwe, 85; Arabian influence in, 86; Umgabe's kraal, 87; direful experience of a swamp, 90; archæology of ruined cities, 95; ancient gold-mines, 99; situation of the Great Zimbabwe ruins, 103; architecture, 148; description of temples, ib.; religious symbolism of birds, 186; commerce of the ancients,

MAS

204; gold-mining, 215; ancient gold-workings, 218; Arabian gold-diggers, 220; geography and ethnology of ruins, 223; ancient output of gold, 228; confusion in topography, 234; Portuguese accounts of ruins, 238; first pioneers of Chartered Company, 240; Toroa ruins, ib.; early Arab trading, 241; Boer expeditions, 242; unoccupied fertile land, 269; scanty population, ib.; highest point in the country, 272; future capital of gold-fields, 279; planting of British flag, ib.; the 'Mashonaland Times and Zambesia Herald,' 280; government stores, ib.; hospital huts, ib.; native engineering skill in Mazoe valley, 288; Mr. E. A. Maund's lecture on ancient gold-mining in the 'Mewezwe district, 290; eland meat, 291; destruction of early Portuguese mission, 296; winter in, 298; native tattooing, 305; native fishing, 311; forest monotony, 315; domestic animals, 318; politics and religion, 326; privations of expedition, 348; highest inhabited spot, 354; magnificence of country, 362; tsetse fly, 363; Scotch enterprise, 365; Heany and Johnson's pioneer work, 371; Portuguese convicts, 378; native bearers, ib.; Pungwe route, 878; fauna, 380; proposed railway from Beira port to the interior, 386; geography and meteorology, 889; list of stations astronomically observed, with altitudes, 398; progress from November 1891 to May 1893, 405. See also Zimbabwe.

MAS

Masoudi, El, Arabian historian, 116; on the Sabæan temples, 148; on ancient stone-worship in Arabia, 194; on Zindj tribes of East Africa, 232

Masoupa in the Ba-Ngwatetse country, 11; native dancing and music, *ib.*; heathenism, 12

Masonvo river, and Mazoe valley, 295

Massapa mines and the Queen of Sheba's gold, 295; ancient Portuguese market in Mazoe valley, *ib.*

Massi-Kessi, early Portuguese influence at, 298; journey to, 366; its Portuguese reminiscences, 367; golden bullets, 368; Chartered Company at, *ib.*; engagement between Portuguese and English, 869; treaty concerning, *ib.*; Portuguese hospitality, 870

Masunsgwe, Mount, visit to, 837

Matabeleland, King of, 6; native raids on Shoshong, 22; raid upon Cherumbila's tribe, 90; raids on Chekatu, 254; raids in Mazoe valley, 288

Matimbi, village of, 277; description of chief, *ib.*

Matindela, ruins at, 100, 136, 262; baobab trees, 135; temple and walls, 137, 156; meaning of the word, guineafowl, 263; curious fruit, *ib.*; gigantic trees, 264; honeybirds, 265; destruction around, *ib.*; profusion of game, *ib.*; hunting parties in locality, *ib.*; game laws of the Makalangas, 266

Matzaire, chief of Chekatu village, 254

Mauch, Karl, German traveller in Mashonaland, 117, 244

MET

Maund, Mr. E. A., on the ruins at Tati and on the Impakwe, 99; on ancient gold-mining in Mashoonland, 290

Maunga tribe, 854

Mazoe valley, ruins in, 99, 135; ruins of fort in gold-fields, 100; author's trip to, 284; native kraals, 286; Mr. Selous' hunting expedition, *ib.*; huts and their inhabitants, 287; handmade pottery of natives, *ib.*; native beer, *ib.*; huts of Mr. Fleming, gold prospector, 288; ancient gold-mines, *ib.*; mountain caves, *ib.*; Matabele raids, *ib.*; native engineering skill, 288; enormous output of gold in ancient times, 289; modern invasion, *ib.*; Rothschild's, Cherry's, and Lockner's settlements, 291; lemontrees in, *ib.*; Mr. Nesbit's hospitality, *ib.*; visit to Yellow Jacket mine, *ib.*; kindness of prospectors, *ib.*; meat of the eland, *ib.*; lion-shooting, 292; curious birds, *ib.*; description of ruin, *ib.*; valuable agricultural country, 294; Chipadzi's village, *ib.*; Mapandera's kraal, *ib.*; Portuguese in, 295; ancient Portuguese markets in, *ib.*; Major Forbes's punishment of Kaffirs, 299; modern agricultural farms 300

Mecca, Kaaba stone at, 195

Mediterranean, prehistoric excavations on the, 209

Meshed, Mohammedan burial at, 121

Mesopotamia, temple at Hierapolis, 117; Sabæan temples, 148

Metemo fort, ruins of, 100, 135, 261

Metzwandira, author's Makalanga body-servant, 248
Midianites, sacred tower of the, 116
Mineni river, accident on, 871
Mines, Royal School of, cast of ingot of tin found in Falmouth Harbour, 216
M'lala, village of, 44; stomach decoration among women, 40; costumes of natives, 49; witch doctor, *ib.*
Mocaranga tribe, land of, 32; Dos Santos' account, 237; Bocarro's description of race, 389
Moffat, Dr., at Shoshong, 23
Moffat, Mr., political agent in Matabeleland, 90
Molopolole river, 15
Mondoro, or lion priest, in 'Mtokoland, 826; interviews with, 827
Monomatapa, empire of, 32; civilisation, 215; Portuguese travellers on wealth of emperor, 234; confusion of name, *ib.*; Father dos Santos' description of the people, 236; Leo Africanus' account of ruins, 240; Da Costa's letter to the King of Portugal concerning ruins, 242; stronghold for chief's wives at Chiburga, 267; Portuguese account of Monomatapa, 331, 332; their treaty with chief, 352
Monteiro, Portuguese traveller, on the Zambesi tribes, 237; on lion worship, 331
Montfaucon, M., on tower worship, 118
Montsoia, native chief, 7
M'shagashi river, 58
'Msweswe, shafts in river district, 299; Mr. E. A. Maund on ancient gold-mining at, 290
'Mtasa, lord of the Nica tribe, 856; mountains in country of, *ib.*; British in possession of kraal, 857; conflicting interests of England and Portugal in land of, 857, 859; Bushman drawings in village, 859
'Mtigeza, chiefs around Mount Wedza, 273; their fortress, *ib.*; interior of huts, 270
'Mtoko country, presents for chief, 284; author's embassy to, 301; births and marriages, 818; marauding transactions, 817; native costoms, *ib.*; language, 818; cattle, *ib.*; chief's kraal, 319; description of women, *ib.*; Zambesi influence, 321; chief's indignation with author, *ib.*; a state visit, 323; nervousness of chief, 324; description of presents, *ib.*; chief's opinion of the white lady, 325; hospitality of the natives, *ib.*; politics and religion, 326; the Mondoro, or lion priest, 827; bucolic prosperity, *ib.*; imminence of civil war, 328; early struggles with the Portuguese, 331; Bushman drawings, 333
Muali, the god of the Makalangas, 57, 841
Muchienda, village of, 258; native game-hunting, *ib.*
Musungaikwa country, tattooed women in, 305
Mwairari river, crossing the, 268
Mycene, Dr. Schliemann's discoveries at, 185

Naka pass, 43
Nakab al Hajar, Arabia, ruins of castle at, 105; temple, 177

NAN

Nankin china in Mazoe Valley, 396

Natal, Bakalanga tribes in, 83

Naucratis, *lebes* from temple at, in British Museum, 200

Necho, Pharaoh, B.C. 600, 225

Nejed, Lower, monoliths in, 119

Nesbit, Mr., mining commissioner, in Mazoe valley, 291

Neves Fereira, English immigrants' boycotted by Portuguese governor of, 879

Nhaya, Pedro de, Portuguese commander, 231; his capture of Sofala, *ib.*

Nica tribe, lord of the, 806

'Nyagowe river, gold in quill found in, 809

Nyanger, camping at, 843; curious grotto, 844; Bushman drawings on rocks, *ib.*; graves in cave, *ib.*; cemeteries in the open, 845; ruins of temple, 846

Nyangombwe mountains, 875

'Nyatzetse river, crossing the, 261; agriculture near, *ib.*

Odzani river, dangerous crossing of, 300

Odxi river, the boundary between Mashonaland and Manicaland, 856

Ophir, land of, theory concerning, 228

Palapwe, migration of natives to, 21; Ba-mangwato tribe at, 23; description of country, 24; mission-house, *ib.*; cascade, *ib.*; babooks, *ib.*; native services, *ib.*; church building, *ib.*; discipline of chief, 26; native women, 27; departure of expedition, 29

PTO

Palgrave, Arabian traveller, 118

Paphos, Cyprus, excavations at, 204

Payva, Alfonso de, Portuguese explorer, 280

Pegado, Captain Vicento, Portuguese governor of Sofala, 239

Pelasgi, mythical race of, 222

Penuel, the sacred tower of the Midianites, 116

'Periplus of the Red Sea,' anonymous author of, 224; his geographical speculations, 225

Perrot and Chipiez, MM., on art history in Sardinia, 117, 118; their work on 'Phœnicia,' 186; on the Phœnician column in the Louvre, 180

Parsia, Mohammedan burial in, 121

Philips, Mr. G., on the Zimbabwe and Tati ruins, 96

Phœnicia, temple construction in, 116; coin found in Cyprus, 186; symbols, 188; Biblical allusions to wealth of Arabia and, 227; intimacy with Sabæa, *ib.*; ancient enterprise, 229

Pigafetta's description of Mashonaland ruins, 240

Pilan, chief of Masoupa, 6, 12

Pliny, vagueness of information as to source of ancient merchandise, 224

Portuguese in Mashonaland, 83; expeditions in Africa, 280; failure of expeditions through Arab jealousy, 285

Providential Pass, 50, 75; Cherumbila's tribe at, 90; Matabele raid upon, *ib.*

Ptolemy, vagueness of information as to source of ancient merchandise, 224; mention of Agizymba nation, 230; on

PUN

Roman penetration through Africa, *ib.*
Pungwe river, early Portuguese influence on the, 298; at Sarmento, 378; its imposing appearance, 379; infested with crocodile and hippopotami, 379, 385; fauna of adjacent country, 380; dangerous sandbanks, 384
Punt, kingdom of, its doubtful whereabouts, 221; wealth of the people, *ib.*; ingots of gold sent to Queen Hatasou, *ib.*; conquered by Egyptians, 226; theory concerning the land of Punt, 228

QUILOA, Sir John Kirk at, 205; Arab settlement at, 241

RAMATLABAMA river, 7
Red Sea, Egyptian commerce on the, 226; Arabian and Phœnician enterprise in region of, 228
Renaudot, M., on Arab experience of savage tribes in East Africa, 233
Revwe river and valley, 367
Rhapta, Arab settlement at, 224; Dean Vincent on the situation of, *ib.*
Rome, its importation of gold from Arabia, 227
Rothschild's settlement in Mazoe valley, 291
Rusapi river, Chipunza's kraal on the, 348

SABÆA, its intimacy with Phœnicia, 227; wealth of, *ib.*; Arabian and Æthiopian cities named alike, 280
Sabi river, 82; ruins of forts, 100;

SAN

situation of ruins, 103; author's expedition to region of, 247; valley scenery, 259; view of mountains, 261; ruined villages and deserted fields near, 263; Zulu raids on Makalanga villages, *ib.*; its magnificence, 268; bathing and washing in, 269
Salisbury fort, daub huts of, 279; fever and famine, 280; growth of townships around, *ib.*; newspaper established, *ib.*; civil and military administration, *ib.*; hospital huts, *ib.*; Benedictine sisters and Jesuit father, *ib.*; anniversary dinner of pioneers at hotel, 281; the question of supplies, *ib.*; Chartered Company's difficulty in catering, 282; influx of adventurers, *ib.*; danger of famine, 283; Mr. Selous in search of food waggons, *ib.*; arrival of provisions, *ib.*; climate of, *ib.*; author's departure for Mazoe valley, 284; his return therefrom, 294; farewell to friends, 303; trading with Kunziland natives, 309
Salt, Mr., in Abyssinia, 229
Salvador, San, iron bells discovered at, 212
Sangwe river, Mapandera's kraal on, 294
Santos, Father dos, Portuguese traveller, 82; on Kaffir instruments, 212; his description of the Monomatapa tribe, 286; allusion to lemon-trees in Mazoe valley, 291; on sacrifice among the Mocarangas, 341; on feasting in Mangwendi's country, 341; burial of chiefs, 346; on early Portuguese travellers, 352

INDEX

SAR

Sardinia, round towers in, 116; MM. Perrot and Chipiez on history of art in, 117
Sargon, annals of, 227
Sarmento, deserted coaches at, 878; climate of, 880
Schliemann, Dr., discoveries of, at Mycene, 185
Science, British Association for the Advancement of, expedition assisted by, 4
Sechele, native chief, 6, 14; capital and residence, 15
Sechuana language, 8; superstition, 10; dancing, 11; marriage laws, 12; religion, 25
Sekatu, village of, 255; growth of cucumbers at, ib.
Selous, Mr., at Providential Pass, 50; in search of provisions for Fort Salisbury, 283; hunting expedition in Mazoe valley, 286; in chief 'Mtoko's kraal, 321; at Kalimazondo's kraal, 335
Selynia, pond of, 20
Semitic nations, monopolising policy of, 228
Shamsi, Queen of Arabia, 227
Shangan tribes, 32; raids on Sabi river region, 263
Shashi river, 80; ruins in vicinity, 95
Sheba, Queen of, and the Masapa gold-mines, 295
Shoshong, journey to, 17; arrival at, 20; hills of, ib.; missionaries at, 21; traders at, ib.; exodus of natives from, ib.; water famine, ib.; tribal raids on, 22; ruins of, ib.; Dr. Livingstone and Dr. Moffat at, 23
Sibibabira, village of, 251
Sikkoma, father of Khama, 26
Silveira, Father, Portuguese Jesuit, martyrdom of, 235, 206
Sindito, chief of Sekatu village, 255; hospitality of, ib.
Siorma, in occupation of Zendj tribes, 238
Sirwah, elliptic temple at, 177
Smet, village of, 272
Sofala, Arabian writers on gold of, 280; Portuguese in possession, 231; Duarte Barbosa on the gold trade, ib.; ancient historian's account of, ib.; tribes of cannibals near, 282; golden mountains near, 234; manufacture of brass ornaments, ib.; Portuguese governor at, 239
Solomon, King, expedition of, 226
Soudan, carving from the, 186
Stonehenge, mythical builders of, 222
Swan, Mr. Robert McNair Wilson, cartographer to expedition, 5; on the orientation and measurements of Zimbabwe ruins, 141; on the geography and meteorology of Mashonaland, 880; his astronomical observat'ons, with altitudes of station., 808
Syria, Phœnician temple of the sun at Emesa, 204

THE

Taif, Arabia, stone-worship at, 105
Tatagora valley, scenery in, 285; the machabel tree, ib.; junction of river with Mazoe, 290
Tati, ruins of, 95; description thereof by Mr. G. Philips and Mr. E. A. Maund, 96
Taungs, native settlement at, 6
Thebes, Bœotia, relics from, 205

TIG

Tiglath Pileser II., Assyrian inscriptions concerning, 227
Todd, Dr., of the 'Magicioune,' succours English immigrants in Mapanda's country, 379
Tokwe river, 50
Toroa, Leo Africanus on ruins of, 246
Torrend, Father, on Mashonaland, 38
Transvaal, ruins of stone huts in the Marico district, 189
Truro Museum, ingot of tin from Falmouth Harbour, 216
Tuli fort, 80
Tyre, Ezekiel's denunciation of, 227; Zechariah on wealth of, 228

UMPANIPATZA, village of, 251
Umgabe, chief of Zimbabwe, 65; his personal appearance, 66; his brother Ikomo, 78; visit to Umgabe's kraal, 86; his intoxicated condition, ib.; uncomfortable quarters, ib.; situation of kraal, 87; his well-filled granaries, 88; domestic commodities, ib.
Umliwan district, fertility of, 371
Umtali, trip to, 284; ancient gold-mining at, 290; B.S.A. camp at, 860; arrival of author, 801; importance of, 803; Portuguese remains near fort, 804; journey to Beira, 805
Umzilikatze, Zulu warrior, 237

VAROMA, Mount, at Zimbabwe, 160
Victoria fort, fever at, 50; dearness of provisions, ib.; horse sickness, 51; sour grass, 52;

ZEY

discovery of gold near, ib.; bridge-building in vicinity, 53; Sir John Willoughby at, 74; departure for Sabi river, 251; prospecting for gold, 280
Vincent, Dean, on the situation of Rhapta, 224
Vryberg, arrival and departure of expedition, 5; native settlement at, 6

WADI ALLAGA gold-mines, 218
Wedza, Mount, highest point in Mashonaland, 272; iron-smelting at, ib.; chiefs in vicinity, 273
Willoughby, Sir John, at Fort Victoria, 74; visits the expedition at Zimbabwe, ib.; interviews the chief's brother, Ikomo, and threatens him, ib.
'Wissenschaft, Akademie der,' by Herr Kremer, 180, 195

YANDORO, a village in Kunzi's country, 312
Yellow Jacket mine, visit to, 298
Yemen, temples and fortresses in, 176
Yenya mountains, 856

ZAMBESI river, Zimbabwe in region of, 297; early Portuguese influence on the, 298
Zamopera, village of, 270; its inhabitants, ib.
Zechariah on the wealth of Tyre, 228
Zendj tribes, 233; iron trade with Indians, 234
Zeyd, Abou, on the wild Zindj tribes of East Africa, 233

Zimbabwe, tribes around, 32; sickness among oxen, 51; adjacent forests, 54; description of the country, 55; fever in camp, ib.; character of natives, 55; arrival of expedition, 59; camp life, 60; flora of, ib.; alarming fire, 63; visitors in camp, 64; ruins, 64, 99, 103; daily work, 64; evening concerts, 65; visit of Umgabe, district chief, ib.; native wages, 69; difficulties with workmen, ib.; provisions and marketing, 70; native ingenuity, 71; ornaments and snuff-boxes, 72; the chief's brother in camp, 73; trouble with natives, ib.; kraal of Ikomo, 75; Amazonian dance, ib.; graves among the ruins, 79; musical instruments, 80, 81; excursions from, 82; beer-making, 83; locust eating, 84; migratory spirit of the natives, ib.; scenery around, 85; Mr. G. Philips's description of the ruins, 90; prominent features of the Great Zimbabwe ruins, 104; excavation work, ib.; religious purport of ruined towers, 115; sacrifice, 117; Kaffir cemetery, 121; description of hill fortress, 122; labyrinthine nature of buildings, 128; gold-smelting furnaces and caves, 131; ruins of Little Zimbabwe, 135; orientation and measurements of ruins by Mr. R. M. W. Swan, 141; nature worship, ib.; astronomical observations, 147, 170, 173; architectural features, 148; coin of Byblos, 150; soapstone monoliths, 167; ancient builders, 176; discoveries during excavation, 179; traces of recent Kaffir habitation, ib.; soapstone carvings, ib.; religious symbolism of birds, 186; circumcision practised by the ancients, 188; ancient veneration for stones, 191; geological fragments, 193, 194; old-world worship, 194; artistic skill of the ancients, 196; fragments of soapstone bowls, 197; Phœnician work, ib.; proto-Arabian lettering on bowls, 200; world-wide commerce of the ancients, 204; Celadon pottery from China, ib.; Persian and Arabian wares, ib.; Monomatapa rule, 205; ceramic art, 207; bronze and iron weapons and implements, 209; ruins scoured by Kaffirs for centuries, 210; excavation of iron weapons and implements, 211; discovery of iron bells, ib.; gold-smelting furnace, 215; Arabian origin of gold-diggers, 220; discovery of gold-smelting crucibles, 221; derivation of name, 234; modern exploration of ruins by a German traveller, 244; thirst for gold among the ancients, 279

Zindj tribes in Africa, 231; Abou Zeyd's description of, 233

Zulu raids in Mashonaland, 43; successes under Umzilikatze, 237

Zygabenus on Ishmaelite stone-worship, 195

MESSRS. LONGMANS, GREEN, & CO.'S
CLASSIFIED CATALOGUE
OF
WORKS IN GENERAL LITERATURE.

History, Politics, Polity, Political Memoirs, &c.

Abbott.—A HISTORY OF GREECE. By EVELYN ABBOTT, M.A., LL.D.
Part I.—From the Earliest Times to the Ionian Revolt. Crown 8vo., 10s. 6d.
Part II.—500-445 B.C. Cr. 8vo., 10s. 6d.

Acland and Ransome.—A HANDBOOK IN OUTLINE OF THE POLITICAL HISTORY OF ENGLAND TO 1894. Chronologically Arranged. By A. H. DYKE ACLAND, M.P., and CYRIL RANSOME, M.A. Cr. 8vo., 6s.

ANNUAL REGISTER (THE). A Review of Public Events at Home and Abroad, for the year 1894. 8vo., 18s.
Volumes of the ANNUAL REGISTER for the years 1863-1893 can still be had. 18s. each.

Armstrong.—ELIZABETH FARNESE: The Termagant of Spain. By EDWARD ARMSTRONG, M.A. 8vo., 16s.

Arnold.—Works by T. ARNOLD, D.D., formerly Head Master of Rugby School.
INTRODUCTORY LECTURES ON MODERN HISTORY. 8vo., 7s. 6d.
MISCELLANEOUS WORKS. 8vo., 7s. 6d.

Bagwell.—IRELAND UNDER THE TUDORS. By RICHARD BAGWELL, LL.D. 3 vols. Vols. I. and II. From the first Invasion of the Northmen to the year 1578. 8vo., 32s. Vol. III. 1578-1603. 8vo., 18s.

Ball.—HISTORICAL REVIEW OF THE LEGISLATIVE SYSTEMS OPERATIVE IN IRELAND, from the Invasion of Henry the Second to the Union (1172-1800). By the Rt. Hon. J. T. BALL. 8vo., 6s.

Besant.—THE HISTORY OF LONDON. By WALTER BESANT. With 74 Illustrations. Crown 8vo., 1s. 9d. Or bound as a School Prize Book, 2s. 6d.

Brassey.—PAPERS AND ADDRESSES. By LORD BRASSEY.
NAVAL AND MARITIME, 1872-1893. 2 vols. Crown 8vo., 10s.
MERCANTILE MARINE AND NAVIGATION, 1871-1894. Crown 8vo., 5s.
POLITICAL AND MISCELLANEOUS, 1861-1894. Crown 8vo., 5s.

Bright.—A HISTORY OF ENGLAND. By the Rev. J. FRANCK BRIGHT, D.D.,
Period I. MEDIÆVAL MONARCHY: A.D. 449 to 1485. Crown 8vo., 4s. 6d.
Period II. PERSONAL MONARCHY: 1485 to 1688. Crown 8vo., 5s.
Period III. CONSTITUTIONAL MONARCHY: 1689 to 1837. Cr. 8vo., 7s. 6d.
Period IV. THE GROWTH OF DEMOCRACY: 1837 to 1880. Cr. 8vo., 6s.

Buckle.—HISTORY OF CIVILISATION IN ENGLAND AND FRANCE, SPAIN AND SCOTLAND. By HENRY THOMAS BUCKLE. 3 vols. Crown 8vo., 24s.

Burke.—A HISTORY OF SPAIN, from the Earliest Times to the Death of Ferdinand the Catholic. By ULICK RALPH BURKE, M.A. 2 vols. 8vo., 32s.

Chesney.—INDIAN POLITY: a View of the System of Administration in India. By General Sir GEORGE CHESNEY, K.C.B., M.P. With Map showing all the Administrative Divisions of British India. 8vo., 21s.

Creighton.—HISTORY OF THE PAPACY DURING THE REFORMATION. By MANDELL CREIGHTON, D.D., LL.D., Bishop of Peterborough. Vols. I. and II., 1378-1464, 32s. Vols. III. and IV., 1464-1518, 24s. Vol. V., 1517-1527. 8vo., 15s.

Cuningham.—A SCHEME FOR IMPERIAL FEDERATION: a Senate for the Empire. By GRANVILLE C. CUNINGHAM, of Montreal, Canada. Cr. 8vo., 3s. 6d.

Curzon.—PERSIA AND THE PERSIAN QUESTION. By the Hon. GEORGE N. CURZON, M.P. With 9 Maps, 96 Illustrations, Appendices, and an Index. 2 vols. 8vo., 42s.

History, Politics, Polity, Political Memoirs, &c.—*continued*.

De Tocqueville.—DEMOCRACY IN AMERICA. By ALEXIS DE TOCQUEVILLE. 2 vols. Crown 8vo., 16*s*.

Dickinson.—THE DEVELOPMENT OF PARLIAMENT DURING THE NINETEENTH CENTURY. By G. LOWES DICKINSON, M.A. 8vo. 7*s*. 6*d*.

Ewald.—THE HISTORY OF ISRAEL. By HEINRICH EWALD, Professor in the University of Göttingen. 8 vols. 8vo., Vols. I. and II., 24*s*. Vols. III. and IV., 21*s*. Vol. V., 18*s*. Vol. VI., 16*s*. Vol. VII., 21*s*. Vol. VIII., 18*s*.

Fitzpatrick.—SECRET SERVICE UNDER PITT. By W. J. FITZPATRICK, F.S.A., Author of 'Correspondence of Daniel O'Connell'. 8vo., 7*s*. 6*d*.

Froude.—Works by JAMES A. FROUDE.
THE HISTORY OF ENGLAND, from the Fall of Wolsey to the Defeat of the Spanish Armada. 12 vols. Cr. 8vo., 3*s*. 6*d*. each.
THE DIVORCE OF CATHERINE OF ARAGON: the Story as told by the Imperial Ambassadors resident at the Court of Henry VIII. Crown 8vo., 6*s*.
THE SPANISH STORY OF THE ARMADA, and other Essays. Cr. 8vo., 3*s*. 6*d*.
THE ENGLISH IN IRELAND IN THE EIGHTEENTH CENTURY.
Cabinet Edition, 3 vols. Cr. 8vo., 18*s*.
Silver Library Edition. 3 vols. Cr. 8vo., 10*s*. 6*d*.
ENGLISH SEAMEN IN THE SIXTEENTH CENTURY. Lectures delivered at Oxford, 1893-94. Crown 8vo., 6*s*.
SHORT STUDIES ON GREAT SUBJECTS. 4 vols. Cr. 8vo., 3*s*. 6*d*. each.
CÆSAR: a Sketch. Cr. 8vo., 3*s*. 6*d*.

Gardiner.—Works by SAMUEL RAWSON GARDINER, D.C.L., LL.D.
HISTORY OF ENGLAND, from the Accession of James I. to the Outbreak of the Civil War, 1603-1642. 10 vols. Crown 8vo., 6*s*. each.
HISTORY OF THE GREAT CIVIL WAR, 1642-1649. 4 vols. Cr. 8vo., 6*s*. each.
HISTORY OF THE COMMONWEALTH AND THE PROTECTORATE, 1649-1660. Vol. I., 1649-1651. With 14 Maps. 8vo., 21*s*.

Gardiner.—Works by SAMUEL RAWSON GARDINER, D.C.L., LL.D., Edinburgh—*continued*.
THE STUDENT'S HISTORY OF ENGLAND. With 378 Illustrations. Cr. 8vo., 12*s*.
Also in Three Volumes, price 4*s*. each.
Vol. I. B.C. 55—A.D. 1509. With 173 Illustrations. Crown 8vo. 4*s*.
Vol. II. 1509-1689. With 96 Illustrations. Crown 8vo. 4*s*.
Vol. III. 1689-1885. With 109 Illustrations. Crown 8vo. 4*s*.

Greville.—A JOURNAL OF THE REIGNS OF KING GEORGE IV., KING WILLIAM IV., AND QUEEN VICTORIA. By CHARLES C. F. GREVILLE, formerly Clerk of the Council. 8 vols. Crown 8vo., 6*s*. each.

Hearn.—THE GOVERNMENT OF ENGLAND: its Structure and its Development. By W. EDWARD HEARN. 8vo., 16*s*.

Herbert.—THE DEFENCE OF PLEVNA, 1877. Written by One who took Part in it. By WILLIAM V. HERBERT. With Maps. 8vo., 18*s*.

Historic Towns.—Edited by E. A. FREEMAN, D.C.L., and Rev. WILLIAM HUNT, M.A. With Maps and Plans. Crown 8vo., 3*s*. 6*d*. each.
BRISTOL. By the Rev. W. HUNT.
CARLISLE. By MANDELL CREIGHTON, D.D., Bishop of Peterborough.
CINQUE PORTS. By MONTAGU BURROWS.
COLCHESTER. By Rev. E. L. CUTTS.
EXETER. By E. A. FREEMAN.
LONDON. By Rev. W. J. LOFTIE.
OXFORD. By Rev. C. W. BOASE.
WINCHESTER. By Rev. G. W. KITCHIN, D.D.
YORK. By Rev. JAMES RAINE.
NEW YORK. By THEODORE ROOSEVELT.
BOSTON (U.S.) By HENRY CABOT LODGE.

Joyce.—A SHORT HISTORY OF IRELAND, from the Earliest Times to 1608. By P. W. JOYCE, LL.D. Crown 8vo., 10*s*. 6*d*.

Lang.—ST. ANDREWS. By ANDREW LANG. With 8 Plates and 24 Illustrations in the Text, by T. HODGE. 8vo., 15*s*. net.

History, Politics, Polity, Political Memoirs, &c.—continued.

Lecky.—Works by WILLIAM EDWARD HARTPOLE LECKY, M.P.

HISTORY OF ENGLAND IN THE EIGHTEENTH CENTURY.
Library Edition. 8 vols. 8vo., £7 4s.
Cabinet Edition. ENGLAND. 7 vols. Cr. 8vo., 6s. each. IRELAND. 5 vols. Crown 8vo., 6s. each.

HISTORY OF EUROPEAN MORALS FROM AUGUSTUS TO CHARLEMAGNE. 2 vols. Crown 8vo., 16s.

HISTORY OF THE RISE AND INFLUENCE OF THE SPIRIT OF RATIONALISM IN EUROPE. 2 vols. Crown 8vo., 16s.

THE EMPIRE: Its Value and Its Growth. An Inaugural Address delivered at the Imperial Institute, November 20, 1893. Crown 8vo., 1s. 6d.

Macaulay.—Works by LORD MACAULAY.

COMPLETE WORKS.
Cabinet Edition. 16 vols. Post 8vo., £4 16s.
Library Edition. 8 vols. 8vo., £5 5s.

HISTORY OF ENGLAND FROM THE ACCESSION OF JAMES THE SECOND.
Popular Edition. 2 vols. Cr. 8vo., 5s.
Student's Edit. 2 vols. Cr. 8vo., 12s.
People's Edition. 4 vols. Cr. 8vo., 16s.
Cabinet Edition. 8 vols. Post 8vo., 48s.
Library Edition. 5 vols. 8vo., £4.

CRITICAL AND HISTORICAL ESSAYS, WITH LAYS OF ANCIENT ROME, in 1 volume.
Popular Edition. Crown 8vo., 2s. 6d.
Authorised Edition. Crown 8vo., 2s. 6d., or 3s. 6d., gilt edges.
Silver Library Edition. Crown 8vo., 3s. 6d.

CRITICAL AND HISTORICAL ESSAYS.
Student's Edition. 1 vol. Cr. 8vo., 6s.
People's Edition. 2 vols. Cr. 8vo., 8s.
Trevelyan Edit. 2 vols. Cr. 8vo., 9s.
Cabinet Edition. 4 vols. Post 8vo., 24s.
Library Edition. 3 vols. 8vo., 36s.

ESSAYS which may be had separately, price 6d. each sewed, 1s. each cloth.

Addison and Walpole.	Lord Clive.
Frederick the Great.	The Earl of Chatham (Two Essays).
Lord Bacon.	Ranke and Gladstone.
Croker's Boswell's Johnson.	Milton and Machiavelli.
Hallam's Constitutional History.	Lord Byron, and The Comic Dramatists of the Restoration.
Warren Hastings (3d. swd., 6d. cl.).	

Macaulay.—Works by LORD MACAULAY,—continued.

MISCELLANEOUS WRITINGS AND SPEECHES.
Popular Edition. Cr. 8vo., 2s. 6d.
Cabinet Edition. Including Indian Penal Code, Lays of Ancient Rome, and Miscellaneous Poems. 4 vols. Post 8vo., 24s.

SELECTIONS FROM THE WRITINGS OF LORD MACAULAY. Edited, with Occasional Notes, by the Right Hon. Sir G. O. Trevelyan, Bart. Crown 8vo., 6s.

May.—THE CONSTITUTIONAL HISTORY OF ENGLAND since the Accession of George III. 1760-1870. By Sir THOMAS ERSKINE MAY, K.C.B. (Lord Farnborough). 3 vols. Crown 8vo., 18s.

Merivale.—Works by the Very Rev. CHARLES MERIVALE, late Dean of Ely.

HISTORY OF THE ROMANS UNDER THE EMPIRE.
Cabinet Edition. 8 vols. Cr. 8vo., 48s.
Silver Library Edition. 8 vols. Cr. 8vo., 3s. 6d. each.

THE FALL OF THE ROMAN REPUBLIC: a Short History of the Last Century of the Commonwealth. 12mo., 7s. 6d.

Montague.—THE ELEMENTS OF ENGLISH CONSTITUTIONAL HISTORY. By F. C. MONTAGUE, M.A. Cr. 8vo., 3s. 6d.

Richman.—APPENZELL: Pure Democracy and Pastoral Life in Inner-Rhoden. A Swiss Study. By IRVING B. RICHMAN, Consul-General of the United States to Switzerland. With Maps. Crown 8vo., 5s.

Seebohm.—Works by FREDERIC SEEBOHM.

THE ENGLISH VILLAGE COMMUNITY Examined in its Relations to the Manorial and Tribal Systems, &c. With 13 Maps and Plates. 8vo., 16s.

THE TRIBAL SYSTEM IN WALES: being Part of an Inquiry into the Structure and Methods of Tribal Society. With 3 Maps. 8vo., 12s.

History, Politics, Polity, Political Memoirs, &c.—continued.

Sharpe.—LONDON AND THE KINGDOM: a History derived mainly from the Archives at Guildhall in the custody of the Corporation of the City of London. By REGINALD R. SHARPE, D.C.L., Records Clerk in the Office of the Town Clerk of the City of London. 3 vols. 8vo. 10s. 6d. each.

Sheppard.—MEMORIALS OF ST. JAMES'S PALACE. By the Rev. EDGAR SHEPPARD, M.A. Sub-Dean of the Chapels Royal. With 41 full-page Plates (8 photo-intaglio), and 32 Illustrations in the Text. 2 Vols. 8vo. 36s. net.

Smith.—CARTHAGE AND THE CARTHAGINIANS. By R. BOSWORTH SMITH, M.A., Assistant Master in Harrow School. With Maps, Plans, &c. Cr. 8vo., 3s. 6d.

Stephens.—A HISTORY OF THE FRENCH REVOLUTION. By H. MORSE STEPHENS, Balliol College, Oxford. 3 vols. 8vo. Vols. I. and II., 18s. each.

Stubbs.—HISTORY OF THE UNIVERSITY OF DUBLIN, from its Foundation to the End of the Eighteenth Century. By J. W. STUBBS. 8vo., 12s. 6d.

Sutherland.—THE HISTORY OF AUSTRALIA AND NEW ZEALAND, from 1606 to 1890. By ALEXANDER SUTHERLAND, M.A., and GEORGE SUTHERLAND, M.A. Crown 8vo., 2s. 6d.

Todd.—PARLIAMENTARY GOVERNMENT IN THE BRITISH COLONIES. By ALPHEUS TODD, LL.D. 8vo., 30s. net.

Wakeman and Hassall.—ESSAYS INTRODUCTORY TO THE STUDY OF ENGLISH CONSTITUTIONAL HISTORY. Edited by HENRY OFFLEY WAKEMAN, M.A., and ARTHUR HASSALL, M.A. Crown 8vo., 6s.

Walpole.—Works by SPENCER WALPOLE.

HISTORY OF ENGLAND FROM THE CONCLUSION OF THE GREAT WAR IN 1815 TO 1858. 6 vols. Cr. 8vo., 6s. each.

THE LAND OF HOME RULE: being an Account of the History and Institutions of the Isle of Man. Cr. 8vo., 6s.

Wood-Martin.—PAGAN IRELAND: an Archæological Sketch. A Handbook of Irish Pre-Christian Antiquities. By W. G. WOOD-MARTIN, M.R.I.A. 412 Illustrations. 8vo., 15s.

Wylie.—HISTORY OF ENGLAND UNDER HENRY IV. By JAMES HAMILTON WYLIE, M.A., one of H. M. Inspectors of Schools. 3 vols. Crown 8vo. Vol. I., 1399-1404, 10s. 6d. Vol. II. 15s. Vol. III. 15s. Vol. IV. (In the press.

Biography, Personal Memoirs, &c.

Armstrong.—THE LIFE AND LETTERS OF EDMUND J. ARMSTRONG. Edited by G. F. ARMSTRONG. Fcp. 8vo., 7s. 6d.

Bacon.—LETTERS AND LIFE OF FRANCIS BACON, INCLUDING ALL HIS OCCASIONAL WORKS. Edited by J. SPEDDING. 7 vols. 8vo., £4 4s.

Bagehot.—BIOGRAPHICAL STUDIES. By WALTER BAGEHOT. Cr. 8vo., 3s. 6d.

Blackwell.—PIONEER WORK IN OPENING THE MEDICAL PROFESSION TO WOMEN: Autobiographical Sketches. By ELIZABETH BLACKWELL. Crown 8vo., 6s.

Boyd.—Works by A. K. H. BOYD, D.D., LL.D.

TWENTY-FIVE YEARS OF ST. ANDREWS. 1865-1890. 2 vols. 8vo. Vol. I., 12s. Vol. II., 15s.

ST. ANDREWS AND ELSEWHERE: Glimpses of Some Gone and of Things Left. 8vo., 15s.

Buss.—FRANCES MARY BUSS AND HER WORK FOR EDUCATION. By ANNIE E. RIDLEY. With 5 Portraits and 4 Illustrations. Crown 8vo., 7s. 6d.

Carlyle.—THOMAS CARLYLE: a History of his Life. By JAMES A. FROUDE.
1795-1835, 2 vols. Crown 8vo., 7s.
1834-1881. 2 vols. Crown 8vo., 7s.

Erasmus.—LIFE AND LETTERS OF ERASMUS. By JAMES A. FROUDE. Crown 8vo., 6s.

Fox.—THE EARLY HISTORY OF CHARLES JAMES FOX. By the Right Hon. Sir G. O. TREVELYAN, Bart., M.P.
Library Edition. 8vo., 18s.
Cabinet Edition. Crown 8vo., 6s.

Halford.—THE LIFE OF SIR HENRY HALFORD, Bart., G.C.H., M.D., F.R.S. By WILLIAM MUNK, M.D., F.S.A. 8vo, 12s. 6d.

Hamilton.—LIFE OF SIR WILLIAM HAMILTON. By R. P. GRAVES. 3 vols.

Havelock.—MEMOIRS OF SIR HENRY HAVELOCK, K.C.B. By JOHN CLARK MARSHMAN. Crown 8vo., 3s. 6d.

Luther.—LIFE OF LUTHER. By JULIUS KÖSTLIN. With Illustrations from Authentic Sources. Translated from the German. Crown 8vo., 7s. 6d.

Macaulay.—THE LIFE AND LETTERS OF LORD MACAULAY. By the Right Hon. Sir G. O. TREVELYAN, Bart., M.P.
Popular Edit. 1 vol. Cr. 8vo., 2s. 6d.
Student's Edition. 1 vol. Cr. 8vo., 6s.
Cabinet Edition. 2 vols. Post 8vo., 12s.
Library Edition. 2 vols. 8vo., 36s.

Biography, Personal Memoirs, &c.—*continued*.

Marbot.—THE MEMOIRS OF THE BARON DE MARBOT. Translated from the French by ARTHUR JOHN BUTLER, M.A. Crown 8vo., 7s. 6d.

Seebohm.—THE OXFORD REFORMERS —JOHN COLET, ERASMUS AND THOMAS MORE: a History of their Fellow-Work. By FREDERIC SEEBOHM. 8vo., 14s.

Shakespeare.—OUTLINES OF THE LIFE OF SHAKESPEARE. By J. O. HALLIWELL-PHILLIPPS. With numerous Illustrations and Fac-similes. 2 vols. Royal 8vo., £1 1s.

Shakespeare's TRUE LIFE. By JAS. WALTER. With 500 Illustrations by GERALD E. MOIRA. Imp. 8vo., 21s.

Stephen.—ESSAYS IN ECCLESIASTICAL BIOGRAPHY. By Sir JAMES STEPHEN. Crown 8vo., 7s. 6d.

Turgot.—THE LIFE AND WRITINGS OF TURGOT, Comptroller-General o' France, 1774-1776. Edited for English Readers by W. WALKER STEPHENS. 8vo., 12s. 6d.

Verney.—MEMOIRS OF THE VERNEY FAMILY. Compiled from the Letters and Illustrated by the Portraits at Claydon House, Bucks.

Vols. I. and II. DURING THE CIVIL WAR. By FRANCES VERNEY. With 38 Portraits. Royal 8vo., 42s.

Vol. III. DURING THE COMMONWEALTH. 1650-1660. By MARGARET M. VERNEY. With 10 Portraits, &c. 8vo., 21s.

Walford.—TWELVE ENGLISH AUTHORESSES. By L. B. WALFORD. Cr. 8vo., 4s. 6d.

Wellington.—LIFE OF THE DUKE OF WELLINGTON. By the Rev. G. R. GLEIG, M.A. Crown 8vo., 3s. 6d.

Wolf.—THE LIFE OF JOSEPH WOLF, ANIMAL PAINTER. By A. H. Palmer, Author of 'The Life of Samuel Palmer'. With 53 Plates and 14 Illustrations in the Text. Royal 8vo., 21s.

Travel and Adventure, the Colonies, &c.

Arnold.—Works by Sir EDWIN ARNOLD, K.C.I.E.
SEAS AND LANDS. With 71 Illustrations. Cr. 8vo., 3s. 6d.
WANDERING WORDS. With 45 Illustrations. 8vo., 18s.

AUSTRALIA AS IT IS, or Facts and Features, Sketches and Incidents of Australia and Australian Life, with Notices of New Zealand. By A CLERGYMAN, thirteen years resident in the interior of New South Wales. Cr. 8vo., 5s.

Baker.—Works by Sir SAMUEL WHITE BAKER.
EIGHT YEARS IN CEYLON. With 6 Illustrations. Crown 8vo., 3s. 6d.
THE RIFLE AND THE HOUND IN CEYLON. 6 Illustrations. Cr. 8vo., 3s. 6d.

Bent.—Works by J. THEODORE BENT.
THE RUINED CITIES OF MASHONALAND: being a Record of Excavation and Exploration in 1891. With Map, 13 Plates, and 104 Illustrations in the Text. Crown 8vo., 3s. 6d.
THE SACRED CITY OF THE ETHIOPIANS: being a Record of Travel and Research in Abyssinia in 1893. With 8 Plates and 65 Illustrations in the Text. 8vo., 18s.

Bicknell.—TRAVEL AND ADVENTURE IN NORTHERN QUEENSLAND. By ARTHUR C. BICKNELL. With 24 Plates and 22 Illustrations in the text. 8vo. 15s.

Brassey.—VOYAGES AND TRAVELS OF LORD BRASSEY, K.C.B., D.C.L., 1862-1894. Arranged and Edited by Captain S. EARDLEY-WILMOT. 2 vols. Cr. 8vo., 10s.

Brassey.—Works by the late LADY BRASSEY.

A VOYAGE IN THE 'SUNBEAM'; OUR HOME ON THE OCEAN FOR ELEVEN MONTHS.

Library Edition. With 8 Maps and Charts, and 118 Illustrations. 8vo., 21s.

Cabinet Edition. With Map and 66 Illustrations. Crown 8vo., 7s. 6d.
Silver Library Edition. With 66 Illustrations. Crown 8vo., 3s. 6d.

Popular Edition. With 60 Illustrations. 4to., 6d. sewed, 1s. cloth.

School Edition. With 37 Illustrations. Fcp., 2s. cloth, or 3s. white parchment.

Travel and Adventure, the Colonies, &c.—*continued*.

Brassey.—Works by the late LADY BRASSEY—*continued*.

SUNSHINE AND STORM IN THE EAST.
- *Library Edition.* With 2 Maps and 141 Illustrations. 8vo., 21*s.*
- *Cabinet Edition.* With 2 Maps and 114 Illustrations. Crown 8vo., 7*s.* 6*d.*
- *Popular Edition.* With 103 Illustrations. 4to., 6*d.* sewed, 1*s.* cloth.

IN THE TRADES, THE TROPICS, AND THE 'ROARING FORTIES'.
- *Cabinet Edition.* With Map and 220 Illustrations. Crown 8vo., 7*s.* 6*d.*
- *Popular Edition.* With 183 Illustrations. 4to., 6*d.* sewed, 1*s.* cloth.

THREE VOYAGES IN THE 'SUNBEAM'. Popular Edition. 346 Illustrations. 4to., 2*s.* 6*d.*

THE LAST VOYAGE TO INDIA AND AUSTRALIA IN THE 'SUNBEAM'. With Charts and Maps, and 40 Illustrations in Monotone, and nearly 200 Illustrations in the Text. 8vo., 21*s.*

Froude.—Works by JAMES A. FROUDE.

OCEANA: or England and her Colonies. With 9 Illustrations. Crown 8vo., 2*s.* boards, 2*s.* 6*d.* cloth.

THE ENGLISH IN THE WEST INDIES: or the Bow of Ulysses. With 9 Illustrations. Cr. 8vo., 2*s.* bds., 2*s.* 6*d.* cl.

Howitt.—VISITS TO REMARKABLE PLACES. Old Halls, Battle-Fields, Scenes Illustrative of Striking Passages in English History and Poetry. By WILLIAM HOWITT. With 80 Illustrations. Crown 8vo., 3*s.* 6*d.*

Knight.—Works by E. F. KNIGHT.

THE CRUISE OF THE 'ALERTE': the Narrative of a Search for Treasure on the Desert Island of Trinidad. 2 Maps and 23 Illustrations. Cr. 8vo., 3*s.* 6*d.*

WHERE THREE EMPIRES MEET: a Narrative of Recent Travel in Kashmir, Western Tibet, Baltistan, Ladak, Gilgit, and the adjoining Countries. With a Map and 54 Illustrations. Cr. 8vo., 3*s.* 6*d.*

Lees and Clutterbuck.—B. C. 1887: A RAMBLE IN BRITISH COLUMBIA. By J. A. LEES and W. J. CLUTTERBUCK. With Map and 75 Illustrations. Cr. 8vo., 3*s.* 6*d.*

Murdoch.—FROM EDINBURGH TO THE ANTARCTIC: An Artist's Notes and Sketches during the Dundee Antarctic Expedition of 1892-93. By W. G. BURN MURDOCH. With 2 Maps and numerous Illustrations. 8vo., 18*s.*

Nansen.—Works by Dr. FRIDTJOF NANSEN.

THE FIRST CROSSING OF GREENLAND. With numerous Illustrations and a Map. Crown 8vo., 3*s.* 6*d.*

ESKIMO LIFE. Translated by WILLIAM ARCHER. With 31 Illustrations. 8vo., 16*s.*

Peary.—MY ARCTIC JOURNAL: a Year among Ice-Fields and Eskimos. By JOSEPHINE DIEBITSCH-PEARY. With 19 Plates, 3 Sketch Maps, and 44 Illustrations in the Text. 8vo., 12*s.*

Quillinan.—JOURNAL OF A FEW MONTHS' RESIDENCE IN PORTUGAL, and Glimpses of the South of Spain. By Mrs. QUILLINAN (Dora Wordsworth). New Edition. Edited, with Memoir, by EDMUND LEE, Author of 'Dorothy Wordsworth.' etc. Crown 8vo., 6*s.*

Smith.—CLIMBING IN THE BRITISH ISLES. By W. P. HASKETT SMITH. With Illustrations by ELLIS CARR.
- Part I. ENGLAND. 16mo., 3*s.* 6*d.*
- Part II. WALES AND IRELAND. 16mo., 3*s.* 6*d.*
- Part III. SCOTLAND. [*In preparation.*

Stephen.—THE PLAYGROUND OF EUROPE. By LESLIE STEPHEN, formerly President of the Alpine Club. New Edition, with Additions and 4 Illustrations. Crown 8vo., 6*s.* net.

THREE IN NORWAY. By Two of Them. With a Map and 59 Illustrations. Cr. 8vo., 2*s.* boards, 2*s.* 6*d.* cloth.

Whishaw.—Works by FRED. J. WHISHAW.

THE ROMANCE OF THE WOODS: Reprinted Articles and Sketches. Crown 8vo., 6*s.*

OUT OF DOORS IN TSARLAND: a Record of the Seeings and Doings of a Wanderer in Russia. Cr. 8vo., 7*s.* 6*d.*

Sport and Pastime.

THE BADMINTON LIBRARY

Crown 8vo., 10*s*. 6*d*., each volume.

Edited by the DUKE OF BEAUFORT, K.G., assisted by ALFRED E. T. WATSON.

ARCHERY. By C. J. LONGMAN and Col. H. WALROND, &c. 195 Illusts.

ATHLETICS AND FOOTBALL. By MONTAGUE SHEARMAN. 51 Illusts.

BIG GAME SHOOTING. By C. PHILLIPPS-WOLLEY, F. C. SELOUS, &c.
  Vol. I. Africa and America. With 77 Illus.
  Vol. II. Europe, Asia, and the Arctic Regions. With 73 Illus.

BILLIARDS. By Major W. BROADFOOT, R.E. [*In the Press.*

BOATING. By W. B. WOODGATE. With 49 Illustrations.

COURSING AND FALCONRY. By HARDING COX and the Hon. GERALD LASCELLES. With 76 Illustrations.

CRICKET. By A. G. STEEL, the Hon. R. H. LYTTELTON, ANDREW LANG, W. G. GRACE, &c. With 64 Illustrations.

CYCLING. By the Earl of Albemarle and G. LACY HILLIER. With 59 Illus.

DANCING. By Mrs. LILLY GROVE, F.R.G.S., &c. With 131 Illustrations.

DRIVING. By the DUKE OF BEAUFORT. With 65 Illustrations.

FENCING, BOXING, AND WRESTLING. By WALTER H. POLLOCK, F. C. GROVE, WALTER ARMSTRONG. With 42 Illustrations.

FISHING. By H. CHOLMONDELEY-PENNELL, the Marquis of EXETER, G. CHRISTOPHER DAVIES, &c.
  Vol. I. Salmon, Trout, and Grayling. With 158 Illustrations.
  Vol. II. Pike and other Coarse Fish. With 133 Illustrations.

GOLF. By HORACE G. HUTCHINSON, the Rt. Hon. A. J. BALFOUR, M.P., Sir W. G. SIMPSON, Bart., ANDREW LANG, &c. With 89 Illustrations.

HUNTING. By the DUKE OF BEAUFORT, K.G., MOWBRAY MORRIS, the EARL OF SUFFOLK AND BERKSHIRE, and ALFRED E. T. WATSON, &c. 53 Illustrations.

MOUNTAINEERING. By C. T. DENT, Sir F. POLLOCK, Bart., W. M. CONWAY, DOUGLAS FRESHFIELD, C. E. MATHEWS, &c. With 108 Illustrations.

RACING AND STEEPLE-CHASING. By the EARL OF SUFFOLK AND BERKSHIRE, ARTHUR COVENTRY, &c. With 58 Illustrations.

RIDING AND POLO. By Captain ROBERT WEIR, J. MORAY BROWN, the DUKE OF BEAUFORT, K.G., the EARL of SUFFOLK AND BERKSHIRE, &c. With 59 Illustrations.

SEA FISHING. By JOHN BICKERDYKE. With Contributions by Sir H. GORE-BOOTH, Bart., ALFRED C. HARMSWORTH, and W. SENIOR. With 197 Illustrations.

SHOOTING. By Lord WALSINGHAM and Sir RALPH PAYNE-GALLWEY, Bart. LORD LOVAT, LORD C. L. KERR, and A. J. STUART-WORTLEY, &c.
  Vol. I. Field and Covert. With 105 Illustrations.
  Vol. II. Moor and Marsh. With 65 Illustrations.

SKATING, CURLING, TOBOGANING, AND OTHER ICE SPORTS. By J. M. HEATHCOTE, C. G. TEBBUTT, T. MAXWELL WITHAM, the Rev. JOHN KERR, &c. With 284 Illustrations.

SWIMMING. By ARCHIBALD SINCLAIR and WILLIAM HENRY. With 119 Illus.

TENNIS, LAWN TENNIS, RACQUETS, AND FIVES. By J. M. and C. G. HEATHCOTE, E. O. PLEYDELL-BOUVERIE, the Hon. A. LYTTELTON, Miss L. DOD, &c. With 79 Illustrations.

YACHTING.
  Vol. I. Cruising, Construction, Racing, Rules, Fitting-Out, &c. By Sir EDWARD SULLIVAN, Bart., LORD BRASSEY, K.C.B., C. E. SETH-SMITH, C.B., &c. With 114 Illustrations.
  Vol. II. Yacht Clubs, Yachting in America and the Colonies, Yacht Racing, &c. By R. T. PRITCHETT, the EARL OF ONSLOW, G.C.M.G., &c. With 195 Illustrations.

Sport and Pastime—*continued*.

FUR AND FEATHER SERIES.
Edited by A. E. T. WATSON.
Crown 8vo., 5s. each Volume.

THE PARTRIDGE. Natural History, by the Rev. H. A. MACPHERSON; Shooting, by A. J. STUART-WORTLEY; Cookery, by GEORGE SAINTSBURY. With 11 Illustrations and various Diagrams.

THE GROUSE. Natural History by the Rev. H. A. MACPHERSON; Shooting, by A. J. STUART-WORTLEY; Cookery, by GEORGE SAINTSBURY. With 13 Illustrations and various Diagrams.

THE PHEASANT. Natural History by the Rev. H. A. MACPHERSON; Shooting, by A. J. STUART-WORTLEY; Cookery, by ALEXANDER INNES SHAND. With 10 Illustrations and various Diagrams.

THE HARE AND THE RABBIT. By the Hon. GERALD LASCELLES, &c. [*In preparation*.

WILDFOWL. By the Hon. JOHN SCOTT-MONTAGU, M.P., &c. [*In preparation*.

THE RED DEER. By CAMERON OF LOCHIEL, LORD EBRINGTON, &c. [*In preparation*.

Bickerdyke.—DAYS OF MY LIFE ON WATERS FRESH AND SALT; and other Papers. By JOHN BICKERDYKE. With Photo-Etched Frontispiece and 8 Full-page Illustrations. Crown 8vo., 6s.

Campbell-Walker.—THE CORRECT CARD: or, How to Play at Whist; a Whist Catechism. By Major A. CAMPBELL-WALKER. Fcp. 8vo., 2s. 6d.

DEAD SHOT (THE): or, Sportsman's Complete Guide. Being a Treatise on the Use of the Gun, with Rudimentary and Finishing Lessons on the Art of Shooting Game of all kinds. By MARKSMAN. Crown 8vo., 10s. 6d.

Ellis.—CHESS SPARKS; or, Short and Bright Games of Chess. Collected and Arranged by J. H. ELLIS, M.A. 8vo., 4s. 6d.

Falkener.—GAMES, ANCIENT AND ORIENTAL, AND HOW TO PLAY THEM. By EDWARD FALKENER. With numerous Photographs & Diagrams. 8vo., 21s.

Ford.—THE THEORY AND PRACTICE OF ARCHERY. By HORACE FORD. New Edition, thoroughly Revised and Rewritten by W. BUTT, M.A. With a Preface by C. J. LONGMAN, M.A. 8vo., 14s.

Francis.—A BOOK ON ANGLING: or, Treatise on the Art of Fishing in every Branch; including full Illustrated List of Salmon Flies. By FRANCIS FRANCIS. With Portrait and Plates. Cr. 8vo., 15s.

Gibson.—TOBOGGANING ON CROOKED RUNS. By the Hon. HARRY GIBSON. With Contributions by F. DE B. STRICKLAND and 'LADY-TOBOGGANER'. With 40 Illustrations. Crown 8vo., 6s.

Hawker.—THE DIARY OF COLONEL PETER HAWKER, author of "Instructions to Young Sportsmen". With an Introduction by Sir RALPH PAYNE-GALLWEY, Bart. 2 vols. 8vo., 32s.

Lang.—ANGLING SKETCHES. By A. LANG. With 20 Illus. Cr. 8vo., 3s. 6d.

Longman.—CHESS OPENINGS. By FRED. W. LONGMAN. Fcp. 8vo., 2s. 6d.

Maskelyne.—SHARPS AND FLATS a Complete Revelation of the Secrets of Cheating at Games of Chance and Skill. By JOHN NEVIL MASKELYNE. With 62 Illustrations. Crown 8vo., 6s.

Payne-Gallwey.—Works by Sir RALPH PAYNE-GALLWEY, Bart.
LETTERS TO YOUNG SHOOTERS (First Series). On the Choice and Use of a Gun. With 41 Illustrations. Cr. 8vo., 7s. 6d.
LETTERS TO YOUNG SHOOTERS. (Second Series). On the Production, Preservation, and Killing of Game. With Directions in Shooting Wood-Pigeons and Breaking-in Retrievers. With 104 Illustrations. Crown 8vo., 12s. 6d.

Pole.—Works by W. POLE, F.R.S.
THE THEORY OF THE MODERN SCIENTIFIC GAME OF WHIST. Fcp. 8vo., 2s. 6d.
THE EVOLUTION OF WHIST. Cr. 8vo., 6s.

Proctor.—Works by R. A. PROCTOR.
HOW TO PLAY WHIST: WITH THE LAWS AND ETIQUETTE OF WHIST. Crown 8vo., 3s. 6d.
HOME WHIST: an Easy Guide to Correct Play. 16mo., 1s.

Ronalds.—THE FLY-FISHER'S ENTOMOLOGY. By ALFRED RONALDS. With 20 Coloured Plates. 8vo., 14s.

Wilcocks.—THE SEA FISHERMAN: Comprising the Chief Methods of Hook and Line Fishing in the British and other Seas, and Remarks on Nets, Boats, and Boating. By J. C. WILCOCKS. Illustrated. Crown 8vo., 6s.

Veterinary Medicine, &c.

Steel.—Works by JOHN HENRY STEEL.
A TREATISE ON THE DISEASES OF THE DOG. 88 Illustrations. 8vo., 10s. 6d.
A TREATISE ON THE DISEASES OF THE OX. With 119 Illustrations. 8vo., 15s.
A TREATISE ON THE DISEASES OF THE SHEEP. With 100 Illustrations. 8vo., 12s.
OUTLINES OF EQUINE ANATOMY: a Manual for the use of Veterinary Students in the Dissecting Room. Crown 8vo., 7s. 6d.

Fitzwygram.—HORSES AND STABLES. By Major-General Sir F. FITZWYGRAM, Bart. With 56 pages of Illustrations. 8vo., 2s. 6d. net.

"Stonehenge."—THE DOG IN HEALTH AND DISEASE. By "STONEHENGE". With 78 Illustrations. 8vo., 7s. 6d.

Youatt.—Works by WILLIAM YOUATT.
THE HORSE. With 52 Illustrations. 8vo., 7s. 6d.
THE DOG. With 53 Illustrations. 8vo., 6s.

Mental, Moral, and Political Philosophy.
LOGIC, RHETORIC, PSYCHOLOGY, ETC.

Abbott.—THE ELEMENTS OF LOGIC. By T. K. ABBOTT, B.D. 12mo., 3s.

Aristotle.—Works by.
THE POLITICS: G. Bekker's Greek Text of Books I., III., IV. (VII.), with an English Translation by W. E. BOLLAND, M.A.; and short Introductory Essays by A. LANG, M.A. Crown 8vo., 7s. 6d.
THE POLITICS: Introductory Essays. By ANDREW LANG (from Bolland and Lang's 'Politics'). Cr. 8vo., 2s. 6d.
THE ETHICS: Greek Text, Illustrated with Essay and Notes. By Sir ALEXANDER GRANT, Bart. 2 vols. 8vo., 32s.
THE NICOMACHEAN ETHICS: Newly Translated into English. By ROBERT WILLIAMS. Crown 8vo., 7s. 6d.
AN INTRODUCTION TO ARISTOTLE'S ETHICS. Books I.-IV. (Book X. c. vi.-ix. in an Appendix.) With a continuous Analysis and Notes. By the Rev. E. MOORE, D.D. Cr. 8vo., 10s. 6d.

Bacon.—Works by FRANCIS BACON.
COMPLETE WORKS. Edited by R. L. ELLIS, J. SPEDDING, and D. D. HEATH. 7 vols. 8vo., £3 13s. 6d.
LETTERS AND LIFE, including all his occasional Works. Edited by JAMES SPEDDING. 7 vols. 8vo., £4 4s.
THE ESSAYS: with Annotations. By RICHARD WHATELY, D.D. 8vo. 10s. 6d.
THE ESSAYS: Edited, with Notes. By F. STORR and C. H. GIBSON. Cr. 8vo., 3s. 6d.
THE ESSAYS. With Introduction, Notes, and Index. By E. A. ABBOTT. D.D. 2 vols. Fcp. 8vo., 6s. The Text and Index only, without Introduction and Notes, in One Volume. Fcp. 8vo., 2s. 6d.

Bain.—Works by ALEXANDER BAIN, LL.D.
MENTAL SCIENCE. Crown 8vo., 6s. 6d.
MORAL SCIENCE. Crown 8vo., 4s. 6d.
The two works as above can be had in one volume, price 10s. 6d.
SENSES AND THE INTELLECT. 8vo., 15s.
EMOTIONS AND THE WILL. 8vo., 15s.
LOGIC, DEDUCTIVE AND INDUCTIVE. Part I., 4s. Part II., 6s. 6d.
PRACTICAL ESSAYS. Crown 8vo., 3s.

Bray.—Works by CHARLES BRAY.
THE PHILOSOPHY OF NECESSITY: or Law in Mind as in Matter. Cr. 8vo., 5s.
THE EDUCATION OF THE FEELINGS: a Moral System for Schools. Crown 8vo., 2s. 6d.

Bray.—ELEMENTS OF MORALITY, in Easy Lessons for Home and School Teaching. By Mrs. CHARLES BRAY. Cr. 8vo., 1s. 6d.

Davidson.—THE LOGIC OF DEFINITION, Explained and Applied. By WILLIAM L. DAVIDSON, M.A. Crown 8vo., 6s.

Green.—THE WORKS OF THOMAS HILL GREEN. Edited by R. L. NETTLESHIP.
Vols. I. and II. Philosophical Works. 8vo., 16s. each.
Vol. III. Miscellanies. With Index to the three Volumes, and Memoir. 8vo., 21s.

LECTURES ON THE PRINCIPLES OF POLITICAL OBLIGATION. With Preface by BERNARD BOSANQUET. 8vo., 5s.

Mental, Moral and Political Philosophy—*continued*.

Hodgson.—Works by SHADWORTH H. HODGSON.
  TIME AND SPACE: a Metaphysical Essay. 8vo., 16s.
  THE THEORY OF PRACTICE: an Ethical Inquiry. 2 vols. 8vo., 24s.
  THE PHILOSOPHY OF REFLECTION. 2 vols. 8vo., 21s.

Hume.—THE PHILOSOPHICAL WORKS OF DAVID HUME. Edited by T. H. GREEN and T. H. GROSE. 4 vols. 8vo., 56s. Or separately, Essays. 2 vols. 28s. Treatise of Human Nature. 2 vols. 28s.

Justinian.—THE INSTITUTES OF JUSTINIAN: Latin Text, chiefly that of Huschke, with English Introduction, Translation, Notes, and Summary. By THOMAS C. SANDARS, M.A. 8vo. 18s.

Kant.—Works by IMMANUEL KANT.
  CRITIQUE OF PRACTICAL REASON, AND OTHER WORKS ON THE THEORY OF ETHICS. Translated by T. K. ABBOTT, B.D. With Memoir. 8vo., 12s. 6d.
  FUNDAMENTAL PRINCIPLES OF THE METAPHYSIC OF ETHICS. Translated by T. K. ABBOTT, B.D. (Extracted from 'Kant's Critique of Practical Reason and other Works on the Theory of Ethics.' Cr. 8vo. 3s.
  INTRODUCTION TO LOGIC, AND HIS ESSAY ON THE MISTAKEN SUBTILTY OF THE FOUR FIGURES. Translated by T. K. ABBOTT, and with Notes by S. T. COLERIDGE. 8vo., 6s.

Killick.—HANDBOOK TO MILL'S SYSTEM OF LOGIC. By Rev. A. H. KILLICK, M.A. Crown 8vo., 3s. 6d.

Ladd.—Works by GEORGE TRUMBULL LADD.
  ELEMENTS OF PHYSIOLOGICAL PSYCHOLOGY. 8vo., 21s.
  OUTLINES OF PHYSIOLOGICAL PSYCHOLOGY. A Text-Book of Mental Science for Academies and Colleges. 8vo., 12s.
  PSYCHOLOGY, DESCRIPTIVE AND EXPLANATORY: a Treatise of the Phenomena, Laws, and Development of Human Mental Life. 8vo., 21s.
  PRIMER OF PSYCHOLOGY. Crown 8vo., 5s. 6d.
  PHILOSOPHY OF MIND: an Essay on the Metaphysics of Physiology. 8vo., 16s.

Lewes.—THE HISTORY OF PHILOSOPHY, from Thales to Comte. By GEORGE HENRY LEWES. 2 vols. 8vo., 32s.

Max Müller.—Works by F. MAX MÜLLER.
  THE SCIENCE OF THOUGHT. 8vo., 21s.
  THREE INTRODUCTORY LECTURES ON THE SCIENCE OF THOUGHT. 8vo., 2s. 6d.

Mill.—ANALYSIS OF THE PHENOMENA OF THE HUMAN MIND. By JAMES MILL. 2 vols. 8vo., 28s.

Mill.—Works by JOHN STUART MILL.
  A SYSTEM OF LOGIC. Cr. 8vo., 3s. 6d.
  ON LIBERTY. Cr. 8vo., 1s. 4d.
  ON REPRESENTATIVE GOVERNMENT. Crown 8vo., 2s.
  UTILITARIANISM. 8vo., 2s. 6d.
  EXAMINATION OF SIR WILLIAM HAMILTON'S PHILOSOPHY. 8vo., 16s.
  NATURE, THE UTILITY OF RELIGION, AND THEISM. Three Essays. 8vo., 5s.

Romanes.—MIND AND MOTION AND MONISM. By the late GEORGE JOHN ROMANES, M.A. LL.D., F.R.S. Cr. 8vo., 4s. 6d.

Stock.—DEDUCTIVE LOGIC. By ST. GEORGE STOCK. Fcp. 8vo., 3s. 6d.

Sully.—Works by JAMES SULLY.
  THE HUMAN MIND: a Text-book of Psychology. 2 vols. 8vo., 21s.
  OUTLINES OF PSYCHOLOGY. 8vo., 9s.
  THE TEACHER'S HANDBOOK OF PSYCHOLOGY. Crown 8vo., 5s.
  STUDIES OF CHILDHOOD. 8vo., 12s. 6d.

Swinburne.—PICTURE LOGIC: an Attempt to Popularise the Science of Reasoning. By ALFRED JAMES SWINBURNE, M.A. With 23 Woodcuts. Post 8vo., 5s.

Thomson.—OUTLINES OF THE NECESSARY LAWS OF THOUGHT: a Treatise on Pure and Applied Logic. By WILLIAM THOMSON, D.D. formerly Lord Archbishop of York. Post 8vo., 6s.

Mental, Moral and Political Philosophy—*continued*.

Whately.—Works by R. WHATELY, D.D.
  BACON'S ESSAYS. With Annotation. By R. WHATELY. 8vo., 10s. 6d.
  ELEMENTS OF LOGIC. Cr. 8vo., 4s. 6d.
  ELEMENTS OF RHETORIC. Cr. 8vo., 4s. 6d.
  LESSONS ON REASONING. Fcp. 8vo., 1s. 6d.

Zeller.—Works by Dr. EDWARD ZELLER, Professor in the University of Berlin.
  THE STOICS, EPICUREANS, AND SCEPTICS. Translated by the Rev. O. J. REICHEL, M.A. Crown 8vo., 15s.
  OUTLINES OF THE HISTORY OF GREEK PHILOSOPHY. Translated by SARAH F. ALLEYNE and EVELYN ABBOTT. Crown 8vo., 10s. 6d.
  PLATO AND THE OLDER ACADEMY. Translated by SARAH F. ALLEYNE and ALFRED GOODWIN, B.A. Crown 8vo., 18s.
  SOCRATES AND THE SOCRATIC SCHOOLS. Translated by the Rev. O. J. REICHEL, M.A. Crown 8vo., 10s. 6d.

MANUALS OF CATHOLIC PHILOSOPHY.
(Stonyhurst Series.)

A MANUAL OF POLITICAL ECONOMY. By C. S. DEVAS, M.A. Cr. 8vo., 6s. 6d.

FIRST PRINCIPLES OF KNOWLEDGE. By JOHN RICKABY, S.J. Crown 8vo., 5s.

GENERAL METAPHYSICS. By JOHN RICKABY, S.J. Crown 8vo., 5s.

LOGIC. By RICHARD F. CLARKE, S.J. Crown 8vo., 5s.

MORAL PHILOSOPHY (ETHICS AND NATURAL LAW). By JOSEPH RICKABY, S.J. Crown 8vo., 5s.

NATURAL THEOLOGY. By BERNARD BOEDDER, S.J. Crown 8vo., 6s. 6d.

PSYCHOLOGY. By MICHAEL MAHER, S.J. Crown 8vo., 6s. 6d.

History and Science of Language, &c.

Davidson.—LEADING AND IMPORTANT ENGLISH WORDS: Explained and Exemplified. By WILLIAM L. DAVIDSON, M.A. Fcp. 8vo., 3s. 6d.

Farrar.—LANGUAGE AND LANGUAGES. By F. W. FARRAR, D.D., F.R.S. Cr. 8vo., 6s.

Graham.—ENGLISH SYNONYMS, Classified and Explained: with Practical Exercises. By G. F. GRAHAM. Fcap. 8vo., 6s.

Max Müller.—Works by F. MAX MÜLLER.
  THE SCIENCE OF LANGUAGE, Founded on Lectures delivered at the Royal Institution in 1861 and 1863. 2 vols. Crown 8vo., 21s.
  BIOGRAPHIES OF WORDS, AND THE HOME OF THE ARYAS. Crown 8vo., 7s. 6d.

Max Müller.—Works by F. MAX MÜLLER—*continued*.
  THREE LECTURES ON THE SCIENCE OF LANGUAGE, AND ITS PLACE IN GENERAL EDUCATION, delivered at Oxford, 1889. Crown 8vo., 3s.

Roget.—THESAURUS OF ENGLISH WORDS AND PHRASES. Classified and Arranged so as to Facilitate the Expression of Ideas and assist in Literary Composition. By PETER MARK ROGET, M.D., F.R.S. Recomposed throughout, enlarged and improved, partly from the Author's Notes, and with a full Index, by the Author's Son, JOHN LEWIS ROGET. Crown 8vo., 10s. 6d.

Whately.—ENGLISH SYNONYMS. By E. JANE WHATELY. Fcap. 8vo., 3s.

Political Economy and Economics.

Ashley.—ENGLISH ECONOMIC HISTORY AND THEORY. By W. J. ASHLEY, M.A. Crown 8vo, Part I., 5s. Part II., 10s. 6d.

Bagehot.—ECONOMIC STUDIES. By WALTER BAGEHOT. Cr. 8vo., 3s. 6d.

Barnett.—PRACTICABLE SOCIALISM: Essays on Social Reform. By the Rev. S. A. and Mrs. BARNETT. Cr. 8vo., 6s.

Brassey.—PAPERS AND ADDRESSES ON WORK AND WAGES. By Lord BRASSEY. Edited by J. POTTER, and with Introduction by GEORGE HOWELL, M.P. Crown 8vo., 5s.

Devas.—A MANUAL OF POLITICAL ECONOMY. By C. S. DEVAS, M.A. Crown 8vo., 6s. 6d. (*Manuals of Catholic Philosophy.*)

Dowell.—A HISTORY OF TAXATION AND TAXES IN ENGLAND, from the Earliest Times to the Year 1885. By STEPHEN DOWELL (4 vols. 8vo.) Vols. I. and II. The History of Taxation, 21s. Vols. III. and IV. The History of Taxes, 21s.

Macleod.—Works by HENRY DUNNING MACLEOD, M.A.
BIMETALISM. 8vo., 5s. net.
THE ELEMENTS OF BANKING. Crown 8vo., 3s. 6d.
THE THEORY AND PRACTICE OF BANKING. Vol. I. 8vo., 12s. Vol. II. 14s.

Macleod.—Works by HENRY DUNNING MACLEOD, M.A.
THE THEORY OF CREDIT. 8vo. Vol. I. 10s. net. Vol. II., Part I., 10s. net. Vol. II. Part II., 10s. 6d.
A DIGEST OF THE LAW OF BILLS OF EXCHANGE, BANK NOTES, &c.

Mill.—POLITICAL ECONOMY. By JOHN STUART MILL.
Popular Edition. Crown 8vo., 3s. 6d.
Library Edition. 2 vols. 8vo., 30s.

Symes.—POLITICAL ECONOMY: a Short Text-book of Political Economy. With Problems for Solution, and Hints for Supplementary Reading. By Prof. J. E. SYMES, M.A., of University College, Nottingham. Crown 8vo., 2s. 6d.

Toynbee.—LECTURES ON THE INDUSTRIAL REVOLUTION OF THE 18th CENTURY IN ENGLAND. By ARNOLD TOYNBEE. With a Memoir of the Author by BENJAMIN JOWETT, D.D. 8vo., 10s. 6d.

Webb.—THE HISTORY OF TRADE UNIONISM. By SIDNEY and BEATRICE WEBB. With Map and full Bibliography of the Subject. 8vo., 18s.

Evolution, Anthropology, &c.

Babington.—FALLACIES OF RACE THEORIES AS APPLIED TO NATIONAL CHARACTERISTICS. Essays by WILLIAM DALTON BABINGTON, M.A. Crown 8vo., 6s.

Clodd.—Works by EDWARD CLODD.
THE STORY OF CREATION: a Plain Account of Evolution. With 77 Illustrations. Crown 8vo., 3s. 6d.

A PRIMER OF EVOLUTION: being a Popular Abridged Edition of 'The Story of Creation'. With Illustrations. Fcp. 8vo., 1s. 6d.

Lang.—CUSTOM AND MYTH: Studies of Early Usage and Belief. By ANDREW LANG, M.A. With 15 Illustrations. Crown 8vo., 3s. 6d.

Lubbock.—THE ORIGIN OF CIVILISATION and the Primitive Condition of Man. By Sir J. LUBBOCK, Bart., M.P. With 5 Plates and 20 Illustrations in the Text. 8vo. 18s.

Romanes.—Works by GEORGE JOHN ROMANES, M.A., LL.D., F.R.S.
DARWIN, AND AFTER DARWIN: an Exposition of the Darwinian Theory, and a Discussion on Post-Darwinian Questions.
Part I. THE DARWINIAN THEORY. With Portrait of Darwin and 125 Illustrations. Crown 8vo., 10s. 6d.
Part II. POST-DARWINIAN QUESTIONS: Heredity and Utility. With Portrait of the Author and 5 Illustrations. Cr. 8vo., 10s. 6d.
AN EXAMINATION OF WEISMANNISM. Crown 8vo., 6s.
MIND AND MOTION AND MONISM. Crown 8vo., 4s. 6d.

Classical Literature and Translations, &c.

Abbott.—HELLENICA. A Collection of Essays on Greek Poetry, Philosophy, History, and Religion. Edited by EVELYN ABBOTT, M.A., LL.D. 8vo., 16s.

Æschylus.—EUMENIDES OF ÆSCHYLUS. With Metrical English Translation. By J. F. DAVIES. 8vo., 7s.

Aristophanes.—THE ACHARNIANS OF ARISTOPHANES, translated into English Verse. By R. Y. TYRRELL. Cr. 8vo., 1s.

Becker.—Works by Professor BECKER.

GALLUS; or, Roman Scenes in the Time of Augustus. Illustrated. Cr. 8vo., 3s. 6d.

CHARICLES; or, Illustrations of the Private Life of the Ancient Greeks. Illustrated. Cr 8vo., 3s. 6d.

Cicero.—CICERO'S CORRESPONDENCE. By R. Y. TYRRELL. Vols. I., II., III. 8vo., each 12s. Vol. IV., 15s.

Farnell.—GREEK LYRIC POETRY: a Complete Collection of the Surviving Passages from the Greek Song-Writing. By GEORGE S. FARNELL, M.A. With 5 Plates. 8vo., 16s.

Lang.—HOMER AND THE EPIC. By ANDREW LANG. Crown 8vo., 9s. net.

Mackail.—SELECT EPIGRAMS FROM THE GREEK ANTHOLOGY. By J. W. MACKAIL. 8vo., 16s.

Rich.—A DICTIONARY OF ROMAN AND GREEK ANTIQUITIES. By A. RICH, B.A. With 2000 Woodcuts. Crown 8vo., 7s. 6d.

Sophocles.—Translated into English Verse. By ROBERT WHITELAW, M.A., Assistant Master in Rugby School; late Fellow of Trinity College, Cambridge. Crown 8vo., 8s. 6d.

Tyrrell.—TRANSLATIONS INTO GREEK AND LATIN VERSE. Edited by R. Y. TYRRELL. 8vo., 6s.

Virgil.—THE ÆNEID OF VIRGIL. Translated into English Verse by JOHN CONINGTON. Crown 8vo., 6s.

THE POEMS OF VIRGIL. Translated into English Prose by JOHN CONINGTON. Crown 8vo., 6s.

THE ÆNEID OF VIRGIL, freely translated into English Blank Verse. By W. J. THORNHILL. Crown 8vo., 7s. 6d.

THE ÆNEID OF VIRGIL. Books I. to VI. Translated into English Verse by JAMES RHOADES. Crown 8vo., 5s.

Wilkins.—THE GROWTH OF THE HOMERIC POEMS. By G. WILKINS. 8vo., 6s.

Poetry and the Drama.

Acworth.—BALLADS OF THE MARATHAS. Rendered into English Verse from the Marathi Originals. By HARRY ARBUTHNOT ACWORTH. 8vo., 5s.

Allingham.—Works by WILLIAM ALLINGHAM.

BLACKBERRIES. Imperial 16mo., 6s.

IRISH SONGS AND POEMS. With Frontispiece of the Waterfall of Asaroe. Fcp. 8vo., 6s.

LAURENCE BLOOMFIELD. With Portrait of the Author. Fcp. 8vo., 3s. 6d.

Allingham.—Works by WILLIAM ALLINGHAM—continued.

FLOWER PIECES; DAY AND NIGHT SONGS; BALLADS. With 2 Designs by D. G. ROSSETTI. Fcp. 8vo., 6s.; large paper edition, 12s.

LIFE AND PHANTASY: with Frontispiece by Sir J. E. MILLAIS, Bart., and Design by ARTHUR HUGHES. Fcp. 8vo., 6s.; large paper edition, 12s.

THOUGHT AND WORD, AND ASHBY MANOR: a Play. Fcp. 8vo., 6s.; large paper edition, 12s.

Sets of the above 6 vols. may be had in uniform half-parchment binding, price 30s.

Poetry and the Drama—*continued*.

Armstrong.—Works by G. F. SAVAGE-ARMSTRONG.
POEMS: Lyrical and Dramatic. Fcp. 8vo., 6s.
KING SAUL. (The Tragedy of Israel, Part I.) Fcp. 8vo. 5s.
KING DAVID. (The Tragedy of Israel, Part II.) Fcp. 8vo., 6s.
KING SOLOMON. (The Tragedy of Israel, Part III.) Fcp. 8vo., 6s.
UGONE: a Tragedy. Fcp. 8vo., 6s.
A GARLAND FROM GREECE: Poems. Fcp. 8vo., 7s. 6d.
STORIES OF WICKLOW: Poems. Fcp. 8vo., 7s. 6d.
MEPHISTOPHELES IN BROADCLOTH: a Satire. Fcp. 8vo., 4s.
ONE IN THE INFINITE: a Poem. Cr. 8vo., 7s. 6d.

Armstrong.—THE POETICAL WORKS OF EDMUND J. ARMSTRONG. Fcp. 8vo., 5s.

Arnold.—Works by Sir EDWIN ARNOLD, K.C.I.E.
THE LIGHT OF THE WORLD: or, the Great Consummation. Cr. 8vo., 7s. 6d. net.
THE TENTH MUSE, AND OTHER POEMS. Crown 8vo., 5s. net.
POTIPHAR'S WIFE, and other Poems. Crown 8vo., 5s. net.
ADZUMA: or, the Japanese Wife. A Play. Crown 8vo., 6s. 6d. net.

Beesly.—BALLADS, AND OTHER VERSE. By A. H. BEESLY. Fcp. 8vo., 5s.

Bell.—CHAMBER COMEDIES: a Collection of Plays and Monologues for the Drawing Room. By Mrs. HUGH BELL. Crown 8vo., 6s.

Carmichael.—POEMS. By JENNINGS CARMICHAEL (Mrs. FRANCIS MULLIS). Crown 8vo., 6s. net.

Cochrane.—THE KESTREL'S NEST, and other Verses. By ALFRED COCHRANE. Fcp. 8vo., 3s. 6d.

Goethe.
FAUST, Part I., the German Text, with Introduction and Notes. By ALBERT M. SELSS, Ph.D., M.A. Cr. 8vo., 5s.
FAUST. Translated, with Notes. By T. E. WEBB. 8vo., 12s. 6d.

Ingelow.—Works by JEAN INGELOW.
POETICAL WORKS. 2 vols. Fcp. 8vo., 12s.
LYRICAL AND OTHER POEMS. Selected from the Writings of JEAN INGELOW. Fcp. 8vo., 2s. 6d.; cloth plain, 3s. cloth gilt.

Kendall.—SONGS FROM DREAMLAND. By MAY KENDALL. Fcp 8vo., 5s. net.

Lang.—Works by ANDREW LANG.
BAN AND ARRIÈRE BAN. A Rally of Fugitive Rhymes Fcp. 8vo., 5s. net.
GRASS OF PARNASSUS. Fcp. 8vo., 2s. 6d. net.
BALLADS OF BOOKS. Edited by ANDREW LANG. Fcp. 8vo., 6s.
THE BLUE POETRY BOOK. Edited by ANDREW LANG. With 12 Plates and 88 Illustrations in the Text by H. J. FORD and LANCELOT SPEED. Crown 8vo., 6s.
Special Edition, printed on Indian paper. With Notes, but without Illustrations. Crown 8vo., 7s. 6d.

Lecky.—POEMS. By W. E. H. LECKY. Fcp. 8vo., 5s.

Peek.—Works by HEDLEY PEEK (FRANK LEYTON).
SKELETON LEAVES: Poems. With a Dedicatory Poem to the late Hon. Roden Noel. Fcp. 8vo., 2s. 6d. net.
THE SHADOWS OF THE LAKE, and other Poems. Fcp. 8vo., 2s. 6d. net.

Lytton.—Works by THE EARL OF LYTTON (OWEN MEREDITH).
MARAH. Fcp. 8vo., 6s. 6d.
KING POPPY: a Fantasia. With 1 Plate and Design on Title-Page by Sir ED. BURNE-JONES, A.R.A. Crown 8vo., 10s. 6d.
THE WANDERER. Cr. 8vo., 10s. 6d.
LUCILE. Crown 8vo., 10s. 6d.
SELECTED POEMS. Cr. 8vo., 10s. 6d.

Poetry and the Drama—*continued*.

Macaulay.—LAYS OF ANCIENT ROME, &c. By Lord MACAULAY.
Illustrated by G. SCHARF. Fcp. 4to., 10s. 6d.
——— Bijou Edition. 18mo., 2s. 6d., gilt top.
——— Popular Edition. Fcp. 4to., 6d. sewed, 1s. cloth.
Illustrated by J. R. WEGUELIN. Crown 8vo., 3s. 6d.
Annotated Edition. Fcp. 8vo., 1s. sewed, 1s. 6d. cloth.

Murray.—(ROBERT F.), Author of 'The Scarlet Gown'. His Poems, with a Memoir by ANDREW LANG. Fcp. 8vo., 5s. net.

Nesbit.—LAYS AND LEGENDS. By E. NESBIT (Mrs. HUBERT BLAND). First Series. Crown 8vo., 3s. 6d. Second Series, with Portrait. Crown 8vo., 5s.

Piatt.—Works by SARAH PIATT.
POEMS. With portrait of the Author. 2 vols. Crown 8vo., 10s.
AN ENCHANTED CASTLE, AND OTHER POEMS: Pictures, Portraits and People in Ireland. Crown 8vo., 3s. 6d.

Piatt.—Works by JOHN JAMES PIATT.
IDYLS AND LYRICS OF THE OHIO VALLEY. Crown 8vo., 5s.
LITTLE NEW WORLD IDYLS. Cr. 8vo., 5s.

Rhoades.—TERESA AND OTHER POEMS. By JAMES RHOADES. Crown 8vo., 3s. 6d.

Riley.—Works by JAMES WHITCOMB RILEY.
OLD FASHIONED ROSES: Poems. 12mo., 5s.
POEMS HERE AT HOME. Fcap. 8vo., 6s. net.

Shakespeare.—BOWDLER'S FAMILY SHAKESPEARE. With 36 Woodcuts. 1 vol. 8vo., 14s. Or in 6 vols. Fcp. 8vo., 21s.
THE SHAKESPEARE BIRTHDAY BOOK. By MARY F. DUNBAR. 32mo., 1s. 6d.

Sturgis.—A BOOK OF SONG. By JULIAN STURGIS. 16mo., 5s.

Works of Fiction, Humour, &c.

Anstey.—Works by F. ANSTEY, Author of 'Vice Versâ'.
THE BLACK POODLE, and other Stories. Crown 8vo., 2s. boards, 2s. 6d. cloth.
VOCES POPULI. Reprinted from 'Punch'. First Series. With 20 Illustrations by J. BERNARD PARTRIDGE. Cr. 8vo., 3s. 6d.
THE TRAVELLING COMPANIONS. Reprinted from 'Punch'. With 25 Illus. by J. B. PARTRIDGE. Post 4to., 5s.
THE MAN FROM BLANKLEY'S: a Story in Scenes, and other Sketches. With 24 Illustrations by J. BERNARD PARTRIDGE. Fcp. 4to., 6s.

Arnold.—THE STORY OF ULLA, and other Tales. By EDWIN LESTER ARNOLD. Crown 8vo., 6s.

Astor.—A JOURNEY IN OTHER WORLDS. a Romance of the Future. By JOHN JACOB ASTOR. With 10 Illustrations. Cr. 8vo., 6s.

Baker.—BY THE WESTERN SEA. By JAMES BAKER, Author of 'John Westacott'. Crown 8vo., 3s. 6d.

Beaconsfield.—Works by the Earl of BEACONSFIELD.
NOVELS AND TALES. Cheap Edition. Complete in 11 vols. Cr. 8vo., 1s. 6d. each.

Vivian Grey.	Henrietta Temple.
The Young Duke, &c.	Venetia. Tancred.
Alroy, Ixion, &c.	Coningsby. Sybil.
Contarini Fleming, &c.	Lothair. Endymion.

NOVELS AND TALES. The Hughenden Edition. With 2 Portraits and 11 Vignettes. 11 vols. Cr. 8vo., 42s.

Boulton.—JOSEPHINE CREWE. By HELEN M. BOULTON. Cr. 8vo., 6s.

Carmichael.—POEMS. By JENNINGS CARMICHAEL (Mrs. FRANCIS MULLIS). Crown 8vo. 6s. net.

Clegg.—DAVID'S LOOM: a Story of Rochdale life in the early years of the Nineteenth Century. By JOHN TRAFFORD CLEGG. Crown 8vo., 2s. 6d.

Works of Fiction, Humour, &c.—continued.

Deland.—PHILIP AND HIS WIFE. By MARGARET DELAND, Author of 'John Ward'. Cr. 8vo., 6s.

Dougall.—Works by L. DOUGALL.
BEGGARS ALL. Crown 8vo., 3s. 6d.
WHAT NECESSITY KNOWS. Crown 8vo., 6s.

Doyle.—Works by A. CONAN DOYLE.
MICAH CLARKE: a Tale of Monmouth's Rebellion. With 10 Illustrations. Cr. 8vo., 3s. 6d.
THE CAPTAIN OF THE POLESTAR, and other Tales. Cr. 8vo., 3s. 6d.
THE REFUGEES: a Tale of the Huguenots. With 25 Illustrations. Crown 8vo., 3s. 6d.
THE STARK-MUNRO LETTERS. Cr. 8vo., 6s.

Farrar.—Works by F. W. FARRAR, Dean of Canterbury.
DARKNESS AND DAWN: or, Scenes in the Days of Nero. An Historic Tale. Cr. 8vo., 7s. 6d.
GATHERING CLOUDS: a Tale of the Days of St. Chrysostom. 2 vols. 8vo., 28s.

Froude.—THE TWO CHIEFS OF DUNBOY: an Irish Romance of the Last Century. By J. A. FROUDE. Cr. 8vo., 3s. 6d.

Fowler.—THE YOUNG PRETENDERS. A Story of Child Life. By EDITH H. FOWLER. With 12 Illustrations by PHILIP BURNE-JONES. Crown 8vo., 6s.

Gerard.—AN ARRANGED MARRIAGE. By DOROTHEA GERARD. Cr. 8vo., 6s.

Gilkes.—THE THING THAT HATH BEEN: or, a Young Man's Mistake. By A. H. GILKES, M.A. Crown 8vo., 6s.

Haggard.—Works by H. RIDER HAGGARD.
JOAN HASTE. With 20 Illustrations. Cr. 8vo., 6s.
THE PEOPLE OF THE MIST. With 16 Illustrations. Crown 8vo., 6s.
MONTEZUMA'S DAUGHTER. With 24 Illustrations. Crown 8vo., 6s.
SHE. 32 Illustrations. Cr. 8vo., 3s. 6d.
ALLAN QUATERMAIN. With 31 Illustrations. Crown 8vo., 3s. 6d.
MAIWA'S REVENGE. Crown 8vo., 1s. boards; 1s. 6d. cloth.
COLONEL QUARITCH, V.C. Cr. 8vo., 3s. 6d.
CLEOPATRA. With 29 Illustrations Crown 8vo., 3s. 6d.
BEATRICE. Cr. 8vo., 3s. 6d.
ERIC BRIGHTEYES. With 51 Illustrations. Cr. 8vo., 3s. 6d.

Haggard.—Works by H. RIDER HAGGARD—continued.
NADA THE LILY. With 23 Illustrations. Cr. 8vo., 3s. 6d.
ALLAN'S WIFE. With 34 Illustrations. Crown 8vo., 3s. 6d.
THE WITCH'S HEAD. With 16 Illustrations. Crown 8vo., 3s. 6d.
MR. MEESON'S WILL. With 16 Illustrations. Crown 8vo., 3s. 6d.
DAWN. With 16 Illustrations. Crown 8vo., 3s. 6d.

Haggard and Lang.—THE WORLD'S DESIRE. By H. RIDER HAGGARD and ANDREW LANG. With 27 Illustrations by M. GREIFFENHAGEN. Cr. 8vo., 3s. 6d.

Harte.— IN THE CARQUINEZ WOODS, and other Stories. By BRET HARTE. Cr. 8vo., 3s. 6d.

Hornung.—THE UNBIDDEN GUEST. By E. W. HORNUNG. Cr. 8vo., 3s. 6d.

Lang.—A MONK OF FIFE: a Romance of the Days of Jeanne D'Arc. Done into English, from the Manuscript in the Scots College of Ratisbon, by ANDREW LANG. With Illustrations and Initial Letters by SELWYN IMAGE. Crown 8vo., 6s.

Lemon.—MATTHEW FURTH. By IDA LEMON. Crown 8vo., 6s.

Lyall.—Works by EDNA LYALL, Author of 'Donovan,' &c.
THE AUTOBIOGRAPHY OF A SLANDER. Fcp. 8vo., 1s. sewed.
Presentation Edition. With 20 Illustrations by LANCELOT SPEED. Cr. 8vo., 2s. 6d. net.
DOREEN: The Story of a Singer. Cr. 8vo., 6s.

Matthews.—HIS FATHER'S SON: a Novel of the New York Stock Exchange. By BRANDER MATTHEWS. With Illus. Cr. 8vo., 6s.

Melville.—Works by G. J. WHYTE MELVILLE.

The Gladiators.	Holmby House.
The Interpreter.	Kate Coventry.
Good for Nothing.	Digby Grand.
The Queen's Maries.	General Bounce.

Cr. 8vo., 1s. 6d. each.

Oliphant.—Works by Mrs. OLIPHANT.
MADAM. Cr. 8vo., 1s. 6d.
IN TRUST. Cr. 8vo., 1s. 6d.

Payn.—Works by JAMES PAYN.
THE LUCK OF THE DARRELLS. Cr. 8vo., 1s. 6d.
THICKER THAN WATER. Cr. 8vo., 1s. 6d.

Works of Fiction, Humour, &c.—continued.

Phillipps-Wolley.—SNAP: a Legend of the Lone Mountain. By C. PHILLIPPS-WOLLEY. With 13 Illustrations by H. G. WILLINK. Cr. 8vo., 3s. 6d.

Prince.—THE STORY OF CHRISTINE ROCHEFORT. By HELEN CHOATE PRINCE. Crown 8vo., 6s.

Quintana.—THE CID CAMPEADOR: an Historical Romance. By D. ANTONIO DE TRUEBA Y LA QUINTANA. Translated from the Spanish by Henry J. Gill, M.A., T.C.D. Crown 8vo., 6s.

Rhoscomyl.—THE JEWEL OF YNYS GALON: being a hitherto unprinted Chapter in the History of the Sea Rovers. By OWEN RHOSCOMYL. Cr. 8vo., 6s.

Robertson.—NUGGETS IN THE DEVIL'S PUNCH BOWL, and other Australian Tales. By ANDREW ROBERTSON. Cr. 8vo., 3s. 6d.

Sewell.—Works by ELIZABETH M. SEWELL.
A Glimpse of the World. | Amy Herbert.
Laneton Parsonage. | Cleve Hall.
Margaret Percival. | Gertrude.
Katharine Ashton. | Home Life.
The Earl's Daughter. | After Life.
The Experience of Life. | Ursula. Ivors.
Cr. 8vo., 1s. 6d. each cloth plain. 2s. 6d. each cloth extra, gilt edges.

Stevenson.—Works by ROBERT LOUIS STEVENSON.
STRANGE CASE OF DR. JEKYLL AND MR. HYDE. Fcp. 8vo., 1s. sewed. 1s. 6d. cloth.
THE DYNAMITER. Cr. 8vo., 3s. 6d.

Stevenson and Osbourne.—THE WRONG BOX. By ROBERT LOUIS STEVENSON and LLOYD OSBOURNE. Cr. 8vo., 3s. 6d.

Suttner.—LAY DOWN YOUR ARMS *Die Waffen Nieder*: The Autobiography of Martha Tilling. By BERTHA VON SUTTNER. Translated by T. HOLMES. Cr. 8vo., 1s. 6d.

Trollope.—Works by ANTHONY TROLLOPE.
THE WARDEN. Cr. 8vo., 1s. 6d.
BARCHESTER TOWERS. Cr. 8vo., 1s. 6d.

TRUE, A, RELATION OF THE TRAVELS AND PERILOUS ADVENTURES OF MATHEW DUDGEON, Gentleman: Wherein is truly set down the Manner of his Taking, the Long Time of his Slavery in Algiers, and Means of his Delivery. Written by Himself, and now for the first time printed. Cr. 8vo., 5s.

Walford.—Works by L. B. WALFORD.
MR. SMITH: a Part of his Life. Crown 8vo., 2s. 6d.
THE BABY'S GRANDMOTHER. Crown 8vo., 2s. 6d.
COUSINS. Crown 8vo., 2s. 6d.
TROUBLESOME DAUGHTERS. Crown 8vo., 2s. 6d.
PAULINE. Crown 8vo. 2s. 6d.
DICK NETHERBY. Crown 8vo., 2s. 6d.
THE HISTORY OF A WEEK. Crown 8vo., 2s. 6d.
A STIFF-NECKED GENERATION. Crown 8vo. 2s. 6d.
NAN, and other Stories. Cr. 8vo., 2s. 6d.
THE MISCHIEF OF MONICA. Crown 8vo., 2s. 6d.
THE ONE GOOD GUEST. Cr. 8vo. 2s. 6d.
'PLOUGHED,' and other Stories. Crown 8vo., 6s.
THE MATCHMAKER. Cr. 8vo., 6s.

West.—Works by B. B. WEST.
HALF-HOURS WITH THE MILLIONAIRES: Showing how much harder it is to spend a million than to make it. Cr. 8vo., 6s.
SIR SIMON VANDERPETTER, AND MINDING HIS ANCESTORS. Two Reformations. Crown 8vo., 5s.
A FINANCIAL ATONEMENT. Cr. 8vo.,

Weyman.—Works by S. J. WEYMAN.
THE HOUSE OF THE WOLF. Cr. 8vo., 3s. 6d.
A GENTLEMAN OF FRANCE. Cr. 8vo., 6s.
THE RED COCKADE. Cr. 8vo., 6s.

Popular Science (Natural History, &c.).

Butler.—OUR HOUSEHOLD INSECTS. An Account of the Insect-Pests found in Dwelling-Houses. By EDWARD A. BUTLER, B.A., B.Sc. (Lond.). With 113 Illustrations. Crown 8vo., 6s.

Clodd.—A PRIMER OF EVOLUTION: being a Popular Abridged Edition of 'The Story of Creation'. By EDWARD CLODD. With Illus. Fcp. 8vo., 1s. 6d.

Furneaux.—Works by W. FURNEAUX.
BUTTERFLIES AND MOTHS (British). With 12 coloured Plates and 241 Illustrations in the Text. Crown 8vo., 12s. 6d.
THE OUTDOOR WORLD; or, The Young Collector's Handbook. With 18 Plates, 16 of which are coloured, and 549 Illustrations in the Text. Crown 8vo., 7s. 6d.

Popular Science (Natural History, &c.).

Graham.—COUNTRY PASTIMES FOR BOYS. By P. ANDERSON GRAHAM. With numerous Illustrations from Drawings and Photographs. Crown 8vo., 6s.

Hartwig.—Works by Dr. GEORGE HARTWIG.

   THE SEA AND ITS LIVING WONDERS. With 12 Plates and 303 Woodcuts. 8vo., 7s. net.

   THE TROPICAL WORLD. With 8 Plates and 172 Woodcuts. 8vo., 7s. net.

   THE POLAR WORLD. With 3 Maps, 8 Plates and 85 Woodcuts. 8vo., 7s. net.

   THE SUBTERRANEAN WORLD. With 3 Maps and 80 Woodcuts. 8vo., 7s. net.

   THE AERIAL WORLD. With Map, 8 Plates and 60 Woodcuts. 8vo., 7s. net.

Hayward.—BIRD NOTES. By the late JANE MARY HAYWARD. Edited by EMMA HUBBARD. With Frontispiece and 15 Illustrations by G. E. LODGE. Cr. 8vo., 6s.

Helmholtz.—POPULAR LECTURES ON SCIENTIFIC SUBJECTS. By HERMANN VON HELMHOLTZ. With 68 Woodcuts. 2 vols. Crown 8vo., 3s. 6d. each.

Hudson.—BRITISH BIRDS. By W. H. HUDSON, C.M.Z.S. With a Chapter on Structure and Classification by FRANK E. BEDDARD, F.R.S. With 17 Plates (8 of which are Coloured), and over 100 Illustrations in the Text. Crown 8vo., 12s. 6d.

Proctor.—Works by RICHARD A. PROCTOR.

   LIGHT SCIENCE FOR LEISURE HOURS. Familiar Essays on Scientific Subjects. 3 vols. Crown 8vo., 5s. each.

   CHANCE AND LUCK: a Discussion of the Laws of Luck, Coincidence, Wagers, Lotteries and the Fallacies of Gambling, &c. Cr. 8vo., 2s. boards, 2s. 6d. cloth.

   ROUGH WAYS MADE SMOOTH. Familiar Essays on Scientific Subjects. Silver Library Edition. Cr. 8vo., 3s. 6d.

   PLEASANT WAYS IN SCIENCE. Cr. 8vo., 5s. Silver Library Edition. Crown 8vo., 3s. 6d.

Proctor.—Works by RICHARD A. PROCTOR—*continued*.

   THE GREAT PYRAMID, OBSERVATORY, TOMB AND TEMPLE. With Illustrations. Crown 8vo., 5s.

   NATURE STUDIES. By R. A. PROCTOR, GRANT ALLEN, A. WILSON, T. FOSTER and E. CLODD. Crown 8vo., 5s. Sil. Lib. Ed. Cr. 8vo., 3s. 6d.

   LEISURE READINGS. By R. A. PROCTOR, E. CLODD, A. WILSON, T. FOSTER, and A. C. RANYARD. Cr. 8vo., 5s.

Stanley.—A FAMILIAR HISTORY OF BIRDS. By E. STANLEY, D.D., formerly Bishop of Norwich. With Illustrations. Cr. 8vo., 3s. 6d.

Wood.—Works by the Rev. J. G. WOOD.

   HOMES WITHOUT HANDS: a Description of the Habitation of Animals, classed according to the Principle of Construction. With 140 Illustrations. 8vo., 7s. net.

   INSECTS AT HOME: a Popular Account of British Insects, their Structure, Habits and Transformations. With 700 Illustrations. 8vo., 7s. net.

   INSECTS ABROAD: a Popular Account of Foreign Insects, their Structure, Habits and Transformations. With 600 Illustrations. 8vo., 7s. net.

   BIBLE ANIMALS: a Description of every Living Creature mentioned in the Scriptures. With 112 Illustrations. 8vo., 7s. net.

   PETLAND REVISITED. With 33 Illustrations. Cr. 8vo., 3s. 6d.

   OUT OF DOORS; a Selection of Original Articles on Practical Natural History. With 11 Illustrations. Cr. 8vo., 3s. 6d.

   STRANGE DWELLINGS: a Description of the Habitations of Animals, abridged from 'Homes without Hands'. With 60 Illustrations. Cr. 8vo., 3s. 6d.

Works of Reference.

Longmans' GAZETTEER OF THE WORLD. Edited by GEORGE G. CHISHOLM, M.A., B.Sc., Fellow of the Royal Geographical and Statistical Societies. Imp. 8vo. £2 2s. cloth, £2 12s. 6d. half-morocco.

Maunder's (Samuel) Treasuries.

BIOGRAPHICAL TREASURY. With Supplement brought down to 1889. By Rev. JAMES WOOD. Fcp. 8vo., 6s.

TREASURY OF NATURAL HISTORY: or, Popular Dictionary of Zoology. With 900 Woodcuts. Fcp. 8vo., 6s.

TREASURY OF GEOGRAPHY, Physical, Historical, Descriptive, and Political. With 7 Maps and 16 Plates. Fcp. 8vo., 6s.

THE TREASURY OF BIBLE KNOWLEDGE. By the Rev. J. AYRE, M.A. With 5 Maps, 15 Plates, and 300 Woodcuts. Fcp. 8vo., 6s.

HISTORICAL TREASURY: Outlines of Universal History, Separate Histories of all Nations. Fcp. 8vo., 6s.

Maunder's (Samuel) Treasuries —continued.

TREASURY OF KNOWLEDGE AND LIBRARY OF REFERENCE. Comprising an English Dictionary and Grammar, Universal Gazetteer, Classical Dictionary, Chronology, Law Dictionary, &c. Fcp. 8vo., 6s.

SCIENTIFIC AND LITERARY TREASURY. Fcp. 8vo., 6s.

THE TREASURY OF BOTANY. Edited by J. LINDLEY, F.R.S., and T. MOORE, F.L.S. With 274 Woodcuts and 20 Steel Plates. 2 vols. Fcp. 8vo., 12s.

Roget.—THESAURUS OF ENGLISH WORDS AND PHRASES. Classified and Arranged so as to Facilitate the Expression of Ideas and assist in Literary Composition. By PETER MARK ROGET, M.D., F.R.S. Crown 8vo., 10s. 6d.

Willich.—POPULAR TABLES for giving information for ascertaining the value of Lifehold, Leasehold, and Church Property, the Public Funds, &c. By CHARLES M. WILLICH. Edited by H. BENCE JONES. Crown 8vo., 10s. 6d.

Children's Books.

Crake.—Works by Rev. A. D. CRAKE.
EDWY THE FAIR; or, the First Chronicle of Æscendune. Crown 8vo., 2s. 6d.
ALFGAR THE DANE: or, the Second Chronicle of Æscendune. Cr. 8vo., 2s. 6d.
THE RIVAL HEIRS: being the Third and Last Chronicle of Æscendune. Cr. 8vo., 2s. 6d.
THE HOUSE OF WALDERNE. A Tale of the Cloister and the Forest in the Days of the Barons' Wars. Crown 8vo., 2s. 6d.
BRIAN FITZ-COUNT. A Story of Wallingford Castle and Dorchester Abbey. Cr. 8vo., 2s. 6d.

Lang.—Works edited by ANDREW LANG.
THE BLUE FAIRY BOOK. With 138 Illustrations. Crown 8vo., 6s.
THE RED FAIRY BOOK. With 100 Illustrations. Cr. 8vo., 6s.
THE GREEN FAIRY BOOK. With 101 Illustrations. Crown 8vo., 6s.
THE YELLOW FAIRY BOOK. With 104 Illustrations. Crown 8vo., 6s.
THE BLUE POETRY BOOK. With 100 Illustrations. Crown 8vo., 6s.
THE BLUE POETRY BOOK. School Edition, without Illustrations. Fcp. 8vo., 2s. 6d.
THE TRUE STORY BOOK. With 66 Illustrations. Crown 8vo., 6s.

Lang.—Works edited by ANDREW LANG —continued.
THE RED TRUE STORY BOOK. With 100 Illustrations. Crown 8vo., 6s.

Meade.—Works by L. T. MEADE.
DADDY'S BOY. Illustrated. Crown 8vo., 3s. 6d.
DEB AND THE DUCHESS. Illustrated. Crown 8vo., 3s. 6d.
THE BERESFORD PRIZE. Crown 8vo., 3s. 6d.

Molesworth.—Works by Mrs. MOLESWORTH.
SILVERTHORNS. Illustrated. Cr. 8vo., 5s.
NEIGHBOURS. Illus. Crown 8vo., 2s. 6d.

Stevenson.—A CHILD'S GARDEN OF VERSES. By ROBERT LOUIS STEVENSON. Small fcp. 8vo., 5s.

Upton.—THE ADVENTURES OF TWO DUTCH DOLLS AND A 'GOLLIWOGG'. Illustrated by FLORENCE K. UPTON, with Words by BERTHA UPTON. With 31 Coloured Plates and numerous Illustrations in the Text. Oblong 4to., 6s.

Wordsworth.—THE SNOW GARDEN, and other Fairy Tales for Children. By ELIZABETH WORDSWORTH. With Illustrations by TREVOR HADDON. Cr. 8vo., 5s.

Longmans' Series of Books for Girls.

Crown 8vo., price 2s. 6d. each.

ATELIER (THE) DU LYS: or an Art Student in the Reign of Terror.
BY THE SAME AUTHOR.
MADEMOISELLE MORI.
THAT CHILD.
UNDER A CLOUD.
THE FIDDLER OF LUGAU.
A CHILD OF THE REVOLUTION.
HESTER'S VENTURE.
IN THE OLDEN TIME.
THE YOUNGER SISTER.

THE THIRD MISS ST. QUENTIN. By Mrs. MOLESWORTH.

THE PALACE IN THE GARDEN. Illustrated. By Mrs. MOLESWORTH.

ATHERSTONE PRIORY. By L. N. COMYN.

THE STORY OF A SPRING MORNING, &c. By Mrs. MOLESWORTH. Illustrated.

NEIGHBOURS. By Mrs. MOLESWORTH.

VERY YOUNG; and QUITE ANOTHER STORY. By JEAN INGELOW.

CAN THIS BE LOVE? By Louis A. PARR.

KEITH DERAMORE. By the Author of 'Miss Molly'.

SIDNEY. By MARGARET DELAND.

LAST WORDS TO GIRLS ON LIFE AT SCHOOL AND AFTER SCHOOL. By Mrs. W. GREY.

STRAY THOUGHTS FOR GIRLS. By LUCY H. M. SOULSBY. 16mo., 1s. 6d. net.

The Silver Library.

CROWN 8vo. 3s. 6d. EACH VOLUME.

Arnold's (Sir Edwin) Seas and Lands. With 71 Illustrations. 3s. 6d.

Bagehot's (W.) Biographical Studies. 3s. 6d.

Bagehot's (W.) Economic Studies. 3s. 6d.

Bagehot's (W.) Literary Studies. 3 vols. 3s. 6d. each. With Portrait.

Baker's (Sir S. W.) Eight Years in Ceylon. With 6 Illustrations. 3s. 6d.

Baker's (Sir S. W.) Rifle and Hound in Ceylon. With 6 Illustrations. 3s. 6d.

Baring-Gould's (Rev. S.) Curious Myths of the Middle Ages. 3s. 6d.

Baring-Gould's (Rev. S.) Origin and Development of Religious Belief. 2 vols. 3s. 6d. each.

Becker's (Prof.) Gallus: or, Roman Scenes in the Time of Augustus. Illus. 3s. 6d.

Becker's (Prof.) Charicles: or, Illustrations of the Private Life of the Ancient Greeks. Illustrated. 3s. 6d.

Bent's (J. T.) The Ruined Cities of Mashonaland: being a Record of Excavation and Exploration in 1891. With 117 Illustrations. 3s. 6d.

Brassey's (Lady) A Voyage in the 'Sunbeam'. With 66 Illustrations. 3s. 6d.

Clodd's (E.) Story of Creation: a Plain Account of Evolution. With 77 Illustrations. 3s. 6d.

Conybeare (Rev. W. J.) and Howson's (Very Rev. J. S.) Life and Epistles of St. Paul. 46 Illustrations. 3s. 6d.

Dougall's (L.) Beggars All; a Novel. 3s. 6d.

Doyle's (A. Conan) Micah Clarke: a Tale of Monmouth's Rebellion. 10 Illus. 3s. 6d.

Doyle's (A. Conan) The Captain of the Polestar, and other Tales. 3s. 6d.

Doyle's (A. Conan) The Refugees: A Tale of The Huguenots. With 25 Illustrations. 3s. 6d.

Froude's (J. A.) Short Studies on Great Subjects. 4 vols. 3s. 6d. each.

Froude's (J. A.) Cæsar: a Sketch. 3s. 6d.

Froude's (J. A.) Thomas Carlyle: a History of his Life.
1795-1835. 2 vols. 7s.
1834-1881. 2 vols. 7s.

Froude's (J. A.) The Two Chiefs of Dunboy: an Irish Romance of the Last Century. 3s. 6d.

Froude's (J. A.) The History of England, from the Fall of Wolsey to the Defeat of the Spanish Armada. 12 vols. 3s. 6d. each.

Froude's (J. A.) The English in Ireland. 3 vols. 10s. 6d.

Froude's (J. A.) The Spanish Story of the Armada, and other Essays. 3s. 6d.

Gleig's (Rev. G. R.) Life of the Duke of Wellington. With Portrait. 3s. 6d.

Haggard's (H. R.) She: A History of Adventure. 32 Illustrations. 3s. 6d.

Haggard's (H. R.) Allan Quatermain. With 20 Illustrations. 3s. 6d.

Haggard's (H. R.) Colonel Quaritch, V.C.: a Tale of Country Life. 3s. 6d.

Haggard's (H. R.) Cleopatra. With 29 Full-page Illustrations. 3s. 6d.

Haggard's (H. R.) Eric Brighteyes. With 51 Illustrations. 3s. 6d.

Haggard's (H. R.) Beatrice. 3s. 6d.

Haggard's (H. R.) Allan's Wife. With 34 Illustrations. 3s. 6d.

Haggard's (H. R.) The Witch's Head. With Illustrations. 3s. 6d.

Haggard's (H. R.) Mr. Meeson's Will. With Illustrations. 3s. 6d.

Haggard's (H. R.) Dawn. With 16 Illustrations. 3s. 6d.

Haggard's (H. R.) and Lang's (A.) The World's Desire. With 27 Illus. 3s. 6d.

The Silver Library—*continued.*

Haggard's (H. R.) Nada the Lily. With Illustrations by C. H. M. Kerr. 3s. 6d.
Harte's (Bret) In the Carquinez Woods, and other Stories. 3s. 6d.
Helmholtz's (Hermann von) Popular Lectures on Scientific Subjects. With 68 Woodcuts. 2 vols. 3s. 6d. each.
Hornung's (E. W.) The Unbidden Guest. 3s. 6d.
Howitt's (W.) Visits to Remarkable Places. 80 Illustrations. 3s. 6d.
Jefferies' (R.) The Story of My Heart: My Autobiography. With Portrait. 3s. 6d.
Jefferies' (R.) Field and Hedgerow. With Portrait. 3s. 6d.
Jefferies' (R.) Red Deer. 17 Illus. 3s. 6d.
Jefferies' (R.) Wood Magic: a Fable. 3s. 6d.
Jefferies' (R. The Toilers of the Field. With Portrait from the Bust in Salisbury Cathedral. 3s. 6d.
Knight's (E. F.) The Cruise of the 'Alerte': a Search for Treasure on the Desert Island of Trinidad. 2 Maps and 23 Illustrations. 3s. 6d.
Knight's (E. F.) Where Three Empires Meet: a Narrative of Recent Travel in Kashmir, Western Tibet, etc. With a Map and 54 Illust. 3s. 6d.
Lang's (A.) Angling Sketches. 20 Illus. 3s. 6d.
Lang's (A.) Custom and Myth: Studies of Early Usage and Belief. 3s. 6d.
Lees (J. A.) and Clutterbuck's (W. J.) B.C. 1887, A Ramble in British Columbia. With Maps and 75 Illustrations. 3s. 6d.
Macaulay's (Lord) Essays and Lays of Ancient Rome. With Portrait and Illustrations. 3s. 6d.
Macleod's (H. D.) The Elements of Banking. 3s. 6d.
Marshman's (J. C.) Memoirs of Sir Henry Havelock. 3s. 6d.
Max Müller's (F.) India, what can it teach us? 3s. 6d.
Max Müller's (F.) Introduction to the Science of Religion. 3s. 6d.

Merivale's (Dean) History of the Romans under the Empire. 8 vols. 3s. 6d. ea.
Mill's (J. S.) Political Economy. 3s. 6d.
Mill's (J. S.) System of Logic. 3s. 6d.
Milner's (Geo.) Country Pleasures. 3s. 6d.
Nansen's (F.) The First Crossing of Greenland. With Illustrations and a Map. 3s. 6d.
Phillipps-Wolley's (C.) Snap: a Legend of the Lone Mountain. With 13 Illustrations. 3s. 6d.
Proctor's (R. A.) The Orbs Around Us. Essays on the Moon and Planets, Meteors and Comets, the Sun and Coloured Pairs of Suns. 3s. 6d.
Proctor's (R. A.) The Expanse of Heaven. Essays on the Wonders of the Firmament. 3s. 6d.
Proctor's (R. A.) Other Worlds than Ours. 3s. 6d.
Proctor's (R. A.) Rough Ways made Smooth. 3s. 6d.
Proctor's (R. A.) Pleasant Ways in Science. 3s. 6d.
Proctor's (R. A.) Myths and Marvels of Astronomy. 3s. 6d.
Proctor's (R. A.) Nature Studies. 3s. 6d.
Rossetti's (Maria F.) A Shadow of Dante: an Essay towards studying Himself, his World and his Pilgrimage. 3s. 6d.
Smith's (R. Bosworth) Carthage and the Carthaginians. 3s. 6d.
Stanley's (Bishop) Familiar History of Birds. 160 Illustrations. 3s. 6d.
Stevenson (Robert Louis) and Osbourne's (Lloyd) The Wrong Box. 3s. 6d.
Stevenson (Robt. Louis) and Stevenson's (Fanny van de Grift) More New Arabian Nights.—The Dynamiter. 3s. 6d.
Wayman's (Stanley J.) The House of the Wolf: a Romance. 3s. 6d.
Wood's (Rev. J. G.) Petland Revisited. With 33 Illustrations. 3s. 6d.
Wood's (Rev. J. G.) Strange Dwellings. With 60 Illustrations. 3s. 6d.
Wood's (Rev. J. G.) Out of Doors. 11 Illustrations. 3s. 6d.

Cookery, Domestic Management, &c.

Acton.—MODERN COOKERY. By ELIZA ACTON. With 150 Woodcuts. Fcp. 8vo., 4s. 6d.
Bull.—Works by THOMAS BULL, M.D.
 HINTS TO MOTHERS ON THE MANAGEMENT OF THEIR HEALTH DURING THE PERIOD OF PREGNANCY. Fcp. 8vo., 1s. 6d.
 THE MATERNAL MANAGEMENT OF CHILDREN IN HEALTH AND DISEASE. Fcp. 8vo., 1s. 6d.

De Salis.—Works by Mrs. DE SALIS.
 CAKES AND CONFECTIONS À LA MODE. Fcp. 8vo., 1s. 6d.
 DOGS: a Manual for Amateurs. Fcp. 8vo., 1s. 6d.
 DRESSED GAME AND POULTRY À LA MODE. Fcp. 8vo., 1s. 6d.
 DRESSED VEGETABLES À LA MODE. Fcp. 8vo., 1s. 6d.
 DRINKS À LA MODE. Fcp. 8vo., 1s. 6d.
 ENTRÉES À LA MODE. Fcp. 8vo., 1s. 6d.

Cookery, Domestic Management, &c.—continued.

De Salis.—Works by Mrs. DE SALIS—*continued*.
    FLORAL DECORATIONS. Fcp. 8vo., 1s. 6d.
    GARDENING À LA MODE. Part I. Vegetables, 1s. 6d.; Part II. Fruits, 1s. 6d.
    NATIONAL VIANDS À LA MODE. Fcp. 8vo., 1s. 6d.
    NEW-LAID EGGS: Hints for Amateur Poultry Rearers. Fcp. 8vo., 1s. 6d.
    OYSTERS À LA MODE. Fcp. 8vo., 1s. 6d.
    PUDDINGS AND PASTRY À LA MODE. Fcp. 8vo., 1s. 6d.
    SAVOURIES À LA MODE. Fcp. 8vo., 1s. 6d.
    SOUPS AND DRESSED FISH À LA MODE. Fcp. 8vo., 1s. 6d.
    SWEETS AND SUPPER DISHES À LA MODE. Fcp. 8vo., 1s. 6d.
    TEMPTING DISHES FOR SMALL INCOMES. Fcp. 8vo., 1s. 6d.
    WRINKLES AND NOTIONS FOR EVERY HOUSEHOLD. Cr. 8vo., 1s. 6d.

Lear.—MAIGRE COOKERY. By H. L. SIDNEY LEAR. 16mo., 2s.

Poole.—COOKERY FOR THE DIABETIC. By W. H. and Mrs. POOLE. With Preface by Dr. PAVY. Fcp. 8vo., 2s. 6d.

Walker.—Works by JANE H. WALKER, L.R.C.P.
    A HANDBOOK FOR MOTHERS: being Simple Hints to Women on the Management of their Health during Pregnancy and Confinement, together with Plain Directions as to the Care of Infants. Cr. 8vo., 2s. 6d.

    A BOOK FOR EVERY WOMAN. Part I. The Management of Children in Health and out of Health. Crown 8vo., 2s. 6d.

Miscellaneous and Critical Works.

Allingham.—VARIETIES IN PROSE. By WILLIAM ALLINGHAM. 3 vols. Cr. 8vo. 18s. (Vols. 1 and 2, Rambles, by PATRICIUS WALKER. Vol. 3, Irish Sketches, etc.)

Armstrong.—ESSAYS AND SKETCHES. By EDMUND J. ARMSTRONG. Fcp. 8vo., 5s.

Bagehot.—LITERARY STUDIES. By WALTER BAGEHOT. With Portrait. 3 vols. Crown 8vo., 3s. 6d. each.

Baring-Gould.—CURIOUS MYTHS OF THE MIDDLE AGES. By Rev. S. BARING-GOULD. Crown 8vo., 3s. 6d.

Battye.—PICTURES IN PROSE OF NATURE, WILD SPORT, AND HUMBLE LIFE. By AUBYN TREVOR BATTYE, F.L.S., F.Z.S. Crown 8vo., 6s.

Baynes.—SHAKESPEARE STUDIES, AND OTHER ESSAYS. By the late THOMAS SPENCER BAYNES, LL.B., LL.D. With a biographical Preface by Prof. LEWIS CAMPBELL. Crown 8vo., 7s. 6d.

Boyd ('A. K. H. B.').—Works by A. K. H. BOYD, D.D., LL.D.
    And see MISCELLANEOUS THEOLOGICAL WORKS, p. 31.
    AUTUMN HOLIDAYS OF A COUNTRY PARSON. Crown 8vo., 3s. 6d.
    COMMONPLACE PHILOSOPHER. Crown 8vo., 3s. 6d.
    CRITICAL ESSAYS OF A COUNTRY PARSON. Crown 8vo., 3s. 6d.
    EAST COAST DAYS AND MEMORIES. Crown 8vo., 3s. 6d.

Boyd ('A. K. H. B.').—Works by A. K. H. BOYD, D.D., LL.D.—*continued*.
    LANDSCAPES, CHURCHES AND MORALITIES. Crown 8vo., 3s. 6d.
    LEISURE HOURS IN TOWN. Crown 8vo., 3s. 6d.
    LESSONS OF MIDDLE AGE. Cr. 8vo., 3s. 6d.
    OUR LITTLE LIFE. Two Series. Cr. 8vo., 3s. 6d. each.
    OUR HOMELY COMEDY: AND TRAGEDY. Crown 8vo., 3s. 6d.
    RECREATIONS OF A COUNTRY PARSON. Three Series. Cr. 8vo., 3s. 6d. each. Also First Series. Popular Ed. 8vo., 6d.

Butler.—Works by SAMUEL BUTLER.
    EREWHON. Cr. 8vo., 5s.
    THE FAIR HAVEN. A Work in Defence of the Miraculous Element in our Lord's Ministry. Cr. 8vo., 7s. 6d.
    LIFE AND HABIT. An Essay after a Completer View of Evolution. Cr. 8vo., 7s. 6d.
    EVOLUTION, OLD AND NEW. Cr. 8vo., 10s. 6d.
    ALPS AND SANCTUARIES OF PIEDMONT AND CANTON TICINO. Illustrated. Pott 4to., 10s. 6d.
    LUCK, OR CUNNING, AS THE MAIN MEANS OF ORGANIC MODIFICATION? Cr. 8vo., 7s. 6d.
    EX VOTO. An Account of the Sacro Monte or New Jerusalem at Varallo-Sesia. Crown 8vo., 10s. 6d.

Miscellaneous and Critical Works—*continued.*

Gwilt.—An Encyclopædia of Architecture. By Joseph Gwilt, F.S.A. Illustrated with more than 1100 Engravings on Wood. Revised (1888), with Alterations and Considerable Additions by Wyatt Papworth. 8vo., £2 12s. 6d.

Jefferies.—Works by R. Jefferies.
Field and Hedgerow: Last Essays. With Portrait. Crown 8vo., 3s. 6d.
The Story of My Heart: With Portrait and New Preface by C. J. Longman. Crown 8vo., 3s. 6d.
Red Deer. 17 Illusts. Cr. 8vo., 3s. 6d.
The Toilers of the Field. With Portrait. Crown 8vo., 3s. 6d.
Wood Magic. With Frontispiece and Vignette by E. V. B. Cr. 8vo., 3s. 6d.
Thoughts from the Writings of Richard Jefferies. Selected by H. S. Hoole Waylen. 16mo., 3s. 6d.

Johnson.—The Patentee's Manual: a Treatise on the Law and Practice of Letters Patent. By J. & J. H. Johnson, Patent Agents, &c. 8vo., 10s. 6d.

Lang.—Works by Andrew Lang.
Letters to Dead Authors. Fcp. 8vo., 2s. 6d. net.
Letters on Literature. Fcp. 8vo., 2s. 6d. net.
Books and Bookmen. With 19 Illustrations. Fcp. 8vo., 2s. 6d. net.
Old Friends. Fcp. 8vo., 2s. 6d. net.
Cock Lane and Common Sense. Fcp. 8vo., 6s. 6d. net.

Laurie.—Historical Survey of Pre-Christian Education. By S. S. Laurie, A.M., LL.D. Crown 8vo., 12s.

Leonard.—The Camel: Its Uses and Management. By Major Arthur Glyn Leonard. Royal 8vo., 21s. net.

Macfarren.—Lectures on Harmony. By Sir Geo. A. Macfarren. 8vo., 12s.

Max Müller.—Works by F. Max Müller.
India: What can it Teach us? Cr. 8vo., 3s. 6d.
Chips from a German Workshop.
Vol. I., Recent Essays and Addresses. Cr. 8vo., 6s. 6d. net.
Vol. II., Biographical Essays. Cr. 8vo., 6s. 6d. net.
Vol. III., Essays on Language and Literature. Cr. 8vo., 6s. 6d. net.
Vol. IV., Essays on Mythology and Folk Lore. Crown 8vo., 8s. 6d.

Milner.—Works by George Milner.
Country Pleasures: the Chronicle of a Year chiefly in a Garden. Cr. 8vo., 3s. 6d.
Studies of Nature on the Coast of Arran. With Illustrations by W. Noel Johnson. Cr. 8vo., 6s. 6d. net.

Poore.—Essays on Rural Hygiene. By George Vivian Poore, M.D., F.R.C.P. With 13 Illustrations. Cr. 8vo., 6s. 6d.

Proctor.—Works by R. A. Proctor.
Strength and Happiness. With 9 Illustrations. Crown 8vo., 5s.
Strength: How to get Strong and keep Strong, with Chapters on Rowing and Swimming, Fat, Age, and the Waist. With 9 Illus. Cr. 8vo., 2s.

Richardson.—National Health. A Review of the Works of Sir Edwin Chadwick, K.C.B. By Sir B. W. Richardson, M.D. Cr. 8vo., 4s. 6d.

Rossetti.—A Shadow of Dante: being an Essay towards studying Himself, his World, and his Pilgrimage. By Maria Francesca Rossetti. Cr. 8vo., 10s. 6d. Cheap Edition, 3s. 6d.

Solovyoff.—A Modern Priestess of Isis (Madame Blavatsky). Abridged and Translated on Behalf of the Society for Psychical Research from the Russian of Vsevolod Sergyeevich Solovyff. By Walter Leaf, Litt. D. With Appendices. Crown 8vo., 6s.

Stevens.—On the Stowage of Ships and their Cargoes. With Information regarding Freights, Charter-Parties, &c. By Robert White Stevens, Associate Member of the Institute of Naval Architects. 8vo. 21s.

Van Dyke.—A Text-Book of the History of Painting. By John C. Van Dyke, of Rutgers College, U.S. With Frontispiece and 109 Illustrations in the Text. Crown 8vo., 6s.

West.—Wills, and How Not to Make Them. With a Selection of Leading Cases. By B. B. West. Fcp. 8vo., 2s. 6d.

Miscellaneous Theological Works.

*** *For Church of England and Roman Catholic Works see* MESSRS. LONGMANS & CO.'s *Special Catalogue.*

Balfour.—THE FOUNDATIONS OF BELIEF: being Notes Introductory to the Study of Theology. By the Right Hon. ARTHUR J. BALFOUR, M.P. 8vo., 12s. 6d.

Boyd.—Works by A. K. H. BOYD, D.D.
COUNSEL AND COMFORT FROM A CITY PULPIT. Crown 8vo., 3s. 6d.
SUNDAY AFTERNOONS IN THE PARISH CHURCH OF A SCOTTISH UNIVERSITY CITY. Crown 8vo., 3s. 6d.
CHANGED ASPECTS OF UNCHANGED TRUTHS. Crown 8vo., 3s. 6d.
GRAVER THOUGHTS OF A COUNTRY PARSON. Three Series. Crown 8vo., 3s. 6d. each.
PRESENT DAY THOUGHTS. Crown 8vo., 3s. 6d.
SEASIDE MUSINGS. Cr. 8vo., 3s. 6d.
'TO MEET THE DAY' through the Christian Year: being a Text of Scripture, with an Original Meditation and a Short Selection in Verse for Every Day. Crown 8vo., 4s. 6d.
OCCASIONAL AND IMMEMORIAL DAYS. Cr. 8vo., 7s. 6d.

De La Saussaye.—A MANUAL OF THE SCIENCE OF RELIGION. By Prof. CHANTEPIE DE LA SAUSSAYE. Crown 8vo., 12s. 6d.

Kalisch.—Works by M. M. KALISCH.
BIBLE STUDIES. Part I. The Prophecies of Balaam. 8vo., 10s. 6d. Part II. The Book of Jonah. 8vo., 10s. 6d.
COMMENTARY ON THE OLD TESTAMENT: with a new Translation. Vol. I. Genesis. 8vo., 18s. Or adapted for the General Reader. 12s. Vol. II. Exodus. 15s. Or adapted for the General Reader. 12s. Vol. III. Leviticus, Part I. 15s. Or adapted for the General Reader. 8s. Vol. IV. Leviticus, Part II. 15s. Or adapted for the General Reader. 8s.

Martineau.—Works by JAMES MARTINEAU, D.D., LL.D.
HOURS OF THOUGHT ON SACRED THINGS: Sermons. 2 Vols. Crown 8vo., 7s. 6d. each.
ENDEAVOURS AFTER THE CHRISTIAN LIFE. Discourses. Cr. 8vo., 7s. 6d.
THE SEAT OF AUTHORITY IN RELIGION. 8vo., 14s.
ESSAYS, REVIEWS, AND ADDRESSES. 4 Vols. Crown 8vo., 7s. 6d. each. I. Personal; Political. II. Ecclesiastical; Historical. III. Theological; Philosophical. IV. Academical; Religious.
HOME PRAYERS, with Two Services for Public Worship. Crown 8vo. 3s. 6d.

Macdonald.—Works by GEORGE MACDONALD, LL.D.
UNSPOKEN SERMONS. Three Series. Crown 8vo., 3s. 6d. each.
THE MIRACLES OF OUR LORD. Crown 8vo., 3s. 6d.
A BOOK OF STRIFE, IN THE FORM OF THE DIARY OF AN OLD SOUL: Poems 18mo., 6s.

Max Müller.—Works by F. MAX MÜLLER.
HIBBERT LECTURES ON THE ORIGIN AND GROWTH OF RELIGION, as illustrated by the Religions of India. Crown 8vo., 7s. 6d.
INTRODUCTION TO THE SCIENCE OF RELIGION: Four Lectures delivered at the Royal Institution. Cr. 8vo., 3s. 6d.
NATURAL RELIGION. The Gifford Lectures, delivered before the University of Glasgow in 1888. Cr. 8vo., 10s. 6d.
PHYSICAL RELIGION. The Gifford Lectures, delivered before the University of Glasgow in 1890. Cr. 8vo., 10s. 6d.
ANTHROPOLOGICAL RELIGION. The Gifford Lectures, delivered before the University of Glasgow in 1891. Cr. 8vo., 10s. 6d.
THEOSOPHY OR PSYCHOLOGICAL RELIGION. The Gifford Lectures, delivered before the University of Glasgow in 1892. Cr. 8vo., 10s. 6d.
THREE LECTURES ON THE VEDANTA PHILOSOPHY, delivered at the Royal Institution in March, 1894. 8vo., 5s.

Phillips.—THE TEACHING OF THE VEDAS. What Light does it Throw on the Origin and Development of Religion? By MAURICE PHILLIPS, London Mission, Madras. Crown 8vo., 6s.

Romanes.—THOUGHTS ON RELIGION. By the late GEORGE J. ROMANES, author of 'Darwin and After Darwin,' &c. Crown 8vo., 4s. 6d.

SUPERNATURAL RELIGION: an Inquiry into the Reality of Divine Revelation. 3 vols. 8vo., 36s.
REPLY (A) TO DR. LIGHTFOOT'S ESSAYS. By the Author of 'Supernatural Religion'. 8vo., 6s.
THE GOSPEL ACCORDING TO ST. PETER: a Study. By the Author of 'Supernatural Religion'. 8vo., 6s.

Thom.—A SPIRITUAL FAITH. Sermons. By JOHN HAMILTON THOM. With a Memorial Preface by JAMES MARTINEAU, D.D. With Portrait. Crown 8vo. 5s.